D1727005

European Yearbook of International Economic Law

EYIEL Monographs - Studies in European and International Economic Law

Volume 15

Series Editors

Marc Bungenberg, Saarbrücken, Germany

Christoph Herrmann, Passau, Germany

Markus Krajewski, Erlangen, Germany

Jörg Philipp Terhechte, Lüneburg, Germany

Andreas R. Ziegler, Lausanne, Switzerland

EYIEL Monographs is a subseries of the European Yearbook of International Economic Law (EYIEL). It contains scholarly works in the fields of European and international economic law, in particular WTO law, international investment law, international monetary law, law of regional economic integration, external trade law of the EU and EU internal market law. The series does not include edited volumes. EYIEL Monographs are peer-reviewed by the series editors and external reviewers.

More information about this subseries at http://www.springer.com/series/15744

Andrea Lucia Tapia-Hoffmann

Legal Certainty and Central Bank Autonomy in Latin American Emerging Markets

 Springer

Andrea Lucia Tapia-Hoffmann
Martin Luther University Halle-Wittenberg
Halle (Saale), Germany

ISSN 2364-8392   ISSN 2364-8406   (electronic)
European Yearbook of International Economic Law
ISSN 2524-6658   ISSN 2524-6666   (electronic)
EYIEL Monographs - Studies in European and International Economic Law
ISBN 978-3-030-70985-3   ISBN 978-3-030-70986-0   (eBook)
https://doi.org/10.1007/978-3-030-70986-0

Dissertation zur Erlangung des Grades eines Doktors der Rechte (Dr. iur.) der Juristischen und
Wirtschaftswissenschaftlichen Fakultät der Martin-Luther-Universität Halle-Wittenberg
Vorgelegt von: Andrea Lucia Tapia-Hoffmann, Leipzig
Erstgutachter: Prof. Dr. Christian Tietje, LL.M.
Zweitgutachter: Prof. Dr. Matthias Lehmann, D.E.A., LL.M., J.S.D.
Tag der öffentlichen Verteidigung: 15. Oktober 2019, Halle an der Saale

This Springer imprint is published by the registered company Springer Nature Switzerland AG.
The registered company address is: Gewerbestrasse 11, 6330 Cham, Switzerland

To my family

Acknowledgments

This book benefited from comments of many colleagues, friends, and professionals. First and foremost, I am thankful for the support of Prof. Christian Tietje. He is a wonderful teacher and great academic guide. I am also thankful to Prof. Matthias Lehmann for important discussions and comments on this project, especially when I got started, as well as my former colleagues Julia Schaarschmidt and Lina Lorenzoni for their friendship and support.

I am grateful to Prof. Richard Epstein, NYU Law, and Prof. Mario Rizzo, NYU Economics, for being great hosts during my research stay at the Classical Liberal Institute at NYU Law. I am thankful to Prof. Aaron Simowitz, fellow at the Classical Liberal Institute, as well as many others for discussing my research and providing hints on how to move forward.

Further, I thank Carlos Gustavo Cano, former board member of the Bank of the Republic of Colombia, and Alberto Boada Ortiz, general secretary of the board, for their hospitality during my research visit at the bank and the many insights they provided.

Contents

About the Author

Andrea Lucia Tapia-Hoffmann is an Ecuadorian-German attorney. She holds a law degree from the Pontifical Catholic University of Ecuador (PUCE) in Quito, Ecuador and a doctoral degree from the Martin Luther University Halle-Wittenberg in Germany. She has broad international experience after working for several years in Ecuador and the USA. Since 2017, she has worked as an in-house lawyer and data protection specialist in Germany. Her interests are in economic law, comparative law, human rights, and privacy law.

Abbreviations

ACHR	American Convention on Human Rights
Art.	Article
BPBA	Bank of the Province of Buenos Aires
BRC	Bank of the Republic of Colombia
BRC Act	Act of the Bank of the Republic of Colombia
BM	Bank of Mexico
BM Law	Law of the Bank of Mexico
CAV	Corporación de Ahorro y Vivienda
BCRA	Central Bank of the Argentine Republic
BCRA Law	Organic Charter of the BCRA
CBB	Central Bank of Brazil
CBCH	Central Bank of Chile
CBCH Law	Constitutional Organic Law of the Central Bank of Chile
CCC	Constitutional Court of Colombia
CDU	Código Disciplinario Único (de Colombia)
CEO	Chief Executive Officer
CER	Coeficiente de Estabilización de Referencia
Civ. Code	Civil Code
CRBP	Central Reserve Bank of Peru
CRBP Law	Organic Law of the Central Reserve Bank of Peru
CMN	Conselho Monetário Nacional (do Brasil)
CONFIS	Consejo Superior de Política Fiscal
CONPES	Consejo Nacional de Política Económica y Social
Const. Argentina	Constitution of Argentina
Const. Brazil	Constitution of Brazil
Const. Chile	Constitution of Chile
Const. Colombia	Constitution of Colombia
Const. Mexico	Constitution of Mexico
Const. Peru	Constitution of Peru
CSJN Argentina	Corte Suprema de Justicia de la Nación

DSU	Dispute Settlement Understanding
Eds	Editors
ECB	European Central Bank
ESCB	European System of Central Banks
EU	European Union
FED	Federal Reserve
ICCPR	International Covenant on Economic, Social and Cultural Rights
IMF	International Monetary Fund
LFRSP México	Ley Federal de Responsabilidades Administrativas de los Servidores Públicos
LSFN Brazil	Lei do Sistema Financeiro Nacional (Brazil)
N/A	Not applicable, not available
para	Paragraph
RIBC Brazil	Regimento Interno do Banco Central do Brasil
RSRM	Reglamento del Senado de la República de México
Sec.	Section
SCJN México	Suprema Corte de Justicia de la Nación
SELIC	Sistema Especial de Liquidação e Custodia
STF Brasil	Supremo Tribunal Federal
TC Chile	Tribunal Constitucional de Chile
TC Peru	Tribunal Constitucional de Peru
UDHR	Universal Declaration of Human Rights
UPAC	Unidad de Poder Adquisitivo Constante
U.S. Constitution	Constitution of the United States of America
UVR	Unidad de Valor Real
WTO	World Trade Organization

List of Figures

List of Tables

Chapter 1
Introduction

1.1 Monetary Stability in Latin America

Monetary instability has been endemic throughout the twentieth century in Latin America. Inflation, the fall of domestic purchasing power, was particularly high in the 1970s and 1980s, when central banks engaged in expansionary monetary policies to finance government expenditures.[1] In addition, currency crashes caused financial crises and inflationary spurs, specifically in the 1990s. Because the threat of inflation increased contractual risks and put a drag on investment and economic growth, episodes of monetary instability motivated the sovereigns, with the power to create and regulate money, to reforms of central bank laws. Price stability has gradually become the *raison d'etre* of monetary policy.[2] An increasing number of central banks in Latin America have been granted autonomy in the law to allow central banks to pursue monetary policy independent from political intervention.

Since the 1990s, price stability has improved in Latin America. Figure 1.1 illustrates the development of inflation rates in Latin America's emerging markets from 1995 to 2015. In 1995, inflation in most Latin American countries was lower than it was in the 1970s and 1980s, but still much higher than that in developed countries, such as Germany or the United States. In the 2000s, inflation dropped to below five percent per annum in Chile, Colombia, Mexico, and Peru. At the same time, these Latin American countries experienced substantially higher rates of economic growth than the developed countries. Figure 1.2 shows that, particularly

---

[1]See, e.g., Rosenn (1979), p. 270. Rosenn explains that during the sixties the annual average inflation rates of Brazil was of 58%, Chile 25%, Argentina 24%. In Argentina and Chile inflation rates increased further during the seventies. In Brazil, Colombia and Peru inflation rates were 28.6%, 22.4% and 21.5%. In Chile and Argentina, they were above 100%.

[2]Lastra (2015), p. 61.

© The Author(s), under exclusive license to Springer Nature Switzerland AG 2021
A. L. Tapia-Hoffmann, *Legal Certainty and Central Bank Autonomy in Latin American Emerging Markets*, European Yearbook of International Economic Law 15, https://doi.org/10.1007/978-3-030-70986-0_1

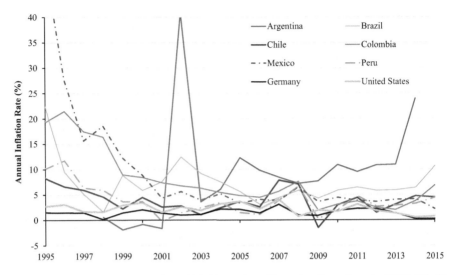

Fig. 1.1 Inflation in Latin America (1995–2015) (Own illustration, Data from the IMF's World Economic Outlook Database, available at https://www.imf.org/en/publications/weo)

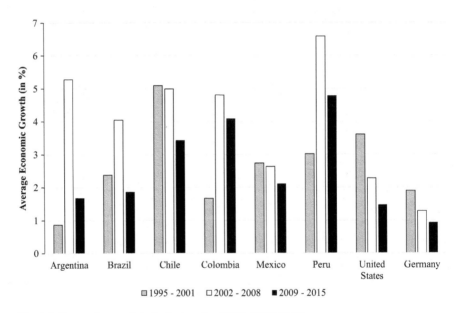

Fig. 1.2 Economic growth in Latin America (1995–2015) (*Ibid*)

up to the financial crisis of 2008, Argentina, Brazil, Peru, Chile, and Colombia grew substantially faster than, for example, Germany or the United States.

Improvements in economic activity and the convergence of inflation rates with those in the United States and Germany suggest that some of the emerging market economies might gain developed country status in the near future. However, notably, *Reinhart* and *Rogoff* warn from drawing such premature conclusions in their well-known book, *This Time Is Different*. They emphasize that to graduate from developing country status, countries must be able to maintain levels of stability over longer periods.[3] And the history of monetary instability in Latin America casts some doubts on the ability of the Latin American countries to enter a period of prolonged monetary stability.[4]

In the early 1980s, many governments in Latin America's emerging markets had accumulated large amounts of foreign debt to increase spending, as they could refinance relatively cheaply in international markets after opening the economy to foreign investors. There was great hope they would eventually catch up with the United States and Western Europe. But when inflation and interest rates for funding in international markets, especially in the United States, rose, debt servicing became difficult. Worried about government defaults, investors withdrew capital from the emerging markets, triggering currency crashes. The devaluation of the currencies made imports and debt-service, denominated in foreign currency, expensive. Governments had to default on external debt.[5]

In the 1990s, governments in a number of Latin American emerging market economies had pegged their currencies more tightly to the U.S. dollar to import monetary stability from the United States. Exchange rate pegging was seen as a means to delegate monetary policy to a foreign central bank, in particular the U.S. Federal Reserve, and prevent the abuse of monetary policy to finance government spending.[6] This worked just fine for a while. But the pegs were not as credible as hoped. When political goals conflicted with exchange rate pegs, investors began to distrust the exchange rate pegs and withdrew capital from the countries.[7] A second wave of currency crises swept the region, leading to the abandonment of the pegged exchange rate systems. For example, Mexico experienced a crisis in 1994 that ended its dreams of a rapid development. Similarly, Brazil and Colombia had to give up their exchange rate pegs in 1999.[8] And although the currency board in Argentina seemed promising in terms of providing monetary stability, the currency board failed in 2001.[9]

Looking at these historical patterns we might conclude that the recent improvements in price stability in Latin America are hardly sustainable and merely reflect the high rates of economic growth. Perhaps governments simply did not see a need to

---

[3]For preconditions to graduate from emerging market status, see Reinhart and Rogoff (2011), p. 283.

[4]*Ibid.*, p. 284.

[5]*Ibid.*, p. 261.

[6]Bernhard et al. (2001), p. 15.

[7]Frankel (2003), pp. 3–5.

[8]Frenkel (2003), p. 48.

[9]Thomas and Cachanosky (2006), pp. 71–72. More generally for several examples, see also Reinhart and Rogoff (2011), p. 284.

finance spending via the central banks because the rates of economic growth were high, such that central banks were allowed to focus on lowering inflation.[10] As such, monetary stability might be at risk when economic development stagnates.

The data in Figs. 1.1 and 1.2 could be interpreted along the same lines. In countries like Peru, Chile, and Colombia, economic growth remained high compared to the developed countries between 2009 and 2015. Inflation stayed at moderate levels in these countries. In Argentina and Brazil, however, growth rates were lower between 2009 and 2015 than in prior years. Inflation rates also went up. Argentina's government has moved from left to right and then again from right to left in recent years because of the conflicts triggered by social consequences of inflation as well as anti-inflationary policies.

This book provides evidence that the move toward central bank autonomy to tackle monetary instability provides a legal–institutional reason to be confident of a sustainable decline in inflation in some Latin American countries, e.g., Chile and Peru. Indeed, the economics literature has long taught us that central bank autonomy is an important means to shield central banks from government intervention and to provide them with the necessary dose of credibility in committing toward non-inflationary policies. However, that is not the full story. The book also suggests that, e.g., in Colombia, we should not be too confident about a sustainable decline in inflation even though the central bank was granted autonomy in the country's constitution and has been given an inflation target.

This book argues that legal certainty concerning the rules that guarantee central bank autonomy is of utter importance. In a nutshell, there is legal certainty when legal rules allow people to form expectations, to guide their actions and to plan. Only when there is legal certainty concerning central bank autonomy, the law provides reasons to be confident that central banks operate independent from political influence and will be able to pursue the objective of maintaining monetary stability. For there to be legal certainty, the set of rules that ought to guarantee central bank autonomy must be clear, consistent and coherent with the broader legal framework.

Considering the complexity of legal frameworks surrounding central banks, this book provides a granular legal-institutional analysis of the central banks of Argentina, Brazil, Chile, Colombia, Mexico and Peru (status as of 2019) to determine how central bank autonomy is embedded in the respective legal frameworks of the countries and to draw implications for reforms and proper arrangements that can help cure monetary instability. The analysis indicates that the strength of the legal commitment that grants autonomy to the central banks differs across countries and points to inconsistent or conflicting rules within the broader legal frameworks, as well as exceptions in the law that may jeopardize the autonomy and credibility of central banks in guaranteeing price stability.

---

[10]In personal communication with central bankers from Colombia, some suggested that the central bank may be allowed to follow price stability targets only if there is no need to deviate from them from the perspective of the government.

Let us summarize three such differences upfront: First, countries give central banks different objectives, which might provide either more, or less room for government interference. Second, the modification of rules may require different procedures in different countries. Central bank autonomy certainly cannot be the means to achieve monetary stability as implied by political economists if the organ's autonomous status can be altered at will. And third, legal frameworks may be consistent or not. If the law states that a central bank is autonomous but there are statutory provisions that suggest otherwise or important other laws that are in conflict with autonomy, the law might provide little certainty concerning central bank autonomy even if the central bank law was meant to.

1.2   Outline

The book is comprised of three main parts. The first part serves to set the stage for the key argument in explaining the importance of legal certainty. Chapter 2 summarizes the different notions of legal certainty, its characteristics, and its relationship to other principles of law, such as the principle of non-retroactivity and the protection of legitimate expectations. Chapter 3 elaborates on the link between legal certainty and the idea of credible commitments, implying that legal certainty is a precondition for credibility. We will see that modification costs of legal-commitment devices differ within and between the six Latin American countries considered, implying a different degree of legal certainty concerning legal rules. Differences in modification costs primarily imply differences in strength and durability of commitments.

Part two links the importance of the strength of legal commitments to the objectives of central banks (Chap. 4) and shows that prescriptions in the statutes of the monetary authorities in the region differ dramatically (Chap. 5). Specifically, the lack of coherence of the legal status of an autonomous central bank with its arrangements regarding, personal, financial, and operational autonomy are striking feature of several but not all Latin American central banks considered.

The last part of the book draws attention to threats to central bank autonomy that are not immediately obvious from studying constitutional provisions and central bank statutes. In Colombia, court decisions regarding the central bank's use of monetary policy show that there may be a conflict between the social rule of law and central bank autonomy that may lead activist courts to rule against operational decisions of the central bank and threaten its credibility (Chap. 6). In Argentina, the use of economic emergency decrees undermined certainty concerning central bank autonomy (Chap. 7).

The final chapter (Chap. 8) summarizes the differences between institutional frameworks and suggests ways for improvement.

References

Bernhard W, Broz JL, Roberts Clark W (2001) The political economy of monetary institutions: an introduction. Urbana 15. Available at https://pages.ucsd.edu/~jlbroz/pdf_folder/BBC_IO.pdf

Frankel J (2003) Experience of and lessons from exchange rate regimes in emerging economies. NBER Working Paper No. 10032

Frenkel R (2003) Globalización y Crisis Financieras en América Latina. Revista de la Cepal 80:41-54

Lastra R (2015) International financial and monetary law, 2nd edn. Oxford University Press

Reinhart C, Rogoff K (2011) This time is different: eight centuries of financial folly. Princeton University Press

Rosenn K (1979) The effect of inflation in the law obligations in Argentina, Brazil, Chile and Uruguay. Bost Coll Int Comp Law Rev 2:269. Available at https://lawdigitalcommons.bc.edu/iclr/vol2/iss2/4

Thomas C, Cachanosky N (2006) Argentina's Post-2001 economy and the 2014 default. Q Rev Econ Financ 60:70–80. https://doi.org/10.1016/j.qref.2015.08.002

Chapter 2
Legal Certainty

2.1 Introduction

This chapter serves to define and elaborate on different notions of legal certainty. Explaining legal certainty presupposes an understanding of the objectives and importance of the rule of law. The first chapter, therefore, briefly reviews what the rule of law means and how a legal system under the rule of law is organized. Legal certainty is an important element of it (Sect. 2.2). In outlining different notions of legal certainty (Sect. 2.3) and elaborating on the relationship between the legal certainty, the rule of law and other principles of law (Sect. 2.4) the chapter refers to peculiarities regarding the Latin American legal systems.

2.2 The Principle of Legal Certainty and the Rule of Law

2.2.1 The Rule of Law and the Law

The terms *rule of law* and *the law* are often used like synonyms. However, there is a difference between them: the rule of law is the political and philosophical ideal of a system of predictable general legal rules, in which people can seek for defense of their rights through an established process.[1] The law, on the other hand, are positive rules (rights, processes, institutions, judicial decisions and sanctions) enacted by authorized officials, whose violation face coercion. In this sense, the rule of law can be equated to a moral dimension of how the law should be. The law can be equated to

---

[1] Waldron (2008), pp. 45–47.

established standards of validity.[2] The fact that some elements of the law are not in perfect shape does not threaten the entire ideal of the rule of law. They are in fact fixable. When we claim that the rule of law fails, we usually mean the systematical failure of more than one element of the law that threatens the general ideal of governance under the law.[3]

The very origins of the rule of law as summarized by *Clark* help us clarify the essence of the ideal: The ancient Greek philosophers Aristotle and Plato envisaged the rule of law as mechanism that would promote a moral society by setting the standards of conduct. At the same time, the rule of law was supposed to constrain the power of potentially tyrant authorities. The idea of the rule of law as a power-constraining devise further progressed during the late Roman period because of the abuse of power of the Prince. The power of the Prince was first questioned during the Christian era and replaced by the will of God. However, during the medieval period, there was not a clear separation of the figures of the God and the King. Indeed, the King had the power of expressing the voice of God. Taking the ancient thought as the departing point of the modern conception of the rule of law it is possible to define it as a canon whose central premise is the supremacy of objective standards (laws) over the will of men.[4]

Legal scholars have contributed to the evolution of the rule of law along time by adding other elements to the concept. Dicey added the elements of equality in front of the law and the role of the courts of justice.[5] Equality in front of the law ensures that the rule of law reigns over all men. Thus, both, citizens and government officials are subject to the same set of general rules, fundamental rights and obligations. In a common-law system, the courts of justice are the creator and adjudicator of law. In civil law systems, as present in Latin America, the courts are not the main creator of legal rules. Therefore, we must include another element that is concerned with the role of the legislature, the legitimate authority in charge of law-making. The existence of previously written, general laws that are enacted by a legitimate authority on which people can base their decisions is a pre-condition to achieve legal equality in civil law systems. The courts are guarantors of legal equality because they have the

---

[2]Lyons explains the classic and contemporary ideas about positivism. He reviews the differences between divine law, positive law and positive morality according to Austin, Hart and Dworkin. See Lyons (1977), pp. 416–418.

[3]According to Waldron, there is a threshold for the existence of the rule of law. These minimal requirements are described by Waldron in part V of his essay. They are: Courts as norm applying institutions, public norms, positive rules, orientation to the public good, and systematicity. For more detail, see Waldron (2008), pp. 19–36.

[4]Clark writes that the importance of the state in ancient Greece relied on its authority to enact the laws that would organize social life and would limit the selfishness of individuals. At that point in history, the first notions of the social contract were born to separate moral from law and to allow legal rules to organize society without the interference of individual preferences. According to the author, Epicureo developed the ideas of separating the state from the individual whose main role in life is pursuing his own happiness and the necessity of preserving people from the tyranny of the authorities. See Clark (1999), pp. 28–29. See also De la Hidalga (2008), pp. 215–218.

[5]Beaulac (2007), pp. 3–4.

obligation of providing via adjudication, identical treatment to every legal person, regardless of social, economic or political position.[6]

2.2.1.1   Objectives of the Rule of Law

According to *Frederic Bastiat* the rule of law—or simply *the law*—is

> the organization of the natural right of lawful defense; it is the substitution of collective for individual forces, for the purpose of acting in the sphere in which they have a right to act, of doing what they have the rights to do, to secure persons, liberties and property and to maintain each on its right, so as to cause justice to reign over us all.[7]

From this quote, we can infer the two main objectives of the rule of law: (1) to organizing society so that people know "the sphere in which they have a right to act, of doing what they have the rights to do" and (2) to achieve justice by "securing persons, liberties and property and to maintain each on its right".

Both objectives of the rule of law, ordering society and accomplishing justice, have in common that they seek the general good of a society. Pursuing the society's general wellbeing is what makes legal rules accepted as part of the legal system.[8] To effectively organize society, legal systems must meet some structural and formal characteristics. In this respect, many authors mention Lon Fuller's list of legal requirements. Among them are the generality, receptiveness, publicity and certainty of the legal rules. Moreover, they must be subject to judicial review.[9] Other authors have lengthened Fuller's list of characteristics, by also including the independence of the judiciary, access to the administration of justice, etc.[10]

This formal notion of the rule of law has, however, little in common with the notion of justice. Justice entails the specification of rights and liberties, which are the substantive content of the law.[11] Justice is not directly related to the formal aspects of the rule of law but to its substantive dimension. These substantive elements are the set of rights and obligations of people and also guarantees of the neutrality in the administration of justice. Examples are the independence of the judiciary, the due process or rules for the use of precedents, etc. According to *Waldron*, the substantive dimension does not include the organizational aspects of the law, but the process and argumentation in front of the courts and tribunals. This means that the rule of law requires general rules with the characteristics mentioned by Fuller and other authors, but also requires the possibility of challenging these characteristics in front of a judge that helps determine somebody's rights when they are conflicting or at risk.[12]

---

[6]O'Donnell (2004), pp. 32–33. See also Gribnau (2013), p. 53.

[7]Bastiat (1968), p. 3.

[8]Waldron (2008), p. 31.

[9]*Ibid.*, p. 7. *See* also Beaulac (2007), p. 7; Epstein (2007), pp. 19–20.

[10]Clark (1999), p. 32.

[11]Beaulac (2007), pp. 5–6.

[12]Waldron (2008), pp. 55–56.

The substantial aspect of the rule of law complements the formal rule of law. Indeed, the formal rule of law is necessary to assure government attachment to the legal rules. However, legal rules are not product of any uncontrollable force of the nature, like physic laws, but made by humans[13] prompt to mistake, failure and the temptation of ruling for individual benefits. Lacking substantive content, the formal rule of law would be unable to restrain political regimes from using the law-making apparatus as a mean of abuse. Indeed, abusive regimes often perform their function under a set of formal legal rules that do not respect human rights and are unjust or unequal.[14]

Understanding the relevance of the substantive content of the law allows to have a more accurate sense of what the rule of law is. In this regard, *Waldron* distinguishes ideas of Hart, Austin or Bentham who saw the law as simply a set of organized orders and commands that come from an authorized authority from the less positivist point of view of Cicero, Thomas of Aquinas, Locke or Pashukanis. The latter group underlined that a system of the rule of law does not exist if this system is plagued with legal formalities, but it is substantively unjust.[15]

2.2.1.2   The State and the Law

The central figure of contemporary political organization is the nation state. The law and the state have a very close relationship. The law governs the state and organizes the affairs and scope of power of state organs. The state organs make and enforce law, but even law-making and law-enforcing require a legal basis.[16]

The state can be understood in three different dimensions that interact with each other: political, juridical and organizational. In its political dimension, the state is the *people* or the group of habitants that live in a territory. In its juridical dimension, the state has *legal personality*. That the state is a legal person means that it has rights and obligations specified in the law.[17] The state as an apparatus is a unity that acts through several organs that make feasible the performance of its functions.[18]

The sovereign people grant public power through the law and, as means of safety, the constitution establishes people's subjective rights that the state must respect.[19] The guidelines of legal rules allow for a balance between the private affairs of the

---

[13]Waldron mentions that positivity requires the lawmaker's use of imagination and creativity. See Waldron (2008), p. 31.

[14]Clark criticizes some modern doctrines of the rule of law that prefer formal aspects of law over substantive aspects. Laws based on mere formality are, according to him, usually unfair and compatible with tyrannic regimes. See Clark (1999), pp. 32–33.

[15]Waldron (2008), pp. 14–16.

[16]See, e.g., Ungar (2002), p. 20, on how the law is the basis for state action.

[17]Gordillo (2012), IADA–II–1–3.

[18]See, e.g., López Guerra (1980), pp. 22–23, for more on the legal personality of the state.

[19]Gordillo (2012), IADA–II–1–3.

individuals and the performance of public functions of authorities. *Epstein* explains that individuals should have more leeway in their actions than the state. The reason is that individuals do not hold the monopoly of power and, instead, face the restrictions established by other social institutions, e.g., the markets. The state, on the other hand, as holder of power that can be imposed on others, is less vulnerable to competition. Therefore, the law must substantially restrict the authorities' power.[20]

This raises the question of how the law may constrain authorities. The law requires, in the first place, the valid swearing-in of the authorities.[21] In Latin America, the constitutions prescribe different ways of electing state officials. Some of them are democratically elected like presidents (e.g. in Colombia), members of the parliament, mayors and so on.[22] Judges are not elected by popular election but appointed through processes that involve the executive, legislative branches and the Supreme Court itself.[23] The heads of other state institutions like control organs, superintendence, electoral courts, among others, have a legal way of appointment of their own.[24] Legal rules typically regulate the scope of the competences of state officials by distributing competences among several organs.[25]

---

[20]Epstein (2011), pp. 190–192.

[21]See, for instance, Constitution of Chile Art. 7 para 1 [English Translation of Constitución Política de la República de Chile, Gazeta Oficial, 24 October 1980] [hereinafter Const. Chile]: *"[T]he organ of the State act validly, with the prior regular investiture of their members, within their field of competence, and in the form that the law prescribes."*

[22]See, for instance, Constitution of Colombia with Amendments through 2015 Art. 260 [English Translation of Constitución Política de Colombia, Diario Oficial No. 49.554, 25 June 2015] [hereinafter Const. Colombia] that lays out that the citizens *"elect in a direct manner the President and Vice President of the Republic, senators, representatives, governors, deputies, mayors [. . .]"* among others.

[23]Const. Chile Art. 78 on Supreme Court selection: *"Ministers and judicial prosecutors of the Supreme Court shall be appointed by the President of the Republic, choosing from a list of five people that, in each case, will be proposed by the same Court with the agreement of the Senate. [. . .]"* According to Art. 239 Const. Colombia, the *"judges of the Constitutional Court shall be elected by the Senate of the Republic [. . .] from lists presented to it by the President of the Republic, the Supreme Court of Justice and the Council of State."*

[24]For instance, according to Art. 98 Const. Chile, the General Comptroller *"[. . .] will be designated by the President of the Republic with the agreement of the Senate [. . .]"*. According to Art. 264 Const. Colombia, the members of the National Election Commission, *"are elected by the Congress of the Republic [. . .] on the basis of proposals submitted by the political parties or movements with legal personality or by coalitions formed between them."*

[25]Article IV of the Ley de Procedimiento Administrativo General [General Act of Administrative Procedure of Peru, Official Diary of 10 April 2001] lays down *legality* as one of the principles that govern the competences of the public administration. This article states that *"the administrative authorities must respect the Constitution, the legislation and the law, within scope of the allocated powers and in accordance with the purposes for which they were conferred on them. (1.1) [Own Translation]"* See also Rafael Selume Sacaan v. Congreso Nacional de Chile, TC Chile, Sentencia Rol No. 472, 30 August 2006.

2.2.1.3 The Problems of the Estado de Derecho in Latin America

The *rule of law* is mainly characterized by elements that allow for the ordering of society and the achievement of justice. The role of the state under the rule of law is implicit. However, the institution that prevails according to the concept of the rule of law are the courts of justice. The Latin American *estado de derecho* entails the function of the state in a more general sense. It is related with the state governance under the law and democracy.[26] Under such a *democratic rule of law*, perhaps the best way of translating *estado de derecho*, the law guarantees the civil as much as the political rights of the citizens and creates the strings that attach state officials to the legal rules. Authorities are subject to electoral accountability, to the scrutiny of social organization and to the control of other state branches and organs and subject to a process of legal accountability.[27]

The *democratic rule of law* works to the extent that the state is subject to the law. The courts of justice play a critical role in establishing both, democracy and the rule of law in a country. The courts overview a correct distribution of power among state organs, guarantee the accountability of public officials and, consequently, restrain authoritarian rulers and keeps politics under public scrutiny. When courts of justice fail at doing so, the electoral accountability is the only one that remains. In such a situation, politicians can make decisions to gain popularity while the rule of law is transformed into a rule of the majority. The poor role the courts of justice play in many Latin American countries allow powerful politicians to be de facto exempted from subjecting to the law and treating dissidents in a discriminatory fashion.[28] In fact, the courts of justice have been inefficient at guarantying the accountability of state officials because very often the independence of the judiciary has been a mere statement and the courts have supported either private or political interests.[29]

As long as there is a clear delimitation between politics and law, this mix of the rule of law and democracy should not cause problems. In many Latin American countries, however, the line that divides politics and law is often rather blurred. In fact, "many individuals are citizens with respect to political rights but not in terms of civil rights. They are as poorly legally as materially."[30] The problem of not drawing clear legal limits for politics on paper and in practice is that democracy often sets goals and objectives that can be contradictory to the prescriptions of the legal rules.

---

[26]Epstein explains that there is a direct connection between the rule of law and democracy because the rule of law prevents the tyranny of autocratic rulers. Moreover, in the context of democracy the rule of law shall avoid the "tyranny of the majority" by setting some minimum standards that must be respected even by the majority of people deciding in elections. See Epstein (2011), p. 13 and pp. 190–191.

[27]O'Donnell (2004), pp. 32–33.

[28]Prillaman (2000), pp. 1–2; see also O'Donnell (2004), pp. 36–42.

[29]To read more about impunity within the Latin American judicial system, see Mainwaring (2003), p. 22.

[30]O'Donnell (2004), p. 42.

In this context, institutions are created to accomplish a specific task but end up performing a different role.[31]

Right from the beginning of the existence of the Latin American countries as independent states the relationship between the rule of law and democracy has not been an easy one. It was not easy to create institutions in a society used to a self-centered way of authority and a legal system full of impunity and disorder, inherited from Spanish colonialism. Further, the population was, and still is, marked by deep differences that make it hard to keep countries together and to prevent civil wars. The outcome of this environment is that from the beginning the citizens of Latin American countries have felt like the victims of an unequal system and their main objective has been to achieve social justice through their elected officials rather than through the law.[32] These phenomena contributed to the weakness of the rule of law in Latin America, distorted the rules of the democratic game and triggered constant public disappointment and a permanent search of the democratic government that will eventually make everybody happy.[33]

The lack of rule of law tends to show in high rates of corruption. It starts at the lowest levels, where bribing authorities is the rule, and works its way up to governmental levels, where fraud and nepotism are also a common practice.[34] There are even reported instances of presidents abusing their power to remain head of state or to accommodate other institutions to return favors. Several examples come to mind. One of them is the former President of Mexico Ernesto Zedillo, who modified, through a constitutional amendment, the Supreme Court's procedures of judicial review. The excuse was the need of improving the administration of justice. However, as a side-effect the Supreme Court was filled with executive-friendly judges.[35] In Peru, former President Alberto Fujimori—in a so-called *self-coup d'état*—dissolved Congress and fired the constitutional authorities that declared a third reelection unconstitutional. Furthermore, disrespecting the separation of branches, Carlos Menem, a former Argentinian President, passed emergency acts to create and modify legislation. To make this possible he replaced independent judges of the Supreme Court with friends of his government.[36]

---

[31]Prillaman (2000), p. 2. See also Shirk and Rios Cazares (2007), pp. 3–7, explaining how during the transition from dictatorships to democracy that took place in the 1980s and 1990s the new political authorities focused on enhancing the perception of a legitimate delegation of sovereignty rather than on the traditional elements of the rule of law. State representatives had incentives to satisfy people's expectations and favored a system of redistribution of wealth to legitimize the new regimes at the expense of the rule of law. People, on the other hand, accepted violations of the key elements of the rule of law to achieve "social justice".

[32]Ungar (2002), pp. 20–23.

[33]Shirk and Rios Cazares (2007), pp. 3–7.

[34]Morris (1992), pp. 11–12.

[35]Schedler (1999), p. 159.

[36]Schor (2006), p. 4.

2.2.2 *Legal Certainty and the Rule of Law*

2.2.2.1 Understanding Legal Certainty

Legal certainty is at the center of the ideal of the rule of law. The objective of the law is to bring certainty to the uncertainty of social relationships. Specifically, legal certainty is related to the rule of law's objective of organizing society. To organize society legal consequences of actions must be predictable. Predictability entails that legal subjects cannot only understand individual legal rules but also the big picture of the legal system. People must be able to follow the directions of legal rules and themselves be able to foresee the consequences of their actions. As *Waldron* explains, when legal rules are predictable, the law "respects their dignity as beings capable of explaining themselves."[37]

Legal rules that provide legal certainty are "a great public good"[38] because they reduce the uncertainties of individuals' lives. When the legal rules are certain, people can avoid getting immersed in conducts that can produce negative legal consequences.[39] Thus, the ideal legal rules must be understandable by legal professionals and adjudicators, but also by people without legal training.[40] Legal certainty is a relevant principle in administrative law because its application seeks to protect individual citizens from the power of the state. To *Hayek* legal rules should "make it possible to foresee with a fair degree of certainty how the authority will use its coercive powers in given circumstances, and to plan one's individual affairs on the basis of this knowledge."[41]

Government needs a set of clearly systematized legal rules that are applied regularly to create consistent public policy. Even the discretion of public authorities needs to be subject to limits by the law in order to be predictable. Predictability of the rules that govern the actions of the state guarantees people's liberty. In this sense, it is a requirement of the law to be certain enough to validate the actions of state officials and it is an obligation of state officials to attach to those legal rules to provide certainty of their actions.[42]

Nowadays, guaranteeing legal certainty has become more complicated since the law regulates complex aspects, such as those related to the economy. It would be naive to think that it is possible to achieve perfect certainty in the law in a continuously evolving legal system that keeps on adapting to changes in society.[43] Legal certainty cannot be taken for granted. Aiming for legal certainty does not have

---

[37]Waldron (2008), p. 28.

[38]O'Donnell (2004), p. 35.

[39]According to Maxeiner, even if Americans have resignated to live with legal indeterminacy, the opposite, legal certainty is still a guiding principle of European law. See Maxeiner (2006), p. 543.

[40]Epstein (2011), p. 14.

[41]Von Hayek (2005), pp. 75–76.

[42]Epstein (2011), pp. 20–21.

[43]See Popelier (2000), p. 339.

to be understood as trying to achieve an absolute goal, because legal certainty is a *matter of degree*.[44] However, even though a legal system cannot provide total certainty, the more it provides, the better.

Hence, legal certainty does not mean that the law cannot be modified and adapted to a new environment. Legal certainty entails reasonable parameters of stability of the legal rules and responsibility of the law makers. In order to preserve legal certainty, the law makers must evaluate the reliability and validity of the legal rules and get sufficient information before creating or amending them. Certainty in the law is amidst the necessary steadiness of the legal rules and the unavoidable constant evolution of society that demands some *flexibility* to change and adapt to different times and necessities.[45]

2.2.2.2 Legal Certainty in Latin American Law

The closest term for legal certainty in, both, Spanish and Portuguese legal theory is *seguridad* or *segurança jurídica*, which can be literally translated as legal security (like the German *Rechtssicherheit*).[46] The terms legal certainty and legal security differ semantically. While the dictionary defines the word *certainty* as the clear knowledge and reliability on something,[47] *security* is the conviction of being safe from any threat, in other words, the absence of fear.[48] Therefore, *seguridad jurídica* entails more than just the knowledge and predictability of the law. Legal certainty, in this sense, also comprises the belief of being out of danger that determines the social behavior of people.[49] In other words, the equivalent of legal certainty in Spanish (and Portuguese) calls for a legally determinate setting where people can trust that their dignity is protected because they can rely on the ordering role of legal institutions.[50]

The importance of the principle of legal certainty is known and recognized in Latin America. According to the Constitutional Court of Colombia (CCC), the principle of legal certainty is a basic principle of a legal framework subject to the Constitution.[51] The principle of legal certainty is not directly mentioned in the

---

[44]Levy (1996), p. 189.

[45]Krajewski explains how the GATS (General Agreement on Trade and Services) embody certain elements of legal certainty such as transparency and clear and precise scheduling. At the same time, the GATS recognize the right of state members to introduce new regulations. See Krajewski (2014), pp. 89–90.

[46]See, e.g., Wroblewsky (1975), pp. 318–319. Wroblewsky explains that legal security and legal certainty are often considered the same.

[47]*Oxford Dictionary*, Definition of *certainty* in English.

[48]*Oxford Dictionary*, Definition of *security* in English.

[49]Wroblewsky (1975), p. 314.

[50]Sarlet (2010), pp. 8–9.

[51]Francisco Javier Lara Sabogal v. Congreso de la República de Colombia, CCC, Sentencia C-634-11, 24 August 2011.

Colombian Constitution, but it is implicit in the first articles. From the point of view of legal certainty as an instrument to protect people's dignity and integrity, Article 1[52] of the Colombian constitution establishes that Colombia is a state based on the respect of people's dignity. Articles 2[53] and 5[54] establish the role of the state regarding the respect and protection of constitutional principles. Article 3[55] explicitly binds the state to the law, particularly to the constitution. Article 4[56] establishes the supremacy of the constitution and that all laws of regulations have to remain coherent with constitutional provisions to be valid. Finally, Article 6[57] makes every individual responsible in case of legal violations.

References to legal certainty can also be found for the other countries. The Constitution of Mexico mentions the principle of legal certainty in relation to the protection of communal property of land.[58] The Constitutional Tribunal of Peru recognizes legal certainty as an implicit constitutional principle,[59] which is the basis for several decisions made by that Court.[60] In Argentina, the Supreme Court of Justice (CSJN Argentina) is in charge of interpreting and preserving constitutional principles like legal certainty.[61] According to the courts, a way of ensuring legal certainty in society is by protecting property rights, contractual obligations and

---

[52]Const. Colombia Art. 1.

[53]According to the Art. 2 Const. Colombia, "[t]he essential goals of the state are [. . .] to guarantee the effectiveness of the principles, rights and duties stipulated by the Constitution [. . .]."

[54]The Const. Colombia Art. 5 states that state authorities are obliged to "recognize, without any discrimination whatsoever, the primacy of the inalienable rights of the individual [. . .]."

[55]According to the Const. Colombia Art. 3, the representatives of the people must perform their functions "within the limits established in the Constitution."

[56]The Const. Colombia Art. 4 establishes: "The Constitution provides the norm of regulations. In all cases of incompatibility between the Constitution and the statute or other legal regulations, the constitutional provisions shall apply." Furthermore, "[i]t is the duty of citizens and of aliens in Colombia to obey the Constitution and the laws, and to respect and obey the authorities."

[57]In consonance with the Const. Colombia Art. 6: "Individuals are solely responsible before the authorities for violations of the Constitution and the laws."

[58]In this sense, according to the Constitution of Mexico Art. 27 (XIX) [English Translation of the Political Constitution of the Mexican States, Gazeta de la Federación, 5 February 1917] [hereinafter Const. Mexico]: "the State shall establish the measures required to provide agrarian justice in a prompt and honest manner, in order to guarantee legal certainty in land ownership."

[59]Percy Rogelio Zevallos Fretel v. Sala Civil Transitoria de la Corte Superior de Justicia de Huánuco, TC Peru, Sentencia Exp. No. 05448, 13 June 2012.

[60]Colegio de Notarios de Junín v. Congreso de la República de Perú, TC Perú, Sentencia Exp. No. 016, 30 April 2013. See also Scotiabank Perú S.A.A. v. Quinta Sala de lo Civil de la Corte Superior de Justicia de Lima, TC Perú, Sentencia Exp. No. 037, 25 January 2012, and Corporación Pesquera San Fermín S.A. v. Cuarta Sala de lo Civil de la Corte Superior de Justicia de Lima, TC Perú, Sentencia Exp.No. 02835, 13 December 2012.

[61]Arpires Luis Daniel v. Estado Nacional Ministerio de Justicia Seg y Der. Humanos Policía Federal s/Accidente en el ámbito militar y Fzas. de Seg, CSJN Argentina, Fallos: 7944:2004, 5 February 2009.

investment.[62] And last but not least, the Constitutional Tribunal of Chile (TC Chile) even claimed that guaranteeing legal certainty is part of the state's duty of promotion of the common good.[63]

2.2.2.3 A Brief Note on Legal Rules Versus Principles

The legal system includes rules and principles.[64] Principles of law may be considered to be something like the pillars of the legal system. Legal rules are its bricks. The general principles of law—like the principle of legal certainty[65]—are not invented by legislation; legislation may refer to them. They are abstract and do not need to fulfil the requirements of positive law.[66] Legal certainty—along with other principles of law—is taken into account in legal frameworks by mere invocation in the constitution, statutes or case law.[67]

In contrast, legal rules, the very products of legislation, shall influence people's choices and decisions by limiting possibilities of action.[68] They are also devices to assign competences and attributions among the traditional branches of the state and other state institutions.[69] To fulfill these functions legal rules need to be embedded in a hierarchical structure, on top of which is the constitution.[70] Legal rules are either mandates, prohibitions or authorizations. A *mandate* describes an action as compulsory; a *prohibition* expresses an omission as compulsory and an *authorization* states a conduct as permitted.[71] Legal rules are prompt to disagreements concerning their content and contestable in front of the courts when applied to particular cases.

Legal principles, however, are not contestable and, in case of conflict, they require to be balanced against each other.[72] In adjudication, the application of principles is not as straight forward as the application of legal rules. While legal

---

[62]*Irene Gwendoline and others v. Instituto de Educación Integral San Patricio S.R.L*, CJSN Argentina, Fallos: 330:5345, 18 December 2007.

[63]*Control constitucionalidad "Ley Tasa de Aranceles a las Importaciones"*, TC Chile, Sentencia Rol No. 280, 20 October 1998.

[64]Waldron (2008), p. 34.

[65]This is also considered this way in Latin America. For instance, *Banco de Crédito e Inversiones v. Congreso Nacional de Chile*, TC Chile, Sentencia Rol No. 574, 13 March 2007, the TC Chile refers to the principle of legal certainty as a general principle of public law that demands a reasonable stability of the legal situations and a "correct access to the rights."

[66]Bernitz et al. (2008), p. 26.

[67]Raitio (2003), p. 125.

[68]Wroblewsky (1975), pp. 313–314.

[69]Braithwaite (2002), p. 69.

[70]O'Donnell (2004), p. 34.

[71]Burgoa and Carlos (2011), pp. 62–63.

[72]Ratio explains that legal certainty requires a balance with other principles of law, like the principles of legality and proportionality. The search for proportionality demands a balance between the private and the public interest. See Raitio (2003), pp. 116–117.

rules are directly applied to a case, principles only show the path that a decision must follow.[73] *Paunio* explains that in judicial adjudication, the principles of law, such as legal certainty, are the underlining reasons that judges use to explain why their decisions are right.[74] They are the *spirit of the law* or the purpose that the legislator had at the moment of creating law.[75]

2.3 Notions of Legal Certainty

It is possible to analyze legal certainty from two points of view: the characteristics of the legal framework and the individual perception of legal certainty. The first is the *objective* (formal and substantive legal certainty) and the second is the *subjective* perspective of legal certainty.[76] We speak of objective legal certainty when the functional and structural characteristics of the legal system provide a sounds basis for the predictability, accessibility and acceptability of the legal rules.[77] Objective legal certainty focuses on the "process of law making, law finding, and law applying."[78]

---

[73]Bernitz et al. (2008), p. 26.

[74]Paunio explains that there are two different "reasons" that judges apply to justify their decisions: authority reasons (rules, precedent, and doctrine) and substantive reasons (principles). Furthermore, Paunio explains that in the context of adjudication there is also an important difference between principles and policies. From a judicial reasoning perspective, principles prevail over policies because they are linked to individual rights while policies are linked to society goals. Legal certainty falls within substantive reasons for adjudication and while being a principle, legal certainty has also deep importance for policy. For this reason, legal certainty can be considered a "meta-principle". See Paunio (2013), pp. 60–63.

[75]Federal Civil Code of Mexico Art. 19 [Código Civil Federal de México, Diario Oficial de la Federación, 26 May, 14 July, 31 August, 1928] [hereinafter Civ. Code Mexico] prescribes that *"when the meaning of the law is clear, its wording cannot be disregarded under the excuse of consulting its spirit. But it is possible to interpret an obscure legal expression by consulting the intentions or spirit clearly manifested in the law, or in the reliable history of its establishment* [Own Translation]." See also the Civil Code of Colombia Art. 27 [Código Civil de Colombia, Diario Oficial No. 46.494, 27 December 2006] [hereinafter Civ. Code Colombia] for instance, in case of legal gaps or obscurity in civil cases in Mexico, judicial decisions must be made according to the general principles of law. The Const. Mexico Art. 14 para 4: *"In civil trials, final sentence must agree with the law writing or the legal interpretation thereof. In the case of lack of the appropriate law, sentence must be based on the general principles of law."*

[76]Calderón (2009), p. 183.

[77]Popelier (2000), p. 340.

[78]In Europe, specifically in Germany, there is a huge interest in the prevalence of the principle of legal certainty. Legal certainty is entrenched in the German legal framework through practical methods of law making and law applying. See Maxeiner (2006), pp. 551–552.

2.3.1 Formal Legal Certainty

2.3.1.1 Definition and Importance

The most commonly referred to notion of objective legal certainty is formal legal certainty. The legal framework provides formal legal certainty when the law is determinate; it is able to answer legal inquiries and therefore allows for predictability of legal outcomes. Legal indeterminacy, by contrast, relates to the lack of precision that makes legal consequences difficult to predict. Legal indeterminacy produced by obscurity, incongruence and legal vacuums prevents people from understanding the law and leaves room for arbitrariness.[79]

2.3.1.2 Formal Legal Certainty and Law Making

The drafters of constitutional and legal rules have the main responsibility in providing legal certainty in the process of law making.[80] In the ideal scenario the representatives of the people, have the knowledge required to perform their task. They recognize that legal rules do not work in isolation because modifying one law affects the entire legal framework. They have a deep understanding about the issue the law is going to regulate.[81] Legislators must also take into account the existence of precedents that determine how the legal rules will be applied. And it is critical to evaluate the costs and outcomes of the new legal rules in the social and economic setting.[82]

The awareness of the context and impact of the law allows legal drafters to enact legal rules that apply the conditions of proper law making. Such laws are free of ambiguity, coherent with the legal framework, proportionate, reasonable and well-motivated.[83] They allow individuals to identify two extremes of the range of legality: what is legal and what is illegal; and make decisions that prevent them from negative outcomes.[84]

The ideal scenario of law making rarely exists. It is often the case that the spectrum of legality is full of nuances and fails to guide people's conduct and to prevent them from committing illegal actions and facing the consequences thereof. The lack of certain laws also make enforcement hardly possible. *De Logue* explains how uncertainties in tax law affect compliance and make tax enforcement

---

[79]Maxeiner (2006), p. 543. See also Maxeiner (2008), p. 35.

[80]Popelier (2000), p. 328.

[81]Waldron (2008), pp. 34–35.

[82]Popelier (2000), p. 340.

[83]For conditions of proper law making, see Popelier (2000), pp. 321–323. See also Calderón (2009), p. 184.

[84]De Logue (2005), pp. 251–252.

complicated.[85] These issues arise in Latin America because of the phenomena called "legislative motorization",[86] a common practice that seeks to improve legislation through deep and innovative changes. Yet, constant modifications produce a normative chaos instead of a simplified legal system that everybody can understand and assimilate.[87] Seeking clarity and coherence of the legal framework, the countries subject to this study have codified their legislation. For example, the Civil Code of Mexico dictates that when a newly enacted law prescribes something completely or partially different from an old one, this automatically abolishes the old one.[88]

2.3.1.3 Characteristics

Determinate legal rules best allow predicting legal outcomes because they are clear, precise, stable and coherent.[89]

Clarity

Clarity demands the absence of obscurities or imprecisions so that legal provisions leave no room for guessing. To avoid vague answers, the legislator must have sufficient knowledge about the topic the new legislation addresses. Further, the wording of the legal prescriptions must be precise enough to avoid linguistic indeterminacy produced when rules are too general, obscure or ambiguous.[90] Linguistic determinacy is important for legal interpretation. One of the main aspects to take into account when interpreting a law is the literal grammatical sense and the ordinary meaning of the words.

Note that, however, it is impossible to write up determinate legal rules for every instance the legislator might have in mind. In some cases, wording has to be vague. A vague standard, which is subject to interpretation by a court, is preferable if the alternative would be a clear rule that does not represent the intentions of the legislator or creates uncertainty by those subject to the rule.[91] Indeed, in cases of

---

[85]De Logue explains that when the substantive content of tax law is uncertain people tend to calculate their probability of a sanction for noncompliance and decide accordingly whether to attach to the legal rules or not. They also calculate the probabilities of "detection" and when it is low, they tend to take the risk of non-complying with the law. See *Ibid.*, pp. 245–252, 267, 278.

[86]Rivero Ortega (2013), pp. 51–52.

[87]Villegas (1993), p. 40.

[88]Civ. Code Mexico Art. 9: *"The law is repealed only by a subsequent law that expressly declares so or that contains provisions that are wholly or partially incompatible with the previous law.* [Own Translation]*"*.

[89]Maxeiner (2008), p. 32. See also Popelier (2000), pp. 321–323.

[90]For more on "uncertainties in language and law", see Paunio (2013), p. 12.

[91]Raban explains the differences between clearly written rules and flexible standards. See Raban (2010), pp. 175–190.

obscurity, courts infer from the *spirit of the law*, which is the intention of the legislator at the moment of creating the legal rule.[92]

Coherence

A coherent legal system is made up by legal rules that are "'hanging together', 'making sense as a whole', [with] 'cohesion', 'consonance' and 'speaking with one voice'."[93] Legal coherence means that the legal rules are coherent when analyzed individually but also when they are analyzed altogether.[94] Like pieces of a puzzle, the growing body of rules builds on each other and should fit with the rest to produce one picture. This body of rules includes the constitution, legislation, case law, administrative acts as well as policy.[95] In a coherent legal system, legal rules must not only be consistent with each other, but also with the underlining values that are the essence of the rule of law, i.e. the division of branches, equality under the law, and independence of judiciary, etc.[96] To have a coherent legal system it is necessary to get rid of archaic legal rules that may make it harder to determine which rules belong together.[97] Contextual coherence of the entire law and of the legal system itself is necessary for interpretation because even in case of obscurity of a particular legal rule the context can help recognize its real sense.[98]

Coherence is critical for predictability of the prevailing legal framework and also of future legal changes, because it is only possible to predict modifications of the legal rules when changes fit in a pre-existing coherent legal framework.[99]

---

[92]Civ. Code Colombia Art. 27: *"Grammatical interpretation. When the meaning of the law is clear, it is not possible to disregard its literal wording as an excuse to consult its spirit. But it is possible to interpret a dark legal expression by interpreting its clearly manifested intention or spirit or the reliable story of its establishment* [Own Translation].*"* Furthermore the Civ. Code Colombia Art. 28 states: *"Meaning of the words. The words of the law will be understood in their natural and obvious sense, according to their general use, but when the legislator has expressly defined them in some subjects, they will be given their legal sense* [Own translation].*"*

[93]Paunio (2013), p. 83.

[94]Braithwaite (2002), p. 55.

[95]Waldron (2008), pp. 32–33.

[96]Paunio departs from Dworkin's idea of law as an integrity or global coherence of the legal system. For more on the different notions of coherence, see Paunio (2013), pp. 83–84.

[97]Popelier (2000), p. 330.

[98]Civ. Code Colombia Art. 30: *"The context of the law will help to illustrate the sense of each one of its parts, so there must be among them due correspondence and harmony. The dark passages of a law can be illustrated by other laws, particularly if they are concerned with the same subject* [Own Translation].*"*

[99]Popelier (2000), p. 335.

Stability

Stability of the legal rules enhances people's confidence because if the law remains the same over time the expected legal consequences are also maintained.[100] However, legal rules cannot enjoy absolute stability because they regulate an evolving society. Technological or social changes may make it necessary to modify and adapt rules to new circumstances.[101] To provide stability, the law should be changed only in specific cases related with the common good, like a situation of evident necessity or potential threat to people's rights.[102]

Restrictions in the modification of the legal rules are important because legal change carries transition costs. At the core of the transition costs of creating and modifying legal rules is the idea that "a legal system will experience transitional friction simply in adjusting to the existence of a new positive law norm."[103] These costs include the cost of acquiring knowledge about the new rule, insecurity about the effects of the new legal rule, interpretative errors, private adjustment to the new rules and the cost in which state institutions incur to apply the new legal rule.[104] The sudden modification of private conventions can carry extra costs that were unforeseeable at the time agreements were made and affect private conventions that private parties can establish and apply in an environment of legal stability, like processes of contracting and conflict settlements. These changes carry also extra costs for the state that needs to establish a system of compensation and a process to protect "reliance interests".[105] Further, judiciary revision should be able to avoid the implementation of the new legal rule if the common good does not satisfactorily justify a reform.[106] Such changes can even trigger conflicts and disputes that challenge the capacity of the judiciary.[107]

2.3.2 Substantive Legal Certainty

2.3.2.1 Definition and Importance

There is substantive legal certainty when legal outcomes and judicial decisions can be *rationally accepted* by those directly affected and by the community in

---

[100]For a clarification on the importance of a stable taxation regime for entrepreneur, see Epstein (2003), pp. 81–82.

[101]*Ibid.*, p. 69.

[102]Oropeza Barboza (n.d.), p. 70.

[103]Van Alstine (2001), p. 1305.

[104]*Ibid.*, p. 1306.

[105]Epstein (2003), p. 76.

[106]For more on the costs of legal transitions, see Epstein (2003), pp. 81–85.

[107]For more on how legal transition costs affect the administration of justice, see Van Alstine (2001), pp. 1314–1316.

general.[108] *Suominen* claims that "legal certainty is understood as entailing a state having legislation", but also,

> a legal system that protects the individual against arbitrary measures from the state itself. Such measures include not being prosecuted or sentenced without sufficient evidence, not being sentenced without legal support and that all individuals are considered and treated equal regardless of their social status and origin.[109]

Thus, legal certainty is also related to the process of judicial adjudication that permits people, corporations and public bodies to dispute their rights and obligations in front of a court and to question whether or not a primary rule has been broken.[110] Substantive legal certainty challenges the traditional notion of formal legal certainty. It relates legal certainty to the ideal of justice.[111]

2.3.2.2 Substantive Legal Certainty and Law Applying

> Clear, general public norms are valueless if they are not properly administered, and fair procedures are not good if the applicable rules keep changing or are ignored altogether.[112]

The courts of justice can provide legal certainty through adjudication in three ways: (1) by adjudicating following a due process that respects substantial guarantees like the right to argue in a hearing; being equal in front of an independent court, etc. (2) by solving the unavoidable uncertainties of legislation. Judicial decisions are supposed to fill the gaps that the legislator was not able to cover at drafting the

---

[108]Paunio (2013), p. 2.

[109]Suominen (2014), pp. 6–7.

[110]Waldron (2008), pp. 20–21.

[111]It is claimed that legal certainty and justice are not the same. Even though foreseeability of the legal outcomes protects people from the arbitrary action of public officials it does not guarantee fairness in the content of the legal provisions nor in the judicial adjudication. Legal certainty and justice are two objectives of the rule of law that can be in conflict. Some argue that it is more important for the rule of law to be certain than to be just. The reason is that if people know with certainty that acting in some way will produce negative consequences, they can prevent themselves from committing deeds that can trigger negative legal outcomes. Moreover, even though people may feel distressed by a conflicting situation, it is a much greater distress for people to find themselves at risk of committing an illegal act and carrying the consequences. This can be the case when the law is obscure, the legal provisions are not consistent among each other or because the law was changed from one day to the other. Nevertheless, legal certainty and justice are complementary concepts because both are pillars of a system under the rule of law. The president of the Supreme Court of Justice of Brazil has manifested that legal certainty is a pivotal principle for the effectiveness of justice. Legal rules must provide predictability and the legal decisions must be rationally acceptable to increase the likelihood of fair judicial decisions. See Krajewski (2014), p. 79; see also Neuhaus (1963), p. 796.

[112]Waldron (2008), p. 8.

primary rule,[113] and (3) by including the characteristics of formal legal certainty in their drafting. Judicial decisions must be coherent with the broad legal system. This means that judicial decisions must be clearly written; the judicial reasoning must also be stable and permanent (*res iudicata*)[114] and coherent within the legal system. To be coherent a judicial decision must respect the primary legal rules but also take precedent into account.[115]

Formal and substantive legal certainty are closely related because the courts of justice are supposed to adjudicate according to what the legislators have defined as legal conducts. Judicial decisions are not the outcome of an established process of law making. Judges must apply general laws made by legislators to a particular case in order to solve a legal disagreement.[116] Therefore, formal legal certainty sets the conditions for substantive legal certainty to arise. To be acceptable judicial decisions must be motivated and show that the procedural guarantees have been respected. Only when a decision is justified it can be acceptable for the legal community in general.[117] The argumentation must respect precedent as much as possible, must be transparent, detailed and potentially show a priority order. Only a decision with these characteristics would be acceptable for those directly affected by decisions and the legal community in general.[118]

Other substantive characteristics of the system of adjudication, like independence of the judges counts at providing substantive legal certainty. Judges in courts are in charge of enforcing the generally existing laws and solving conflicts in particular cases[119] where there are doubts and disagreement about the application of the law.[120] Judicial decisions have to be based on the law and not on personal or political influences. That is why judges have to decide in strict attachment to the law and be

---

[113]Maxeiner explains that legal rules have unavoidably legal vacuums because it is impossible for legislators to address all the cases, all the conditions for a legal situation to arise, use an accurate language and avoid subjectivity at doing all this. See Maxeiner (2006), p. 555.

[114]Rodriguez Yong (2008), p. 422.

[115]Levi (2013), p. 502.

[116]Maxeiner (2006), p. 558.

[117]Paunio (2013), p. 3.

[118]*Ibid.*, p. 87.

[119]Waldron (2008), p. 20. If the courts must decide cases of civil nature, they determine rights of private parties. In criminal cases, they must act like the coercive arm of the society against actions that disturb the peaceful life of a community. In administrative cases the courts may protect the interests of the in front of the state. In constitutional cases, they may determine the attachment of the actions, functions and duties of authorities to the constitution. Among the countries in analysis only Mexico and Colombia have specialized courts to deal with administrative issues between government officials or administrative agencies. Mexico has the "Tribunal de lo Contencioso Administrativo" and Colombia the "Consejo de Estado." In the other countries, the competence to decide about administrative controversies lies with civil courts or tribunals.

[120]Waldron explains that judges decide by projecting the inherent logic of the law to the controversy or uncertainty of a case. See Waldron (2008), p. 35.

independent decisionmakers.[121] An independent judicial system is an effective control of the actions of the government, other political institutions and the bureaucracy. An independent judiciary increases the legitimacy of government decisions because it guarantees that they are made in conformity with the law. This role of independent courts not only guarantees the protection of people's rights but also the proper functions of the government in the performance of technical tasks that require broader discretion.[122]

The quality of the judicial decisions and their degree of acceptability by the legal subjects depends, at least partly, on the quality of the legal rules that define the legal situation and the methods of adjudication. Judges cannot make decisions based on their own conscience and understanding of the situation. In the process of judicial interpretation, the first thing that a judge does is a textual analysis of the legal rules. When analyzing the textual content of the law there are two aspects to take into account. First, it is necessary to attribute to the words their original meaning. This means that it is necessary to think about what the original writer meant by it and not more than that.[123] In words of *Richard Epstein*, "[i]t is usually dangerous business to put a modern gloss on a traditional term."[124] The general values reflected in established legal rules are the pattern to follow for judicial decisions.[125] These rules have to be clear, determinate and written in accurate language because the *ordinary meaning of words* is the most used argument in adjudication.[126]

However, even in the ideal scenario of an accurate process of lawmaking even for the best legislator is impossible to draft the law in a way to allow for perfect legal certainty in all possible circumstances. Legislators will never be able to avoid obscurity[127] and include all situations in the law that might be applied in the future.

---

[121]According to Dam, there are two types of judicial independence: "structural independence" and "behavioral independence." Structural independence entails the autonomy of the courts as an institution within the state. Behavioral independence entails the real freedom in the practice that individual judges have to make decisions. See Dam (2006), p. 16. Shetreet explains that to achieve an accurate degree of behavioral independence the judicial branch must enjoy leeway to decide about the appointment and dismissal of their members, their salaries, or their tenure. See Shetreet (1979), p. 57.

[122]Jordao and Rose-Ackerman explain that the role of the courts of justice should go beyond the protection of people's rights and try to balance democracy with those rights and with the technical functions of state organisms. See Jordao and Rose-Ackerman (2014), p. 4.

[123]Epstein (2007), p. 9.

[124]*Ibid.*

[125]Neuhaus (1963), pp. 802–803.

[126]Paunio (2013), p. 32.

[127]The Civil Code of Peru [Código Civil de Perú, Official Journal, 25 July 1984] [hereinafter Civ. Code Peru] made it an obligation for the Supreme Court, the Constitutional Court and the General Fiscal of the Nation to report cases of obscurity that complicate the clear interpretation and application of the law to Congress. Civ. Code Peru Art. X: *"The Supreme Court, the Constitutional Court (*) and the Attorney General are required to report to the Congress the gaps or deficiencies in legislation. Judges and prosecutors have the same obligation with respect to the corresponding upper court. [Own Translation]".*

It is impossible to categorize all cases without missing a single case using a language that describes each case in so much detail that no doubts may arise.[128] It is common and often preferable from the perspective of legal certainty to have primary rules or ambiguous legal standards that do not effectively determine the legality of a conduct[129] and make it impossible to develop judicial reasoning by following a simple formula: legislation + facts = decision.[130]

For this reason, the textual analysis of the legal rules is only the first phase of the process of judicial interpretation.[131] The next phase demands that the courts exercise some degree of discretion and solve the uncertainty through interpretation.[132] For instance, judicial interpretation may require the introduction of principles that do not exist in the constitutional text but are necessary to explain the mere existent of the constitutional prescription. *Epstein* mentions the doctrine of the *police power of the state* as a doctrine that is not mentioned in the U.S. Constitution but has been widely used by the American courts to justify the state's intervention in economic aspects to pursue welfare objectives.[133] Indeed, during interpretation adjudicators have to take into account that the legal system is multifaceted and does not only consist of a simple set of legal rules, but other elements like principles of law, the constitution, administrative acts, case law, etc. which have to be balanced in particular cases.[134]

In the case of common law systems, judging by precedent is the main technic to preserve legal certainty.[135] It entails that in each new case the adjudicator has to look for comparable judicial decisions made in the past about the same factual situation and apply analogically the same reasoning to the new case.[136] However, not every judicial decisions becomes an obligatory precedent right away, but after showing a clear influence on other decisions of the same kind along a timeline.[137] Precedent is also mandatory for a lower court when the decision has been made by a higher court.[138] Thus, judges are not only guided by the wording of *primary rules* that describe a particular conduct and impose a legal consequence but also by *secondary rules* which are preexisting judicial decisions. The secondary rules have the judge's insights in a particular case that influence future decisions on similar cases and

---

[128]Maxeiner (2006), p. 555.

[129]Paunio explains how multilingualism is a challenge for courts (in this case the ECJ) whose semantic discussions about the meaning of single words show that judges most of the time try to attach to the wording of the law. See Paunio (2013), p. 32.

[130]Maxeiner (2006), pp. 577–578.

[131]Epstein (2007), p. 9.

[132]On more about discretion as an essential element of positivism, see Kress (1984), pp. 372–373.

[133]Epstein (2007), p. 9.

[134]Kress (1984), p. 378. Lyons explains Dworkin's critics on positivism since a legal system is not only made of positive rules but also of principles. See also Lyons (1977), p. 418.

[135]Steiner (2005), p. 31; see also López Daza (2011), p. 174.

[136]Levi (2013), p. 2.

[137]Braithwaite (2002), p. 51.

[138]Steiner (2005), p. 32.

connect them to the entire legal system. Precedents must limit the court's decisions,[139] give a sense of *equal treatment* and provide predictability, steadiness and coherence with regard to the legal system[140] and saves time by avoiding constant constitutional litigation and contradictory decisions in cases in which the result should be predictable based on analogous cases.[141]

2.3.2.3 Accessibility of the Legal Rules and Law Finding

> Good laws are of little value, if the legal system does not provide an accessible, convenient, and efficient method of enforcing laws and obtaining redress for violation of rights.[142]

For legal rules to be accessible, they must be public[143] and understandable for everybody. Even though the technicality and heterogeneity of some legal rules can make them hard to understand for people without the required expertise, the structure and organization of the legal framework should assure, at least, a minimal degree of comprehensibility. A disorganized set of rules causes different sides of a conflict to have different conceptions of the law. Then, the meaning of the law is undetermined

---

[139]Paunio (2013), p. 95.

[140]To read more on an analysis of Scalia's Argument for Discretion-Constraining Norms, see Solum (2002), pp. 10–12.

[141]Dam mentions that in Brazil cases are seldom decided based on precedent. In Brazil cases are mostly decided on a fully individual basis, without considering previous decisions on the same topic. The consequence is the increased uncertainty on issues whose outcome should be clear from the beginning. See Dam (2006), p. 14.

[142]Shetreet (1979), pp. 62–63.

[143]According to Oropeza Barboza the publication must follow a process of promulgation. See Oropeza Barboza (n.d.), p. 68. This process is specified in the Civil Codes of the countries: Consolidated, Coordinated and Systematized Text of the Civil Code Law No. 4,808; about the Civil Registry Law No. 17,344; Minors Law No. 14,908; about Family Abandonment and Payment of Food Pensions and the Law No. 16,271 about Tax on Inheritance, Allocations and Donations [Texto Refundido, Coordinado y Sistematizado del Código Civil; de la Ley No. 4.808, sobre Registro Civil, de la Ley No. 17.344, que Autoriza Cambio de Nombres y Apellidos, de la Ley No. 16.618, Ley de Menores, de la Ley No. 14.908, sobre Abandono de Familia y Pago de Pensiones Alimenticias, y de la Ley No. 16.271, de Impuesto a las Herencias, Asignaciones y Donaciones, Diario Oficial, 30 May 2000] [hereinafter Civ. Code Chile]. According to Art. 6 Civ. Code Chile, *"the law is only binding once it is enacted according to the Constitution State and published in accordance with the following precepts.* [Own Translation]*"* Civ. Code Chile Art. 7: *"The law shall be published in the Official Journal, and from the date hereof the law is known and mandatory to all. For all legal purposes, the date of the law is the date of its publication in the Official Journal. However, any law may establish different rules about publication and the date or dates on which it takes effect.* [Own Translation]*".*
   Civil and Commercial Code of the Argentine Republic [Código Civil y Comercial de la Nación, Boletín Oficial, 8 October 2014] [hereinafter Civ. Code Argentina] Art. 2: *"Laws are only mandatory after their publication and from the date that is determined. If there is not determined date, they will be mandatory after eight days following their official publication.* [Own Translation]*"* See also Civ. Code Mexico Art. 3; Civ. Code Colombia Art. 12.

and the outcome unforeseeable. Further, the lack of systematization considerably increases money and time spend in solving cases.[144]

The publication of the legal rules is supposed to document the rule-making process and to inform about the changes. The "documentary function"[145] of legal publication seeks to increase transparency of the legal rules. In this sense, the publication has to reproduce a reliable version of the legal document enacted by the authorities, as well as the date of enactment. Its "informative function"[146] is to make subjects of the law aware that new rules have been created and also that other legal rules have been replaced or abolished. Because of the informative function of the publication of legal rules it is possible to assume that they are known by everybody and, therefore, mandatory for all legal subjects. This assumption is fundamental for legal certainty because it represents the assurance of the binding effect of the legal rules over people's behavior.[147]

Besides fulfilling the requirement of publication, legal rules are accessible and manageable for people when they are comprehensible. Extremely technical and heterogeneous legal rules can only be understood by legal professionals. They are inaccessible for people with little economic resources or without sophisticated legal education and, in the practice, they fail to guide people's behavior. Then, people are more likely to disobey the law and to get undesirable legal consequences.[148]

When new legal rules are constantly created, modified or difficult to understand, the informative function of the publication is not so effective to make people aware of the legal environment. Moreover, citizens are not so familiarized with the official publication as with the information obtained through the media, which is helpful but not a precise, impartial and accurate means of legal information.[149]

The legal system is accessible when there is access to the broad system of administration of justice. It does not only concern courts but also the police, investigators, prosecutors, and in general the entire apparatus of justice. It further entails good training of judges and lawyers and sufficient resources.[150] Efficient processes to avoid inefficiency problems that a broad access to justice could bring, such as an excessive amount of cases, court overcrowding and delay and economic arrangements that assure judicial service at a reasonable price or even at public expense.[151]

In Latin America, the judiciary system is less open to the general public than in Germany or the United States. For instance, in Mexico's judicial system lawyers and judges are, on average, insufficiently prepared, there are not enough resources and

---

[144]Maxeiner (2006), p. 603.

[145]Popelier (2000), p. 329.

[146]Ibid.

[147]Ibid., pp. 329–330.

[148]Braithwaite (2002), p. 57.

[149]Rhode (2001), p. 1793.

[150]Shetreet (1979), p. 63.

[151]Ibid., pp. 55–56.

procedures are ineffective.[152] Further, people in Latin America typically face high uncertainty about the judicial services that they are going to receive. Very often they do not know their natural judges, nor can they predict the outcomes of their cases.[153] Therefore, the legal system is widely perceived to be for a group of people and inaccessible for the most disadvantaged social groups that are priced out of the market for justice. The resulting lack of accessibility reflects inequality in front of the law.[154]

2.3.3 Subjective Legal Certainty

> The evaluation of legal certainty is determined by the attitude of the individual to the reality he lives in, and especially to the socio-political system and the law in force.[155]

The main difference to objective legal certainty is the change in perspective. From a subjective point of view what matters is this perception of legal certainty that makes people generate expectations about legal results.[156] While objective legal certainty is related to the inherent characteristics of the legal system, subjective legal certainty stems from the certitude and feeling of security that people have if they know that they are free of unforeseeable legal risks.[157] The perspective of subjective legal certainty goes from legal certainty in the books to the legal certainty in the society.[158] There is subjective legal certainty when legal subjects know that their

---

[152]To read more about the necessary changes in the judicial system in Mexico, see Shirk and Rios Cazares (2007), p. 1.

[153]Braithwaite (2002), p. 57. Maxeiner explains how even in legal indeterminate environments, legal certainty is improved when people can identify the appliers (in this case their natural judges) of the law. See Maxeiner (2006), pp. 559–560.

[154]O'Donnell (2004), p. 40.

[155]Wroblewsky (1975), p. 314.

[156]The principle of protection of legitimate expectations could be argued as the subjective perspective of legal certainty. According to Popelier, provided there is a perception of objective legal certainty people build legitimate expectations which are defined as "the certainty a subject of law has about the realization of his own expectations and what legal consequences will follow from his actions." See Popelier (2000), p. 340. See also Craig (1996), p. 303 claiming: "The natural role of legitimate expectations is, however, to reflect individual's perspective and the value of legal certainty."

[157]Villegas (1993), p. 36.

[158]For more on real legal certainty as the objective of implementation of the law, see Otto (2002), pp. 23–25.

rights are protected by the law and they have the ability to predict how and when authorities are going to apply it.[159] This certitude represents the most effective restriction of government power and promotes people's confidence in the law.

In Latin American law, the concept of legal certainty includes the predictability of the legal rules and acceptability of the judicial decisions, but also the confidence of people in the reliability of the legal system. The Constitutional Court of Colombia (CCC) has claimed that legal certainty is the certitude that people have about the authorities' protection and respect of their lives, freedom and property. Therefore, when state officials affect citizens' rights, legal certainty is a safeguard that demands the strict adherence of the authorities to the conditions and processes laid down beforehand in the constitution and the laws.[160] Subjective legal certainty requires trust in the courts of justice.

When legal rules are accessible, people have the required knowledge and are able to apply the law to themselves. Formal legal certainty makes the legal system trustworthy and people can rely on it if people can believe in the steadiness of the legal rules that protect their legal relationships and vested rights from sudden modifications. Then, predictability of legal outcomes is possible and legal subjects can develop expectations based on confidence. To sum up, from a subjective point of view, there is legal certainty when the state has been able to protect the relationship of trust with its citizens by accurately developing its law making, finding and applying roles.[161]

---

[159]Villegas (1993), p. 33.

[160]*Santiago Huertas Bequis v. Colegio Ateneo Moderno de Santa Marta y su Rector Alfredo Almenares Barros*, CCC, Sentencia T-256, 13 June 1993.

[161]Rodriguez Yong (2008), p. 422. See also Calderón (2009), pp. 183–184.

2.4 Legal Certainty and Other Principles of Law[162]

2.4.1 Legal Certainty and the Principle of Non-Retroactivity[163]

Legal rules that impose sanctions retrospectively cause uncertainty. They undermine predictability and affect people's plans much more than those that rule the future.[164] The *principle of non-retroactivity* of the law is a guarantee of legal certainty, because it prescribes that legal rules have to be prospective to not affect conducts or actions previously undertaken.[165] Economically, the application of retrospective rules may

---

[162]The discussion in this part of the chapter focuses on analyzing legal certainty as a general principle of law that has to be taken into consideration in the enactment of legal rules. However, it is important to mention the argument about principles providing more legal certainty than the rules themselves. John Braithwaite defends the idea that principles of law are more certain than detailed legal rules about topics related to a continuously modifying and dynamic environment like that of business and economics. The reason is that it is difficult to draw out all the possible details in situations that hardly remain unchanged. Attempting to do this only adds obscurity and inconsistency to the broad picture of the legal system. Therefore, when regulating this kind of areas, it is better to avoid using rules alone. Instead, a mix of precise legal rules backed up by non-binding principles is preferable. It is important the make the rule of law work and prevent adjudicators form ignoring legal prescriptions without justification in cases when the application of a legal rule in unreasonable. See Braithwaite (2002), p. 47.

[163]The legal frameworks of our six Latin American countries include the principle of non-retroactivity of the law in their constitutions. For instance, the Const. Colombia Art. 29, establishes that *"Due process shall be applied in all cases of legal and administrative measures. Guarantee of due process No one may be judged except in accordance with previously written laws which shall provide the basis of each decision before a competent judge or tribunal following all appropriate forms."* The Const. Mexico Art. 14 para 1: *"No law will have retroactive effect in detriment of any person."* See also *Juan Rafael Bravo Arteaga v. Congreso de la República de Colombia*, CCC, Sentencia C-549, 29 November 1993. See also Constitution of Peru Art. 2 [English Translation of Constitución Política del Perú, Diario Oficial, 30 December 1993] [hereinafter Const. Peru], prescribes that as part of people's right to freedom and personal security *"a. No one is obliged to do what the law does not command, nor prevented from doing what the law does not prohibit. b. No restrictions whatsoever to personal freedom shall be permitted, except in cases provided by the law. Slavery, servitude, and traffic in human beings are prohibited in any form. [...] d. No one shall be prosecuted or convicted for any act or omission that, at the time of its commission, was not previously prescribed in the law expressly and unequivocally as a punishable violation, or did not constitute an offense penalized by law.[...]"* The Constitution of Brazil Art. 5 [English translation of the Constituição da República Federativa do Brasil, Diario Oficial da União, 5 October 1988] [hereinafter Const. Brazil], prescribes that all persons are equal before the law, without any distinction whatsoever, Brazilians and foreigners residing in the country being ensured of inviolability of the right to life, to liberty, to equality, to security and to property, on the following terms: *"XXXIX. - There is no crime without a previous law to define it, nor a punishment."*

[164]Maxeiner (2006), p. 559.

[165]Popelier (2000), p. 333.

be extremely costly for, e.g., firms engaging in international trade that based calculations of profit and loss on assumptions no longer valid.[166]

The Constitutional Tribunal of Chile has recognized that the principle of non-retroactivity entails a fundamental guarantee for legal certainty, because predictability is only possible when the legal principle is known in advance. According to the Tribunal, attributing legal consequences to certain acts that an individual could not take into account at the moment of acting, because they were not part of the current legal framework, is in conflict with certainty of the law.[167]

There are two types of retroactivity of the law: "true-retroactivity" and "quasi-retroactivity",[168] also known as "apparent retroactivity".[169] True retroactivity refers to a new legal rule that applies to a legal situation that was concluded in the past, that is, before the publication of the legal rule. Quasi-retroactivity refers to legal rules that are prospective but have retroactive effects. This is the case when a new legal rule is applied to a legal situation that has not yet been completed.[170] It also can be seen in adjudication, when a prospective judicial decision outweighs previous precedents.[171]

Quasi-retroactivity is often seen in the area of public policy, when a new policy adopted by an administration has retroactive effects over the plans that people made based on a previous policy choice.[172] Examples of quasi-retroactivity are for instance when new taxes, that are effective prospectively, affect the prices of goods that were purchased before the new tax was in force,[173] or if, e.g., legislation that established the possibility of tax deductions is repealed after people performed transactions expecting a tax deduction in the future.[174] We may also think of examples when governments imposed product liability on firms for the harm their products might cause that was not in place when the product was actually sold so that a firm is punished based on an ex-ante unforeseeable legal rule. This may happen, e.g., when products do not obviously harm anyone right away but perhaps over longer periods or if used in a bad manner, e.g., in medicine.[175]

In criminal law, the principle of non-retroactivity is known as *nullum crimen, nulla poena sine lege stricta, (scripta), praevia* which means those criminal activities and their sanctions must be prescribed as unlawful before an action was

---

[166]Craig (1996), p. 304.

[167]*Banco de Crédito e Inversiones v. Congreso Nacional de Chile*, TC Chile, Sentencia Rol No. 574, 13 March 2007.

[168]For the wording, see Raitio (2003), p. 129.

[169]Craig (2006), p. 553.

[170]Raitio (2003), p. 129.

[171]Steiner (2005), p. 1.

[172]Craig (1996), p. 305.

[173]For a comprehensive understanding of legal retroactivity in the context of tax law, see Graetz (1977), p. 49.

[174]Epstein (2003), pp. 78–82.

[175]Epstein (2003), pp. 86–87.

undertaken. People should not be criminalized, convicted or punished for conducts that were legal at the time of being carried out.[176] The principle of non-retroactivity is related to legal certainty because a basic aspect of certainty in the law is that people should be able to rely on the rules that are valid when they act and not the ones created later be it by legislators or a judicial decision (in common law countries).[177] The principle literally demands legal certainty because it requires a strict design of criminal law, where the crimes and sanctions are specified without obscurity or ambiguity. In this regard, the Constitutional Tribunal of Chile maintains that to achieve legal certainty a precise description of conduct that is criminally punishable is necessary.[178] An exception to this principle is applicable in the case of modifications that are advantageous to the accused[179] but never when it is to a disadvantage.

2.4.2 Legal Certainty and the Protection of Legitimate Expectations

> A person must be able to rely on an established administrative practice or policy. If the government or administration raises certain expectations it must honor them.[180]

The quote implies that the protection of legitimate expectations guarantees that people who act lawfully do not find their expectations frustrated by policy or changes in the law.[181] In particular, expectations may turn out to be disappointed when people cannot foresee a change in legislation, public policy, and case law precedents or when a new administrative act comes into force.[182]

Reynolds outlines that in the common law tradition, the principle of protection of legitimate expectations is related to ideals of "fairness" *and* "the principle of good administration".[183] The principle of legitimate expectations is related to the principle of fairness particularly in adjudication to prevent that people face unfair outcomes

---

[176]For a more detailed explanation of the principle nullum crimen, nulla peoena sine lege stricta, (scripta), praevia, see Mokhtar (2005), pp. 41–47.

[177]Steiner (2005), p. 2.

[178]*Control constitucionalidad "Ley de Caza"*, TC Chile, Sentencia Rol No. 244, 26 August 1996. The *nulla poena sine lege* apllies also for administrative sanctions because they are also punitive. Administrative sanctions "are punitive in nature cannot be imposed unless they have a clear and unambiguous legal basis. *See:* Raitio (2003), p. 159.

[179]Const. Colombia Art. 29 para 3: *"In criminal law, permissive or favorable law, even when ex post facto, shall be applied in preference to restrictive or unfavorable alternatives."* See also Const. Brazil Art. 5 (XL), *"penal law shall not be retroactive, except to benefit the defendant."* See also Mokhtar (2005), p. 49.

[180]Popelier (2000), p. 327.

[181]Raitio (2003), p. 200.

[182]Popelier (2000), pp. 333–334.

[183]Reynolds (2011), pp. 330–337.

triggered by e.g. court decisions that overrule precedents laid down in past decisions.[184]

In the civil law systems, the principle of protection of legitimate expectations is closely related to legal certainty, because the instability of the law harms people's expectations.[185] "The law can only be certain when people know what to expect."[186] According to Argentina's Supreme Court of Justice, it is important that the legal actions that produce an expectation are kept to not disappoint the people that trusted them. The linkage between the trust of people's legitimate expectations and the certainty of the legal rules is that reciprocal promises, between for instance contractual parts, are based on clear and foreseeable legal rules.[187]

Reynolds mentions that the ECJ has repeatedly equated the principle of legal certainty and legitimate expectations to the point of invoking them as if they were the same. However, in the practice the protection of legitimate expectations challenges the clarity, stability and consistency of established legal rules. The reason is that legal certainty functions as a broad principle that underlies the entire legal system. Legitimate expectations, on the other hand, takes into account the point of view of the individual that considers his or her expectations disappointed. It follows that seeking to protect somebody's legitimate expectations could have as a result uncertainty about the legal framework applied in the particular case.[188]

Instead of claiming that the principles of protection of legitimate expectations and legal certainty are the same, it is more accurate to say that they are closely linked.[189] Consider public policy. Public policy is part of the legal framework. Therefore, public policy should not be considered acts of unconstrained discretion of the public authority but to reflect the main goals of society and ideals established in the law.[190] It is necessary to balance legal stability to protect legitimate expectations that might be upset by public policy with the necessary flexibility of regulation via accurate devices that provides public policy institution leeway to act, preserving a safe legal setting.[191]

To this end, the law must set constraints on discretion at conducting public policy because personal expectations can be threatened by excessive leeway of authorities. The fact that the actions of the public administration enjoy some degree of freedom can trigger sudden changes of administrative decisions that affect the plans of people. Given the complexity of modern legal systems people cannot have constant and accurate information about legal change or the content of the law at all times.

---

[184]Steiner (2005), p. 2.

[185]*Ibid.*, p. 23, 2.

[186]*Ibid.*, pp. 1–2.

[187]*Ibid.*

[188]Reynolds (2011), pp. 337–341.

[189]Craig (1996), p. 305; see also Craig (2006), p. 549.

[190]Paunio (2013), pp. 61–62.

[191]Krajewski (2014), pp. 80–81.

Therefore, the way authorities apply legal rules is of high importance for the perception of what the law is and for its future application.[192]

The common good is the main element that a court must take into account to equilibrate legitimate expectations with the needs of altering the legal environment.[193] In this sense, to make discretionary decisions also the public administration has to weight the common good versus somebody's legitimate expectations.[194]

Legal certainty is critical for protecting legitimate expectations especially when discretion is exercised on behalf of the *common good*. The law should provide constraints to discretion. For instance, it should be clear about a list of options among which the authority can freely choose, the accountability of public officials and even the fulfillment of preconditions to exercise discretion.[195] In this way, even the actions of discretionary administrative bureaucracies can be predictable insofar as the actions of the public officials attach to an objectively certain legal framework.[196]

The principle of protection of legitimate expectations and legal certainty are applied in international and domestic law. In international investment law, these two principles are linked to the standard of a *fair and equitable treatment* that has been invoked as a natural expectation of investors that states must respect. The *fair and equitable treatment* standard entails that investors should be able to rely on the state organs to decide homogenously.[197]

The development of expectations is closely related to the subjective perspective of legal certainty. It is in fact claimed that "the natural role of legitimate expectations is, however, to reflect the individual's perspective and the value of legal certainty."[198] Even though, for example, in German law[199] the principles of legal certainty and legitimate expectations are clearly differentiated, they overlap in

---

[192]Craig (1996), p. 298.

[193]*Ibid.*, p. 292.

[194]*Ibid.*, p. 303.

[195]Maxeiner (2006), pp. 561–562.

[196]Lachmann (1971), p. 114.

[197]Kingsbury and Schill (2009), pp. 8–12. See also *CMS Gas Transmission Company. v. The Republic of Argentina*, ICSID, Case No. ARB/01/8, Award, 12 May 2005, para 274. Similarly, *Occidental Exploitation and Production Company (OEPC) v. the Republic of Ecuador*, UNCITRAL, LCIA Case No. UN3467, Final Award, July 2004, para 183. Those cases are used in Kingsbury and Schill (2009), p. 10.

[198]Craig (1996), p. 303.

[199]Reynolds explains that both, the principle of legal certainty and the protection of legitimate expectations are creations of German law. Within the German legal framework, they are clearly differentiated. Legal certainty (Rechtssicherheit) stresses the importance of certainty of the content of the law. The protection of legitimate expectations (Vertrauensschutz) focuses on protecting people who trusted that the actions of the public authorities are legal. The principle of protection of legitimate expectations has in this context a specific target that is the actions of the public administration. However, the protection of legitimate expectations can be applied even against legislation threatening the basic requirements of legal certainty such as stability of the legal rules. See Reynolds (2011), pp. 340–341.

Latin American legal frameworks.[200] In Brazilian law they are treated almost like synonyms.[201] According to the Constitutional Court of Colombia, the principle of the protection of legitimate expectations (confianca or confianza legitima) is a crucial requirement for the existence of legal certainty.[202]

In a similar manner, the Constitutional Tribunal of Chile (TC Chile) has linked the principle of legal certainty to the protection of legitimate expectations as follows:

> Among the characteristic elements of the rule of law are legal certainty and the protection of legitimate expectations, that must be enjoyed by whom develop their activities under principles and positive rules. This entails that everybody must be able to trust that their behavior, if it is subject to the existing law, must be recognized by the legal order and, therefore, produce all the legal effects related to their actions [Own Translation].[203]

2.5 Summary

Legal certainty is a general principle of law that guides how the law has to be made, interpreted and applied. In Latin America, constitutional provisions or judicial decisions of the courts refer to the principle of legal certainty. Even though legal

---

[200]The principle of protection of legitimate expectations overlaps also with other principle like proportionality, fairness, abuse of power, good administration. See Reynolds (2011), p. 330. Retroactivity and good faith. The principle of proportionality requires a deeper understanding of the influence that legal rules and public decisions can have on people. See Thomas (2000), pp. 15–16.

Proportionality also requires that legal rules are realistic in their demands. See Popelier (2000), p. 337. From the perspective of law enforcement, the principle of proportionality seeks to avoid arbitrariness in the actions of state officials. Then authorities' actions cannot override fundamental rights and should not do more than what is necessary to achieve their goals. See Raitio (2003), pp. 97–98.

The principle of protection of legitimate expectations is considered the "technical form" of the principle of fairness. It specifically means "the right to fair treatment at the hands of the public authority." Further, it is argued that the principle of protection of legitimate expectations is an "application of the principle of abuse of power" that seeks to avoid "unfairness of the public authority". Reynolds (2011), p. 332.

At the center of the principle of good faith of the administration is the idea of that even though ignorance about the law does not exclude people from the consequences of not applying the law, this is not only in the responsibility of the individual if the authorities have contributed to unlawful action by providing the wrong information either through inaccurate advice or inconsistency in the public actions. See Kuusikko (2001), pp. 458–459, 469.

[201]The Supreme Federal Tribunal of Brazil (the organ in charge of constitutionality control) considers the protection of legitimate expectations as version of legal certainty especially regarding electoral topics. See *Vicente de Paula de Souza Guedes v. Ministério Público Eleitoral*, STF Brasil, Recurso Extraordinario No. 637.485. 1 August 2012.

[202]Rodriguez Yong (2008), p. 422. See also *Carlos A. Ballesteros B v. Gobierno de la República de Colombia*, CCC, Sentencia C-314, 1 April 2004.

[203]*Banco de Crédito e Inversiones v. Congreso Nacional de Chile*, TC Chile, Sentencia Rol No. 574, 13 March 2007.

certainty is not directly related to the goal of achieving justice, it is critical for achieving the rule of law's objective of organizing society. Certainty about the law contributes to the institutional wide order by gathering accurate information about the legality or illegality of actions, which facilitates the interaction in society.

The chapter has also outlined different notions of legal certainty. For there to be formal legal certainty legal rules must be clear, stable and consistent. It is the role of lawmakers to create legislation with these characteristics to enable those who are subject to the law to predict the legal outcomes of their actions. To provide certainty the law also has to be accessible. This implies a duty of the state in publishing the legal rules and establishing means that make the law reachable and understandable for the layman. Further, law adjudicators are supposed to enact coherent judicial decisions that are in harmony with the legal framework and promote the social acceptability of their verdicts, i.e., substantive legal certainty. A legal system that is able to achieve a high degree of objective (formal and substantive) legal certainty is also able to promote legal certainty from the point of view of those subject to the law, i.e., subjective legal certainty.

Finally, the principle of legal certainty is touched when the courts invoke other related principles like the principle of non-retroactivity and the principle of the protection of legitimate expectations. The latter is often considered the practical consequence of legal certainty especially in Latin American legal systems.

Legal References

Constitutions

Constitution of Colombia with Amendments through 2015 [English Translation of Constitución Política de Colombia, Diario Oficial No. 49.554, 25 June 2015]. Constitute Project, University of Texas at Austin, available at https://www.constituteproject.org/constitution/Colombia_2015.pdf

Constitution of Mexico [English Translation of the Political Constitution of the Mexican States, Gazeta de la Federación, 5 February 1917], Constitute Project, University of Texas at Austin, available at https://www.constituteproject.org/constitution/Mexico_2015.pdf?lang=en

Constitution of Peru [English Translation of Constitución Política del Perú, Diario Oficial, 30 December 1993], Congress of the Republic of Peru, available at http://www.congreso.gob.pe/Docs/files/CONSTITUTION_27_11_2012_ENG.pdf [Last accessed on November 11, 2018].

Legislation

Argentina

Civil and Commercial Code of the Argentine Republic [Código Civil y Comercial de la Nación, Boletín Oficial, 8 October 2014].

Colombia

Civil Code of Colombia [Código Civil de Colombia, Diario Oficial No. 46.494, 27 December 2006].

Chile

Consolidated, Coordinated and Systematized Text of the Civil Code Law No. 4,808; about the Civil Registry Law No. 17,344; Minors Law No. 14,908; about Family Abandonment and Payment of Food Pensions and the Law No. 16,271 about Tax on Inheritance, Allocations and Donations [Texto Refundido, Coordinado y Sistematizado del Código Civil; de la Ley No. 4.808, sobre Registro Civil, de la Ley No. 17.344, que Autoriza Cambio de Nombres y Apellidos, de la Ley No. 16.618, Ley de Menores, de la Ley No. 14.908, sobre Abandono de Familia y Pago de Pensiones Alimenticias, y de la Ley No. 16.271, de Impuesto a las Herencias, Asignaciones y Donaciones, Diario Oficial, 30 May 2000].

Mexico

Federal Civil Code of Mexico [Código Civil Federal de México, Diario Oficial de la Federación, 26 May, 14 July, 31 August 1928].

Peru

Civil Code of Peru [Código Civil de Perú, Diario Oficial, 25 July 1984].
General Act of Administrative Procedure of Peru [Ley de Procedimiento Administrativo General, Official Journal, 10 April 2001].

Case Law

ICSID

CMS Gas Transmission Company v. The Republic of Argentina, ICSID, Case No. ARB/01/8, Award of 12 May 2005, para 274.

UNCITRAL

Occidental Exploitation and Production Company (OEPC) v. the Republic of Ecuador, UNCITRAL, LCIA Case No. UN3467, Final Award of July 2004, para 183.

Corte Suprema de Justicia de la Nación [Supreme Court of Justice of Argentina]

Arpires Luis Daniel v. Estado Nacional Ministerio de Justicia Seg y Der. Humanos Policía Federal s/Accidente en el ámbito militar y Fzas. de Seg,CJSN Argentina, Fallos: 7944:2004, 5 February 2009.
Irene Gwendoline y otros v. Instituto de Educación Integral San Patricio S.R.L, CJSN Argentina Fallos: 330:5345, 18 December 2007.

Supremo Tribunal Federal do Brazil [Supreme Federal Court of Brazil]

Vicente de Paula de Souza Guedes v. Ministério Público Eleitoral, Supreme Federal Court of Brazil, Recurso Extraordinario No. 637.485. 1 August 2012.

Tribunal Constitucional de Chile [Constitutional Tribunal of Chile]

Control constitucionalidad "Ley de Caza", TC Chile, Sentencia Rol No. 244, 26 August 1996.
Control constitucionalidad "Ley Tasa de Aranceles a las Importaciones", TC Chile, Sentencia Rol No. 280, 20 October 1998.
Rafael Selume Sacaan v. Congreso Nacional de Chile, TC Chile, Sentencia Rol No. 472,30 August 2006.
Banco de Crédito e Inversiones v. Congreso Nacional de Chile, TC Chile, Sentencia Rol No. 574, 13 March 2007.

Corte Constitucional de Colombia [Constitutional Court of Colombia]

Santiago Huertas Bequis v. Colegio Ateneo Moderno de Santa Marta y su Rector Alfredo Almenares Barros, CCC, Sentencia T-256, 13 June 1993.
Juan Rafael Bravo Arteaga v. Congreso de la República de Colombia, CCC, Sentencia C-549, 29 November 1993.
Carlos A. Ballesteros B v. Gobierno de la República de Colombia, CCC, Sentencia C-314,1 April 2004.
Francisco Javier Lara Sabogal v. Congreso de la República de Colombia, CCC, Sentencia C-634-11, 24 August 2011.

Tribunal Constitucional del Perú [Constitutional Tribunal of Peru]

Scotiabank Perú S.A.A. v. Quinta Sala de lo Civil de la Corte Superior de Justicia de Lima, TC Perú, Sentencia Exp. No. 037, 25 January 2012.

Percy Rogelio Zevallos Fretel v. Sala Civil Transitoria de la Corte Superior de Justicia de Huánuco, TC Peru, Sentencia Exp. No. 05448, 13 June 2012.

Corporación Pesquera San Fermín S.A. v. Cuarta Sala de lo Civil de la Corte Superior de Justicia de Lima, TC Perú, Sentencia Exp.No. 02835, 13 December 2012.

Colegio de Notarios de Junín v. Congreso de la República de Perú, TC Perú, Sentencia Exp. No. 016, 30 April 2013.

References

Bastiat F (1968) The law. Laissez Faire Books

Beaulac S (2007) An inquiry into the international rule of law, EUI Max Weber Program Services Working Paper 14. Available at http://papers.ssrn.com/sol3/papers.cfm?abstract_id=1074562

Bernitz U, Nergelious J, Cardner C, Groussot X (2008) General principles of EC law in a process of development: reports from a conference in Stockholm 23–24 March. Swedish Network for Legal Studies, Kluwer Law International

Braithwaite J (2002) Rules and principles: a theory of legal certainty. Aust J Legal Philosophy 27:47–82. Available at http://heinonline.org/HOL/LandingPage?handle=hein.journals/ajlph27&div=6&id=&page=

Burgoa T, Carlos A (2011) La Deóntica Jurídica como Clave de la Interpretación de las Leyes Fiscales. Contaduría y Administración 235:57–76. Available at http://www.cya.unam.mx/index.php/cya/article/view/419

Calderón G (2009) Seguridad Jurídica y Derecho Penal. Revista de Estudios de la Justicia 11:181–199. Available at http://web.derecho.uchile.cl/cej/rej11/OLIVER%20_14_.pdf

Clark D (1999) The many meanings of the rule of law. In: Jayasuriya K (ed) Law, capitalism and power in Asia: the rule of law and legal institutions. Routledge, New York, pp 28–44

Craig P (1996) Substantive legitimate expectations in domestic community law. Cambridge J 55 (2):289–312. https://doi.org/10.1017/S0008197300098184

Craig P (2006) EU Administrative Law. Oxford University Press

Dam K (2006) The Judiciary and Economic Development. University of Chicago Law School, Chicago Unbound, Coase-Sandor Working Paper Series in Law and Economics No. 287. Available at http://chicagounbound.uchicago.edu/cgi/viewcontent.cgi?article=1536&context=law_and_economics

De la Hidalga L (2008) Teoría General del Estado. Editorial Porrúa, México

De Logue K (2005) Optimal tax compliance and penalties when the law is uncertain. Virginia Tax Rev 25(339):241–296. Available at http://repository.law.umich.edu/law_econ_archive/art66/

Epstein R (2003) Beware of Legal transitions: a presumptive vote for the reliance interest. J Contemp Legal Iss 13(69):69–92. Available at http://heinonline.org/HOL/LandingPage?handle=hein.journals/contli13&div=9&id=&page=

Epstein R (2007) How progressives rewrote the constitution. Cato Institute

Epstein R (2011) Design for liberty: private property, public administration and the rule of law. Harvard University Press

Fondation pour le droit continental (2015) Index of Legal Certainty: Report for the Civil Law Initiative. Available at http://www.fondation-droitcontinental.org/en/wp-content/uploads/2015/06/NS_Rapport-complet-5-juin-2015_EN.pdf

Gordillo A (2012) Tratado de Derecho Administrativo y Obras Selectas. Tomo 5, Primeras Obras, Fundación de Derecho Administrativo. Available at http://www.gordillo.com/pdf_tomo5/tomo5.pdf

Graetz M (1977) Legal transitions: the case of retroactivity in income tax revision. Univ Pa Law Rev 126(1):47–87. https://doi.org/10.2307/3311758

Gribnau H (2013) Equality, legal certainty and tax legislation in the Netherlands. Fundamental legal principles as checks on legislative power: a case study. Utrecht Law Rev 9(2):52–74

Jordao E, Rose-Ackerman S (2014) Judicial review of executive policy making in advanced democracies: beyond rights review. Adm Law Rev 66(1):1–71. Available at https://papers.ssrn.com/sol3/papers.cfm?abstract_id=2419994

Kingsbury B, Schill S (2009) Investor-State Arbitration as Governance: Fair and Equitable Treatment, Proportionality and the Emerging Global Administrative Law. NYU School of Law, Public Law and Legal Theory Research Paper Series, Working Paper 9(46). Available at http://papers.ssrn.com/sol3/papers.cfm?abstract_id=1466980

Krajewski M (2014) Balancing legal certainty with regulatory flexibility. In: Lim A, De Meester B (eds) WTO domestic regulation and services trade–putting principles into practices. Edward Elgar, pp 79–94

Kress K (1984) Legal reasoning and Coherence: Dworkin's rights thesis, retroactivity and the linear order of decisions. Calif Law Rev 72(3):369–402. https://doi.org/10.2307/3480482

Kuusikko K (2001) Advice, good administration and legitimate expectations: some comparative aspects. Eur Public Law 7(3):455–472

Lachmann L (1971) The legacy of Max Weber. The Glendessary Press. Available at https://mises.org/system/tdf/The%20Legacy%20of%20Max%20Weber_2.pdf?file=1&type=document

Levi E (2013) An introduction to legal reasoning. University of Chicago Press

Levy D (1996) Does an independent Central Bank violate democracy? J Post Keynes Econ 18 (2):189–210. https://doi.org/10.1080/01603477.1995.11490068

López Daza GA (2011) El juez constitucional colombiano como legislador positivo: ¿un gobierno de los jueces? Revista Mexicana de Derecho Constitucional 24:169–193. Available at http://www.scielo.org.mx/scielo.php?pid=S1405-91932011000100005&script=sci_arttext

López Guerra L (1980) Sobre la Personalidad Jurídica del Estado. Revista del Departamento de Derecho Político, Universidad de Extremadura 6:17–35. Available at https://pdfs.semanticscholar.org/39c0/87cb40675664b2c4c5b06babad47faae99d0.pdf

Lyons D (1977) Principles, positivism and legal theory. Yale Law J 87(2):415–435. https://doi.org/10.2307/795657

Mainwaring S (2003) Introduction: Democratic accountability in Latin America. In: Mainwaring S, Welna C (eds) Democratic accountability in Latin America. Oxford University Press, pp 3–33

Maxeiner J (2006) Legal certainty: a European alternative to American legal indeterminacy. Tulane J Int Law Company Law 15(541):545–607. Available at http://heinonline.org/HOL/LandingPage?handle=hein.journals/tulicl15&div=20&id=&page=

Maxeiner J (2008) Some realism about legal certainty. Houst J Int Law 31(1):27–46. Available at https://papers.ssrn.com/sol3/papers.cfm?abstract_id=1230457

Mokhtar A (2005) Nullum Crimen, Nulla Poena Sine Lege: aspects and prospects. Statute Law Rev Oxford University Press 26(1):41–55. https://doi.org/10.1093/slr/hmi005

Morris SD (1992) Corrupción y Política en el México contemporáneo. Siglo XXI

Neuhaus P (1963) Legal certainty and equity in the conflict of laws. Law Contemp Probl 28 (4):795–807. https://doi.org/10.2307/1190565

O'Donnell G (2004) The quality of democracy: why the rule of law matters. J Democr 15(4):32–46. https://doi.org/10.1353/jod.2004.0076

Oropeza Barboza A (n.d.) La Seguridad Jurídica en el Campo del Derecho Privado. Revista de la Escuela de Derecho de Puebla 2:61–80. Available at https://revistas-colaboracion.juridicas.unam.mx/index.php/juridica-libre-puebla/article/view/570/520

Otto J (2002) Toward an analytical framework: real legal certainty and its explanatory factors. In: Chen J, Li Y, Otto J (eds) Implementations of law in the People's Republic of China. Martinus Nijhoff Publishers, pp 23–34

Paunio E (2013) Legal certainty in multilingual EU law: language, discourse and reasoning at the European Court of Justice. Ashgate Publishing Limited

Popelier P (2000) Legal certainty and the principles of proper law making. Eur J Law Reform 2 (3):321–342. Available at http://heinonline.org/HOL/LandingPage?handle=hein.journals/ ejlr2&div=27&id=&page=

Prillaman W (2000) The Judiciary and democratic decay in Latin America: declining confidence in the rule of law. Greenwood Publishing Group

Raban O (2010) The fallacy of legal certainty: why vague legal standards may be better for capitalism and liberalism. Public Interest Law J 19(175):175–190

Raitio J (2003) The principle of legal certainty in EC law. Kluwer Academic Publishers

Reynolds P (2011) Legitimate expectations and the protection of trust in public officials. Public Law 2:330–352

Rhode D (2001) Access to Justice. Fordham Law Rev 69(1785):1785–1819. Available at http:// heinonline.org/HOL/LandingPage?handle=hein.journals/flr69&div=65&id=&page

Rivero Ortega R (2013) Derecho Administrativo Económico. Sexta Edición, Marcial Pons

Rodriguez Yong C (2008) Enhancing legal certainty in Colombia: the role of the Andean community. Mich State J Int Law 17(407):408–463. Available at http://heinonline.org/HOL/ LandingPage?handle=hein.journals/mistjintl17&div=17&id=&page=

Sarlet WI (2010) A eficácia do Direito Fundamental à Segurança Jurídica: Dignidade da Pessoa Humana, Direitos Fundamentais e Proibição de Retrocesso Social no Direito Constitucional Brasileiro. Revista di Direito Social 14(21):1–38. Available at http://www.direitodoestado.com/ revista/rere-21-marco-2010-ingo-sarlet.pdf

Schedler A (1999) The self-restraining state: power and accountability in new democracies. Lynne Rienner Publishers. Available at https://books.google.de/books?id=MD8Vx1HLOZgC& dq=zedillo+judicial+reform+abuse+of+power&lr=&hl=de&source=gbs_navlinks_s

Schor M (2006) Constitutionalism through the looking glass of Latin America. Texas Int Law J 41 (1):1–38. Available at http://heinonline.org/HOL/LandingPage?handle=hein.journals/tilj41& div=6&id=&page=

Shetreet S (1979) The administration of justice: practical problems, value conflicts and changing concepts. I.B.C. Law Rev 13(52):52–80. Available at http://heinonline.org/HOL/LandingPage? handle=hein.journals/ubclr13&div=8&id=&page

Shirk D, Rios Cazares A (2007) Introduction: reforming the administration of Justice in Mexico. In: Cornelius W, Shirk D (eds) Reforming the administration of Justice in Mexico. University of Notre Dame Press, pp 1–50. Available at http://www3.undpress.nd.edu/excerpts/P01130-ex.pdf

Solum L (2002) A Law of Rules: A Critique and Reconstruction of Justices Scalia's View of the Rule of Law. Loyola Law School (Los Angeles) Public Law and Legal Theory, Research Paper No. 5. Available at http://www.researchgate.net/profile/Lawrence_Solum/publication/ 228168419_A_Law_of_Rules_A_Critique_and_Reconstruction_of_Justice_Scalia's_View_ of_the_Rule_of_Law/links/540a06a40cf2d8daaabf9ebf.pdf

Steiner E (2005) Judicial ruling with prospective effect – from comparison to systematization. In: Steiner E (ed) Comparing the prospective effect of judicial ruling across Jurisdictions, Ius Comparatum – Global Studies in Comparative Law 3:1–23. Available at http://link.springer. com/book/10.1007/978-3-319-16175-4

Suominen A (2014) What role for legal certainty in criminal law within the area of freedom, security and Justice in the EU? Bergen J Crim Law Just 2(1):1–31. https://doi.org/10.15845/bjclcj.v2i1. 615

Thomas R (2000) Legitimate expectations and proportionality in administrative law. Hart

Ungar M (2002) Elusive reform: democracy and the rule of law in Latin America. Lynne Rienner Publishers

Van Alstine M (2001) Treaty law and legal transition costs. Chicago-Kent Law Rev 77:1303–1324. Available at http://heinonline.org/HOL/LandingPage?handle=hein.journals/chknt77& div=43&id=&page=

Villegas H (1993) El Contenido de la Seguridad Jurídica. Revista Impuestos. Available at http:// www.ipdt.org/editor/docs/02_Rev26_HBV.pdf

Von Hayek F (2005) The Road to Serfdom, Reprint 2005. Routledge Classics, London and New York

Waldron J (2008) The concept of the rule of law. Georgia Law Rev 43(1):1–54. Available at http:// heinonline.org/HOL/LandingPage?handle=hein.journals/geolr43&div=4&id=&page

Wroblewsky J (1975) Functions of law and legal certainty. Anuario de Filosofía del Derecho 17:313–321

Chapter 3
Legal Certainty and Legal Commitment Mechanisms

3.1 Introduction

The dictionary defines the word *commitment* as "the engagement or obligation that restricts freedom of action" and "the state or quality of being dedicated to a cause, activity, etc."[1] Credibility is "the quality to be trusted and believed in."[2] Therefore, a credible commitment is a promise that can be assumed to be fulfilled. For governments, a *problem of credible commitments* arises if people distrust the government's promises. A reliable incentive scheme can help make government commitments credible.[3]

A country's legal framework guides and limits the actions of the state and defines the relationship between rulers and ruled, helping, for instance, public institutions to commit to predictable actions. To prevent abuse of power by the rulers, legal frameworks include commitments of the state, e.g., "to guarantee full enjoyment of human rights, to protect the population from threats to their security, and to promote general welfare based on justice and the comprehensive and balanced development of the Nation."[4] More specific examples are the legal commitment of the General Comptroller of Colombia who "oversees the fiscal management of the administration and of individuals or entities that manage funds or assets of the Nation";[5] of the Colombian National Attorney General "to protect human rights and ensure their effectiveness";[6] and of the deputies in Brazil to not "be the owners, controllers or directors of a company which enjoys benefits arising from a contract

---

[1] *Oxford Dictionary*, Definition of *Commitment* in English.
[2] *Oxford Dictionary*, Definition of *Credibility* in English.
[3] Miller (2002), p. 297.
[4] Const. Peru Art. 44.
[5] Const. Colombia Art. 267 para 1.
[6] *Ibid.*, Art. 277.

with a public legal entity or perform a remunerated position therein".[7] Thus, the legal system provides incentives to solve the central dilemma around the credibility of commitments, which is "how to bind the players to agreements across space and time."[8]

However, the mere embedment of commitments in the legal framework does not in itself solve the problem of credibility. Legal certainty is a precondition for credible commitments. This chapter shows that the degree of legal certainty that legal rules provide determines the credibility of legal commitments in two ways. First, legal rules that provide a high degree of legal certainty help governments make predictable decisions. Second, such legal rules will prevent abuse and give people reason to believe that state officials will fulfill their legal commitments—the subjective notion of legal certainty.

To show the relationship between legal certainty and credible commitments, this chapter reviews the function of legal rules as institutions in providing incentives for governments to act according to their legal mandate and explains what kind of legal mechanisms are more suitable to incorporate credible commitments in terms of the degree of legal certainty that they provide.

3.2 Legal Framework and Commitments

3.2.1 Legal Rules and Institutions

People collaborate to achieve both private and social goals. Cooperation is best possible when social actors have information about other people's plans and actions. According to the institutional economics literature, institutions are structures that act as communication channels that provide people with information. Institutions, such as legal rules, encapsulate people's expectations about how others are going to behave and condense the set of guidelines that different groups of people will follow.[9] Institutions give orientation. They may limit the range of actions of each player. However, institutions also allow guessing "with greater confidence what others will do."[10]

---

[7]Const. Brazil Art. 54 (II a).

[8]North (1993), p. 11. Of course, this does not necessarily mean that contracts or promises cannot be breached. But the legal system shall provide incentives to discourage deviating from promises made by the government.

[9]Lachmann (1971), pp. 49–50.

[10]*Ibid.*, p. 61. By contrast, the institutional economics literature considers the players which are composed of people who seek to achieve a joint goal, organizations. Such organizations can be the state and its organs, private enterprises, churches, universities, or clubs. See North (1993), p. 12. For more detail on why it is not easy to fully disentangle the idea of organizations and institutions, see Khalil (1995), p. 448. Following the common usage of the term, monetary authorities are referred to as institutions.

Institutions are firmly entrenched in society when they are the consequence of a continual pattern of social relationships, and individuals and organizations[11] have followed the guidance of an institution for a long time and have passed it along for generations. Hence, institutions require a degree of endurance or stability. To be useful, they should not change rapidly or not all the time. Moreover, the many institutions must also form a coherent system to help guide people's behavior and to be relied upon by society.[12]

As such, *informal institutions* or formalized informal institutions are naturally entrenched in society. Traditions, the language of a community, families[13] and so on have helped people cope with everyday lives for generations. People know that other people will understand the words they use and can act upon this understanding. There will be misunderstandings, but as long as a language remains dominant in a society, expectations will rarely be disappointed, so that a language will continue to be a useful institution. The problem with *formal institutions*, such as legal rules, is that they can change more rapidly.[14] They are sophisticated institutions that were crafted by people, who produce, implement, and apply them. Therefore, for formal institutions to be entrenched in society, they must be widely accepted, which can be hard to achieve. There may also be issues of misunderstanding if the rules may be interpreted inconsistently.[15]

Institutions do not remain completely immutable over time. Some institutions must adapt to new circumstances.[16] Institutions may change endogenously as a result of the interdependent relationships of different organizations or as a response of the members of society to the incentives created by institutions.[17]

3.2.2 Legal Commitments

Believing that whoever makes a promise will keep it would be naïve. Commitments help to make promises credible when they raise the costs of deviating from the promises made.[18] *North* suggests that people's decisions are constrained by a commitment when incentives are aligned with the commitment. When incentives

---

[11] *"While ends define the organization, means include besides material and technological resources – para-digms and conventions or, in short institutions. Agents act according to ends – some of them objective, others entrepreneurial – in light of means – some of them give other potential."* Khalil (1995), p. 447.

[12] Lachmann (1971), p. 51.

[13] *Ibid.*, p. 53.

[14] North (1993), p. 16. See also Lachmann (1971), pp. 72–73.

[15] *Ibid.*, p. 62.

[16] *Ibid.*, p. 51. See also North (1990), p. 6.

[17] North (1993), p. 17.

[18] For more on credibility and commitment, see Weimer (1997), p. 23.

are such that following the commitment means following personal interests,[19] a commitment makes a promise credible in the "motivational"[20] sense. People may also be forced to comply with their promises. When discretion to disregard a commitment is impossible, commitments make promises "credible in the imperative sense".[21] Increasing the costs via the threat of unpleasant consequences in the case of deviating may give motivational commitments an imperative notion.

Motivational commitments bear uncertainty about their future fulfillment, as it is possible that, when a promise was made, the person making the promise had incentives to comply that no longer exist when compliance is required.[22] For example, *Chapman* shows that it is possible that two parties may want to commit to acting in a way that will yield the best outcome for each of them. However, when decisions are made, deviation from the commitment is the rational choice.[23]

State officials are subject to such *pre-commitment problems*.[24] On the one hand, the credibility of government commitments can be influenced by factors that do not depend on state officials. For example, the state may decide not to carry out a previously announced reform, because the potential benefits are determined to be lower than the costs at the time of implementation.[25] On the other hand, state officials may pursue personal benefits or have to be prevented from acting imprudently when the time of implementation arrives.[26] The problem of credibility triggered by economic and personal factors requires states to send a robust indication of commitment if they want to make their promises credible.[27]

Legal rules entail legal commitments. They may change people's incentives from being merely based on their own self-interest to be "normatively required."[28]

---

[19]Of course, we do this all the time. For example, people tend to lend money to friends rather than strangers. We risk losing the money, but we can be sure that the friend will try to repay. His incentive is to keep the friendship. Some do not. Some never do. But the losses are limited. We will not lend high amounts to friends we know that will not repay. If so, it will be considered a gift. When the stakes are higher, we may not want to take that risk, which is why banks ask for collateral and lots of proof to provide loans.

[20]North (1993), p. 13.

[21]*Ibid.*

[22]North explains that according to game theory "players can be bound when the gains from living up to agreements exceed the gains from defecting." See *ibid.*, p. 11.

[23]Chapman (2004), p. 478. In this game-theoretic approach to law, deviation is shown to be rationale, undermining commitments made earlier.

[24]Ginsburg (2005), pp. 721–722.

[25]Campos and Esfahani (2000), p. 221.

[26]Miller (2002), pp. 291–292; see also Ginsburg (2005), pp. 721–722.

[27]Simmons discusses reasons for international monetary commitments with the IMF following current account liberalization, suggesting that such commitments send a signal to markets. Countries seem to send such signals when reputation is at stake and other countries choose to commit to similar agreements. The article suggests that market pressure works as "enforcement mechanism" of such commitments. See Simmons (2000a), p. 821.

[28]See, e.g., Chapman (2004), pp. 474–483 for Chapman's example of the "Centipede Game." See also Khalil (1995), p. 448; Simmons (2000b), p. 325.

Legalizing commitments is usually the most effective way of sending a stronger signal of government commitment. Legal rules bind, although hardly ever perfectly, state officials through the scrutiny and control of state performance and through coercion in case of non-compliance.[29]

Legal rules state in advance both the commitments of authorities, such as the central bank objective of preserving the stability of prices, and the punishment that public authorities will face if they do not fulfil the commitments, such as political costs like dismissal or pecuniary penalties or a loss in reputation[30] that operate in a "motivational" sense.[31] Providing *ex-ante* credible legal commitments may help to prevent *ex-post* deviation.[32] Guidelines for public policy, procedures and mechanisms to supervise the actions of authorities and deal with due process in court, accountability rules or rules for legislative procedures can help to reassure government commitments.[33] Rules may, for instance, delegate the development of public policy to organizations that are not influenced by government authorities, such as independent central banks.[34] Rules may also provide incentives or oblige new governments to embrace commitments made by former governments.[35] As such, legal rules incentivize public officials to adhere to their promises and induce state officials to respect agreements.[36]

Absent a high degree of objective legal certainty, the legal system lacks legitimacy and cannot allow for credible commitments. As *Finnemore* explains, the

> [l]aw is legitimate only to the extent that it produces rules that are generally applicable, exhibit clarity or determinacy, are coherent with other rules, are publicized (so that people know where they are), seek to avoid retroactivity, are relatively constant over time, are possible to perform, and are congruent with official action. [37]

To allow for credible commitments, legal rules need to provide a clear and consistent picture of what they are trying to command. They should also be difficult to modify,[38] or as *North* and *Weingast* put it, "[r]ules the sovereign can readily revise differ significantly in their implications for performance from exactly the same rules

---

[29]Egebo and Englander (1992), p. 53. See also Gaubatz (1996), pp. 111–112.

[30]Finnemore and Toope (2001), p. 748. See also Simmons (2000b), p. 325.

[31]Brunner et al. (2011), p. 3.

[32]Williamson writes of how to avoid opportunism using credible commitments. See Williamson (1994), p. 183.

[33]Miller (2002), p. 318.

[34]Egebo and Englander (1992), p. 53.

[35]Campos and Esfahani (2000), p. 225.

[36]Tinbergen (1952), p. 75.

[37]Finnemore and Toope (2001), p. 749. Finnemore further explains that "legal claims are legitimate and persuasive only if they are rooted in reasoned argument that creates analogies to past practice, demonstrate congruence with the overall systemic logic of existing law, and attend to contemporary social aspirations and the large moral fabric of society."

[38]Weimer (1997), p. 20.

when not subject to revision."[39] To achieve a degree of stability, legal rules need to be protected from the influences of state officials. Legal rules cannot be credible when the entity that creates them has the power to change them at will.[40]

Preserving legal certainty can be a motivational constraint for the state itself.[41] Certainty of the legal environment gives state authorities a good reputation in the eyes of the constituents and the international community that may have a greater benefit than betraying citizens' confidence.[42] For example, a sudden modification of rules may harm investors by triggering high economic costs in terms of money and time invested,[43] which may not be in the interest of governments. One reason for the harm is the costs derived from legal transitions, among which are the costs of having to absorb the content of the new provisions and of mistakes in enforcement.[44] With regard to economic benefits, legal certainty in guaranteeing property rights assures investors that their property rights are actually protected and allows them to foresee costs and benefits.[45] By contrast, if investors expect extra risks and losses triggered by potential non-compliance of governments with their promises, they most likely will try to protect themselves by exercising restraint in immersing in new investments and requiring higher risk premiums.[46] Building reputation takes time and demands high political capital. Repetitively behaving in a responsible manner may in fact make commitments credible.[47]

---

[39]North and Weingast (1989), p. 803.

[40]Miller (2002), pp. 291–292.

[41]North and Weingast (1989), p. 804.

[42]For further detail, see how Simmons explains in this article how reputation influences the fulfillment of legal commitments even in a situation of lack of central enforcement, like it is the case of committing to the rule of international treaties. See Simmons (2000b), pp. 325–327. To read about how stability of the policies does not guarantee credibility of government commitments, see Keefer and Stasavage (2003), p. 408.

[43]North sets as an example of how attaching to the legal rules is preferable for long run economic growth. He says that the individual preference of, e.g., a King is to maximize his wealth. He could do so by confiscating property and forcing citizens to work. However, this type of action has a cost in terms of output because people work more and better if they can enjoy the benefits of their own work. On the other hand, giving people freedom to enjoy the fruit of their labour puts an authoritarian ruler in risk because people have more means to get rid of him. People would have a reason to do so if the fear that at some point the ruler is going to change his mind and change the original rule of respecting people's property. Then, if the ruler considers that accumulating wealth is more important than assuring to remain in power, he will choose to create a rule that diminishes his power and bind him permanently. See North (1993), p. 14.

See also Gaubatz (1996). The author explains how the rule of law, as the main characteristic of liberal democracies is a determinant for the state to credibly commit internally and externally.

[44]Van Alstine (2001), p. 1303.

[45]Tamanaha (2007), pp. 11–12. See also Miller (2002), p. 311.

[46]Brunner et al. (2011), p. 5.

[47]North and Weingast (1989), p. 804.

More often than not, legal commitments must be designed to guarantee stability and to prevent states from modifying them.[48] A difficult amendment process or a large number of veto players may make modifications of legal rules costly. When the process of legislative reform is easy, the commitment entrenched in the legal rules is less credible.[49] Thus, the harder the processual requirements to create and modify legal rules are, the costlier it is to alter the legal framework in terms of time, difficulty of implementation and political capital.

In sum, legal rules can be protected from the manipulation or deviations of the government (at least to some extent) (1) when they establish the scope of action of government officials with clarity, so that any deviation is obvious; (2) when they are consistent with the entire legal framework, so that inconsistencies cannot be abused; and (3) when reversing them has a high cost that authorities are not willing to bear. When legal rules fulfill these characteristics of legal certainty, they can be reliable sources of information about the authorities' purposes and can increase the likelihood that the government will comply with them. To *Simmons* there is compliance with the legal rules when an actor, by and large, follows the "prescribed behavior".[50] Hence, compliance or the notion thereof depends strongly on the quality of the legal framework that prescribes the behavior.

3.3 Legal Certainty and the Costs of Modifying Legal Commitment Devices

Documents that express state commitments assure that those commitments will not be disregarded. Embedding commitments in international agreements, a constitution or legislation of lower rank may subtly imply the degree of credibility of legal commitments. Moreover, the diffusion of power in the political sphere and the delegation of authority may increase the costs of modifying legal commitments.

3.3.1 International Agreements

International agreements govern relationships between countries concerning issues as diverse as the tax treatment of multinational firms, international trade, human rights, or international organizations. For instance, by signing an international trade and investment agreement, state authorities may aim to achieve future economic benefits for their citizens from access to foreign goods and capital markets. Most economists believe that, in principle, allowing foreign trade is beneficial, as, for

---

[48]*Ibid.* See also Campos and Esfahani (2000), p. 225.

[49]Ginsburg (2005), p. 727.

[50]Simmons (2000b), p. 333.

instance, removing barriers to trade may improve upon the international division of labor. Foreign trade may encourage competition in product markets and thereby lower prices for consumers.[51] Opening up the economy is associated with institutional improvements, such as reducing corruption.[52] International competition may further trigger innovation[53] and limit the power of interest groups, which makes it less likely for governments to protect large domestic firms that might have an interest in preventing open markets.[54] Political scientists have further provided evidence that foreign trade may help preserve an environment of peace and concord to continue to benefit from the international exchange of goods and services.[55]

In addition to the economic benefits that may follow from increased international trade and investment, governments may hope for reputational benefits by signing international agreements.[56] For example, when a country aims to open its economy to promote economic development, it must assure that it is perceived as a reliable partner.[57] Indeed, all of the signing partners must believe that the other partners will honor the legal commitments made in their treaty.[58] Domestic legal regimes that provide legal certainty and governments that commit to the rule of law domestically are more likely to do the same in the international context.[59]

Countries with a strong rule of law are more likely to adhere to international agreements. International agreements themselves will further bolster this trust. Governments of less stable countries may want to use international agreements to signal that they are trustworthy and reliable. For these governments, agreements with other partner states and international institutions may help to build reputation. It is, therefore, likely that countries will sign such agreements when they are already able to comply.[60] Hence, international agreements influence the credibility of the domestic rule of law and promote a stronger international rule of law.[61]

---

[51]Mankiw and Taylor (2011), pp. 8–9.

[52]Kose et al. (1999), pp. 8–62.

[53]Von Hayek (2002), p. 9.

[54]Rajan and Zingales (2003), p. 5.

[55]Hegre et al. (2010), p. 763.

[56]Simmons (2000b), p. 324.

[57]Simmons (2000b), pp. 324–325.

[58]Campos and Esfahani (2000), pp. 229–230. The authors explain that creating international agreements entails costs. Some of them can be e.g., "transportation costs". The cost of transporting goods and people from one place to other will induce to create international agreements among neighbours. Another example is the "transaction costs" that constantly controlling a countries attachment to the treaty. In this sense, the characteristics of the domestic rule of law of a country signal the potential "costs of transaction". This transaction costs are lower and less worrisome when the country domestically enforces property rights and contracts.

[59]Simmons (2000a), pp. 822, 832.

[60]Simmons (2000b), p. 324. See also Simmons (2000a), pp. 819–822.

[61]Yackee (2008), pp. 805–806. Yackee explains that the idea behind the Bilateral Investment Treaties is to balance the rules of law among different countries to create a "formally strong international rule of law." Generally, the BITs are signed between a developed country and an

International agreements require compliance.[62] They may take some policy decisions and means of enforcement out of the hands of domestic players. Although international agreements may be enforced via *retaliation* against other parties in case of noncompliance or through "financial and material sanctions,"[63] the fear of losing reputation may be sufficient to guarantee compliance. Losing reputation may mean to become less attractive to, for instance, international investors. In this sense, international agreements are often market-enforced. The reaction of the market provides countries with incentives enough to preserve reputation by complying with international treaties.[64]

Treaties have a higher probability of domestic enforcement when they are subject to internal scrutiny. Therefore, international agreements should be ratified to signal compliance. The process of ratification of an international agreement by a country's parliament provides insights to the international community about such factors as the *political capital* that allows governments to stay committed.[65]

The degree of legal certainty is one of the elements that determines if international agreements are weak or strong legal commitment devices. For instance, contracts are regarded as stronger than pledges, because contracts are binding, less flexible, and have more efficient mechanisms of control and accountability. Pledges, on the other hand, are not binding and impose less obligations on states than contracts. Further, pledges are not as widely published as contracts, as the result of which the reputational costs that pledges carry in case on noncompliance are lower. Finally, pledges are easier to negotiate and almost never require ratification by parliaments.[66]

Given the higher degree of legal certainty that contracts provide, they involve a deeper state commitment.[67] Although governments might benefit from the flexibility

---

emerging market or developing country which does not offer the same degree of legal certainty. The BITs seek to assure that if in the future, the contracts and property rights of investors are endangered by e.g., a modification of the legal framework, they can apply dispute settlements provisions that permit initiation of international arbitration against the non-compliant state. Ginsburg (2005), p. 712. Ginsburg explains how international treaties can influence the reliability of domestic commitments in cases of transition from dictatorship to democracy.

[62]Simmons (2000b), p. 351.

[63]Ginsburg (2005), p. 730.

[64]Simmons (2000a), p. 822. See also Ginsburg (2005), p. 730.

[65]Ginsburg (2005), pp. 724–726; see also Raustiala (2005), p. 598.

However, some countries signed treaties but never ratified them. See Yackee (2008), p. 815. Yackee mentions the case of Brazil that signed several Bilateral Investment Treaties and has not ratified them to avoid facing international arbitration courts that are out the control of the national legal and political structure.

[66]Raustiala (2005), pp. 591–592. According to the author, pledges are more flexible than contracts, among other reasons, because pledges set less obligations on states. Therefore, the states can modify international pledges more easily. Because pledges are not as widely published as contracts, the reputational costs in case on noncompliance are much lower. Finally, pledges are easier to negotiate and as pledges almost never require ratification of the legislative, they are directly in force.

[67]Raustiala (2005), pp. 581–587. This author further explains how the elements of legality, substance and structure are intertwined and how they determine the architecture of international

of pledges as opposed to the stringency of contracts, national constituencies tend to prefer contracts over pledges because of the concern that a shortsighted government might come to power.[68] From this perspective, legal certainty may determine whether an international agreement is regarded as soft or hard law.[69] Specifically, a lack of precision and clarity of the prescriptions can cause a legally binding contract to be regarded as soft law instead of hard law.[70]

Not everybody agrees with the importance of formal international agreements. *Yackee*'s analysis of the impact of stronger formal bilateral investment treaties (BIT) on decisions to invest suggests that there is no evidence of an effect of stronger treaties on investment. He argues that "legal ignorance, legal pluralism and legal ambiguity."[71] are the main reasons why stronger contracts do not really matter in the context of international agreements. However, arbitration tribunals are necessary to fill the gaps opened by obscure legal rules in international treaties.[72] Even though arbitrators find it difficult to adjudicate and enforce unclear treaties properly, such as occurs when the degree of formal certainty is low, the author seems to consider substantive legal certainty more relevant in the context of international agreements.

Examples of treaties that seek to assure credibility of state commitments are the World Trade Organization (WTO) agreement and the International Monetary Fund's (IMF) Articles of Agreement. The WTO agreement assures credibility of state commitments towards respecting and remaining open to international trade by increasing transparency and setting up a system of international coercion. The WTO informs about the attachment of the governments to its rules and established the Dispute Settlement Understanding (DSU) that allows for retaliation.[73]

In the area of international monetary policy, the IMF's Articles of Agreement is the treaty regime that seeks to promote a strong international monetary rule of law. Member states[74] that voluntarily adhere to this treaty are legally bound to keep an open and unlimited current account to satisfy international monetary duties. The

---

agreements. He analyses how the design of international agreements determines the deepness of the commitments that states get through international agreements. The formal characteristics of the rule of law are among the elements that determine the deepness of state's legal commitments.

[68]*Ibid.*, pp. 597–599.

[69]There are two ways of understanding the difference between hard and soft law in international law. One of the criteria to differentiate them is that the first is binding and the later non-binding. The critics of this point of view claim that a critical characteristic of the legal rules is their binding force. Thus, rules that are non-binding are not rules at all therefore, soft law cannot be a legal category. Others explain that hard law in the international context has three elements: obligation, precision, and delegation. Thus, soft law has one or more of these elements weakened. This is, either it is nonbinding, or vague or does not delegate authority to any third party to monitor its implementation. For more detail, see Schaffer and Pollack (2010), pp. 712–717.

[70]Raustiala criticizes the notion of soft law as imprecise law. See Raustiala (2005), pp. 586–591.

[71]Yackee (2008), p. 807.

[72]*Ibid.*, pp. 809–813.

[73]Ginsburg (2005), pp. 733–734.

[74]The six countries analysed are IMF members. See International Monetary Fund (n.d.).

rules of this treaty give national governments and monetary authorities incentives to have an open current account and to be able to make payments when due, leaving aside other priorities like increasing employment and promoting economic development via the export-channel.[75]

3.3.2 The Constitution as a Commitment Device

3.3.2.1 The Role of the Constitution

People's diversity, such as their socio-economic situation, makes it hard to get to a consensus about the scope of the state's legal boundaries. Some people may prefer strong state legal boundaries that allow for more individual freedom. Others may be more interested in the redistribution of wealth and prefer a state with more leeway to tax income, for instance. According to *Weingast*, we can think of the "the problem of policing a state or sovereign as a coordination problem."[76] The constitution as an objective standard that concentrates the main interests of the society, among them the limits to state action, can help solve this coordination problem.[77]

In theory, a constitution should be a *precommitment device* binding the actions of social actors, most importantly restraining authorities from committing abuse. It should also limit the influence of majority rule.[78] The basic rights that ought to be protected in the constitution may be derived from a natural law perspective, as it is argued was the case for the U.S. Constitution.[79] On the other hand, *Kelsen*'s rather positivist approach suggests that "[t]he document which embodies the first constitution is a real constitution, a binding norm, only on the condition that the basic norm is presupposed to be valid."[80] It is valid, if it was drafted and signed by the first holders of sovereignty who were delegated to do so. In this respect, free people entrusted the state with the attributions of creating, interpreting, and applying the law via the constitution. The constitution also contains the rules for the state to exercise these attributions.[81]

In democracies, citizens do not need to beg for the respect of the authorities. They are the source of and the reason for government power.[82] Constitutions are designed

---

[75]Simmons (2000a), pp. 819–821.

[76]Weingast (1995), p. 15.

[77]*Ibid.*

[78]Ginsburg (2005), pp. 722–723.

[79]George (2001), p. 2269.

[80]Kelsen (1945), p. 115.

[81]Raz (1970), pp. 95–97. Here we find the legal positivist hypothesis that the basic norm of the legal system was somehow drafted by authorized people.

[82]O'Donnell (2004), p. 38. Here, O'Donnell explains how authority always derives from the citizens, not only the authority of those democratically elected but also those appointed by them.

to make it hard for governments to disrespect constitutional rights.[83] The constitution represents assurance that the state authorities will not modify the rules of the game except as the constitution permits. Constitutions are thought to be "self-enforcing"[84] over generations of people as "lex perpetua".[85] An agreement is self-enforcing when all parties involved want to respect it because it is beneficial to all of them.[86] Therefore, the constitutional mandate must not be easily reversible.

Making modifications of the constitution particularly costly and having the government commit to protecting the constitution[87] shields the constitutional commitments from the inherent instability of electoral politics.[88] As a prerequisite, people must agree about the limits of the government and, at the same time, be willing to punish the authorities that do not fulfill the constitutional mandate.[89] To enable enforcement, the constitutional limits should—as *Weinberg* put it—be designed "appropriately", because "constitutions place limits on governments through structure and processes" that stipulate how state authorities are supposed to act.[90]

However, societies are constantly evolving. Therefore, the aggregated preferences change over time. For instance, after the two World Wars, a public economic order emerged, as governments around the world moved from a neutral to an active position in the economy.[91] Nowadays, many constitutions include provisions on economic policy, social security or education.[92] Alternatively, the constitutions may be interpreted to allow interference by the state in these matters.[93]

---

[83]Ginsburg (2005), pp. 722–723.

[84]North and Weingast (1989), p. 808.

[85]Figueruelo Burrieza (1993), pp. 47–48.

[86]Tesler (1980), pp. 27–44.

[87]Lachmann (1971), p. 104.

[88]Ginsburg (2005), p. 710.

[89]Weingast (1995), p. 26.

[90]Weingast (2005), pp. 10–13.

[91]Yrarrázabal (1987), p. 98.

[92]*Ibid.*, pp. 102–107.

[93]Richard Epstein explains that constitutional interpretation deals with the introduction of principles that are not expressly mentioned in the constitutional text. However, interpretation must make sense of the constitutional prescriptions. For instance, the principle of the "police power of the state" is no mentioned in the U.S. constitution but is the justification for state intervention in education, health care, security and even morals. This practice is a normal part of constitutional interpretation and can be even beneficial if it is performed according to the meaning, functions, and objectives of the original text. See Epstein (2007), pp. 9–11.

3.3.2.2 Objective Legal Certainty and the Constitution: Consistency of the Legal Framework and the Need for Stability

In the legal system, the constitution is—using Kelsen's words—the "basic norm" that has the role of leading and guiding the legal system.[94] The constitution consents and orders the creation of new rules, and it is, therefore, the master link in the *chain of validity* that guarantees the internal coherence and unity of the legal system.[95] In this sense, the constitution guides policy, regulations and case law, which must follow the chain of hierarchy that determines the validity of the legal rules.[96]

The constitution determines the political organization of the state. Beyond the traditional division of the executive, legislative and judiciary branches,[97] modern states divide their power among a broader and more complex group of organs. They include autonomous agencies with specific roles. While all of these organs are differentiated, they remain part of the unity of the state.[98]

The division of power must improve state efficiency and acts as a counterweight system, *checks and balances*, against the concentration of power in only one person or institution. State organs mutually control each other. For instance, the legislative branch oversees the actions of the executive branch; and the highest court controls the legality and constitutionality of the decisions of both other branches. The division of branches must be an obstacle to opportunistic behavior by the government. It restricts the modification of the basic structure of the state and protects people's wealth and property rights. For instance, creating and reforming legislation usually requires the agreement of the executive and legislative branches and often also the judiciary. A divided parliament into different groups can further limit modifications.[99]

There are also institutions especially vested with power to overview state organs, which may improve "horizontal accountability"[100] and further guarantee constitutional commitments. An example of such an institution is a general comptroller that may be put in place to supervise the public budget.

---

[94]Kelsen (1945), p. 115; Raz (1970), pp. 95–97. See also Sepúlveda Iguiniz (2006), p. 227.

[95]To read more about Kelsen's ideas on the constitution and the chain of legal validity, see Raz (1970), pp. 96–108 or look up Kelsen (1945), Parts X and XI.

[96]Lyons (1977), p. 428.

[97]Montesquieu (1989), p. 173.

[98]López Guerra (1980), pp. 22–23.

[99]See, e.g., North and Weingast (1989), pp. 817–819. They explain how the Glorious Revolution improved the credibility of the government to commit because it allowed for a system of "checks and balances" with, for instance, independent judges.

[100]O'Donnell (2004), p. 37. According to the author, "vertical accountability" is, for instance, set up via elections.

3.3.2.3 The Problem of Subjective Legal Certainty in Latin America: Lack of Entrenchment of the Constitution

For there to be subjective legal certainty about the commitments laid out in the constitution, it is a necessary condition that the constitution is entrenched in society. Constitutions are entrenched in society when there is a general understanding among people that politics and law are different. As the constitution also rules the political process, it is critical to understand that the constitution is the limit for ordinary politics. Constitutional rules are based on broad principles, while ordinary or electoral politics is based on votes.[101]

In Latin America, constitutions tend to be only weakly entrenched in society for three reasons. First, there are deep material differences among people that trigger very different preferences and views of the world.[102] These include differences in identity and different views on the role of the state in society. Second, because of the differences, there is no general agreement among people about punishing deviations from the constitutional mandate.[103] Third, many Latin American countries have a centralist tradition. Governments often move from one extreme to the other, and those in power tend to aim for drastic modifications of the law, a situation diametrically opposite to the basic idea of constitutions.

For instance, Chile's current constitution was set up under Pinochet's military dictatorship. A left-wing government led by M. Bachelet aimed to amend that constitution. The official reason was that the constitution was created during the dictatorship and was not legitimately approved.[104] Recurring modifications to the constitutional mandate harm the capacity of legal rules to be a real guideline for people's behavior. The mismatch between the law in the books and the law in action and the inconsistency of the legal prescription with the legal system is almost endemic in Latin America.[105]

In principle, the mandatory attachment of state officials to the constitution is clearly defined within the legal orders of the Latin American countries analyzed in this work. Article 121 of the Constitution of Colombia forbids state officials to exercise other attributions than those specifically ordered by the constitution and the law. Article 6 of the Constitution of Chile binds the actions of state institutions and state officials to the constitutional mandate. It also subjects authorities to legal accountability and includes sanctions if the constitutional limits are surpassed. Article 45 of the Peruvian Constitution clarifies that the power of the state finds

---

[101]For more on the lack of constitutional entrenchment of Latin American constitutions and the difference to the constitution of the United States of America, see Schor (2006), p. 6.

[102]Weingast (1995), p. 14. Weingast explains how material differences among people make a difference in sharing ideas of limiting the power of the state.

[103]*Ibid.*, p. 26.

[104]Gamboa and Segovia (2016), pp. 136–137; see also Verdugo (2014), p. 43.

[105]To read how the constitution and the law evolved historically in Latin America, see Schor (2006), pp. 14–24.

limits in the law. In line with this, Article 46 gives the population the right of insurgency and disobedience if authorities exercise power beyond their mandate.

In a similar vein, Article 49 of the Constitution of the United States of Mexico states that the exercise of power is divided among the powers of the Union. These powers are organisms like the executive, legislative and judicial branch and the internal authorities of the states that are part of the federal republic. Article 41 of the Mexican constitution stresses the requirement of exercising power within the limits of the constitutional and the legal attributions given to the central state and to each state.

In Argentina, Section 31 of the National Constitution of the Republic binds the provincial authorities to the constitutional prescriptions, legally approved international treaties and laws enacted by Congress. Due to recurring political and social turmoil that had broken the Argentinean constitutional order, Article 36 restates the prevalence of the constitutional mandate and the nullity of every act against the constitution. This article also prescribes the legislative creation of the so-called *Law of Ethics*, which, in Article 2, obliges public officials to respect and act according to the constitution and the law. Likewise, the Brazilian constitution requires the adherence of every branch of the state, the individual states, the federal state, and other administrative organizations to a number of principles in Article 37. Among them is the principle of the lawfulness of their acts and decisions. It also defines sanctions for administrative dishonesty and the liability of public authorities for damages caused to third parties.

However, the content and function of a constitution is widely unknown or regarded as of little importance by large shares of the population in Latin America. For instance, *Sepúlveda Iniguez* mentions the result of a poll performed in Mexico in 2004, in which the people's perception of the constitution was evaluated. The results of this study show that only 4.8% of the respondents affirmed to have a vast knowledge of the constitution. More strikingly, 72.6% affirmed to know little about the constitution, and 20.3% claimed not to know anything at all about their constitution.[106]

3.3.3   The Implications of Procedures in Law Making: Organic Laws

Legislation can differ in material content and in its formal process of creation and amendment, which affect the costs of modifications.[107] Modifying some legal rules can be more difficult than others because some of them could require a special organ

---

[106]Sepúlveda Iguiniz (2006), p. 228.

[107]Cordero (2010), p. 128.

to carry out the reform, a longer process or higher approval majorities.[108] To understand Latin American legislation, it is important to distinguish between ordinary laws and organic laws, a differentiation that is also known in the legal frameworks of France,[109] Portugal[110] and Spain.[111]

Organic laws are thought to complement the constitution. Therefore, organic laws in *strictu sensu* have two characteristics. First, they rule specific topics that "in virtue of the Constitution must be object of constitutional organic laws."[112] Thus, they

---

[108]Among the legal frameworks considered it is possible to identify different types of approval majorities. The most common are the simple, absolute, and qualified majority, but there can be other voting requirements. In Chile for instance the absolute majority is equivalent to the majority of the members of the deputies and senators *in office*, this means all the members of the National Congress of Chile and not only the ones attending a session. A simple majority, on the other hand, is equivalent to the majority of the deputies and senators present during the voting. Nevertheless, amending the constitution requires the three-fifths of the deputies and senators in office and reforming and organic law requires the approval of *"four sevenths of the deputies and senators"* in office. See Const. Chile Art. 66 para 2.

In Colombia there are four types of majorities. There are simple and absolute majorities with the same characteristics as in Chile. There are also, qualified, and special majorities. The first requires the vote of two-thirds of the members in office of the Senate and the House of Representatives (to approve amnesties and pardons). The latter requires three quarters of the members in office of the Senate and the House of Representatives (to approve the travel abroad of state officials financed with treasure money). See Regulation of the House of Representatives of Colombia Art. 79 (1), 122 (1) [Reglamento del Congreso de los Diputados, Boletín Oficial No. 237, 4 October 1993]. See also Const. Colombia Art. 145.

In Argentina and Mexico there are three types of majorities. Qualified majority means two-thirds (66%) of the votes of those present in the voting. Absolute majority represents 50%+1 of the vote of those present in the voting. Finally, simple majority is the equivalent to having at least one more vote in favor of an option above other option. See Rules of the Chamber of Deputies of Mexico Art. 3 (XII, XIII, XIV) [Reglamento de la Cámara de Diputados de México, Diario Oficial de la Federación of 24 December 2010].

In Peru, the relative majority (simple majority) requires that the votes in favor of a proposal exceed the votes against it. Absolute majority requires 50%+1 vote of the members in office. Finally, the qualified majority requires two-thirds of the votes of all the members in office. See Standing Rules of the Congress of Peru Art. 81 [Reglamento del Congreso de Perú, Diario Oficial, 10 March 2018].

In Brazil, no decision of the National Congress of Brazil is taken with simple majority. The only options are absolute majority which is equivalent to the 50% plus one of the members in office or qualified majority equivalent to two-thirds of the members in office. See Const. Brazil Art. 47.

[109]Constitution of France Art. 46 [English translation of the Constitution de la République française, 4 October 1958]: *"The acts of the Parliament which are defined by the Constitution as Organic Acts are voted and modified according to the following dispositions."*

[110]Constitution of Portugal Art. 166 [English translation of the Constitution Portuguese, 2 April 1976]: *"Form of Acts). 1. The acts provided for in Art 161a shall take the form of constitutional laws."*

[111]Constitution of Spain Sec. 81: [English translation of Constitución Española, December 29, 1978]: *"Organic Laws are those relating to the implementation of fundamental rights and public liberties, those approving the Statutes of Autonomy and the general electoral system and other laws provided by the Constitution. 2. The approval, amendment or repeal of organic acts shall require the overall majority of the Members of Congress in the final vote of the bill as a whole."*

[112]Const. Chile Art. 63.

regulate aspects that are reserved for them in the constitutional text,[113] such as constitutional rights or the organization of state institutions.[114] By contrast, ordinary laws are common legislation created by the mere initiative of the legislators without direct constitutional order. The main criterion to identify an ordinary law is that it regulates all that is not within the scope of organic laws.[115]

Second, given their level of importance, the process of creation and amendment of organic laws is more difficult in comparison to the process of creating and amending ordinary laws.[116] Therefore, organic laws are commonly thought to be of higher rank than ordinary laws. The Constitutional Court of Colombia places organic laws under the constitution but over other types of legislation in the legal hierarchy. Violating legal precepts of organic laws is considered an indirect violation of the constitution.[117]

Some legal scholars argue against a supra-legal nature of organic laws. They argue that, because ordinary and organic laws are created by the same organ, the legislative branch, they should be considered of the same legal rank unless the constitution is explicit in granting a higher rank to organic laws.[118] In this case, an ordinary law contradicting an organic law is not an indirect but a direct violation of the constitution that grants an extraordinary function to organic laws. In principle, however, they argue that the more stringent process of creation and amendment to safeguard the legal precepts of constitutional nature is the only difference between organic and ordinary law.[119]

Although common in Latin American legal frameworks, organic laws can come with different labels. In Brazil, they are called supplementary laws.[120] The Brazilian constitution commands that a supplementary law regulates, for instance, the Statute of the Judicature[121] and the Armed Forces.[122] Even though Article 59 of the Brazilian constitution does not mention organic laws among the legal documents

---

[113]Freijedo (1981), p. 290.

[114]Rios (1983), pp. 41–43. See also Santamaría Pastor (1979), p. 40; Sepúlveda Iguiniz (2006), pp. 231, 234.

[115]For more detail on the differences between organic and ordinary laws, see Santamaría Pastor (1979), p. 40.

[116]Cordero (2010), p. 136. See also Rios (1983), pp. 41–43; Santamaría Pastor (1979), p. 40.

[117]Francisco José Bautista Villalobos v. Congreso de la República de Colombia, CCC, Sentencia C-557, 20 August 2009. See also Cordero (2010), p. 135.

[118]Santamaría Pastor (1979), pp. 42–43.

[119]For more on the discussion about the principles of legal hierarchy and legal competence of organic laws, see Freijedo (1981), pp. 290–295. See also Santamaría Pastor (1979), pp. 40–46.

[120]The Const. Brazil Art. 59 sole para: Among the legislation enacted by the Congress are the *"supplementary laws"* that *"provide for the preparation, drafting, amendment and consolidation of laws."*

[121]Const. Brazil Art. 93: *"A supplementary law, proposed by the Supreme Federal Court, shall provide for the Statute of the Judicature [. . .]".*

[122]Const. Brazil Art. 142 para 1: *"A supplementary law shall establish the general rules to be adopted in the organization, training and use of the Armed Forces."*

that comprise the legislative process, Article 29 does mention that organic laws should govern municipalities.[123]

Colombian law includes two types of legislation with organic law characteristics. One is labeled organic laws, the other is statutory laws. Statutory laws regulate everything related to the exercise of civil and political rights. In this sense, statutory laws regulate fundamental rights, the administration of justice, political participation, political parties, and states of emergency.[124] Organic laws in Colombia rule the organization of state institutions, such as the legislative branch, and development plans and the general budget.[125]

According to the Constitution of Peru, the substantive content of organic laws is the "structure and operation of the State bodies as defined in the Constitution, as well as other matters whose regulation by such acts are established in the Constitution."[126] This includes, for instance, the General Comptroller,[127] the central bank,[128] the administration of justice,[129] the process of free elections,[130] and the concession of natural resources.[131]

---

[123]Const. Brazil Art. 29: *"Municipalities shall be governed by organic law, voted in two readings, [. . .] and approved by two thirds of the members of the Municipal Chamber [. . .]."*

[124]Const. Colombia Art. 152: *"By way of status Acts (leyes estatuarias) the Congress of the Republic shall regulate the following subject areas: a. Fundamental rights and duties of individuals and the proceedings and resources for their protection; b. Administration of justice; c. Organization and regulations of parties and political movements; the formal statute of the opposition and electoral functions; d. Institutions and machinery of citizen participation; e. States of exception. f. The equal electoral treatment of candidates for the Presidency of the Republic who comply with the requirements established by statute."*

[125]Const. Colombia Art. 151: *"The Congress shall issue Institutional Acts regulating the exercise of legislative activity. Through them, the rules of procedure of Congress and of each House, regulations concerning the preparation, approval, and execution of the Budgetary Revenues and Appropriations Law, and the execution of the general development plan and those relative to the assignment of regulatory responsibilities to the territorial entities shall be established. The Institutional Acts shall require, for their approval, an absolute majority of the votes of the members of both Houses."*

[126]Const. Peru Art. 106: *"Organic acts govern the structure and operation of State bodies as defined in the Constitution, as well as other matters whose regulation by such acts is established in the Constitution."*

[127]Const. Peru Art. 82: *"The office of the Comptroller General is a decentralized body of public law that enjoys autonomy in accordance with its organic act."*

[128]Const. Peru Art. 84: *"The Central Bank is a corporate entity under public law. It is autonomous in conformity with its organic act."*

[129]According to Const. Peru Art. 143, the jurisdictional bodies are the Supreme Court of Justice and tribunals as determined by their organic acts.

[130]Const. Peru Art. 31: *"Citizens are entitled to take part in public affairs by means of referendum, legislative initiative, removal or revocation of authorities, and demands for accountability. They also have the right to be elected and to freely elect their representatives in accordance to the provisions and procedures set forth by the organic act."*

[131]Const. Peru Art. 66 paras 1 and 2: *"Natural resources, renewable and non-renewable, are patrimony of the nation. The State is sovereign in their utilization. An organic law fixes the*

In Chile, constitutional organic laws determine the organization of the public administration (Article 38), the states of exception (Article 44), the functioning of the Nation Congress (Article 52, c. 55), the organization and attributions of tribunals of justice (Article 77), and the composition, organization, and functions of the central bank (Article 108). In the legal framework of Chile, there are also other types of laws that require a special process of creation and amendment. For instance, laws that interpret the constitution and seek to clarify obscure constitutional rules[132] require a special quorum.[133] Moreover, Chilean law knows laws of *qualified major-ity*,[134] which are ordinary laws in terms of material content, as their creation does not derive from a direct constitutional order that require an absolute majority. However, given the importance of the topics embedded in this type of laws, they should have a stiffer process of creation and amendment that guarantees their stability and a broader consensus. Therefore, the required majority is based on all senators and deputies in office to be approved.[135]

Moreover, some organic laws do not fulfill the characteristics of organic laws in *strictu sensu*. This is the case in Mexico, where organic laws regulate aspects ordered by the constitution, but those aspects are not safeguarded by a more stringent process of creation and amendment. The same requirements must be met to create and amend an ordinary law and an organic law.[136]

The case of organic law in Argentina is also particular. Even though the constitution does not have a single reference to organic law, there are organic-like laws in the Argentinean legal framework. Among them are the Organic Law of Political Parties and the Organic Law of the Ministries of the Executive Branch. The

---

conditions of their use and grants them to private individuals. Such a concession grants the title holders a real right subject to those regulations."

[132]Cordero (2010), p. 130.

[133]Const. Chile Art. 66 para 1: *"The legal norms that interpret constitutional precepts will need, for their approval, amendment or repeal, three fifths of the deputies and senators in exercise."*

[134]The laws of qualified quorum are a legal category only existent in the Chilean legal framework. This type of law was introduced in the constitution of 1980. See Cordero (2010), pp. 134–135. Laws of qualified quorum in Chile are in charge of regulating sensitive topics such as all related with terrorism, death penalty or the exercise of fundamental rights. For instance, Const. Chile Art. 9 para 2 states that *"A law of qualified quorum will determine terrorist conduct and its penalty."* Art. 19 Number 1 para 3 sets forth: *"The death penalty can only be stablished for a crime provided for in a law adopted by qualified quorum."* Number 12 para 1 says: *"Freedom to express opinion and to inform, without prior censorship, in any form and by any medium, without prejudice to responsibility for any crimes or abuses committed in the exercise of these freedoms, in conformity with the law which must be of qualified quorum."*

[135]Const. Chile Art. 66 para 3: *"The legal norms of qualified quorum will be established, amended or repealed by the absolute majority of the deputies and senators in exercise."* see also Cordero (2010), p. 135.

[136]Mexico does not differentiate between organic and ordinary laws. *"Every single bill or decree shall be discussed successively at both Houses, except the issues that are within the exclusive jurisdiction of one of the Houses. The House shall observe the methods, periods of time and debating and voting procedures established by the Congress Act and its regulations."* See Const. Mexico Art. 72.

constitution does, however, mention that these institutions should be regulated by a special law that requires a higher majority.[137] The same provision applies to legislation on the structure and functioning of the General Audit of the Nation.[138] By contrast, Argentina's constitution mentions that the federal bank in charge of issuing currency, i.e., the central bank, should be set up by Congress without reference to a special process or a higher quorum. Consequently, the Organic Charter of the Central Bank of the Argentine Republic does not fulfill all characteristics typically associated with organic laws.[139]

Hence, legal commitments embedded in organic law are, *ceteris paribus*, more credible, as they entail a higher degree of formal legal certainty. From the sheer term—*organic*—it is possible to infer that organic laws ought to promote an organized and coherent legal framework.[140] Organic laws contribute to the clarity of the constitution, because they complement constitutional principles and prevent the constitution from being overwhelmed by too much detail. By making organic laws costlier to reverse, the drafters of constitutions aimed to reduce flexibility in ruling on constitutional aspects that are supposed to remain stable in time or are in need of special protection.[141] The stringent process of amendment guarantees stability of legal commitments.[142] It requires a wider agreement on laws of special importance,[143] making short-term legal arrangements or sudden modifications in the future more difficult.[144]

3.3.4 Distribution of Power and Delegation

The degree of concentration of power affects the costs of policy reversals. *Tsebelis*'s *Veto Players: How Political Institutions Work* shows that additional veto players imply more policy stability. Veto players are the people or institutions with the power to make, change or stop a decision. These include the legislature, the

---

[137]See, e.g., Constitution of Argentina Art. 77 para 2 [English translation of the Constitution of the Argentinean Nation, Diario Oficial No. 27.959, 23 August 1994] [hereinafter Const. Argentina]: *"Bills that modify the electoral system and the system of political parties shall be approved by the absolute majority of the totality of the members of the Chambers."*

[138]Const. Argentina Art. 85 para 3: *"This body of technical assistance of the Congress, with functional autonomy, shall be made up in the manner that the law that regulates its creation and operation establishes; such law shall be approved by an absolute majority of the members of each Chamber [. . .]."*

[139]According to Const. Argentina Art. 75 (6), Congress shall be empowered *"[t]o establish and regulate a Federal bank with power to issue money, as well as other National banks."*

[140]Cordero (2010), p. 132.

[141]Sepúlveda Iguiniz (2006), pp. 231, 234.

[142]Cordero (2010), p. 127.

[143]Santamaría Pastor (1979), p. 41.

[144]Sepúlveda Iguiniz (2006), p. 226. See also Rivero Ortega (2013), p. 65.

executive, the courts of justice and even a transitory body elected to create a new constitution such as a constituent assembly.[145] Even if the legal structure provides for several veto players, the real number of veto players depends on their eventual political-ideological division. For instance, if the president of the republic belongs to the same political party or coalition of the majority of the parliament, then the president is not an independent veto player.[146]

Distributing power among several players makes it harder for each of them to follow self-interest and to maximize personal well-being by engaging in opportunistic behavior.[147] In this regard, *North* and *Weingast* explain how removing the possibility of making one-sided decisions from the Crown increased the degree of credibility of its commitments during the Glorious Revolution in England.[148] It is more difficult to follow pure self-interest, as all involved individuals, including those in parliament, have their own personal preferences that they rarely share in common. To achieve their goals, the representatives need to negotiate and reach consensus with one another, which demands greater effort than individual decision-making. A reform, e.g., with the consensus of the executive, the parliament and the oversight of the courts, diminishes the possibility of state authorities to act in their personal benefit and, at the same time, signals that they are in a credible position to commit with the stability of the legal framework.[149]

As *Falaschetti* and *Miller* reason:

> Diffusing authority in political economies can [...] promote efficiency by enhancing the credibility with which external agents can promise (explicitly or implicitly) to forgo opportunistic strategies. To the extent that optimal expropriation is not feasible, a state's constituents have the necessary ex ante assurance to contribute individually costly levels of effort that, in turn, can induce sustainable, efficient outcomes.[150]

---

[145]Tsebelis (2000), pp. 446–447.

[146]*Ibid.*, p. 449.

[147]Falaschetti and Miller (2001), p. 391.

[148]North and Weingast (1989), p. 817. North and Weingast argue that during the Glorious Revolution in England the Crown lost the possibility of legislating and creating policy unilaterally because it always needed the approval of the Parliament. The Parliament was also constrained because it represented several different points of view and interests that made individual rent-seeking more complicated. Further, the judiciary was supposed to be independent which reduced the influence of the Crown in the appointment and control of judges. The Crown was also restricted economically because there were for the first-time restrictions over the loans of the Bank of England. The Bank was only allowed to give loans to the Crown or to buy land that belonged to the Crown with approval of the Parliament.

[149]Falaschetti and Miller (2001), pp. 401–408.

[150]*Ibid., p.* 402. See also Campos and Esfahani (2000), p. 230; Pedroza de la Llave (2002), p. 177.

Another way to diffuse the power of authorities and raise costs of policy reversal is delegation via territorial or functional decentralization, which adds potential veto players.[151]

The most typical example of the delegation of power is territorial decentralization known as *federalism*.[152] Federalism is a system in which the exercise of power is spread among the branches of the central government and the government of the states that form a union.[153] Powers may be further delegated to provincial or even smaller territorial portions that may be free to make decisions and to manage their own resources.[154]

The objective of the territorial political decentralization of power is to create a state setup that limits the power of authorities and promotes their efficiency, improving the distribution of information as governments with a smaller territory and fewer people can have better information about local preferences.[155] In addition, citizens are better informed about the activities of their authorities, which results in increased overall transparency, as people may move from one jurisdiction to another and can choose the most benevolent environment for their economic activities. Having multiple local governments may promote competition for the best institutions and increase costs of creating hostile conditions, such as uncertainty for businesses and investment.[156] As *Yingyi* and *Weingast* put it,

> the decentralization of information and authority and interjurisdictional competition can provide a more credible commitment to secure economic rights and preserve markets.[157]

The most common example of the functional decentralization of power is the creation of administrative autonomies.[158] An administrative autonomy is a state

---

[151]Another way to delegate might be by moving competences to an international organization, when the leeway to make decisions is removed totally or partially from the government. On international delegation, see Ginsburg (2005), p. 734.

[152]Yingyi and Weingast (1997), pp. 85–89.

[153]Rodden (2004), p. 489. See also Guerrero (1979), p. 83.

[154]Hutchcroft (2001), p. 31.

[155]Obviously, this is the case when a unified state decides to distribute powers. In contrast, in the US the States were originally independent and decided to delegate power to the central state. However, the remaining State power does improve transparency and allows for jurisdictional competition.

[156]Yingyi and Weingast (1997), pp. 83–88.

[157]*Ibid.*, p. 85.

[158]The terms used in the Latin American administrative law to define administrative autonomies can be a bit confusing. For instance, the Mexican legal framework states that according to the degree of freedom to develop their activities, administrative autonomies can be "deconcentrated", "decentralized" or "autonomous" organs. The common characteristic that all of them share is that they are opposites to centralized institutions of the public administration, at least to some degree. Among the differences, a deconcentrated institution has relative freedom to act but cannot manage itself because it is an institution that is always within a ministry or sub-secretary. A decentralized organ enjoys higher independence because it has its own legal personality, organizational structure, and administrative faculties to manage itself and handle its own budget. Nevertheless, they are hierarchically inferior and dependent on the organ of central administration that is responsible for the transfer of competences. Thus, the superior organ is the one that decides about the dimension

institution with a smaller scope of public power[159] that has been granted some degree of independence[160] to make technical decisions that achieve a public goal[161] free from political pressure.[162] There are differences in the transfer of power. Governments may transfer some competences to an agency, which is an institution intended to execute policies on behalf of the government. In this case, the scope of power is very limited. On the other hand, governments may delegate broader competences that do not require only executive power but decision-making power to create policies, a delegation of power known as devolution.[163]

The delegation of power to autonomous and ideally apolitical institutions may help deal with *the problem of credible commitment* over time or *time-inconsistency problems* that take place when potentially conflicting objectives or incentives may make it harder for a central government to commit credibly to the achievement of objectives over longer periods of time, especially in economic policy.[164] Being autonomous gives the state organ leeway to cope with demanding and specialized duties and attributions.[165] At the same time, political power is prevented from directing, modifying, changing or blocking the decisions of an autonomous institution.[166]

Furthermore, as administrative autonomies tend to handle specialized tasks, the people in charge may be more likely to possess the necessary knowledge and

---

and duration of the transfer of power. Finally, an autonomous institution has the highest degree of independence. Basically, they can manage themselves, their own budget, and, they also have the attribution of self-regulation. See Pedroza de la Llave (2002), pp. 176–178.

[159]Guerrero (1979), p. 83.

[160]There has been some discussion about whether the legal terms "independence" and "autonomy" can be regarded as synonyms. Some authors argue that they are different because independent institutions have complete freedom and are out of the scope of the legislation enacted by the Congress. On the other hand, the term autonomy is applicable to institutions that have institutional constraints but enjoy some freedom to achieve their goals and to elaborate their own regulation. See Laurens et al. (2007), p. 263 (Footnote 1).

From the perspective of institutional economics, the most accepted notion is to use both terms "interchangeably" because the term autonomy entails "operational freedom", and the term independence entails "absence of political interference". See, e.g., Lybek (2004), p. 1. See also Jácome and Vásquez (2008), p. 788 (Footnote 1).

From a linguistic perspective, the word "autonomy" is related to words such as "self" and "law." Thus, we can understand it as an attribution of self-regulation. It may further be associated with the concepts of "freedom" and "self-government." See Pedroza de la Llave (2002), p. 175.

[161]*Inversora Bursátil, S.A.,* Amparo, SCJN México, Sentencia 2a. XV, Tomo XV, March 2002, p. 430. See also *Jaime Rafael Pedraza Vanegas v. Congreso de la República de Colombia,* CCC, Sentencia C-050, 10 February 1994. For literature, see Ugalde (2010), p. 256. See also Zúñiga (2007), p. 227; Cordero (2012), p. 16.

[162]Miller (2002), p. 321.

[163]Hutchcroft (2001), p. 30.

[164]Keefer and Stasavage (2003), p. 407.

[165]Zúñiga (2007), p. 227. See also Cordero (2012), p. 16.

[166]Zúñiga (2007), p. 231.

expertise to carry out their tasks.[167] To be successful, the law has to provide certainty about the nature and conditions of the delegation to assure that it is effective. The law has to be particularly specific about the scope of the autonomy, because the exceptional legal nature of an autonomous organ demands a particular set of rules that matches its unique characteristics,[168] sets legal constraints that make the degree of autonomy of the institution hard to eliminate or diminish,[169] and clarifies the scope of actions for the autonomy.

Administrative autonomies emerged as a solution to the several new state activities that demand a high degree of specialization to deal with the complex new social and economic functions of the state[170] that developed after the end of World War II. This development seems to have made changes in the traditional structure of the state and the *functional distribution of power* to new institutions necessary.[171] The Supreme Court of Mexico explains the reasons for the existence of administrative autonomies as follows:

> The public power attributions have increased along time. From the rule of law we have moved to the social rule of law because the growing population brought more problems and needs and, therefore, triggered an increasing public intervention in several activities. [Own Translation][172]

The emergence of these new independent state organs[173] may be viewed as incompatible with Montesquieu's classical conception of the state, which is based on dividing the power among the executive, legislative and judiciary,[174] because autonomous organs reduce the scope of power of the traditional branches of the state.[175] However, it is important to clarify that even institutions with a high degree of administrative autonomy should not be confused with sovereign institutions. Sovereign institutions are able to work in isolation from other state organs. They can also expand powers and come in conflict with the other state branches, such as

---

[167]Given the technical character of the decisions, officials in charge are typically not selected via democratic elections. See Hutchcroft (2001), p. 32.

[168]*Control constitucionalidad enmienda "Ley General de Bancos"*, TC Chile, Sentencia Rol No. 216, 17 July 1995.

[169]Brunner et al. (2011), p. 12.

[170]Knill (1999), p. 122.

[171]Control constitucionalidad enmienda "Ley General de Bancos", TC Chile, Sentencia Rol No. 216, 17 July 1995.

[172]*Banco Inbursa, S.A.* and others, Amparo, SCJN México, Sentencia 2a. CCXXIV, Tomo XIV, December 2001.

[173]Const. Colombia Art. 113: *"The branches of government are the legislative, the executive, and the judiciary. In addition to the organs that constitute them, there are others, autonomous and independent, for the execution of other functions of the State. The various organs of the State have separate functions but cooperate harmoniously for the realization of their goals."* See also *René Vargas Pérez v. Congreso de la República de Colombia*, CCC, Sentencia C-481, 7 July 1999.

[174]*Control constitucionalidad enmienda "Ley General de Bancos"*, TC Chile, Sentencia Rol No. 216, 17 July 1995.

[175]Cárdenas et al. (1999), p. 469.

by usurping attributions entrusted to the president of a country. An autonomous institution is not a "state within another state",[176] because, even though other state organs cannot interfere with it, the autonomous institution will preserve links, such as through communication.[177]

The autonomy of the central bank is the paradigm example of the delegation or transfer of power to an autonomous institution. In fact, most central banks enjoy some degree of administrative autonomy to pursue non-inflationary objectives. Before the World Wars, the classical gold standard (1880–1913) helped to shield monetary policy from the political abuse of the printing press. Authorities had to conduct monetary policy within the limits set by the gold standard, if they did not want to risk having to go off the gold standard, which tended to worsen the governments' access to capital markets and to increase the cost of government borrowing.[178]

In Latin America, there are several other examples of institutions that enjoy some degree of autonomy, such as those in charge of administrative control, developing electoral functions (in Colombia),[179] water and sewerage, natural gas, electric power and telecommunications (in Argentina)[180] and tax collection (in Peru and Mexico).[181] In general, any state organism or even public corporation[182] created to fulfill a public function or service can be granted administrative autonomy.[183]

3.4   An Analysis of Procedural Differences in Law Creation and Amendment

3.4.1   Procedural Differences Within Each Legal Framework

Modification costs matter for the persistence of legal rules. To be able to qualitatively assess the political capital necessary to create and amend legislation of different rank in Argentina, Brazil, Chile, Colombia, Peru and Mexico, the book provides an analysis of the number of discussions, quorums required, and veto

---

[176]*Control constitucionalidad "Ley Orgánica Banco central de Chile"*, TC Chile, Sentencia Rol No. 78, 20 September 1989.

[177]Pedroza de la Llave (2002), pp. 175–176. See also *Control constitucionalidad "Ley Orgánica Banco central de Chile"*, TC Chile, Sentencia Rol No. 78, 20 September 1989.

[178]Smits (1997), p. 154.

[179]*Control constitucionalidad "Ley Orgánica Banco central de Chile"*, TC Chile, Sentencia Rol No. 78, 20 September 1989.

[180]Urbiztondo et al. (1998), p. 3.

[181]Taliercio (2004), pp. 213–214.

[182]*Control constitucionalidad "Ley Orgánica Banco central de Chile"*, TC Chile, Sentencia Rol No. 78, 20 September 1989.

[183]*Control constitucionalidad enmienda "Ley General de Bancos"*, TC Chile, Sentencia Rol No. 216, 17 July 1995.

Table 3.1 Legislative procedure in Argentina

	Constitutional	Ordinary laws	Special laws
Role of Congress	Initiative	Initiative Discussion	Initiative Discussion
No. of Discussions	N/A	At least 1 in each chamber	At least 1 in each chamber
Required Voting in Congress	To approve the initiative: 2/3 of the members	To approve the bill in first discussion: Simple majority (at least one more vote in favor of an option above other options) To approve the corrections made in the second chamber: absolute majority To insist on the original bill: 2/3 of the members	To approve the bill in first discussion: Absolute majority (50%+1 of the votes of those present in the voting) To approve the corrections made in the second chamber: absolute majority To insist on the original bill: 2/3 of the members
Role of Executive	N/A	Objections, approval, promulgation	Objections, approval, promulgation
Referendum	N/A	N/A	N/A
Constituent Assembly	Yes	N/A	N/A

Source: Author. Summary of findings from legal analysis as presented in respective country section

players involved in the specific legislative processes. The following tables summarize the processes of creating and amending different legal rules for each country and refer to the relevant articles in the constitutions of the countries (status as of October 2019). The accompanied descriptions interpret the tables in terms of modification costs. As the previous discussion suggests, promises entailed in constitutions are found to be more credible within each legal framework. Constitutional amendments are costlier than the modification of other legislation (as shown below) in each of the six countries.

3.4.1.1 Argentina

The legal framework of Argentina leaves no doubt that it is considerably costlier to amend the constitution than ordinary legislation and special legislation. As summarized in the first column of Table 3.1, Argentina's Congress can declare the need for a constitutional amendment. To pass such a declaration requires the high quorum of two thirds of the members of Congress. In addition, another democratically elected organ, the Constituent Assembly, is in charge of the process of amending the Constitution.[184] Installing a constituent assembly is costly in terms of time and the resources that are required to call for elections, political campaigns, headquarters,

---

[184]Const. Argentina Art. 30.

etc. Not surprisingly, the Argentinean Constitution of 1853 has seen substantial changes only once, in 1994.[185]

In the Argentinean legal framework, special laws can be equated with the organic laws in the other countries. Like organic laws in Colombia and Chile the content of a special law is determined in the constitution and entails a stiffer process of creation and reform. The special legislation is reserved to specific constitutional topics only (see columns 2 and 3 of Table 3.1). Few topics demand special legislation. Examples are issues related to democratic participation and budgetary aspects.[186] This special legislation requires a more complicated process of creation and amendment than ordinary legislation. As can be appreciated in the table, the difference lies in the quorum necessary to approve a bill in the first chamber. Whereas special laws require an absolute majority (50%+1 of the votes of those present in the voting), simple majorities (at least one more vote in favor of an option above other options) are sufficient when legislation does not touch topics reserved to special legislation.

The National Congress of Argentina is bicameral. Two different collective bodies within the Congress must each agree about a bill,[187] which makes it harder to pass and amend legislation. Any bill that originates in the Chamber of Deputies or in the Senate must be approved by both houses before it is passed to the President of the Republic. If the President totally or partially rejects the bill, the bill goes back to the house of origin, which can confirm it with two-thirds of the votes and then send it to the revising house. If the latter also confirms it with two-thirds of the votes, it can be sent to the President who must promulgate the law without more objections.[188]

3.4.1.2   Brazil

In line with the legal rank, amending the Brazilian constitution is more difficult than amending legislation. The main differences lay in the number of discussions needed for approval and that discussing the proposal of constitutional amendments requires voting.[189] Table 3.2 shows that a proposal of a constitutional reform requires the support of one-third of the elected members of Congress to be discussed. Bills for constitutional amendments require four discussions, two in each chamber of Congress. Approval of a bill requires a qualified majority (two-thirds of the members in

---

[185]Negretto (2009), p. 40.

[186]These special laws rule the following specific aspects: Referendum, see Const. Argentina Art. 40; budget allocations, see Const. Argentina Art. 75 (2) and (5); political parties and the electoral system, see Const. Argentina Art. 77 para 2; the General Audit of the Nation, see Const. Argentina Art. 85 para 3; the Judicial Council, see Const. Argentina Art. 114.

[187]Tsebelis (2000), p. 459.

[188]For the participation of the executive branch, see Const. Argentina Arts. 81, 83, and 99 para 3.

[189]Const. Brazil Art. 60 (I): *"The Constitution may be amended on the proposal of: I- at least one third of the members of the Chamber of Deputies or of the Federal Senate."*

Table 3.2 Legislative procedure in Brazil

	Constitutional	Organic laws	Supplementary laws	Ordinary laws
Role of Congress	Initiative Discussion	Initiative and discussion for laws of federal districts	Initiative Discussion	Initiative Discussion
No. of Discussions	4 (2 in each chamber)	2 in the municipal or legislative chamber	Not specified. See ordinary laws	2 (1 in each chamber)
Required Voting	1/3 of the members of one of the chambers to propose the amendment 2/3 of the members of each chamber	2/3 of the members	Approved by absolute majority	Approved by majority Rejected with absolute majority following veto
Role of the Executive	Initiative	N/A	Initiative Revise the bill, sanction it or veto it in case of unconstitutionality and being contrary to public interest	Initiative Revise the bill, sanction it or veto it in case of unconstitutionality and being contrary to public interest
Referendum	N/A	N/A	N/A	N/A
Constituent Assembly	N/A	N/A	N/A	N/A

Source: Author. Summary of findings from legal analysis as presented in respective country section

office).[190] The role of the President is limited to being one of the actors who can initiate a constitutional amendment.[191] The constitution does not give the President any veto power.

---

[190]This is the case for instance of the organic law that governs the Federal District according to Const. Brazil Art. 32. It is also the case of the Municipalities even though their organic law is not enacted by the legislative branch but by the Municipal Chamber. See Const. Brazil Art. 29.

[191]Const. Brazil Art. 60 (II): *"The Constitution shall be amended on the proposal of: II–the President of the Republic"*.

Brazilian law distinguishes among organic, supplementary, ordinary[192] and delegated laws.[193] The creation and amendment processes of supplementary (*Leis Complementares*) and ordinary laws are fairly similar.[194] In both cases, three veto players are involved: the two chambers of the Congress and the President. Create and reform these types of legislation in Brazil requires two readings, one in each of the chambers of the Congress. The Brazilian President may take the initiative by revising or promulgating bills.[195] She may also veto bills if they seem unconstitutional or against public interest. Supplementary laws are approved with absolute majority (50% plus one of the members in office), ordinary laws require the presence of the absolute majority and a majority vote.[196]

According to the Constitution, the federal district and the municipalities are governed by organic laws. The municipality creates and amends its own legislation. The legislative chamber is in charge of legislation for the federal district. The President of the Republic has no role in the creation and amendment of organic laws. However, there are extra requirements when the bill must be discussed (2 readings) and the time interval between the discussions (10 days). Organic laws have to be approved by two-thirds of the votes.

3.4.1.3 Chile

As in all six countries, the costs of amending the Constitution are substantially higher than those of other legislation in Chile. Table 3.3 shows that three or four players are involved: the two chambers of the Congress, the President of the

---

[192]Const. Brazil Art. 59: *"The Legislative Process comprises the preparation of I Amendments to the constitution; II Supplementary laws; III Ordinary laws; IV Delegated laws; V Provisional measures; VI Legislative decrees; VII Resolutions."*

[193]The Const. Brazil Art. 68 establishes that *"[d]elegated laws shall be drawn upon by the President of the Republic, who shall request delegation from the National Congress."* They are not included in the Table as there is not much specific about them in the constitution.

[194]However, the enactment of organic laws in Brazil is reserved for the state legislatures which have legislative powers and not to the National Congress of Brazil. Creating or amending organic laws demand the approval voting of two-thirds of the members in office of the Congress. See Const. Brazil Art. 32.

[195]Const. Brazil Art. 61: *"The initiative of supplementary and ordinary laws is within the competence of any member or committee of the Chamber of Deputies and the Federal Senate of the National Congress, the President of the Republic, the Supreme Federal Court, the Superior Courts, the Attorney-General of the Republic and the citizens in the manner and the cases provided in this Constitution."*

See also Const. Brazil Art. 66 including para 1: *"The House in which voting is concluded shall send the bill of law to the President of the Republic, who, if he concurs, shall sanction it. [...] Paragraph 1. If the President of the Republic considers the bill of law, wholly or in part, unconstitutional or contrary to public interest, he shall veto it, wholly or in part, within fifteen workdays, counted from the day of receipt and he shall, within forty-eight hours, the President of the Senate of the reasons of his veto."*

[196]Const. Brazil Arts. 47 and 69.

Table 3.3 Legislative procedure in Chile

	Constitutional Amendment	Organic law	Ordinary law
Role of Congress	Initiative	Initiative	Initiative
No. of Discussions	2 (1 in each chamber)	2 (1 in each chamber)	2 (1 in each chamber)
Required Voting	3/5 or 2/3 of the members of each chamber	4/7 members of each chamber	Simple majority
Role of Executive	Initiative Reject the project of amendment Make observations Call to plebiscite	If rejected in one chamber, the President can insist that the other chamber approves the bill or reform Approve it and promulgate it Disapprove bills	The same as for organic acts
Referendum	If the President rejects a bill and the legislature insists on it, the President must promulgate the amendment or call a plebiscite	N/A	N/A
Constituent Assembly	N/A	N/A	N/A

Source: Author. Summary of findings from legal analysis as presented in respective country section

Republic and the citizens, if they are consulted in a plebiscite. The Chileans have the last word whenever Congress and the President cannot agree about a constitutional amendment. The vote required to amend the Chilean Constitution depends on how the process comes about. In Congress, a vote of three-fifths (60%) of the deputies and senators in office is required to approve constitutional amendments. However, the voting requirement for approval is higher (two-thirds) when the amendment is related to very sensitive topics, such as the basic institutions, constitutional rights and duties, a public ministry, armed forces, public security and the constitutional prescriptions governing the reform of the Constitution.[197] The same votes are required either to approve or decline the objections of the President of the Republic or to insist on a bill of amendment after it is rejected by the President. If Congress successfully insists on amendments rejected by the President, he will have to promulgate[198] the reform within ten days via a decree or consult the people in a plebiscite.[199]

---

[197]Const. Chile Art. 127.

[198]Const. Chile Art. 128 para 2: *"If the President of the Republic totally rejects a reform project approved by both Chambers and they insist entirely by two thirds of the members in exercise of each Chamber, the President of the Republic shall promulgate that project* [. . .]*"*. The promulgation is a solemn act through which the President of the Republic announces officially the existence of a new law. *The Law Dictionary*, Definition of *promulgation* in English: http://thelawdictionary.org/promulgate/.

[199]Const. Chile Art. 128 para 2.

Chile further distinguishes between two different types of legislation: constitutional organic acts and ordinary acts. The procedure is found in columns 2 and 3 of Table 3.3 Amending an organic act requires the same vote as amending the Constitution, which is 57% of the elected members of Congress.[200] By contrast, to create and approve an ordinary law requires only a simple majority (of representatives attending the session).[201] Apart from the required votes, the process of creating or reforming legislation is similar for constitutional organic laws and ordinary laws. Both can originate in either chamber of Congress, by initiative of the President or by initiative of a member of Congress. Bills must be approved in both chambers of Congress.[202] They are then submitted to the President, who can have objections, approve[203] or reject the bill. If the President has objections or rejects a bill, the bill goes back to the chamber of origin.[204] Congress can either accept the objections raised[205] or insist on the bill as it is with a support of two-thirds of the members of each chambers. Thereafter, the bill is sent back to the President for promulgation.[206]

3.4.1.4   Peru

The Peruvian constitution sets out the entire process for constitutional amendments in Article 206. Congress or the President can propose changes to the Constitution. Alternatively, the citizens of Peru can initiate amendments via elections with the vote of 0.3% of Peruvians (with the right to vote). But the President's role is restricted. Any initiative to amend the Constitution will require the approval of the cabinet.[207]

Table 3.4 indicates that there are several ways and requirements for approval of constitutional amendments. One way to approve a constitutional reform is through two discussions in Congress, the first of which requires an absolute majority vote (50% +1 votes of the members in office). The discussion must be approved by two thirds of the elected members of the Congress. If the two-thirds are missing in the

---

[200]Const. Chile Art. 66 para 2: *"The legal norms to which the Constitution confers the character of organic constitutional laws will require, for their approval, amendment or repeal, of the four sevenths of the deputies and senators in exercise."*

[201]Const. Chile Art. 66 para 4.

[202]Const. Chile Art. 65 para 1 is on the initiative of creating a law. *See* also Const. Chile Art. 69 para 1.

[203]The Const. Chile Art. 72 states that if the President of the Republic *"approves it, [he] will arrange its promulgation as a law."*

[204]According to Art. 73 para 1 Const. Chile, the President of the Republic has to make observations *"within a period of thirty days."*

[205]The Const. Chile Art. 73 para 3 sets forth that *"[i]f both Chambers approve the observations, the project will have the force of law and will be returned to the President for its promulgation."*

[206]Const. Chile Art. 73 para 4 states that *"if both Chambers [. . .] insist by two-thirds of its present members, on all or part of the project approved by them, it will be returned to the President for its promulgation."*

[207]Const. Peru Art. 206 para 2.

Table 3.4 Legislative procedure in Peru

	Constitutional Amendment	Organic law	Ordinary law
Role of Congress	Initiative Discussion Approval	Initiative Discussion Approval	Initiative Discussion Approval
No. of Discussions	1 or 2	2	2
Required Voting	Absolute majority Greater than 2/3	Absolute majority	Simple majority
Role of Executive	Initiative	Initiate the process Send to the Congress bills with urgent char- acter Receive bills for veto.	Initiate the process Send to the Congress bills with urgent char- acter Receive bills for veto.
Referendum	When not approved with absolute majority in two sessions	N/A	N/A
Constituent Assembly	N/A	N/A	N/A

Source: Author. Summary of findings from legal analysis as presented in respective country section

discussion, the way to approve a constitutional amendment is to call for a referendum.[208] The President cannot object to a constitutional reform.[209]

Peru's constitution is significantly more difficult to amend than other legislation. Columns 2 and 3 of Table 3.4 describe the legislative process to amend the two types of legislation in Peruvian law: organic and ordinary laws. The Constitution does not establish the process of creating and amending ordinary legislation.[210] As in most countries, the main difference is in the majorities required to approve them. While ordinary laws require a simple majority (the votes in favor of a proposal exceed the votes against it), organic laws require an absolute majority.[211] The President can

---

[208]Const. Peru Art. 32: "*A referendum may be held in the* [. . .] [p]*artial or complete amendment of the Constitution.*" For the ways to constitutional reform, see Const. Peru Art. 206 para 1.

[209]Const. Peru Art. 206 para 2: "A law concerning a constitutional reform shall not be objected to by the President of the Republic."

[210]In Peru, the Standing Rules of the Congress of Peru Art. 73 [Reglamento del Congreso de Perú, Diario Oficial, 10 March 2018] provide for the process of creating and amending ordinary legislation.

[211]Const. Peru Art. 106 para 2.

Table 3.5 Legislative procedure in Mexico

	Constitutional	Legislation
Role of Congress	Discussion and approval of the bill Remission to the states' legislatures	Discussion and approval of bill
Role of States' Legislatures	Approval of the bill	N/A
No. of Discussions	2 (1 in each chamber of the Congress) 1 in each state legislature	2 (1 in each chamber)
Required Voting	2/3 of the members in office of the Congress 2/3 of the members in office of the states' legislatures	Simple majority 2/3 to approve the presidential objections Absolute majority to reconsider it in the chamber of origin if it was rejected in the second chamber
Role of Executive	Promulgation	Initiative to introduce bills Approval or objection Promulgation and publication
Referendum	N/A	N/A
Constituent Assembly	N/A	N/A

Source: Author. Summary of findings from legal analysis as presented in respective country section

initiate the process[212] and send bills to the legislature that the President considers urgent.[213] The President also receives bills for veto.[214]

3.4.1.5 Mexico

Surprisingly, the Mexican Constitution is silent about who has the initiative to amend the Constitution.[215] But amendments are considered. Table 3.5 indicates that both the Federal House of Representatives and the Federal Senate of Mexico must approve respective bills in one session in each chamber with the vote of two-thirds of the members in office in each chamber.[216] Thereafter, the president

---

[212]Const. Peru Art. 107 para 1 states that *"[b]oth the President of the Republic and the congressmen have the right to initiate in lawmaking."*

[213]Const. Peru Art. 105: *"Bills sent by the Executive branch of an urgent nature should have priority in Congress."*

[214]Const. Peru Art. 108 para 2: *"If the President of the Republic has observations to share regarding the whole or any part of the law passed by the Congress, he shall submit them to the legislature within fifteen days."*

[215]Patino Camarena (2011), p. 176.

[216]Const. Mexico Art. 135: *"This Constitution may be subject to amendments. The vote of two-thirds of the present members of the Congress of the Union is required to make amendments or additions to the Constitution. Once the Congress agrees on the amendments or additions, these*

of the chamber of revision must send the bill to the state legislatures.[217] When at least sixteen of Mexico's thirty-one state legislatures have approved the bill of amendment with the vote of two-thirds of the elected members, the bill is approved.[218] The President of Mexico then has to promulgate and publish the amendment.

The process of creating and amending legislation is much simpler as shown in Table 3.5. The state legislatures are not asked. Two discussions in Congress[219] and only a simple majority are required to pass a bill.[220] But the President has a more active role. The Mexican President can take the initiative to create,[221] amend or reject bills.[222] When a bill is rejected, Congress can either redraft the bill or pass the bill anyway, if there is a qualified majority (two thirds (66%) of the votes of those present in the voting) for it.[223]

3.4.1.6 Colombia

In Colombia, there are three ways to amend the Constitution as shown in column 1 of Table 3.6.[224] First, amendments may be done via the legislature. The amendment process via the legislative branch is divided into two steps. First, the government, the members of the Colombian Congress or a number of citizens may propose a

---

must be approved by the majority of state legislatures." See also Standing Rules of the Senate of Mexico Art. 89 (2) (e) [Reglamento del Senado de la República de México, Diario Oficial de la Federación, 4 June 2010] [hereinafter RSRM]: *"The bill of reform of the constitution approved by the House of Representatives shall be immediately sent to the chamber for revision. [Own Translation]"*

[217]RSRM Art. 225, para 1, I: *"When the Senate, as the chamber of revision in the legislative process of amendment of the Constitution, approves the bill, the President of the Senate [...] send the bill to each of the state legislatures [...] for their consideration. [Own Translation]"*

[218]RSRM Art. 225, 1: *"If the Bill is approved by a minimum of sixteen state legislatures, (the President of the Senate) makes the corresponding calculation reports, informs to the Plenary and makes the corresponding declaration [Own Translation]."* See also Constitution of the State of Baja California Art. 166 para 1: [Own translation of Constitución Política del Estado de Baja California, Periódico Oficial No. 23, 16 August 1953]: *"The present Constitution may be added or amended. The initiatives that have that objective [...] require the approval of at least two-thirds of the total representatives that integrate the legislature [Own Translation]."*

[219]Const. Mexico Art. 72 (a).

[220]RSRM Art. 79.

[221]Const. Mexico Art. 71.

[222]Const. Mexico Art. 72 (a) suggests that after the discussion and approval of a bill in both legislative, *"[...] the bill shall be submitted to the President of the Republic who, after deciding that no further corrections should be made, shall publish it without delay."*

[223]Const. Mexico Art. 72 (c).

[224]Const. Colombia Art. 374: *"The Political Constitution may be reformed by Congress, a Constituent Assembly, or by the people through a referendum."*

Table 3.6 Legislative procedure in Colombia

	Constitutional Amendment	Organic law	Statutory law	Ordinary law
Role of Congress	Initiative Approve the bill Call to Constitutional Assembly Call to referendum	Initiative Approve the bill	Initiative Approve the bill	Initiative Approve the bill
No. of Discussions	2 (to publish the bill, and to approve it)	4 (2 in each chamber)	4 (2 in each chamber)	4 (2 in each chamber)
Required Voting	1st discussion: simple majority 2nd discussion: absolute majority	Absolute majority	Absolute majority	Simple majority
Role of Executive	Initiative of reform publish the bill	Initiative and Amendment Ask to recon-sider Solicit urgent approval Final approval	Dictate and amend Ask to recon-sider Solicit urgent approval Final approval	Dictate and amend Ask to recon-sider Solicit urgent approval Final approval or objection Promulgation
Referendum	Yes	N/A	N/A	N/A
Constituent Assembly	Yes	N/A	N/A	N/A

Source: Author. Summary of findings from legal analysis as presented in respective country section

"legislative act" that has to be discussed[225] and approved by a simple majority (the majority of the deputies and senators present during the voting).[226] The government must publish the proposal in the official legal gazette. In a second step, the approval requires eight months of discussion. The Constitution prescribes that two rounds of debate are necessary during the two legislative periods. The legislative periods in Colombia, generally, take place between July and December and between March and June.[227] The approval also requires an absolute majority in the lower and higher chambers of Congress. Alternatively, amendments may be initiated by a democratically elected constitutional assembly. The decision to call for elections belongs exclusively to the Congress.[228] Moreover, a constitutional amendment that involves the democratic process, the structure or organization of the legislative branch or fundamental rights and guarantees requires a referendum.[229]

---

[225]Const. Colombia Art. 375 paras 1 and 2.

[226]Const. Colombia Art. 375 paras 2 and 3.

[227]Congress of Colombia, Frequent Questions: http://www.camara.gov.co/portal2011/preguntas-frecuentes/116-ique-fechas-comprenden-los-periodos-legislativos-de-sesiones.

[228]Const. Colombia Art. 376.

[229]Const. Colombia Art. 377.

The Colombian Constitution recognizes three main types of legislation: organic, statutory and ordinary laws (see Table 3.6). The traditional role of organic laws is divided between organic laws and statutory laws in the Colombian legal framework. Thus, according to the Colombian Constitution, organic laws regulate aspects related to the structure of the state. Specifically, the Constitution determines that organic laws, labeled as "institutional acts" in the law, regulate three aspects: (1) the exercise of the Congress and its chambers of the legislative activity; (2) the preparation and implementation of the national budget, appropriation bills and Colombia's general plan of development; and (3) the allocation and distribution of competences to local authorities.[230]

The President of the Republic can amend a bill, ask for its reconsideration, object to it or approve it. According to the Constitution, both the Colombian Congress and the President of the Republic have the power to create, amend and approve organic laws.[231] The creation and amendment of organic laws are not subject to special mechanisms of approval such as a referendum or an assembly. However, organic laws require two four discussions in Congress and an absolute majority for approval.[232]

The Constitution of Colombia also assigns specific topics of regulation to the statutory laws: (1) the fundamental rights and their mechanisms of protection; (2) the administration of justice; (3) rules about the organization and government of political parties, democratic participation and electoral functions; (4) institutions and mechanisms for participation in the democratic process; and (5) state of exception declared in case of emergencies and threats to the national peace.[233] The Congress is in charge of discussing and approving statutory laws in four sessions (two in each chamber).[234] An absolute majority of the members of the Congress is required for approval.[235] The Constitution gives the President of the Republic the power to "solicit the urgent passage of any legislative bill."[236]

The amendment of ordinary laws in the Colombian framework follows by and large the same procedure as that of organic laws, except for the majority required to approve an ordinary law.[237]

---

[230]Const. Colombia Art. 151.

[231]According to the Const. Colombia Art.157, "[n]o bill will become law without meeting the following requirements: [...] 4. Securing the approval of the government." See also Const. Colombia Art. 165: "Once a legislative bill is approved by both Houses, it shall be transmitted to the government for its approval. [...]".

[232]Const. Colombia Art. 151 in combination with Art. 157.

[233]Const. Colombia Art. 152.

[234]Const. Colombia Art. 157.

[235]Const. Colombia Art. 153. See also Const. Colombia Art 154 para 2 on initiation.

[236]Const. Colombia Art. 163.

[237]Const. Colombia Art. 146: "In Congress as a whole, in the Houses and in their permanent committees, decisions shall be taken by the majority of votes of those attending, unless the Constitution should expressly prescribe a special majority."

3.4.2   Procedural Differences Between Legal Frameworks

The detailed description does not only allow for a qualitative comparison of modification costs of legislation within one country's legal frameworks but also for a comparison between countries. To evaluate the credibility of legal commitments laid down in a constitution, it is important to compare whether it is significantly easier to amend a constitution in one country than in another. For example, if it is not possible to amend a constitution in one country, promises laid down in the constitution can be considered super-binding. It is, however, also possible that constitutional amendments are only slightly costlier than the modification of regular legislation in a country. In this case, constitutional promises may not provide the same credibility. Organic law in one country may be harder to modify than a constitution in another. The differences in modification costs of each type of legislation, therefore, affect both the degree of legal certainty entailed in legal provisions in a specific country and the relative degree of legal certainty in legal commitments between countries.

Based on the legal analysis, the constitution of Argentina seems to be the hardest to modify because the vote required to approve the resolution that declares the necessity of constitutional amendment is high (two-thirds of the members of the legislature). Furthermore, the reform is not carried out by the legislature but by a constitutional assembly that must be democratically elected in general elections. This entails a costly electoral process and uncertainty about the preferences of the future members of the assembly, which are not found as such in the other legal frameworks. In other words, the amendment of the constitution is not in the hands of the government or the legislature.

The Constitution of Mexico is the next most difficult to modify. Although Argentina and Brazil are also federal states (Colombia, Peru and Chile are not), only Mexico uses the territorial distribution of power to add (potential) veto players and increase modification costs for constitutional amendments. More veto players entail not only a longer process but also the necessity of a broader consensus because of the plurality of opinions involved. Furthermore, the vote required to approve the amendment, both in the national legislature and in the state legislatures, is high.

The amendment process of the Chilean constitution demands high majorities in the legislature to approve the amendment. If there is no agreement, a referendum may be necessary. From this perspective, amending the Constitution of Chile seems to differ little from amending the Constitution of Peru. However, although the required votes are still high in Peru, modifications to the constitution involve fewer veto players than in Chile, where the President can reject bills as they are in the first round.

The process of constitutional amendment in Colombia ranks low in terms of difficulty because of its ambiguity. The easiest process of amending the Constitution applies to every aspect not related to the process of political participation, fundamental rights and the constitutional rules of the legislature. Only the amendments of these three aspects require a referendum. Amending the Constitution in all other aspects requires a relatively long process because the discussion lasts two legislative periods, not sessions, but the voting majorities are low compared to those in the legal frameworks of the other countries. The Constitution also provides the opportunity to install a constitutional assembly to amend the Constitution. Yet, deciding its installation is at the discretion of the legislature. The Constitution does not specify in which case and under which conditions this is necessary.

The legal analysis suggests that amending Brazil's Constitution involves the lowest modification costs. Even though the voting requirement is generally higher than in Colombia, the amendment process fully excludes the option of having a referendum or installing a constitutional assembly. The only veto player here is the legislative branch.

According to the legal frameworks of Chile, the modification of the Constitution and constitutional organic law differs greatly only when there is a call to a plebiscite to approve the modification. Therefore, for instance, amending a constitutional organic law in Chile is almost as difficult as amending the Constitution in Brazil, because of the high vote required to create or reform a constitutional organic act in Chile (four-seventh of the members of the Congress versus one-third and two-thirds in Brazil). In fact, most modifications of the Colombian and Peruvian constitutions do not require a constituent assembly or a referendum. In these cases, changes to organic law in Chile and to the constitutions of Peru or Colombia are also comparable in terms of modification costs.

Comparing the countries, it is obvious that procedural differences between the constitutions and legislation of the next lower rank are particularly large in Argentina and Mexico. In the case of Argentina, constitutional amendments are the hardest, while the process of modification of special laws is comparable to that of organic law in Colombia and Peru. In the case of Mexico, there is only ordinary law, which requires smaller majorities than organic law in other countries.

3.5 Summary

There is a strong link between legal certainty and the credibility of legal commitments. The higher the degree of legal certainty that legal devices entail, the better the conditions for authorities to commit and for citizens to believe the legal commitments. To make commitments credible for a longer period, they should be included in the legal framework in such a way that it is hard to modify the commitments.

This chapter explained the implications of embedding commitments in legal documents such as international treaties, constitutions, organic laws and ordinary laws for legal certainty with a special emphasis on the stability of the legal rules. In general, increasing the number of veto players, for instance the number of parties in Congress, several constituencies, and different state organs involved in modifying a legal commitment, adds to the difficulty of completing the amendment process.

The constitution is most effective in restraining authorities domestically. The constitution is designed to be a legal device that enforces society's commitments by setting clear, stable and consistent rules. To guarantee the stability of the constitution, modification costs tend to be high. Although it is harder to modify the constitution than other legislation in each of the six Latin American countries studied here, the analysis in this chapter has provided evidence that the constitution is a particularly strong legal commitment device in Argentina, Mexico and Chile. In Peru, Colombia and Brazil, ambiguities or a small number of veto players make constitutional amendments easier.

However, stability of the rules may come at some cost as well. Although the Argentinian constitution seems very difficult to modify and may provide legal certainty for what is already laid down in the constitution, the procedural rules may make it almost prohibitive to use the constitution as a commitment device for new promises. Hence, the procedural differences between creating and amending laws may help explain why some countries choose to use the constitution to commit credibly to certain goals, while others do not.

Legal References

Constitutions

Constitution of Argentina with Amendments through 1994 [English Translation of Diario Oficial No. 27.959, 23 August 1994]. Constitute Project, University of Texas at Austin, available at http://www.constituteproject.org/constitution/Argentina_1994.pdf

Constitution of Chile with Amendments through 2015 [English Translation of the Constitución Política de la República de Chile, Gazeta Official, 20 October 2015]. Constitute Project, University of Texas at Austin, available at https://www.constituteproject.org/search?lang=en&q=chile

Constitution of Colombia with Amendments through 2015 [English Translation of Constitución Política de Colombia, Diario Oficial No. 49.554, 25 June 2015]. Constitute Project, University of Texas at Austin, available at https://www.constituteproject.org/constitution/Colombia_2015.pdf

Constitution of France [English Translation of the Constitution de la République Française, 4 October 1958].

Constitution of Mexico [English Translation of the Political Constitution of the Mexican States, Gazeta de la Federación, 5 February 1917], Constitute Project, University of Texas at Austin available at https://www.constituteproject.org/constitution/Mexico_2015.pdf?lang=en

Constitution of Peru [English Translation of Constitución Política del Perú, Diario Oficial, 30 December 1993]. Congress of the Republic of Peru, available at http://www.congreso.gob.pe/Docs/files/CONSTITUTION_27_11_2012_ENG.pdf [Last accessed on November 11, 2018].

Constitution of Portugal [English Translation of the Constitution Portuguese, 2 April 1976].

Constitution of Spain [English Translation of Constitución Española, 29 December 1978].

Constitution of the State of Baja California [Constitución Política del Estado de Baja California, Periódico Oficial No. 23, 16 August 1953].

The Constitution of Brazil [English Translation of the Constituição da República Federativa do Brasil, Diario Oficial da União, 5 October 1988]. Chamber of Deputies, available at http://english.tse.jus.br/arquivos/federal-constitution

Legislation

Colombia

Regulation of the House of Representatives of Colombia [Reglamento del Congreso de los Diputados, Diario Oficial No. 237, 4 October 1993].

Mexico

Rules of the Chamber of Deputies of Mexico [Reglamento de la Cámara de Diputados de México, Diario Oficial de la Federación, 24 December 2010].

Standing Rules of the Senate of Mexico [Reglamento del Senado de la República de México, Diario Oficial de la Federación, 4 June 2010].

Peru

Standing Rules of the Congress of Peru [Reglamento del Congreso de la República; Diario Oficial, 10 March 2018].

Case Law

Tribunal Constitucional de Chile [Constitutional Tribunal of Chile]

Control constitucionalidad "Ley Orgánica Banco central de Chile", TC Chile, Sentencia Rol No. 78, 20 September 1989.

Control constitucionalidad enmienda "Ley General de Bancos", TC Chile, Sentencia Rol No. 216, 17 July 1995.

Corte Constitucional de Colombia [Constitutional Court of Colombia]

Jaime Rafael Pedraza Vanegas v. Congreso de la República de Colombia, CCC, Sentencia C-050, 10 February 1994.

Celmira Waldo de Valoyes v. Caja Nacaional de Previsión Social-Seccional Chocó, CCC, Sentencia SU-111, 6 March 1997.

René Vargas Pérez v. Congreso de la República de Colombia, CCC, Sentencia C-4817 July 1999.

Francisco José Bautista Villalobos v. Congreso de la República de Colombia, CCC, Sentencia C-557, 20 August 2009.

Suprema Corte de Justicia de la Nación de México [Supreme Court of Justice of the Nation]

Banco Inbursa, S.A. and others, Amparo, SCJN México,Sentencia 2a. CCXXIV, Tomo XIV, December 2001.

References

Brunner S, Flachsland C, Marschinski R (2011) Credible commitment in carbon policy. Potsdam Institute for Climate Impact Research, Working Paper

Campos JE, Esfahani HS (2000) Credible commitment and success with public enterprise reform. World Dev 28(2):221–243. https://doi.org/10.1016/S0305-750X(99)00128-X

Cárdenas J, Pérez C, Carbonell M (1999) Presente y Futuro de la Autonomía del Instituto Federal Electoral, Administración y Financiamiento de las Elecciones en el Umbral del Siglo XXI. Memoria del Tercer Congreso Internacional de Derecho Electoral 2:467–513

Chapman B (2004) Legal analysis of economics: solving the problem of rational commitment. Chicago-Kent Law Rev 79:471–495. Available at http://heinonline.org/HOL/LandingPage?handle=hein.journals/chknt79&div=25&id=&page=

Cordero E (2010) La Potestad Legislativa, los Tipos de Ley y sus Relaciones con el Derecho Nacional. Revista de Derecho Valdivia 23(1):125–153. https://doi.org/10.4067/S0718-09502010000100006

Cordero (2012) La Administración del Estado en Chile y el Concepto de Autonomía. Contraloría General de la República

Egebo T, Englander AS (1992) Institutional commitments and policy credibility: a critical survey and empirical evidence from the ERM. OECD Econ Stud 18:45–84. Available at https://pdfs.semanticscholar.org/70cc/14d5d76210a4cd57f2d927dad1acb1cd9b02.pdf

Epstein R (2007) How progressives rewrote the constitution. Cato Institute

Falaschetti D, Miller G (2001) Constraining Leviathan: Moral Hazard and credible commitment in constitutional design. J Theoret Polit 13(4):389–411. https://doi.org/10.1177/0951692801013004003

Figueruelo Burrieza A (1993) La Incidencia Positiva del Tribunal Constitucional en el Poder Legislativo. Revista de Estudios Políticos 81:47–72. Available at https://www.semanticscholar.org/paper/La-incidencia-positiva-del-Tribunal-Constitucional-Burrieza/3ec700b7a007805ea1aeed60f2f6aa40429186e9

Finnemore M, Toope S (2001) Alternatives to "Legalization": Richer views of law and politics. Int Org 55(3):743–758. https://doi.org/10.1162/00208180152507614

Freijedo FJ (1981) Comentario Bibliográfico sobre la Naturaleza Jurídica de las Leyes Orgánicas. Revista Española de Derecho Constitucional 1(2):285–311. Available at http://www.cepc.gob.es/Publicaciones/revistas/revistaselectronicas?IDR=6&IDN=304&IDA=24556

Gamboa R, Segovia C (2016) Chile 2015: Falla Política y Desconfianza. Revista de Ciencia Política 36(1):123–144. https://doi.org/10.4067/S0718-090X2016000100006

Gaubatz K (1996) Democratic states and commitment in international relations. Int Org 50 (10):109–139. https://doi.org/10.1017/S0020818300001685

George R (2001) Natural law, the constitution, and the theory and practice of judicial review. Fordham Law Rev 69:2269–2283. Available at http://heinonline.org/HOL/LandingPage?handle=hein.journals/flr69&div=84&id=&page=

Ginsburg T (2005) Locking in democracy: constitutions, commitment, and international law. N Y Univ J Int Law Polit 38:707–759. Available at http://heinonline.org/HOL/LandingPage?handle=hein.journals/nyuilp38&div=20&id=&page=

Guerrero R (1979) La Constitución Económica. Revista Chilena de Derecho 6(1):79–94. Available at https://www.jstor.org/stable/41605244

Hegre H, Oneal J, Russett B (2010) Trade does promote peace: new simultaneous estimates of the reciprocal effects of trade and conflict. J Peace Res 47(6):763–774. https://doi.org/10.1177/0022343310385995

Hutchcroft P (2001) Centralization and decentralization in administration and politics: assessing territorial dimensions of authority and power. Gov Int J Policy Adm 14(1):23–53. https://doi.org/10.1111/0952-1895.00150

International Monetary Fund (n.d.) List of Members' Date of Entry. https://www.imf.org/external/np/sec/memdir/memdate.htm. Accessed 7 Sept 2017

Jácome L, Vásquez F (2008) Is there any link between legal Central Bank independence and inflation? Evidence from Latina America and the Caribbean. Eur J Polit Econ 24(4):788–801. https://doi.org/10.1016/j.ejpoleco.2008.07.003

Keefer P, Stasavage D (2003) The limits of delegation: veto players, central bank independence, and the credibility of monetary policy. Am Polit Sci Rev 97(3):407–423. https://doi.org/10.1017/S0003055403000077

Kelsen H (1945) The general theory of law and state. The Law Book Exchange Ltd

Khalil E (1995) Organizations versus institutions. J Inst Theoret Econ 151(3):445–466. Available at https://www.jstor.org/stable/40751821

Knill C (1999) Explaining cross-national variance in administrative reform: autonomous versus instrumental bureaucracies. J Public Policy 19(2):113–139. https://doi.org/10.1017/S0143814X99000203

Kose A, Prasad E, Rogoff K, Wei S-J (1999) Financial globalization: a reappraisal. IMF Staff Papers. Palgrave Macmillan 56(1):8–62. Available at https://link.springer.com/article/10.1057%2Fimfsp.2008.36

Lachmann L (1971) The legacy of Max Weber. The Glendessary Press. Available at https://mises.org/system/tdf/The%20Legacy%20of%20Max%20Weber_2.pdf?file=1&type=document

Laurens B, Sommer M, Arnone M, Segalotto JF (2007) Central Bank autonomy: lessons from global trends. IMF Staff Pap 56(2):263–296. Available at https://www.imf.org/en/Publications/WP/Issues/2016/12/31/Central-Bank-Autonomy-Lessons-from-Global-Trends-20632

López Guerra L (1980) Sobre la Personalidad Jurídica del Estado. Revista del Departamento de Derecho Político, Universidad de Extremadura 6:17–35. Available at http://www.mpfn.gob.pe/escuela/contenido/actividades/docs/2201_02_personalidad_juridica.pdf

Lybek T (2004) Central Bank autonomy, accountability and governance: conceptual framework. IMF Seminar on Current Developments in Monetary and Financial Law, Washington. Available at https://www.imf.org/external/np/leg/sem/2004/cdmfl/eng/lybek.pdf

Lyons D (1977) Principles, positivism and legal theory. Yale Law J 87(2):415–435. https://doi.org/10.2307/795657

Mankiw G, Taylor M (2011) Economics. Cengage Learning EMEA

Miller G (2002) Above politics. J Public Adm Res Theory 10(2):289–328. https://doi.org/10.1093/oxfordjournals.jpart.a024271

Montesquieu CS (1989) The spirit of laws. Cambridge University Press

Negretto G (2009) Paradojas de la Reforma Constitucional en América Latina. J Democracy en Español 1(1):38–54

North D (1990) Institutions, institutional change and economic performance. Cambridge University Press, Cambridge. https://doi.org/10.1017/CBO9780511808678

North D (1993) Institutions and credible commitment. J Inst Theoret Econ 149(1):11–23. Available at https://www.jstor.org/stable/40751576

North D, Weingast B (1989) Constitutions and commitment: the evolution of institutions governing public choice in seventeenth century England. J Econ Hist 49(4):803–832. https://doi.org/10.1017/S0022050700009451

O'Donnell G (2004) The quality of democracy: why the rule of law matters. J Democr 15(4):32–46. https://doi.org/10.1353/jod.2004.0076

Oxford Dictionary on Lexico.com, Definition of Commitment in English

Oxford Dictionary on Lexico.com, Definition of Credibility in English

Patino Camarena J (2011) Consideraciones en Torno al Mecanismo de Reforma a la Constitución General y a las Constituciones de los Estados. Instituto de Investigaciones Jurídicas de la UNAM, Publicación Electrónica 1:175–187. Available at https://archivos.juridicas.unam.mx/www/bjv/libros/6/2955/16.pdf

Pedroza de la Llave ST (2002) Los Órganos Constitucionales Autónomos en México. In: Serna de la Garza JM, Caballero Juarez JA (eds) Estado de Derecho y Transición Jurídica. Serie Doctrina Jurídica 95:173–194. Available at http://biblio.juridicas.unam.mx/libros/1/306/1.pdf

Rajan R, Zingales L (2003) The great reversals: politics of financial development in the twentieth century. J Financ Econ 69(1):5–50. https://doi.org/10.1016/S0304-405X(03)00125-9

Raustiala K (2005) Form and substance in international agreements. Am J Int Law 99(3):581–614

Raz J (1970) The concept of the legal system. Clarendon Press, Oxford. Available at http://www.asia-comparativelaw.com/manageedit/uploadfile/20108816218555.pdf

Rios L (1983) Las Leyes Orgánicas Constitucionales. Revista Chilena de Derecho 10(1):39–44. Available at https://www.jstor.org/stable/4160809

Rivero Ortega R (2013) Derecho Administrativo Económico, Sexta Edición. Marcial Pons

Rodden J (2004) Comparative federalism on meaning and measurement. Comp Polit 36 (4):481–500. https://doi.org/10.2307/4150172

Santamaría Pastor JA (1979) Las Leyes Orgánicas: Notas en Torno a su Naturaleza y Procedimiento de Elaboración. Revista del Departamento de Derecho Político 4:39–57. https://doi.org/10.5944/rdp.4.1979.7981

Schaffer G, Pollack M (2010) Hard vs. soft law: alternatives, complements and antagonists in international governance. Minn Law Rev 94:706–799. Available at https://papers.ssrn.com/sol3/papers.cfm?abstract_id=1426123

Schor M (2006) Constitutionalism through the looking glass of Latin America. Tex Int Law J 41 (1):1–38. Available at http://heinonline.org/HOL/LandingPage?handle=hein.journals/tilj41&div=6&id=&page=

Sepúlveda Iguiniz R (2006) Una Propuesta para el Establecimiento de las Leyes Orgánicas Constitucionales en México. Cuestiones Constitucionales: Revista Mexicana de Derecho Constitucional 1(15):223–251. https://doi.org/10.22201/iij.24484881e.2006.15.5776

Simmons B (2000a) International law and state behavior: commitment and compliance in international monetary affairs. Am Polit Sci Rev 94(4):819–835. https://doi.org/10.2307/2586210

Simmons B (2000b) Money and the law: why comply with the public international law of money? Yale J Int Law 25:323–362. Available at http://heinonline.org/HOL/LandingPage?handle=hein.journals/yjil25&div=17&id=&page=

Smits R (1997) The European Central Bank: institutional aspects. Kluwer Law International

Taliercio R (2004) Administrative reform as credible commitment: the impact of autonomy on revenue autonomy performance in Latin America. World Dev 32(2):213–232. https://doi.org/10.1016/j.worlddev.2003.08.008

Tamanaha B (2007) A Concise Guide to the Rule of Law. Legal Studies Research Paper Series, St John's University No. 07-0082. Available at https://papers.ssrn.com/sol3/papers.cfm?abstract_id=1012051

Tesler LG (1980) A theory of self-enforcing agreements. J Bus 53(1):27–44. Available at https://www.jstor.org/stable/2352355

Tinbergen J (1952) On the theory of economic policy. North-Holland Publishing Company, Amsterdam

Tsebelis G (2000) Veto players and institutional analysis. Governance: an. Int J Public Adm 13 (4):441–474. https://doi.org/10.1111/0952-1895.00141

Ugalde F (2010) Órganos Constitucionales Autónomos. Revista del Instituto de la Judicatura Federal 29:253–264. Available at http://www.ijf.cjf.gob.mx/publicaciones/revista/29/Filiberto %20Valent%C3%ADn%20Ugalde%20Calder%C3%B3n.pdf

Urbiztondo S, Artana D, Navajas F (1998) La Autonomía de los Entes Reguladores Argentinos: Aguas y Cloacas, Gas Natural, Energía Eléctrica y Telecomunicaciones. Office of the Chief Economist, Inter-American Development Bank No. R-340

Van Alstine M (2001) Treaty law and legal transition costs. Chicago-Kent Law Rev 77:1303–1324. Available at http://heinonline.org/HOL/LandingPage?handle=hein.journals/chknt77& div=43&id=&page=

Verdugo M (2014) ¿Nueva Constitución? Revista de Derecho Público, Edición Especial 43–47. https://doi.org/10.5354/0719-5249.2014.31674

Von Hayek F (2002) Competition as discovery procedure. Q J Aust Econ 5(3):9–23. Available at https://mises.org/library/competition-discovery-procedure-0

Weimer D (1997) The political economy of property rights: institutional change and credibility in the reform of centrally planned economies. Cambridge University Press, Cambridge

Weingast B (1995) The economic role of political institutions: market preserving federalism and economic development. J Law Econ Org 11(1):1–31. Available at https://www.jstor.org/stable/765068

Weingast B (2005) Self-enforcing constitutions: with an application to democratic stability in America's First Century. Stanford University, Department of Political Science. Available at https://papers.ssrn.com/sol3/papers.cfm?abstract_id=1153527

Williamson O (1994) The Institutions and governance of economic development and reform. World Bank Econ Rev 8(1):171–197. https://doi.org/10.1093/wber/8.suppl_1.171

Yackee JW (2008) Bilateral investment treaties, credible commitment, and the rule of (international) law: do BITs promote foreign direct investment? Law Soc Rev 42(2):805–832. https://doi.org/10.1111/j.1540-5893.2008.00359.x

Yingyi Q, Weingast B (1997) Federalism as a commitment to preserving markets incentives. J Econ Perspect 11(4):83–92. Available at https://www.jstor.org/stable/2138464

Yrarrázabal A (1987) Principios Económicos de la Constitución de 1980. Revista Chilena de Derecho 14:97–112. Available at http://heinonline.org/HOL/LandingPage?handle=hein. journals/rechilde14&div=14&id=&page=

Zúñiga F (2007) Autonomías Constitucionales e Instituciones Contramayoritarias (A Propósito de las Aporías de la "Democracia Constitucional"). Revista Ius et Praxis 13(2):223–244. https://doi.org/10.4067/S0718-00122007000200010

Chapter 4
Central Bank Objectives and Autonomy

4.1 Introduction

The central bank's objective and its autonomy work in tandem.[1] Whereas the legal objective reflects the public interest that the monetary institution is supposed to protect, the autonomy is the legal device that prevents the deviation from the legal objective. Seen from another perspective, the central bank's objective is the justification for its autonomy and the main parameter to mark off its competence.

Legal certainty about the objective and the autonomy of the central bank makes monetary policy predictable. Legal certainty about the objective assures that the law effectively orients the efforts of the monetary authority towards the achievement of a specific technical goal. Legal certainty about the autonomy guarantees that the law is adequately equipped to prevent political intervention in the central bank's decisions. Thus, unpredictable political goals will not affect the pursuit of monetary policy objectives.

When a law is able to guide people's expectations about the performance of the monetary authority, there is subjective legal certainty. In other words, legal certainty about central bank law is mirrored in people's belief and trust in two things: (1) the central bank's commitment to achieving the monetary objective; and (2) the monetary authority's autonomy that prevents political and other interventions in the authority's decisions.

For there to be legal certainty about the central bank's objective, the drafting of the objective must consider the main elements of formal legal certainty. The legal objective of the central bank must be clear, stable and consistent. Leaving other factors that may influence the achievement of monetary goals aside, formal legal certainty about the central bank's objective provides a sound foundation for the authority's credible commitment. In fact, the law can make a credible commitment

---

[1]Garcia Herrero and Del Rio (2003), p. 45.

A. L. Tapia-Hoffmann, *Legal Certainty and Central Bank Autonomy in Latin American Emerging Markets*, European Yearbook of International Economic Law 15, https://doi.org/10.1007/978-3-030-70986-0_4

difficult when there are doubts about the objectives that the monetary authority must pursue. This is the case, for example, when the monetary authority has more than one objective, when the objectives are contradictory, or when they lack a clear order of priority.

In many Latin American countries, the central bank was granted autonomy in the constitution. A study by *Gutierrez* provides evidence of the importance of the legal rank of central bank autonomy in reaching central bank objectives. Through a sample of Latin American and Caribbean countries, the author empirically shows that, if the legal arrangements and enforcement of the central bank law is weak, there is no relationship between *de jure* central bank autonomy and low inflation. However, when central bank autonomy is rooted in the constitution of a country, inflation is lower.[2] While *Gutierrez* does not touch the issue, we can interpret the results as an indication that the constitutional entrenchment of central bank autonomy provides legal certainty about the fulfilment of the central bank objective.

Because the main reason for giving central banks a degree of autonomy in Latin America was to bring down inflation, this chapter starts by outlining the importance of monetary stability from a legal perspective to provide a rationale for monetary stability as a central bank objective. The chapter explains why governments face commitment problems when engaging in non-inflationary policies and why installing a central bank as an autonomous institution in charge of monetary stability may help to resolve the commitment problems. The following analysis of objectives and implications of the rank of autonomy in the legal frameworks of our six Latin American central banks is intended to serve as the basis for a detail-oriented legal study of institutional aspects of the central banks.

4.2 Inflation as a Central Bank Objective and the Need for Autonomy

4.2.1 Inflation and Its Costs

4.2.1.1 Money and Inflation

Money is the broad term for assets used to facilitate the business of the market by acting as a common medium of exchange.[3] This medium of exchange function is the main function of money. Derivative, or secondary, functions are the use of money as a store of value, which means that money can encapsulate purchasing power and maintain it over time. If money were not a medium of exchange, this function would not be available. Finally, to work as a medium of exchange, money also serves as a

---

[2]Gutierrez (2004), p. 255.
[3]Von Mises (1953), p. 776.

unit of account, i.e., the value of goods and services or other assets and liabilities are measured in terms of money.[4]

Money and *currency* are not the same. Currency is a subset of money. Currency is a term for the coins and bills that circulate in an economy or the currency reserves held by banks.[5] It is typically the most accepted means of exchange.[6] By contrast, payment via a debit card involves the use of deposits as a medium of exchange. Deposits are also considered part of the money supply and are more likely to be used as a store of value than, for instance, 100-euro bills. But deposits are loans provided to the banking system. Banks are obliged to provide currency against deposits if customers decide to withdraw their funds.[7]

Currencies emerged to enable people to trade a broad range of products when the direct interchange of goods became obsolete.[8] The advantages of bills and coins over direct exchange are that they are movable and easy to transport; fungible, which means that they can be easily interchanged for others of the same kind; durable; and their value is easy to divide.[9] While in the past people used different types of commodities, like silver or gold, to fulfil financial obligations, today all obligations tend to be met using a legal tender defined by governments. The legal tender is the medium of payment used among citizens, the operations of the central bank, the payment of salaries and tax collection within a jurisdiction.[10] In a fiat money system, the nominal value of the currency is typically the number printed by the state on each bill and coin.[11]

As the literal meaning of the word suggests, inflation originally meant an increase in the money supply.[12] Taken the amount of goods and services produced in an economy as given, a larger money supply changes the exchange relation between money and the respective goods and services. As increasing the money supply makes money less scarce relative to goods and services, the purchasing power of money falls. More money is required to purchase the same goods or services. Thus, the term inflation typically does not refer to the mere increase in the amount of currency in circulation but to situations when this increase is not backed by

---

[4]*Ibid.*, pp. 34–37. For a brief textbook explanation, see Mankiw and Taylor (2011), pp. 617–618.

[5]Pistor (2013), p. 317.

[6]Mankiw and Taylor (2011), p. 619.

[7]Gärtner (2009), p. 70.

[8]Montesquieu (1989), p. 407.

[9]Namén Vargas (1998), p. 38.

[10]Pistor (2013), p. 322.

[11]See, e.g., Rosenn (1978), p. 273 for more on the rise of valorims and erosion of nominalism. See also Namén Vargas (1998), p. 43. Before the emergence of fiat money, the value of the currency was determined by the weight of the scarce precious metal that backs it up. Under the gold standard, the value of the currency was tied to gold. Other ways of calling the money that was backed by gold is "commodity money" because of its inherent value. For instance, the value of gold is given by its use in the making of jewellery. See Mankiw and Taylor (2011), pp. 618–619.

[12]Von Mises (2008), p. 420.

additional production.[13] The purchasing power of the currency is the relationship between the nominal value of the currency and the prices of goods and services valued in that currency. It is also determined by the quoted value of the domestic currency in the national territory relative to the value of other foreign currencies.[14] Hence, inflation is considered the process of increases of prices due to a decreasing purchasing power of the nominal amount of money.[15]

4.2.1.2 Costs of Inflation and Inflation Variability

In principle, if all prices and wages in the economy rose at the exact same pace, inflation would not be a problem for the purchasing power of people's income. However, that is never the case. It is possible for some people to avoid inflation by holding less money and more other assets. People may keep money at the bank to get interest and only withdraw as much as they need or invest extra money in assets that rise along with the price level. But some hold more money than others.

There are costs involved in going to the bank for every transaction you want to take because inflation is high. The same is true for firms. Firms do not change prices every second because there are costs to changing prices, such as printing new price tags or menus. This fact implies that there are transaction costs stemming from inflation. In addition, prices do not all jump up at once but gradually adjust when businesses feel additional demand. Inflation will affect those that can adjust prices early less than those that cannot.[16]

High rates of inflation would necessitate continuous price changes which make planning of purchases and comparing prices harder for both consumers and producers. Setting the appropriate price and calculating profits becomes more difficult. Economic uncertainty increases. When price signals are less reliable in providing information, resources may be misallocated. To allow people to plan their actions, the inflation rate should also be stable. For example, to negotiate a wage increase that compensates for inflation the inflation rate has to be anticipated in advance. Unexpected inflation would have distributional effects, lowering the purchasing power of wages. Surprises in inflation would also redistribute wealth from those that provided loans at a predetermined interest rate to borrowers.[17] Therefore, the economics literature provides a rationale for holding inflation rates low and stable.

A study by behavioral economist *Robert Shiller* and a group of students has provided evidence that inflation is also a permanent concern of people. The study

---

[13]Díaz Etienne (1996), p. 345.

[14]Niño Tejada (1995), p. 253.

[15]Díaz Etienne (1996), p. 345. See also Coban (2005), p. 63. Coban defines inflation as *"[. . .] either a sustained rise in an economy's general level of prices or a corresponding fall in the domestic purchasing power of an economy's currency."*

[16]On the costs of inflation, see Mankiw and Taylor (2011), pp. 663–658.

[17]*Ibid.*, p. 658.

analyzed the public's opinions about inflation. Surveying people in the United States, Germany and Brazil, the study found that most people dislike inflation because inflation "hurts their standard of living".[18] People feel that inflation hampers economic growth and might lead to crisis. But Brazilians seem to be less worried about inflation causing trouble than Germans and Americans.[19] People tend to blame the government or greedy businessmen for inflation.[20]

4.2.2 Legal Reasons to Protect Monetary Stability

4.2.2.1 Monetary Instability and Contracts

Because contracts typically state that payment obligations must be met in a specific currency,[21] monetary stability provides legal certainty about transactions and obligations in real terms. When the value of the legal tender is stable, the amount stated in the contract buys the same basket of goods and services. A stable legal tender is conducive to contract enforcement.[22] But the nominal value of the obligation as put down when a contract is signed may deviate from the functional value of the obligation, which is the purchasing power, when the payments are settled. As there is a degree of uncertainty about the functional value of an obligation, expectations of contracting parties may be disappointed.[23]

Conflicts may arise because unexpected inflation tends to have distributional effects. For instance, if a loan contract does not account for changes in the value of the legal tender, the creditor assumes real losses caused by a decreased value of the currency. In such a case, the creditor may perceive the outcome of the exchange based on a contract as unfair even though the debtor fulfills all obligations by repaying the nominal value as laid down in the contract.[24]

Revaluing contracts, signed based on the assumption of stable currencies, following an inflationary shock is possible but usually difficult. Setting a new value for the contracted obligations undermines legal certainty about transactions. However, inflation will put one party at a disadvantage if, for example, the debtor does not also receive a higher wage corresponding to the rate of inflation. Here the trouble begins. A party can make a case for revalorization if it is not clear whether the parties

---

[18]Shiller (1997), p. 57.

[19]*Ibid.*, p. 60.

[20]*Ibid.*, p. 25.

[21]Lastra (2015), p. 14 explains that money should protect the rights of the contractual parties. See also Niño Tejada (1995), p. 253.

[22]Pistor (2013), p. 315.

[23]Rosenn (1982), p. 72.

[24]Niño Tejada (1995), pp. 253–254.

considered currency stability a problem in advance or accounted for inflation in the loan rate.

Rules for revalorization may either clarify the process in advance or leave much of the decision to the courts and adjudication. Either way, legislators and adjudicators face the difficulty of balancing the rights of the contractual parts in a scenario of price and currency instability, which the contracting parties probably had not taken into account.[25] Adjudicating is even more difficult if the value of the currency is very volatile.[26] If revalorization is the norm, creditors face the problem of determining the real value of their claims.[27]

To solve the contractual uncertainty produced by the changing purchasing power of the currency, contracts may include indexation clauses.[28] These clauses adjust the contractual obligations in accordance with the variation of prices[29] to reflect the real value of the obligation.[30] However, even indexation is far from perfect. The law has to allow for indexation. Standard contracts may not include such clauses. Moreover, the problem of a suitable index arises if obligations are indexed. As inflation may not change the prices of all goods and services to the same extent, the subjective inflation rate that each contractor faces may differ.

4.2.2.2 Property Rights Perspective

The rights to property and to own property are considered basic human rights to guarantee individual liberty.[31] The right to work ensures that people have the resources required to live, namely food, clothes and housing.[32] The right to private property is embedded in the Universal Declaration of Human Rights, the European

---

[25]Rosenn (1978), pp. 274–275.

[26]Rosenn (1978), p. 276. Deciding awards in tort law is an example of the challenges that adjudicators face because of inflation. Given that damages are calculated according to the date of breach of the obligation, the changing value of the currency between this day and the date of the judgment can reduce the value of the compensation. The solution to this problem is setting the interest rate higher than the expected inflation rate. Nevertheless, the longer the tort process the more inflation will eat into the real value of the compensation granted. This is even more complicated when calculating the compensation for a future loss of profit. See *ibid.*, p. 291.

[27]*Ibid.*, p. 297.

[28]It is also possible that contracts include clauses that would provide security to the value of the obligation. For instance, gold clauses determine that the obligation must be paid in gold coins or in a foreign hard currency. See Niño Tejada (1995), p. 254.

[29]Rosenn (1978), pp. 275–276.

[30]*Ibid.*, pp. 274–275; see also Civil Code of Peru [Código Civil de Perú, Official Journal, 25 July 1984] Art. 1236.

[31]Locke (1821), para 27 says: *"Though the earth and all inferior creatures, be common to all men, yet every man has a property in his own person: this no body has any right to but himself. The labour of his body, and the work of his hands, we may say, are properly his."*

[32]Donnelly (2013), pp. 44–45.

Convention of Human Rights,[33] the African Charter on Human and People's Rights,[34] and the American Convention on Human Rights.[35] The Universal Declaration of Human Rights and the American Convention (ACHR) forbid the arbitrary appropriation of someone's property.[36] The parties that signed these international human rights instruments must guarantee private property. The only limit on the enjoyment of property is the common good as specified in the law.[37]

Inflation affects property rights. If a government finances public expenditure via the central bank, i.e., prints money, inflation may be the consequence, and money loses exchange value. Those individuals who hold money are worse off and will bear the costs of the public burden. Inflation also poses challenges to courts that aim to protect private property, for instance, in cases related to compensation for expropriated private property. If the state engages in inflationary policies following the expropriation of property, the money recipients might be worse off than they originally thought. The problem arises particularly when there is a longer timespan between expropriation, the determination of the sum paid for compensation and the actual payment of the compensation.

4.2.2.3 Inflation and the Right to Live with Dignity

Human rights instruments and constitutions tend to recognize that people have a right to live with dignity.[38] The concept of human dignity is complex and challenging to apply, as the substantive content differs between jurisdictions. Yet, there are essential elements that define human dignity. These elements are, first, the intrinsic worth of every human being; second, the requirement of recognition and respect of this intrinsic worth by other; and, third, the justification of the existence of the state for the good and the benefit of the people as opposed to the existence of people for the sake of the state.[39]

---

[33]Protocol to the Convention for the Protection of Human Rights and Fundamental Freedoms Art. 1 [Version published by the European Court of Human Rights of the Protocol No. 1 to the European Convention of Human Rights, entry into force on 20 March 1952].

[34]African (Banjul) Charter on Human and People's Rights Art. 14 [Version published by the African Commission on People's Rights of the African (Banjul) Charter on Human and People's Rights, entry into force on 21 October 1986].

[35]American Convention on Human Rights, Pact of San José Costa Rica Art. 23 [Version published by the Organization of American States of the American Convention on Human Rights, Pact of San José Costa Rica, that entry in force on 18 July 1978] [hereinafter ACHR].

[36]Universal Declaration of Human Rights Art. 17 [Version published by the United Nations, 2015 of the Universal Declaration of Human Rights of 10 December 1948] [hereinafter UDHR].

[37]ACHR Art. 21.

[38]The constitutions of the countries analysed also recognize people's right to live with dignity. See Const. Brazil Art. 1 (III); Const. Colombia Art. 1; Const. Mexico Arts. 1 and 2; Const. Peru Arts. 1 and 3; and Const. Chile Art. 1.

[39]McCrudden (2008), pp. 656, 679.

One way to understand the right to live with dignity is to guarantee that people can provide for themselves and their families. In this sense, the Universal Declaration of Human Rights declares that "everyone who works has the right of just and favorable remuneration ensuring [...] an existence worthy of human dignity".[40] Along the same lines, the International Covenant on Economic, Social and Cultural Rights established that people cannot be destitute of their means of subsistence and that everybody has the right to use their wealth and resources freely.[41] In this sense, people might be considered to have the right to enjoy an adequate standard of living, and the state has the obligation to take the necessary measures to allow the realization of this right.[42] From such a human rights perspective, the law must achieve justice and equality even if it is difficult given the economic conditions. Morality and fairness, rather than technical or economic considerations, take center stage in the management of the economy.[43]

In accordance with the above-mentioned human rights treaties, the Constitution of Mexico establishes that, to allow people to live with dignity, the state must develop an economic system that allows for economic growth, competition, a fair distribution of wealth, and employment.[44] Further, the Constitution of Brazil prescribes that, to provide a life with dignity, the minimum wage must be adjusted to preserve its purchasing power.[45] The Constitution of Peru lays down that workers' remuneration must be sufficient to provide them and their families with material and spiritual wellbeing.[46]

A life with dignity understood in this way is hardest to achieve for the poorest in society, if the constitution does not protect them. Specifically, (in Latin America) poor people have less access to information and education, which makes them easier victims of what is called an unfair expropriation of resources by the state via inflation. Inflation does not affect all people equally. The poorer hold most money in cash. Increases in prices will directly translate into a loss in purchasing power.

---

[40]UDHR Art. 23 (3).

[41]International Covenant on Economic, Social and Cultural Rights Art. 1 [Version published by the United Nations of the International Covenant on Economic, Social and Cultural Rights, 3 January 1976] [hereinafter ICCPR].

[42]ICCPR Art. 11.

[43]Díaz Etienne (1996), p. 342.

[44]Const. Mexico Art. 25: *"The State shall command the development of the Nation to: be integral and sustainable; strengthen national sovereignty and democracy; and, through competitiveness, fostering economic growth, employment rates and a fair distribution of income and wealth, to allow the full exercise of liberty and dignity to individuals, groups and social strata, which security is protected by this Constitution. [...]".*

[45]In the context of the rights of urban and rural workers, the Const. Brazil Art. 7 (IV) states that people have the right to a *"nationally uniform minimum monthly wage, established by law, capable of satisfying the basic living needs and those of their families with housing, food, education, health, leisure, clothing, hygiene, transportation, and social security, with periodical adjustments to maintain its purchasing power, it being forbidden to use it as an index for any purpose".*

[46]Const. Peru Art. 24.

Moreover, inflation and inflation volatility tend to be a drag on economic development due to contract problems, which could help take the poorest out of poverty.[47]

Human rights instruments consider a right to a certain standard of material wellbeing as part of the right to live with dignity. Stabilizing the purchasing power of the people can, therefore, be regarded as a policy that is conducive to guaranteeing the right to a life with dignity.

4.2.3 The Government's Problems in Achieving Monetary Stability

4.2.3.1 Knowledge Problems

Developing monetary policy requires special expertise and technical knowledge. The degree of specialization needed to develop monetary policy is difficult to achieve in the legislature, where legislators must deal with a wide range of topics. Given time and budget constraints, engaging in one issue too extensively would mean disregarding other issues that might be of importance to the electorate as well. One way to solve the problem of expertise is to delegate monetary policy to a government ministry that specializes in monetary policy. This ministry would aim to acquire the expertise needed for monetary policy and thereby to adopt and implement the policies needed to bring down inflation.[48] If we were to call this ministry a central bank, we would have a central bank that is part of the executive.

4.2.3.2 Mal-incentives and Commitment Problems

Such a monetary ministry, however, faces incentives that make it difficult for the government to commit credibly to engage in policies that do not undermine monetary stability. *Neumann* emphasizes that

> [g]overnment has a deeply rooted interest in creating inflation, because inflation permits the flow of seigniorage (over a certain inflation rate) to be raised, drives private agents into higher income tax brackets, reduces the real value of outstanding government debt, and promises a transitory stimulation of the economy, hence employment.[49]

---

[47]Díaz Etienne (1996), pp. 346–352. A qualification is in order. In the U.S., the relatively poor people might have access to information via the internet. But their level of education is lower, which may not allow them to protect themselves from inflation like better educated people. The poorest in the U.S. who beg asking for the famous "dollar", are most directly hurt as the value of the dollar falls when prices rise.

[48]Bernhard (1998), p. 312.

[49]Neumann (1991), p. 96.

In this respect, it is important to remember that government is run by politicians with electoral goals. Political candidates need votes that allow them to have access to office or to remain in office. A common way of gaining votes is to promise spending programs that will need to be financed or to please an influential lobby.[50]

Protecting monetary stability may bring about unpleasant consequences for governments. For instance, during a boom period, the central bank may raise interest rate at which banks can refinance themselves at the central bank to prevent inflation. As higher interest rates raise the refinancing costs of banks, banks will extend fewer loans to customers and finance less investment. The growth rate of the economy will decline which may adversely affect tax revenues. The government, therefore, might run a fiscal deficit.

If fiscal policy, i.e., the spending policy of the government, dominates monetary policy, government and the legislature will put pressure on the central bank to finance deficits at the risk of increasing inflation. By contrast, a central bank that can raise interest rates even if it hurts the government may affect government budget decisions. Inflation may be lower in these circumstances.[51] *Buchanan* and other public choice theorists argue that not only the government but also taxpayers and voters favor easy monetary policy and some inflation over, for instance, immediate tax increases that would be necessary to prevent deficits under stricter monetary policy, in part because they are not aware of the costs of inflation.[52] Moreover, to the benefit of governments, inflation tends to pick up with a time lag, which renders it more difficult to make the government accountable for inflationary policies (unless they are consistently in place).[53] Therefore, governments or central banks that are very much controlled by governments have little incentive to engage in policies that make it harder for governments to finance deficits.[54]

Another incentive problem is related to the timing of promises. Governments that promise to hold inflation low may have incentives to disregard that promise after some time has passed, particularly if people believe the government is serious about and capable of promoting monetary stability. If people expect a rising price level, for instance, labor unions will demand higher wages. Inflation is the result. If, however, people expect monetary stability, wage demands might be rather moderate. In this situation, the government may have an incentive to make it easier for banks to refinance at the central bank to stimulate investment and growth. Inflation may lower wage rates in real terms and contribute to a rise in the level of employment. This

---

[50]Buchanan and Wagner (2000), pp. 79–80. See also Guerrero (1979), pp. 82–82 and p. 90; Hasse (1990), p. 125; Gutierrez (2004), p. 258.

[51]Sargent and Wallace (1981), pp. 1–2. See also Buchanan and Wagner (2000), p. 116.

[52]*Ibid.*, pp. 113–114.

[53]Bini Smaghi (2007), p. 48. See also Miller (2005), p. 221.

[54]Public choice economics seems to imply that monetary stability is only possible if the budget is sound. Adding a balanced budget rule to the constitution may be a step toward achieving budgets that do not require expansionary monetary policies to be sustainable. This may reduce pressure on the monetary authority. However, an additional monetary rule might be necessary to prevent the monetary authority from inflating. See Buchanan and Wagner (2000), pp. 183–189.

time-inconsistency problem commonly arises, unless the government has no other objectives than price stability that can be reached using monetary policy. Bringing on such a *surprise inflation* to stimulate employment will not work repeatedly. People will eventually learn and anticipate this sort of behavior by the government. Inflation expectations and wage demands increase, as governments always have the option to change policies.[55]

4.2.3.3 Delegation of Monetary Policy to an Autonomous Institution

Given the knowledge and incentive problems, governments will have a hard time to credibly committing to monetary stability even if they are serious about it.[56]

The basic principle-agent theory helps to explain the rationale of delegation to solve the knowledge problem. When a principle (here the government) cannot perform an activity because, for instance, of lack of expertise, the principal delegates the performance of such activity to a qualified agent (here the central bank).[57] Ideally, from the perspective of the principal, the agent will carry out the delegated functions in a way that fulfills the best interests of the principal. To get there, the principal must find an agent that is capable of doing the job. As the agent's interests might deviate from the principal's interests, the agent should be monitored. A document or *contract* that lays out, for instance, the salary and penalties for the agent depending on performance can help align the interests of the agent with those of the principle.[58]

However, there are good reasons why we may expect that an autonomous central bank may be in a better position to hold inflation low than an agent of the government. First, an autonomous central bank might be able to contradict government preferences.[59] A truly autonomous monetary authority could maintain its policy even if this complicates the situation for the government by reducing the economic profit derived from the production of currency (seigniorage),[60] increasing

---

[55]The time-inconsistency problem of monetary policy is regularly mentioned in justifications for monetary autonomy. See Eijffinger and De Haan (1996), pp. 5–6. The idea of how, in this context, institutional changes can influence people's decision making was developed in Kydland and Prescott (1977).

[56]This is even more so in countries with a history of inflationary episodes, in which it is harder to trust a government no matter how inflation hawkish it seems. As long as governments have the option to use inflation at some point, people might consider that there is a likelihood that inflation goes up, which can lead to increases in wage demands and a rising price level even if the government does not actively engage in inflationary policies.

[57]Sappington (1991), p. 45.

[58]Elgie (2002), pp. 187–189.

[59]Bernhard (1998), p. 314.

[60]Seigniorage is the revenue that the government obtains by issuing currency. It is a tax without legislation. The inflation tax is almost not perceived by the population who do not receive notice as in the case of any normal tax. However, it is considered a tax on money holders. See Mankiw and Taylor (2011), p. 651.

debt-servicing costs and lowering tax revenues by causing a temporary slowdown of the economy to tame inflation.[61] An autonomous monetary authority would also not face the limitation that a political authority might face, when government and the legislature have different views on what is necessary at a point in time. Finally, a central bank that is independent from political pressure and subject to well-established legal rules is more likely to act in a predictable fashion, which enhances its credibility and reputation.[62] *Miller* outlines:

> The central bank's credibility is enhanced when private economic actors perceive that the bank's decisions are irrevocable. In contrast, if private actors perceive that partisan administrators influence the decisions of the central bank, then the credibility of a nominally independent central bank is undermined.[63]

To explain the delegation of power to an autonomous central bank to deal with the incentive problems, the principal-agent theory may need to be modified, because the central bank's interests should not match the preferences of the government or another state institution.[64] Moreover, governments (principals) with different preferences may be voted in and out of office in democratic systems, whereas the contract for the central bank should remain stable across time.[65]

I suggest not to view the government as (only) *principle* in this context to be able to, by and large, stick with the basic principle-agent story. The principal can be viewed as the entity with the authority to first create the contract for the agent. This principle is not necessarily the same for all central banks. The central bank's principal can be the executive branch, the legislature, both of them, or even a constituent assembly, depending on whether the delegation derives from the constitution or legislation. Any of the mentioned principals may have different preferences and, accordingly, set up different types of central banks in the first place. If the principals are the democratically elected representatives of the legislature or a constituent assembly, the central bank is democratically legitimated.[66]

In this context, it is important to determine how the legal rules for the bank must be designed to represent an *optimal contract* for the central bank.[67] The rules for the central bank should ensure that the will of the people is guaranteed through institutional arrangements clearly and consistently laid down by the legislature,[68] preventing the central bank from following its own private interests as opposed to the common goal reflected in its objective and shielding the central bank from other

---

[61]Gutierrez (2004), p. 258.

[62]Bernhard (1998), p. 311.

[63]Miller (2005), p. 211.

[64]Miller argues that the principal-agent theory would have to be "reformulated". See *ibid.*, pp. 218–220.

[65]For more on the principal-agent theory and the critics of the ECB, see Elgie (2002), pp. 192–194.

[66]Elgie (2002), pp. 190–191.

[67]For more on the topic, see Walsh (1995), p. 151.

[68]Hasse (1990), pp. 125–126.

interests, e.g. from government, that might make the central bank deviate from its mandate.[69]

Therefore, an *optimal contract* to align the incentives of the central bank with those of the people will guarantee a degree of autonomy from the government and assure that the central bank can achieve its objectives without fear of retaliation. Central bank officials have to be shielded from the influence of government. The legal arrangements for a central bank must also include the objective that the bank pursues, the operations that the bank performs, the way that its board members are appointed and dismissed, the way in which the budget is managed, and must clarify the relationship of the central bank to other state organs.[70]

Once the central bank exists, multiple players may be involved in amending central bank law, such as the president of the country, or determining whether the central bank satisfies its objectives, such as the courts via adjudication. If so, this is a very diverse group of people who might have very different preferences. A high degree of competition of preferences between the various people involved may help guarantee the autonomy of the central bank over time, as it makes modifications of the rules more difficult, and control is asserted from various sources over how the central bank officials behave.[71]

4.3   Legal Certainty and Central Bank Objectives in Latin America

4.3.1   Clarity of the Legal Objectives

A central bank's legal objectives are the point of reference for the design of its entire legal framework. For there to be legal certainty about the legal objectives, they must be clear, stable and consistent. Having one objective only, such as *price stability* or a specific *inflation target*, would leave no room for speculation. But in many developing and emerging countries, legal documents do not contain such clear-cut objectives. Instead, many objectives exist, some of which are vague, such as "preserving the purchasing power of the currency" or "preserving monetary stability."[72]

The latter objectives may be considered vague because they can mean two things. On the one hand, they may suggest that the central bank should hold inflation at bay (and prevent deflation) to preserve the domestic exchange value of the currency. On the other hand, monetary stability may refer to the stability of the exchange rate, i.e., the international purchasing power of the currency. More importantly, it is

---

[69]Walsh (1995), p. 151.

[70]*Ibid.*

[71]Miller (2005), pp. 211, 221.

[72]Gutierrez (2004), p. 261.

Table 4.1 Legal certainty and central bank objectives

	Single objective	Priority order	Consistency of objectives	Last modification
Argentina	No	No	No	2012
Brazil	No	Yes	No	1964
Chile[a,b]	No	No	Yes	1989
Colombia[a]	Yes	N/A	N/A	1992
Mexico[a]	Yes	N/A	N/A	1993
Peru[a]	Yes	N/A	N/A	1993

Source: Author. Summary of findings from legal analysis as presented in respective country section
[a]Only the constitutional legal objective is considered in the Table
[b]In Chile, preserving the stability of the payment system, which is usually not a monetary policy but indeed a central bank objective, is explicitly mentioned along with the price stability objective

conceivable that these two ways of seeing monetary stability are not compatible. For instance, stabilizing the exchange rate between the domestic currency and an anchor currency to preserve the external value of the currency may trigger changes in the domestic value of the currency, i.e., inflation or deflation.[73]

When a central bank has several, potentially conflicting objectives, a priority order can provide clarity. This may not be enough to allay public distrust about the consistency of monetary policy, but it could at least help the central bank decide which objective to pursue and under what circumstances.[74] While the main objective of the European Central Bank, for example, is "to maintain price stability",[75] the Treaty of the European Union also includes other objectives, although these are denoted as secondary objectives in Article 127:

> The primary objective of the European System of Central Banks [hereinafter referred to as 'the ESCB', shall be to maintain price stability. Without prejudice to the objective of price stability, the ESCB shall support the general economic policies in the Union with a view to contributing to the achievement of the objectives of the Union as laid down in Article 3 of the Treaty on European Union.[76]

The central bank objectives of the six Latin American countries that are subject to this study differ in many respects. Table 4.1 summarizes the main characteristics of the differences in the objectives as analyzed in the following (status as of October 2019).

We can broadly distinguish the countries into two groups. The first group has one monetary policy objective (see also column 1 of Table 4.1). The group is comprised of the central banks of Colombia and Peru, which both have the objective to preserve

---

[73]Gutierrez (2004), p. 277.

[74]Hasse (1990), p. 117. See also Jácome and Vásquez (2008), p. 800.

[75]Moreover, the Eurosystem has the broader objective to maintain the stability of the payment system as found in the Treaty of the EU Art. 105 (2).

[76]Treaty of the EU Art. 105 (2).

the value of the currency. This single objective is identically specified in their constitutions and legislation.[77]

In contrast to the legal frameworks in Colombia and Peru, those of the second group of countries provide a range of objectives for the respective central banks that may be in conflict with one another or lack a priority order. The Central Bank of Chile is included in this group, because the relevant article mentions two objectives with no priority order. It shall ensure "the stability of the currency" and preserve the "normal functioning of internal and external payment systems."[78] The latter is a broader role of most modern central banks that is not an objective of monetary policy itself. The objective implies that the central bank has a role in oversight or regulation of the payment system of Chile. It shall assure that payments between financial institutions clear without problems. The explicit mention of this objective of the Central Bank of Chile may imply a more extended financial stability objective, as issues in settling payments between financial institutions may bring about financial turbulence and may necessitate the use of central bank facilities to prevent market turmoil.[79]

The legal objective of the Bank of Mexico differs in formulation in its constitutional mandate and the legislation that developed it. According to the Mexican constitution, the objective of the monetary institution is limited to ensure "the stability of the purchasing power of the national currency",[80] but the Law of the Bank of Mexico extends the central bank's objective to "promoting the sound development of the financial system and fostering the proper functioning of payment systems."[81] The constitutional objective remains the priority, and the extra objective can be seen as an important means to achieve the main objective as in the case of Chile. Nevertheless, granting the central bank the additional objectives can be considered an extra limitation of the power of the legislative branch that must be subject to the constitutional mandate.

---

[77]Const. Colombia Art. 373: *"The State, through the intermediary of the Bank of the Republic, shall oversee the maintenance of the purchasing power of the currency."* See also Organic Act of the Bank of the Republic of Colombia Art. 2 [Official Translation of the Ley Orgánica del Banco de la Republica, Ley 31 de 1992, Diario Oficial CXXVIII, 29 December 1992] [hereinafter BRC Act]: *"Banco de la Republica, on behalf of the State, will see to the maintenance of the national currency's acquisitive capacity [. . .]."*

Const. Peru Art. 84 states that the aim of its central bank *"is to preserve monetary stability"*. See also Organic Law of the Central Reserve Bank of Peru Art. 2 [Official Translation of the Ley Orgánica del Banco Central de Reserva del Perú, Law No. 26.123, Diario Oficial, 30 December 1992] [hereinafter CRBP Law]: *"The purpose of the Bank is to preserve monetary stability"*.

[78]Basic Constitutional Act of the Central Bank of Chile Sec. 3 [Official Translation of the Ley Orgánica Constitucional del Banco Central de Chile, Diario Oficial, 6 January 1990] [hereinafter CBCH Law].

[79]European Central Bank (2000).

[80]Const. Mexico Art. 28 para 6.

[81]Law of the Bank of Mexico Art. 2 [Official Translation of the Ley del Banco de México, Official Gazette, 23 December 1993] [hereinafter BM Law].

Until 2012, the Central Bank of the Argentine Republic's (BCRA) statutes specified one objective. The central bank was supposed to preserve the value of the currency.[82] In 2012, an amendment granted the central bank additional objectives. Ever since the bank shall provide for financial stability but also promote "employment, and economic development with social equality".[83] Even though the Argentinean central bank officially announces monetary stability as its main objective on its official website,[84] there is no clarity about the objective of the central bank because of the vagueness of the term *economic development* and the lack of a priority order in the statutes (see column 2 of Table 4.1).

Identifying the objectives of the Brazilian monetary authority is not easy. The first difficulty is to understand that, according to the Act No. 4595, two institutions are in charge of monetary policy: the National Monetary Council of Brazil (CMN) and the Central Bank of Brazil (CBB). The second complication is to deal with the plethora of confusing and scattered legal rules in the Brazilian legal framework that triggers a typical problem for legal certainty in administrative law, which is the problem of finding the applicable disposition.[85]

Regarding the first problem, according to the law, only the CMN has *objectives*. The CBB is the executive arm of the CMN[86] and has only functions. The CMN has one principle objective, which is to formulate the "currency and credit policy [. . .] and thereby achieving the economic and social progress of the country."[87] To achieve this main objective, the Brazilian CMN also has secondary objectives with a clear priority order. According to the legislation, its second objective is to adjust "the volume of the money supply to the real needs of the national economy and its development process".[88] Further objectives are the promotion of the stability of the

---

[82]Organic Charter of the Central Bank of the Argentine Republic of 1992 Art. 3 [Carta Orgánica del Banco Central de la República Argentina de 1992, Boletín Oficial, 23 September 1992] [hereinafter BCRA Law (1992)].

[83]Organic Charter of the Central Bank of the Argentine Republic Sec. 3 [Official Translation of the Carta Orgánica del Banco Central de la República Argentina, Boletín Oficial, 28 March 2012] [hereinafter BCRA Law].

[84]Official website of the bank: http://www.bcra.gov.ar/Institucional/CartaOrganica.asp.

[85]Rivero Ortega (2013), p. 52.

[86]Law of the National Financial System of Brazil Art. 9 [Official Translation of the Lei do Sistema Financeiro Nacional, Diário Oficial da União - Seção 1 – Suplemento, 31 December 1964] [hereinafter LSFN Brazil]: *"It is the responsibility of the Central Bank of the Republic of Brazil to comply with and ensure compliance with the provisions attributed to it by current legislation and norms issued by the National Monetary Council."*

[87]LSFN Brazil Art. 2: *"The Council of the current Superintendency of Currency and Credit is abolished and the National Monetary Council is created as its replacement, with the objective of formulating currency and credit policy in accordance with the terms of this law and thereby achieving the economic and social progress of the country."*

[88]LSFN Brazil Art 3 (I).

internal and external value of the currency,[89] the establishment of balance of payment equilibrium,[90] the funding of crucial projects,[91] the promotion of financial development, the provision of liquidity to financial institutions that are need it,[92] and the coordination of policy (in this order).[93] Analyzing the legal document allows to conclude that the main goal of monetary policy in Brazil is the "economic and social progress of the country"[94] and that holding inflation low is only one of many secondary goals (see column 2 of Table 4.1).

4.3.2 Consistency of the Legal Objectives

Inconsistent objectives make it hard for a central bank to credibly commit to the fulfillment of its goals. Furthermore, inconsistencies in the legal fundamental mandate of the central bank spread through the entire legal framework and bring about problems in coordination with other state organs and accountability. The consistency of central bank goals tends to fall with the number of goals, particularly when the law does not provide a clear priority order.

Among the countries analyzed, the central banks of Brazil and Argentina have explicit employment or economic development objectives. These objectives may be highly political and detrimental to the autonomy of the institutions.[95] But even for a central bank with a high degree of autonomy, they pose problems of consistency with other objectives, such as price stability. Creating jobs and stimulating the economy may require short-term policies, while keeping inflation low is a long-term goal.[96] A central bank that aims to tame inflation expectations may raise interest rates, which will lower investment and production. Employment tends to fall.[97]

---

[89]LSFN Brazil Art. 3 (II) and (III) suggest that the CMN Brazil is supposed to set the internal value of the currency, *"preventing or correcting the inflationary or deflationary surges of domestic or foreign origin, economic depressions and other imbalances rooted in situational phenomena."*

[90]LSFN Brazil Art. 3 (V).

[91]LSFN Brazil Art. 3 (IV) establishes that the CMN must orient *"the investment of the resources of both public and private financial institutions, with a view toward generating conditions favorable conditions to harmonious development of the national economy in the diverse regions of the country."*

[92]LSFN Brazil Art. 2 (VI).

[93]LSFN Brazil Art. 2 (VII) establishes that the CMN Brazil is in charge of *"[c]oordinating monetary, credit, budget, fiscal, domestic and external public debt policies."*

[94]LSFN Brazil Art. 2.

[95]According to CCC, 24 July 1999, René Vargas Pérez v. Congreso de la República de Colombia, CCC, Sentencia C-481, 7 July 1999, a central bank cannot be independent and, at the same time, promote government spending, by lowering interest rates, to encourage economic development. See CCC, Judgment of 24 July 1999.

[96]Laurens et al. (2007), p. 282.

[97]Burdekin and Laney (1988), pp. 650–651.

Conversely, an expansionary monetary policy may spur investment and employment but can also result in rising prices. Keeping inflation at bay does not necessarily match employment goals in the short run.[98] Given that there is also no priority order for the objectives of Argentina's central bank in its organic charter, there is a low degree of legal certainty about its objectives (Table 4.1).

The goal of financial stability is explicitly mentioned as a legal objective in the frameworks of the central banks of Mexico, Argentina and Brazil. In the case of the Central Bank of Chile, the goal can be derived from the bank's secondary legal objective of "assuring the normal functioning of internal and external payments."[99] For the Bank of the Republic of Colombia (Colombia's central bank) and the Central Reserve Bank of Peru, financial stability is not a legal objective. Nevertheless, these central banks have competences closely related to financial stability, like the lender of last resort function[100] and, in the case of Peru, "to regulate the currency and credit in the financial system."[101]

According to *Lybeck*, there is a circular relationship between price and financial stability:

> Inadequate monetary policies could lead to inflation and contribute to a shaky financial system. An unsound financial system could lead to a systemic financial crisis and impinge on monetary policy and, thereafter on price stability.[102]

Thus, a central bank cannot effectively preserve price or currency stability if the banking system is unhealthy. On the other hand, it is not possible to have a sound financial system if the national currency is inherently weak.[103]

As a matter of fact, preserving price stability and assuring liquidity to the financial system during a crisis are closely related.[104] *Quintyn* and *Taylor* explain that this closed knit relationship relies on the fact that it is the financial sector

> through which monetary policy is transmitted to the wider economy and therefore the central bank should be concerned with their soundness as a precondition for an effective monetary policy.[105]

---

[98]Hasse (1990), p. 117.

[99]Central Bank of Chile (2007), p. 6: *"The normal functioning of the payment system involves guaranteeing the essential functions of intermediation between credits and saving, provision of payment services and ensuring the appropriate allocation of risks by financial markets."*

[100]The BRC Act Art. 12 (a), (b) and (c) establishes that Colombia's central bank is the lender of last resort. It *"will be entitled to: a) Grant temporary transient liquidity support by means of discounts and rediscounts in such conditions as the Board of Directors may determine; b) Act as an intermediary for external credit lines for its placement through the credit entities; and, c) To provide them with trust, deposit, clearing, and draft services, and such other services as the Board of Directors may determine."*

[101]Const. Peru Art. 84 para 2.

[102]Quintyn and Taylor (2002), p. 10. See also Lybek (2004), p. 5.

[103]Lundberg (2000), p. 4.

[104]Quintyn and Taylor (2002), p. 24. See also Goodhart and Schoenmaker (1995), p. 541.

[105]Quintyn and Taylor (2002), p. 24.

Further, during a financial crisis, the monetary institution's main objective is to recover confidence in the system and calm unrest in the financial markets. These require the central bank to stem illiquidity problems and the failure of systemically important institutions. The central bank may perform this role as the lender of last resort.[106]

Taking these arguments at face value, it seems that the legal objective of preserving financial stability is, by and large, compatible with the objective of price stability. However, there is also research that suggests that central bank independence is in a vulnerable position, if the monetary authority is also in charge of preserving financial stability because the task of safeguarding the stability of the financial system can be at odds with monetary policy.[107] For instance, the *Bundesbank* maintains that there may also be conflicts between the two objectives. In its *Financial Stability Review*, the *Bundesbank* suggests that low interest rates to prevent deflationary pressure in Europe might undermine the profitability of the banking sector. Therefore, banks are incentivized to take more risks, which is a potential threat to financial stability, at least in the long run,[108] because of the trade-off between the use of monetary instruments, such as interest rates, and the stability of the banking system. When the central bank wants to reduce inflation, the central bankers decide to increase interest rates. However, increases in interest rates are among the causes of a banking crisis.[109] *Mishkin* explains that

> a higher interest rate leads to even greater adverse selection; that is, it increases the likelihood that the lender is lending to a bad credit risk.[110]

But the dispute about the compatibility of the price stability objective and hosting banking supervision is much more intense.[111] Those in favor of hosting banking supervision at the central bank claim that price stability and the oversight of the banking system are complementary objectives, especially if the objective of the central bank is clearly stated and the degree of autonomy is high.[112] *Alan Greenspan* defended this position claiming that,

---

[106]For more on the appropriate central bank tools in a crisis, see Corbo (2010), pp. 27–29.

[107]For more on how the objective of financial stability in the context of the ECB, see Apel (2007), pp. 41–42.

[108]Deutsche Bundesbank (2013), pp. 8–9.

[109]Mishkin (1996), p. 18.

[110]*Ibid.* When the central bank increases interest rates only risky debtors, with risky investment projects, are willing to take on additional debt. Then credit institutions have the option of restricting loan supply or to extend loans to any type of debtor without discriminating between good and bad risks.

[111]For a historical review, see Goodhart and Schoenmaker (1995), p. 541. See also Quintyn and Taylor (2002), pp. 3–4; Garcia Herrero and Del Rio (2003), p. 7.

[112]Laurens et al. (2007), p. 284.

Joint responsibilities make for better supervisory and monetary policy than would result from either a supervisory divorce from economic responsibilities or a macroeconomic policy maker with no involvement in the review of individual bank operations.[113]

Here, the compatibility comes from the link between the micro-supervision of the banking institutions conducted by the supervisory authority and the effects on banking of the macro-stability function carried out by the central bank.[114] Thus, hosting banking supervision within the monetary authority has information and expertise-related advantages.[115] Even though the Central Reserve Bank of Peru does not host banking supervision, the Constitutional Tribunal of Peru recognized the importance of a well-informed central bank to develop its financial stability functions:

To preserve the stability of the currency, the Banco Central de la Reserva executes its policy by regulating liquidity through the banking and financial system. To do this [the central bank] needs to know the economic and financial situation of all corporations of the banking system to evaluate the solvency of each one of these corporations at the right time [Own Translation].[116]

The information obtained from banking supervision also helps the central bank to hedge against problems in the internal and external payment system through its function as the lender of last resort (LLR).[117] By being better informed, the central bank will more likely be in the position to decide whether a banking institution is insolvent or illiquid and avoid financing insolvent institutions.[118]

Furthermore, the supervisory authority might benefit from the institutional structure, especially if the monetary authority is autonomous, to supervise the financial system efficiently.[119] The autonomy of the supervisory institution is included among the Basle Core Principles on Banking Supervision.[120]

In contrast, government dependence can lead to the indifference of supervisory authorities about the restructuring and recapitalization of troubled institutions. An inefficient supervision reduces public confidence in the effectiveness of the restructuring of a bank and can prevent the central bank from executing, on time, the reactive policies needed to avoid banking panics or a paralysis of the interbank system. A late response of the LLR can give the public a perception of instability and trigger doubts about the authority's attachment to the legal rules and their prevalence.

---

[113]Greenspan (1994), p. 4.

[114]Quintyn and Taylor (2002), pp. 10–11.

[115]Mersch (2013), pp. 133–144.

[116]*Banco Central de Reserva del Perú v. Superintendencia de Banca, Seguros y Administradoras Privadas de Fondos de Pensiones*, TC Peru, Sentencia Exp. No. 005, 2 September 2005.

[117]Central Bank of Chile (2007), pp. 13–14.

[118]Lundberg (2000), p. 9.

[119]Quintyn and Taylor (2002), p. 24. See also Laurens et al. (2007), p. 284.

[120]Bini Smaghi (2007), p. 49. See also Bank for International Settlements (2012), p. 10.

Expectations of financial stability should not be underestimated, because the financial system relies on public trust. Its absence can deepen a present crisis and trigger future ones. Isolating the supervisory authority from political influence avoids short-term legal arrangements motivated by political fads of the day and benefits the consistency, stability and clarity of the regulation[121] and of the outcomes. In this sense, a high degree of autonomy of the supervisory authority decreases the probability of a systemic bank crisis, even more if the supervisory autonomy is the central bank.[122]

However, bank supervision has the potential of modifying the very basis of central bank autonomy to conduct monetary policy. In this sense, while the orthodox objective of monetary policy seeks stability of prices and of the currency, banking supervision entails more objectives that go beyond stability, such as, for instance, consumer protection and prevention of money laundering. Because the characteristics of a supervisor are different from the characteristics of a central banker, adding a supervisory function as a central bank objective affects other arrangements made for the central bank, such as the personal autonomy of the board members and the means of accountability.[123]

In particular, banking supervision may be a highly political issue that can open the door for government intervention, undermining the central bank's autonomy.[124] There are several reasons to believe that a central bank hosting banking supervision opens the door for government intervention. First, there are usually several interconnected institutions that supervise the banking system. Among these institutions are the ministry of finance and other supervisory institutions. Second, the government has a right to intervene in the supervisory performance of the central bank, if public funds are involved via government bailouts to distressed financial institutions.[125] Third, "the combination of functions might lead to a conflict of interest."[126] During a financial crisis we might see additional liquidity injections to insolvent banks as these central banks see banking stability at risk. In addition, central banks with banking supervision functions might not want to increase interest rates to preserve financial stability after financial crises, or during boom periods.[127] Indeed, a central bank that hosts supervisory functions may even be exposed to the *reputational damage* caused by the failure of a bank under its supervision.[128]

Taking another perspective, there is normally a strong position of the banking sector against inflation. If, however, a central bank acts as supervisor and sets credit

---

[121]Quintyn and Taylor (2002), pp. 7–12.

[122]Garcia Herrero and Del Rio (2003), p. 45.

[123]Lastra (2015), p. 94.

[124]Lundberg (2000), pp. 8–9.

[125]Lastra (2015), p. 94.

[126]Goodhart and Schoenmaker (1995), p. 545.

[127]*Ibid.*, p. 556.

[128]Quintyn and Taylor (2002), p. 24.

limits, banks may try to avoid them. Doing so may become more important to them than the inflationary consequences.[129]

The ideas about the negative effects of hosting banking supervision within the monetary authority have influenced the legal institutional arrangements of some Latin American countries. Chile, Colombia, Mexico and Peru followed the example of many developed economies and moved the banking supervisory functions to other institutions. Chile granted autonomy to the supervisory entities as suggested by Basel. In Chile, a statutory autonomous Superintendence is in charge of the oversight of the banking system. Also in Peru, the Superintendence of Banking, Insurance and Private Pension Funds handles banking supervision as an autonomous institution (according to the constitution and the law).[130]

Despite the separation between the Central Reserve Bank of Peru and the Superintendence of Banking, Insurance and Private Pension Funds, the Constitutional Tribunal of Peru has remarked about the importance of coordination between them, because they have related functions, and it is possible to guarantee monetary and financial stability only when they work in tandem.[131]

On the other hand, the Banking and Securities National Commission of Mexico has only some degree of technical autonomy, since it is an organ within the Ministry of Finance.[132] Furthermore, the Superintendence of Banks in Colombia is dependent on the government, which is responsible for the inspection, supervision and control of the financial system.[133]

Arguments that support housing banking supervision in the monetary authority have prevailed only in Argentina and Brazil, but to different degrees. The Argentina's central bank supervises the banking system through the Superintendence, which is institutionally and operationally dependent on the central bank.[134] Brazil's central bank is directly in charge of the oversight of the financial system.[135]

---

[129]Posen (1995), pp. 258–259.

[130]Const. Peru Art. 87 para 3.

[131]*Banco Central de Reserva del Perú v. Superintendencia de Banca, Seguros y Administradoras Privadas de Fondos de Pensiones*, TC Peru, Sentencia Exp. No. 005, 2 September 2005.

[132]Act of the National Banking and Securities Commission Art.1 [Ley de la Comisión Nacional Bancaria y de Valores, Diario Oficial de la Federación, 28 April 1995]: *"[T]he National Banking and Securities Commission is hereby established as a decentralized body of the Ministry of Finance, with technical autonomy and executive powers [. . .]* [Own Translation]."

[133]Act 35 of 1993 of Colombia Art. 10 [Ley 35 de 1993, Diario Oficial No. 40.710, 5 January 1993].

[134]BCRA Law Sec. 43.

[135]LSFN Brazil Art. 10 (IX).

4.3.3   Stability of Legal Objectives

The stability of the monetary authorities' legal objectives is critical for credible commitment, because that commitment can be credible only in the long run. Thus, the legal objectives should not be subject to continuous change. The objectives of the CMN of Brazil are stable in time. The same objectives have determined the legal mandate of the CMN of Brazil since 1964. The central banks of Chile and Colombia have had the same objectives since 1989 and 1992, respectively, and have seen no change in objectives. Table 4.1 summarizes the last modification dates as evidence of the stability of objectives in column 4.

Having a history of pursuing the same objective should give rise to expectations that a bank is pursuing exactly that objective, i.e., provide subjective legal certainty about the objective pursued by the bank, as there is less confusion to people that might have experienced a central bank that was in charge of doing one thing that is now doing another.

The history of modern central banking in Latin America began after the Federal Reserve Bank of the United States was created in 1913.[136] Issuing currency and preventing any future financial crisis was the goal of the first Bank of Mexico (1925), which also functioned as a public commercial bank.[137] In consonance with their legal mandate today, the first central banks in Peru (Banco de Reserva, 1922),[138] Colombia (Banco de la República, 1923)[139] and Chile (Central Bank of Chile, 1923) had the objective of preserving the stability of the currency. However, this goal was achieved by maintaining the link between national currencies and gold. Being the bank's banker, they also provided flexibility to help the currency circulation, received deposits and offered loans to private banks.[140]

In contrast to the clear role of the central banks in Colombia, Mexico, Chile and Peru, the role of the central banks in Argentina and Brazil was unclear from the beginning. In this sense, the law that regulated the first central bank in Argentina (from 1935) gave the bank a more active position in the economic development instead of limiting its scope of action to preserve the stability of prices. In addition to preserving price and currency stability, the Argentinean central bank had broad discretion to develop anti-cyclical policy to preserve economic activity.[141]

Similarly, the Brazilian central bank had from the beginning an unclear position in the financial structure and lacked clear functions and objectives. The deep level of ambiguity can be a consequence of political forces that opposed the creation of a central bank with orthodox functions. In fact, the creation of the Brazilian central

---

[136]Liddle and Pita (2011), p. 121.

[137]See website: http://www.banxico.org.mx/acerca-del-banco-de-mexico/semblanza-historica.html#des.

[138]For more on the history of creation of the Peruvian Central Bank, see Pereyra (2012), p. 1.

[139]Martínez Neira (2014), p. 24.

[140]Carrasco (2009), pp. 44–45.

[141]Liddle and Pita (2011), pp. 121, 136.

bank took place in 1964. It took 20 years, since 1945, to crystalize the project of the Brazilian central bank because of severe opposition in the National Congress.[142]

This history indicates that the central banks in Argentina and Brazil would be at a disadvantage in credibly pursuing price stability even if this was embedded as the only objective in current or future central bank frameworks.

4.4 Legal Rank of Central Bank Autonomy and Legal Certainty

4.4.1 Implications of the Constitutional Rank for Legal Certainty

The principle of constitutional supremacy states that the constitution is the corner-stone of the entire legal system. The constitution establishes the fundamental set of attributions and limits to the governments and protects the rights of the citizens.[143] Thus, as the Constitution of Peru reminds us, the "Constitution prevails over any other legal rule",[144] and, therefore, is the source from which legislation, administrative acts and case law derive. The formal limit for legislators is the constitution itself and the control of constitutionality conducted by the most qualified and well-known judges of the country. Judges that are part of a Supreme or Constitutional Court are independent from government interference.[145]

An institution has autonomy of constitutional rank when the autonomous status is given directly by the constituent power in the constitution.[146] Institutions are granted constitutional autonomy when they are supposed to perform critical social and economic state functions that are inconvenient for the traditional state organs to perform.[147] Constitutional rules about institutions, such as, for example, central bank autonomy, are "supreme, entrenched and enforced through the power of the judicial review."[148]

The central banks of Chile, Colombia and Peru were granted autonomy in their constitutions. The constitutions of these countries include an extra chapter with

---

[142]Corazza (2006), p. 5.

[143]Gardbaum (2012). For more on the "supremacy of the constitution", see Limbach (2001).

[144]Const. Peru Art. 51.

[145]Gutierrez (2004), p. 256.

[146]Zúñiga (2007), p. 240.

[147]Tesis Aislada: Controversia Constitucional Municipio de Guadalajara, Estado de Jalisco, SCJN México, Sentencia P. VIII, Tomo XXVII, February 2008, p. 1868.

[148]Gardbaum (2012), p. 3.

central bank provisions.[149] The Bank of Mexico also has autonomy of constitutional rank. However, here, the provisions regarding the central bank are immersed among many other economic rules.[150] Yet, among the six central banks analyzed, only Mexico's central bank was autonomous from the beginning.[151]

The constitutional entrenchment of the autonomy of the central banks in Chile, Colombia and Peru can be regarded as similar to the entrenchment of the European Central Bank in the Treaty of Maastricht. The constitution contains a relatively long and separate set of provisions that determine the autonomy and other basic institutional aspects of the monetary institutions. The intention behind this could be to provide the highest possible degree of autonomy, clearly separated from the other institutions, but as part of the broad institutional legal framework of the countries (or the European Union in the case of the European Central Bank).[152]

Neumann addresses the importance of giving the central bank such a high degree of autonomy through a constitutional amendment. He claims that no monetary authority can pre-commit to low inflation with mere declarations, especially when it is rational for economic actors to depart from original announcements. Entrenching the autonomy of the central bank in the constitution is an important

---

[149]Const. Chile Art. 108: *"There will be an autonomous organ, with its own patrimony, technical in character, called Central Bank, whose composition, organization, functions and powers will be determined by a constitutional organic law."* See also CBCH Law Sec. 1: *"The Central Bank of Chile is an autonomous entity of technical nature, with constitutional status, which has full legal capacity, possesses its own assets and has an indefinite duration [...]."* In line with this, Const. Colombia Art. 371: *"The Bank of the Republic [...] shall be organized as a legal public entity with administrative, patrimonial, and technical autonomy, subject to its own legal regime."* See also BRC Act Art.1. According to Const. Peru Art. 84 para 1, *"[t]he Central Bank is a corporate entity under public law. It is autonomous in conformity with it is organic act."* Art. 28 para 6 Const. Mexico states that *"[t]he State shall have a Central Bank that shall be autonomous in the exercise of its functions and its administration."*

[150]Const. Mexico Art. 28.

[151]But the formal autonomy lasted only until 1955 and from then on, there was a de facto autonomy, motivated only by the will of the board members, until 1970, when Mexico's monetary authority recovered the statutory autonomy. See Turrent y Diaz (2005), p. 48.

By contrast, the Central Bank of Chile became officially autonomous several years after its creation with the constitution of 1980. The autonomy was completely institutionalized with the constitutional organic law of 1989 and remains stable until today. See Larre (2008), p. 5.

The Central Reserve Bank of Peru became officially autonomous with the organic law of 1962. Before, the Peruvian central bank had no statutory autonomy but some degree of autonomy in practice because the members of the board believed in the necessity of autonomy in conducting monetary policy based on technical criteria. See Orrego (2007), p. 17.

The early origins of autonomy of the Colombian central bank did not emerge from the law but from a contract based on the Act 30 of 1922. The legislators considered that placing the central bank outside of the public domain was the best way to really isolate the monetary authority from government intervention. The first Colombian central bank had mostly private capital, the board was integrated by representatives of the private banks and state participation was minimal. The private nature of the Bank of the Republic lasted until 1976 when the government bought all the shares and made official the public nature of the monetary institution. See Martínez Neira (2014).

[152]Goebel (2005), pp. 616–617.

mechanism that prevents the monetary authority from deviating from its original promise.[153]

The constitutional rank of central bank autonomy is beneficial for both formal and substantive legal certainty concerning the independence of the monetary authority and the pursuit of its legal objective. The set of formalities required to amend the constitution and the implications for the legislators of the constitutional hierarchy make the constitutional rank a means to guarantee that formal autonomy is also *de facto* or real autonomy.[154]

Constitutional amendments usually require a complicated process, great majorities, more and longer discussions, or even a constituent assembly. For example, the amendment of European Central Bank (ECB) provisions in the Maastricht Treaty demands the ratification of all of the EU member states.[155] Further, any change to the autonomy of the institution must be declared unconstitutional, because the lack of strict adherence to the constitution makes such legislation null and void.[156] Therefore, central bank autonomy of constitutional rank can be assumed to last in time and to benefit from the stability of constitutions.

Central bank autonomy of constitutional rank also benefits the consistency of the broad legal framework of the central bank. It limits the role of the legislature to provide the institution with a specific legal framework within the boundaries set by the constitution. The Colombian constitution states that, in cases of incompatibility between the constitution and the legislation, the constitutional provisions prevail over the legislation.[157]

In practice, however, constitutional entrenchment of central bank autonomy may not be a sufficient condition to provide legal certainty, such as when, for example, other constitutional or legislative provisions contradict themselves. If some constitutional rules guarantee the autonomy of the monetary authority but other constitutional provisions directly or indirectly allow for government intervention in the issues of the central bank's exclusive responsibility, legal certainty is undermined.[158] Moreover, as shown in the previous chapter, amending the constitution may not be as difficult in one country as in another.

---

[153]Neumann (1991), pp. 96–98.

[154]Gutierrez (2004), p. 256.

[155]Goebel (2005), pp. 616–617.

[156]Cordero (2012), p. 23.

[157]Const. Colombia Art. 372 para 2: *"The Congress shall adopt an Act which shall regulate the Bank of the Republic for the exercise of its functions and the regulations under which the government shall issue the statutes of the Bank. These shall determine, among other things, the form of its organization, its legal regime, the functioning of its executive board and its board of directors, the term of the director, the rules for the constitution of its reserves, among them, those of exchange and monetary stabilization, and the future application of its earnings."*
    Const. Colombia Art. 4 entails the obligation of the legislator to subdue to the constitution: *"The Constitution provides the norm of regulations. In all cases of incompatibility between the Constitution and the statute or other legal regulations, the constitutional provisions shall apply."*

[158]Glenny and Dalglish (1973), p. 144.

While the constitutional entrenchment of central bank autonomy is the legal way to assure a high degree of institutional stability,[159] stability should not be mistaken for inflexibility. Central banks have to adapt to changes. They are subject to an internal self-adaptation within the parameters of the legal framework. Such "adjustments are generally incremental and patchy rather than radical and comprehensive."[160]

The constitutional rank confers to an organ an extensive and almost exclusive management and control over its affairs. In this sense, the governing board of the institution exercises authority in all of the internal affairs and excludes the influence of the executive and legislative branches.[161] But the most relevant aspect about constitutional autonomy is that the independence in a normative sense, also understood as self-regulation, implies that the institution can regulate itself and enact regulation that becomes part of the country's legal framework.[162] Constitutionally autonomous institutions may, for example, be able to self-regulate to ensure their freedom to develop their functions, to enforce their decisions without the influence of third parties[163] and to oppose direct or indirect (potential) interference by government and other state institutions.[164]

The high degree of autonomy guaranteed by the constitutional rank does not automatically suggest unlimited autonomy, nor does it isolate the central bank from the other state institutions. Several decisions of the Constitutional Court of Colombia remark that central bank autonomy in Colombia is not absolute but is limited in a formal and material sense. The formal limits are the functions, attributions and scope of action included in the law. The material limit is the obligation to coordinate with the other economic policymakers.[165] The Constitutional Court of Colombia makes clear, for example, that, to maintain an efficient and healthy general economic policy, the Bank of the Republic of Colombia (Colombia's central bank) must collaborate with the President of the Republic and with the organs of the public administration that are in charge of other areas of economic policy.[166] In a similar manner, the Constitutional Tribunal of Chile (TC Chile) remarks that the central

---

[159]Glenny and Dalglish (1973), pp. 1–6, 146. See also Gutierrez (2004), p. 255.

[160]Knill (1999), p. 121.

[161]Glenny and Dalglish (1973), pp. 1–6, 146.

[162]Pedroza de la Llave (2002), p. 179.

[163]Zúñiga (2007), p. 240.

[164]Bernhard (1998), p. 314.

[165]René Vargas Pérez v. Congreso de la República de Colombia, CCC, Sentencia C-481, 7 July 1999; Guillermo Alberto Duarte Quevedo v. Congreso de la República de Colombia, CCC, Sentencia C-827, 8 August 2001; Andrés Quintero Rubiano v. Congreso de la República de Colombia, CCC, Sentencia C-208, 1 March 2000.

[166]Control constitucionalidad del Proyecto de "Ley Orgánica Constitucional del Congreso Nacional", TC Chile, Sentencia Rol No. 91, 18 January 1990.

bank has a duty to coordinate with the President of the Republic of Chile, who is responsible for the economic policy of the country.[167]

In sum, central banks with autonomy of constitutional rank should have the following characteristics: (1) they have the power of self-regulation; (2) a particular statute effectively protects them from political influence;[168] (3) they are neither subsidiary nor assistants to the government;[169] (4) such institutions have the power to appoint their own authorities, handle their own budgets and develop their own organization; (5) the executive branch is not responsible for the measures taken by the central bank; (6) the constitutional rank can be modified only by the judicial branch;[170] and (7) the autonomy is limited by the obligation to coordinate with other state institutions.[171]

4.4.2 Legal Autarchies and Legal Certainty

Autarchy is a term coined to describe the degree of independence of the central banks in Argentina and Brazil.[172] In the Anglo-Saxon literature, this term is known as *statutory autonomy,* and, in some cases, autarchies are referred to as *state agents* or *state departments* in the literature.[173] Statutory autonomy or autarchy is generally granted to institutions that require a certain degree of independence and flexibility to fulfil a public service.[174] According to Latin American administrative law, autarchy is implicit in the broad definition of autonomy[175] and is defined as the capacity of a

---

[167] *Control constitucionalidad enmienda "Ley General de Bancos"*, TC Chile, Sentencia Rol No. 216, 17 July 1995.

[168] Pedroza de la Llave (2002), p. 179.

[169] Zúñiga (2007), p. 237.

[170] Cárdenas et al. (1999), p. 638.

[171] Zúñiga (2007), p. 237.

[172] BCRA Law Sec. 1: *"The Central Bank of the Argentine Republic is a self-administered National Government entity subject to the provisions of this Charter and other related legal rules."*

LSFN Brazil Art. 8: *"The current Superintendency of Currency and Credit is transformed into a semi-autonomous federal agency denominated the Central Bank of the Republic of Brazil, headquartered in and subject to the jurisdiction of the capital of the Republic, with its own legal personality and assets composed of the properties, rights and values transferred to it in accordance with the terms of this law, together with appropriation, on the date on which this law goes into effect, of the interest and incomes resulting from the provision in Art. 9 of Decree No. 8,495, dated 12/28/1945, which is expressly repealed by this instrument."* LSFN Brazil Art. 1: *"Structured and regulated by this law, the National Financial System will be composed of: I - the National Monetary Council; II - the Central Bank of Brazil; (Text given by Del no. 278, dated 02/28/67) III - Banco do Brasil S.A.; IV - the National Bank of Economic Development; V - all other public and private financial institutions."*

[173] See, e.g., Glenny and Dalglish (1973), p. 42, 44–45, 48.

[174] Glenny and Dalglish (1973), pp. 44–45, 48.

[175] Gordillo (2012), p. 12.

state institution to manage itself without the interference of another state branch or organ[176]

The main characteristic of autarchies is that the autonomous status is not granted in a constitution but in a legislative source.[177] The fact that the legislature decides on the autonomous status places the statutory autonomous institutions under the control of the legislative branch.[178]

To provide legal certainty, it is beneficial if the statutory autonomy is explicitly granted in statutes of the entity being granted the autonomy. But this is not always the case. Because autarchies do not necessarily require a specific set of rules to enjoy a certain degree of autonomy, the statutory autonomy of an institution can also be deduced from the legal provisions that allow the institution to enjoy broader discretion or, simply, from withdrawing the institution from some particular control.[179]

The lack of a constitutional entrenchment implies that autarchies are autonomous to the extent that they can develop their public function but that they not autonomous enough to withdraw from the control, guidance and guardianship exercised by the government.[180] Therefore, there is a greater opportunity for radical, instead of gradual, change, that comes from external rather than internal initiatives.[181] On the other hand, not granting autonomy to an institution in the constitution of a country does not by itself mean that the constitution does not regulate the institution at all as is actually the case for the Argentinean central bank. Quite the contrary, Brazil's constitution does rule some institutional aspects of the monetary institution,[182] such as giving it the exclusive faculty to issue currency[183] or prohibiting it from giving loans to the government.[184] Yet, the decision of whether to grant autonomy to Brazil's central bank depends fully on the legislature.[185]

Autarchies are different from constitutional autonomies, because, even though they also have the capacity of self-management (e.g. of their economic resources,

---

[176]Pedroza de la Llave (2002), p. 178.

[177]Zúñiga (2007), p. 235.

[178]Glenny and Dalglish (1973), pp. 43–44.

[179]*Ibid.*, pp. 44–45, 48.

[180]Zúñiga (2007), p. 235.

[181]Knill (1999), p. 117.

[182]Const. Brazil Art. 52 (III) on the Federal Senate gives it the power *"to give prior consent, by secret voting, after public hearing, on the selection of: [. . .] d) president and directors of the Central Bank [. . .]"*.

[183]Const. Brazil Art. 164: *"The competence of the Union to issue currency shall be exercised exclusively by the central bank."*

[184]Const. Brazil Art. 164 para 1: *"It is forbidden for the central bank to grant, either directly or indirectly, loans to the National Treasury and to any body or agency which is not a financial institution."*

[185]The CBB was not supposed to be independent in the first place. When it was set up, the attribution of controlling the currency and the credit, was supposed to be coordinated between the CBB, the Banco do Brazil (public commercial bank), the Superintendence of Currency and Credit and the Treasury. See Corazza (2006), p. 5.

staff), the opportunity to acquire rights and obligations, and the responsibility of providing a public service, they cannot regulate themselves.[186] The legislative branch keeps the regulatory attribution for itself to maintain the power, control and persuasion over the institution.[187] This is clearly the case for the Argentinean central bank, since the Congress of Argentina has the constitutional duty to preserve currency stability and to create a bank that issues money.[188] In Argentina, the conduct of monetary policy by the central bank is merely the result of a delegation or transfer of competences by Congress to the central bank through legislation, which gives the Central Bank of the Argentine Republic the attribution of self-management but not of self-regulation.[189]

Without the limits included in the constitution, legislatures are restricted only by general constitutional rules, not by a specific constitutional framework that incorporates the autonomy of the institution as the basis for designing the monetary authority.[190] Moreover, the process for changing statutes is easier than the process for amending the constitution in each country. A statutory amendment depends on political arrangements within the legislative branch. Only if the president has veto power is there a functioning counterweight to such statutory changes.[191] The stability of central bank autonomy cannot be fully guaranteed.

Bernhard explains how political forces can influence the amendment of the statutory autonomous status of the central bank. He reasons that the prevalence of central bank autonomy depends on political considerations, especially on whether monetary policy incentives of the government match with those of the members of the legislature. *Bernhard* argues that, when there is a divergence between the policy preferences of the two groups, it is more likely that the legislature will prefer an independent monetary institution. In such a situation, however, this position will also be supported by the government to avoid the risk of intense legislative scrutiny of the government's policies that could threaten a potential re-election. In contrast, when preferences of the executive and legislative branches match, both branches might benefit from a dependent central bank.[192]

The behavior of interest groups and voters may also provide incentives to establish an autonomous institution. If interest groups that deal with state branches

---

[186]Gordillo (2012), pp. 12–13; see also Saddi (2008), p. 2.

[187]Christensen and Lægreid (2006), pp. 9–10.

[188]According to Const. Argentina Art. 75 (6), Congress shall be empowered "[t]*o establish and regulate a Federal bank with power to issue money, as well as other National banks.*" Further Const. Argentina Art. 75 (19) attributes, among other things, "*the protection of the value of money*" to Congress.

[189]General Office of the Comptroller of Argentina [Sindicatura General de la Nación] 26 June 2001, Expediente No. 3176/00.

[190]Cordero (2012), pp. 23–24.

[191]De Haan et al. (1999), pp. 180–181.

[192]Bernhard (1998), pp. 315–318. Bernhard also mentions that political ideologies may influence central bank statutes depending on the respective majorities. In this regard, see also Belke and Potrafke (2012).

fear that the government will try to benefit at their expense, such as, for example, by the use of unanticipated inflation, they might be willing to accept higher costs in transactions when the branches of the state credibly commit to hold inflation low by providing autonomy to the monetary institution.[193] Further, a government that needs to pursue unpopular policies might favor an autonomous institution that pursues objectives in line with the needs of the government to relieve pressure from the voters. The government may then be able to blame the decisions of the autonomous institution for restricting its policy options.[194]

As the legislature can restrict or even eliminate central bank autonomy, if this autonomy is granted by the legislative branch in the first place, the legislature can also choose to restrain from interfering with monetary policy or to design sound legal arrangements that guarantee the autonomy of the central bank. In that event, the degree of independence may be considered almost equal to that of a central bank that was granted autonomy in the constitution of the country.[195]

Nevertheless, the sheer possibility that the legislative branch may decide the status of the autonomy illustrates that the stability of a statutory autonomy and the credibility about the legal role of such an institution is always at risk.[196] Hence, there is no need for an actual threat of modifications. The possibility of legislative intervention is enough to influence decisions of board members or cast doubts about credibility.[197] Such disadvantages of statutory autonomy with regard to the political control over the amendment of the central bank status have been exposed for the central banks in developing and emerging market economies. There is, for example, also a discussion about the US Federal Reserve's (FED) degree of independence.

> [A]lthough [the Fed] enjoys great independence by custom, nothing prevents the Congress from adopting legislation mandating certain goals or policies, a power that the Congress has on rare occasion exercised.[198]

In Latin America, however, history shows that there is reason for concerns about how political interest in the legislature can affect the degree of central bank autonomy. For instance, in Mexico, the Congress modified the Law of the Bank of Mexico of 1936 as soon as the legislators considered central bank autonomy distasteful. While the Act of 1936 had provisions that guaranteed the autonomy of the central bank and the achievement of the objective of price stability, the lack of a constitutional rank and the relatively easy amendment process allowed Congress to eliminate several limitations through the new Act of 1941.[199] In the same manner, a current

---

[193]Miller (1998), pp. 435–436.

[194]See, e.g., Belke and Potrafke (2012), p. 1137.

[195]Cordero (2012), p. 23.

[196]Glenny and Dalglish (1973), pp. 48–49.

[197]Neumann (1991), p. 96.

[198]Goebel (2005), p. 621.

[199]Turrent y Diaz (2005), p. 57.

example of the disadvantage of statutory autonomy is the newly amended organic[200] charter of the Argentinean central bank. Beyond giving additional, potentially contradictory objectives to the monetary authority, the legislative amendment of 2012 explicitly put the central bank under the guidance of the executive branch by providing that its legal objectives have to be pursued "within the framework of its powers and the policies set by the National Government."[201]

4.5 Summary

The analysis in this chapter has evaluated the fundamental legal frameworks of the central banks in six Latin American countries in light of the principle of legal certainty.

Taking into account the constitutions only, the legal frameworks of the Bank of the Republic of Colombia and the Central Reserve Bank of Peru seem to provide a high degree of legal certainty. These central banks have a single objective that is often considered the ideal for an autonomous central bank: *preserving price stability*. Moreover, the legal objectives have remained stable since the early 1990s and are entrenched in the constitutions of the countries, which also provide the central banks with autonomy (of constitutional rank). The combination of a single and technical objective with an effective restriction of government intervention provided by the constitutional rank of their autonomy should, in principle, give the Peruvian and Colombian central banks a sound basis to credibly commit towards their legal objectives.

The study has found that the legal framework of the Central Bank of Chile has given the central bank two objectives with no order of priority. But both objectives (stability of the currency and normal functioning of the internal and external payments system) are compatible with one another and have been stable for some time. While central bank objectives are not found in the Chilean constitution, they are entrenched in the Constitutional Organic Act of the Central Bank of Chile, which is a legal document of (almost) constitutional quality. The consistency and stability of the objectives of the Central Bank of Chile and the institution's autonomy of constitutional rank should be a sound basis for the institution to commit credibly to the fulfilment of its goals.

The framework of the Mexican central bank casts some doubts concerning legal certainty. While the objectives of the Bank of Mexico have also been stable since the 1990s, and the monetary institution has autonomy of constitutional rank, there is no clarity about whether the central bank has the single objective of preserving the stability of the purchasing power of the currency as is set out in the constitution of

---

[200]The term organic, in this case, is not used to explain a higher legal hierarchy but rather the organizational nature of the legal document.

[201]BCRA Law Sec. 3.

the country, or whether it shall also follow secondary objectives, such as preserving the health of the financial system as is suggested in its legislation. The two objectives are consistent with each other and have an order of priority, and, in case of doubt, the constitutional prescription should prevail over legislation. Nevertheless, legal certainty also requires that the legislative branch respects the constitutional mandate and that legislative initiatives adhere to the limits set by the constitution. The resulting lack of clarity about the legal mandate of the Mexican central bank might undermine legal certainty and cause problems in credibly committing to the constitutional objective.

The fundamental frameworks of the CMN of Brazil (the CBB) and the Central Bank of the Argentine Republic (BCRA) are particularly troublesome with respect to providing legal certainty. Even though the CMN of Brazil has several objectives with a clear order of priority, its main objective is the economic and social progress of the country. Objectives related to preserving price stability are only in second or third place. While the CBB as an executive arm of the CMN of Brazil has statutory autonomy, the CMN has no autonomy whatsoever. Therefore, the autarchy of the CBB seems meaningless in terms of providing legal certainty about achieving legal objectives, because the central bank does not make any policy decisions.

Finally, the framework of the BCRA provides no legal certainty for at least three reasons. First, the BCRA has multiple objectives: preserving the value of the currency and promoting employment and economic development. Among these objectives, there is no clear order of priority. Second, the objectives have recently been modified. Third, there is plenty of room for political influence that makes credible commitments very hard to achieve. Political influence should not even come as a surprise since monetary policy is delegated to the central bank only by the legislative branch of Argentina. In fact, the Congress of Argentina is in charge of preserving the stability of the currency according to the Argentinean constitution. In sum, a framework that provides legal certainty about central bank objectives and allows the central bank to commit credibly to fighting inflation—as found in most Latin American emerging markets—has not yet been installed in Argentina.

Legal References

Treaties and Conventions

African (Banjul) Charter on Human and People's Rights [Version published by the African Commission on People's Rights of the African (Banjul) Charter on Human and People's Rights, entry into force on 21 October 1986].
American Convention on Human Rights, Pact of San José Costa Rica Art. 23 [Version published by the Organization of American States of the American Convention on Human Rights, Pact of San José Costa Rica, entry in force on 18 July 1978]

International Covenant on Economic, Social and Cultural Rights [Version published by the United Nations of the International Covenant on Economic, Social and Cultural Rights 3 January 1976].

Protocol to the Convention for the Protection of Human Rights and Fundamental Freedoms [Version published by the European Court of Human Rights of the Protocol No. 1 to the European Convention of Human Rights, entry into force on 20 March 1952].

Universal Declaration of Human Rights [Version published by the United Nations of the Universal Declaration of Human Rights of 10 December 1948].

Constitutions

Constitution of Chile with Amendments through 2015 [English Translation of the Constitución Política de la República de Chile, Gazeta Official, October 20, 2015]. Constitute Project, University of Texas at Austin, available at https://www.constituteproject.org/search?lang=en&q=chile

Constitution of Colombia with Amendments through 2015 [English Translation of Constitución Política de Colombia, Diario Oficial No. 49.554, 25 June 2015]. Constitute Project, University of Texas at Austin., available at https://www.constituteproject.org/constitution/Colombia_2015.pdf

Constitution of Mexico [English Translation of the Political Constitution of the Mexican States, Gazeta de la Federación, 5 February 1917]. Constitute Project, University of Texas at Austin. available at https://www.constituteproject.org/constitution/Mexico_2015.pdf?lang=en

Constitution of Peru [English Translation of Constitución Política del Perú, Diario Oficial, 30 December 1993]. Congress of the Republic of Peru, available at http://www.congreso.gob.pe/Docs/files/CONSTITUTION_27_11_2012_ENG.pdf

The Constitution of Brazil [English Translation of the Constituição da República Federativa do Brasil, Diario Oficial da União, 5 October 1988]. Chamber of Deputies, available at http://english.tse.jus.br/arquivos/federal-constitution

Legislation

Argentina

Organic Charter of the Central Bank of the Republic Argentina of 1992 [Carta Orgánica del Banco Central de la República Argentina de 1992, Boletín Oficial, 23 September 1992].

Organic Charter of the Central Bank of the Republic Argentina [Official Translation of the Carta Orgánica del Banco Central de la República Argentina, Boletín Oficial, 28 March 2012], available at https://www.bcra.gob.ar/Institucional/BCRALaw.asp

Brazil

Law of the National Financial System of Brazil [Official Translation of the Lei 4.595, Lei do Sistema Financeiro Nacional, Diário Oficial da União - Seção 1 – Suplemento, 31 December 1964], available at https://www.bcb.gov.br/ingles/norms/LAW4595EN.asp

National Banking and Securities Commission [Lei 6.4.4, Lei da Comissão Nacional de Banca e Valores Mobiliários Ley de la Comisión Nacional Bancaria y de Valores, Diario Oficial da União 28 April 1995].

Chile

Basic Constitutional Act of the Central Bank of Chile [Official Translation of the Ley Orgánica Constitutional del Banco Central de Chile, Diario Oficial 6 January 1990].

Colombia

Organic Act of the Bank of the Republic of Colombia [Official Translation of the Ley Orgánica del Banco de la República, Ley 31 de 1992, Diario Oficial No. CXXVIII, 29 December 1992].

Act 35 of 1993 of Colombia [Ley 35 de 1993, Diario Oficial No. 40.710, 5 January 1993].

Mexico

Law of the Bank of Mexico [Official Translation of the Ley del Banco de México, Official Gazette, 23 December 1993].

Peru

Civil Code of Peru [Código Civil de Perú, Diario Oficial, 25 July 1984].

Organic Law of the Central Reserve Bank of Peru [Official Translation of the Ley Orgánica del banco central de reserve del Perú, Diario Oficial, 30 December 1992].

Other

General Office of the Comptroller of Argentina [Sindicatura General de la Nación] 26 June 2001, Expediente No. 3176/00.

Case Law

Tribunal Constitucional de Chile [Constitutional Tribunal of Chile]

Control constitucionalidad del Proyecto de "Ley Orgánica Constitucional del Congreso Nacional", TC Chile, Sentencia Rol No. 91, 18 January 1990.
Control constitucionalidad enmienda "Ley General de Bancos", TC Chile, Sentencia Rol No. 216,17 July 1995.

Corte Constitucional de Colombia [Constitutional Court of Colombia]

René Vargas Pérez v. Congreso de la República de Colombia, CCC, Sentencia C-481, 24 July 1999.
Andrés Quintero Rubiano v. Congreso de la República de Colombia, CCC, Sentencia C-208, 1 March 2000.
Guillermo Alberto Duarte Quevedo v. Congreso de la República de Colombia, CCC, Sentencia C-827, 8 August 2001.

Suprema Corte de Justicia de la Nación de México [Supreme Court of Justice of the Nation]

Municipio de Guadalajara, Estado de Jalisco, Controversia Constitucional, Supreme Court of Justice of the Nation of Mexico [Suprema Corte de Justicia de la Nación de México], Sentencia P. VIII, Tomo XXVII, February 2008, p. 1868.

Tribunal Constitucional del Perú [Constitutional Tribunal of Peru]

Banco Central de Reserva del Perú v. Superintendencia de Banca, Seguros y Administradoras Privadas de Fondos de Pensiones, TC Peru, Sentencia Exp. No. 005, 2 September 2005.

References

Apel E (2007) Central banking systems compared: the ECB, the Pre-Euro Bundesbank and the Federal Reserve System. Routledge International Studies in Money and Banking
Bank for International Settlements (2012) Basel Core Principles on Banking Supervision, Basel Committee on Banking Supervision. Available at https://www.bis.org/publ/bcbs213.pdf
Belke A, Potrafke N (2012) Does government ideology matter in monetary policy? A panel data analysis for OECD countries. J Int Money Financ 31(5):1125–1139. https://doi.org/10.1016/j.jimonfin.2011.12.014
Bernhard W (1998) A political explanation of variations in Central Bank independence. Am Polit Sci Rev 92(2):311–327. https://doi.org/10.2307/2585666

Bini Smaghi L (2007) Independence and accountability in supervision: general principles and European setting. In: Masciandaro D, Quintyn M (eds) Designing financial supervision institutions: independence, accountability and governance. Edward Elgar, Cheltenham, pp 41–62

Buchanan J, Wagner R (2000) Democracy in deficit. The political legacy of Lord Keynes, The Collection Works of James M. Buchanan, Volume 8

Burdekin R, Laney L (1988) Fiscal policymaking and the Central Bank institutional constraint. Kyklos 41(4):647–662. https://doi.org/10.1111/j.1467-6435.1988.tb02734.x

Cárdenas J, Pérez C, Carbonell M (1999) Presente y Futuro de la Autonomía del Instituto Federal Electoral, Administración y Financiamiento de las Elecciones en el Umbral del Siglo XXI. Memoria del Tercer Congreso Internacional de Derecho Electoral 2:467–513. available at https://archivos.juridicas.unam.mx/www/bjv/libros/1/239/10.pdf

Carrasco C (2009) Banco Central de Chile 1925-1964: Una Historia Institucional. Banco Central de Chile

Central Bank of Chile (2007) Monetary Policy in an Inflation Targeting Framework. Central Bank of Chile Working Paper. Available at http://www.bcentral.cl/eng/publications/policies/pdf/MonetaryPolicyInflationTargeting.pdf

Christensen T, Lægreid P (2006) Autonomy and regulation: coping with agencies in the modern state. Edward Elgar Publishing

Coban A (2005) Inflation and human rights, protection of property rights against inflation under the European Convention on Human Rights. Essex Human Rights Rev 2(1):62–78

Corazza G (2006) O Banco Central do Brazil Evolução Histórica e Institucional. Perspectiva Econômica 2(1):1–23. https://doi.org/10.4013/4372

Corbo V (2010) Financial stability in a crisis: what is the role of the Central Bank. BIS Papers 51:27–30. Available at http://www.bis.org/publ/bppdf/bispap51f.pdf

Cordero E (2012) La Administración del Estado en Chile y el Concepto de Autonomía. Contraloría General de la República. Años de Vida Institucional (1927-2012) 85:15–32

De Haan J, Amtenbrink F, Eijffinger S (1999) Accountability of Central Banks: aspects and quantifications. BNL Quarterly Review, Banca Nazionale del Lavoro 52(209):169–193. Available at http://ideas.repec.org/p/dgr/kubcen/199854.html

Deutsche Bundesbank (2013) Financial Stability Review, 2013. Available at https://www.bundesbank.de/Redaktion/EN/Downloads/Publications/Financial_Stability_Review/2013_financial_stability_review.pdf?__blob=publicationFile

Díaz Etienne A (1996) La Inflación y los Derechos Humanos, Jurídica-Anuario del Departamento de Derechos de la Universidad. Iberoamericana 26:314–358. Available at https://revistas-colaboracion.juridicas.unam.mx/index.php/juridica/article/view/11303/10350

Donnelly J (2013) Universal human rights in theory and practice. Cornell University Press

Eijffinger S, De Haan J (1996) The political economy of Central Bank independence. Princeton Spec Pap Int Econ 19(1):5–6

Elgie R (2002) The politics of the European Central Bank: principal-agent theory and the democratic deficit. J Eur Public Policy 9(2):186–200. https://doi.org/10.1080/13501760110120219

European Central Bank (2000) The role of the eurosystem in the field of payment systems oversight. European Central Bank

Garcia Herrero A, Del Rio P (2003) Financial stability and the design of monetary policy. Communications 33(33.40.62):7–29. Available at https://www.researchgate.net/publication/28065705_Financial_Stability_and_the_Design_of_Monetary_Policy

Gardbaum S (2012) The Place of Constitutional Law in the Legal System. UCLA School of Law Research Paper No. 12-07. Available at http://papers.ssrn.com/sol3/papers.cfm?abstract_id=2024607

Gärtner M (2009) Macroeconomics, 3rd edn. Prentice Hall

Glenny L, Dalglish T (1973) Public universities, state agencies and the law: constitutional autonomy in decline. Center for Research and Development in Higher Education

Goebel R (2005) Court of Justice oversight over the European Central Bank: delimiting the ECB's constitutional autonomy and independence in the OLAF Judgments. Fordham Int Law J 29

(4):610–654. Available at http://heinonline.org/HOL/LandingPage?handle=hein.journals/
frdint29&div=28&id=&page

Goodhart C, Schoenmaker D (1995) Should the functions of monetary policy and banking
supervisions be separated? Oxford Econ Pap 47(4):539–560. Available at https://www.jstor.
org/stable/2663543

Gordillo A (2012) Tratado de Derecho Administrativo y Obras Selectas. Tomo 5, Primeras Obras,
Fundación de Derecho Administrativo. Available at http://www.gordillo.com/pdf_tomo5/
tomo5.pdf

Greenspan A (1994) Testimony Before the Committee on Banking, Housing and Urban Affairs.
Senate of the U.S, March 2, 1994. Available at http://fraser.stlouisfed.org/docs/historical/
greenspan/Greenspan_19940302.pdf

Guerrero R (1979) La Constitución Económica. Revista Chilena de Derecho 6(1):79–94. Available
at https://www.jstor.org/stable/41605244

Gutierrez E (2004) Inflation performance and constitutional Central Bank independence: evidence
from Latin America and the Caribbean. Economía Mexicana Nueva Época 13(2):255–287.
Available at http://www.economiamexicana.cide.edu/num_anteriores/XIII-2/EVA_GUTIER
REZ.pdf

Hasse R (1990) The European Central Bank: perspectives for a further development of the
European Monetary System, strategies and options for the future of Europe. Bertelsmann
Foundation Publishers

Jácome L, Vásquez F (2008) Is there any Link between Legal Central Bank independence and
inflation? Evidence from Latina America and the Caribbean. Eur J Polit Econ 24(4):788–801.
https://doi.org/10.1016/j.ejpoleco.2008.07.003

Knill C (1999) Explaining cross-national variance in administrative reform: autonomous versus
instrumental bureaucracies. J Public Policy 19(2):113–139. https://doi.org/10.1017/
S0143814X99000203

Kydland F, Prescott E (1977) Rules rather than discretion: the inconsistency of optimal plans. J Polit
Econ 85(3):473–491. https://doi.org/10.1086/260580

Larre A (2008) La Autonomía del Banco Central de Chile: Origen y Legitimación. Documentos de
Política Económica 26:1–25. Available at http://dialnet.unirioja.es/servlet/articulo?
codigo=3066037

Lastra R (2015) International financial and monetary law, 2nd edn. Oxford University Press

Laurens B, Sommer M, Arnone M, Segalotto JF (2007) Central Bank autonomy: lessons from
global trends. IMF Staff Papers 56(2):263–296. Available at https://www.imf.org/en/
Publications/WP/Issues/2016/12/31/Central-Bank-Autonomy-Lessons-from-Global-Trends-
20632

Liddle FC, Pita JJ (2011) Historia de la Creación del Banco Central de la República Argentina.
Investigaciones Económicas del BCRA:117–138. Available at http://www.bcra.gov.ar/pdfs/
investigaciones/64_Liddle.pdf

Limbach J (2001) The concept of the supremacy of the constitution. Mod Law Rev 64(1):1–10

Locke J (1821) Two treaties on government. London, Available at https://books.google.de/books/
about/Two_Treatises_on_Government.html?id=AM9qFIrSa7YC&redir_esc=y

Lundberg E (2000) Monetary Policy and Banking Supervision Functions on the Central Bank.
Banco Central do Brazil Working Paper Series, Volume 2, Available at http://papers.ssrn.com/
sol3/papers.cfm?abstract_id=247513

Lybek T (2004) Central Bank autonomy, accountability and governance: conceptual framework.
IMF Seminar on Current Developments in Monetary and Financial Law, Washington. Available
at https://www.imf.org/external/np/leg/sem/2004/cdmfl/eng/lybek.pdf

Mankiw G, Taylor M (2011) Economics. Cengage Learning EMEA

Martínez Neira NH (2014) Cátedra sobre el Banco de la República. Grupo Editorial Ibanez

McCrudden C (2008) Human dignity and judicial interpretation of human rights. Eur J Int Law 19
(4):655–724. Available at http://ejil.org/pdfs/19/4/1658.pdf

Mersch Y (2013) Financial stability policies in Central Banks. Macedonian Policy J 2(3):1–44. Available at http://www.mfa.gov.mk/sites/default/files/publikacii_dokumenti/Crossroads%20Vol.%20III,%20No.%203%20MNR%20web%20July%202013.pdf#page=135

Miller G (1998) An interest-group theory of central bank independence. J Legal Stud 27 (2):433–453. Available at http://www.jstor.org/discover/10.1086/468026?uid=3737864&uid=e2&uid=4&sid=21104509879413

Miller G (2005) The political evolution of principle-agent models. Ann Rev Polit Sci 8:203–225. https://doi.org/10.1146/annurev.polisci.8.082103.104840

Mishkin F (1996) Understanding Financial Crisis: A Developing Country Perspective. NBER Working Paper No. 5600. https://doi.org/10.3386/w5600

Montesquieu CS (1989) The spirit of laws. Cambridge University Press

Namén Vargas W (1998) Obligaciones Pecuniarias y Corrección Monetaria. Revista Derecho Privado 3:31–64. Available at http://heinonline.org/HOL/LandingPage?handle=hein.journals/revdpriv3&div=5&id=&page=

Neumann M (1991) Precommitment by Central Bank Independence. Open Econ Rev 2(2):95–112. Available at http://link.springer.com/article/10.1007%2FBF01886895

Niño Tejada E (1995) La Reajustabilidad. Revista de Derecho de la Universidad Católica de Valparaíso 16:253–269

Orrego F (2007) Autonomía del Banco Central de Reserva del Perú: Una Perspectiva Histórica. Revista Moneda 135:16–22. Available at http://www.bcrp.gob.pe/docs/Publicaciones/Revista-Moneda/Moneda-135/Revista-Moneda-135-04.pdf

Pedroza de la Llave ST (2002) Los Órganos Constitucionales Autónomos en México. In: Serna de la Garza JM, Caballero Juarez JA (eds) Estado de Derecho y Transición Jurídica, Serie Doctrina Jurídica 95:173–194. Available at http://biblio.juridicas.unam.mx/libros/1/306/1.pdf

Pereyra C (2012) La Creación del Banco de Reserva de Perú. Revista Moneda, Banco Central de Reserva de Perú 150:7–11

Pistor K (2013) A legal theory of finance. J Comp Econ 41(2):315–330. https://doi.org/10.1016/j.jce.2013.03.003

Posen A (1995) Declarations are not enough: Financial Sector Sources of Central Bank Independence. NBER Macroeconomics Annual, Vol. 10. MIT Press, pp 253–274. Available at http://www.nber.org/chapters/c11021.pdf

Quintyn M, Taylor M (2002) Regulatory and Supervisory Independence and Financial Stability. IMF Working Paper, No. 02/46, Available at https://www.imf.org/external/pubs/ft/wp/2002/wp0246.pdf

Rivero Ortega R (2013) Derecho Administrativo Económico. Sexta Edición, Marcial Pons

Rosenn K (1978) The effects of inflation on the law of obligations in Argentina, Brazil, Chile, and Uruguay. Bost Coll Int Comp Law J 2(2):269–298. Available at http://lawdigitalcommons.bc.edu/cgi/viewcontent.cgi?article=1631&context=iclr

Rosenn K (1982) Law and inflation. University of Pennsylvania Press. Available at https://books.google.de/books?id=tH2GCgAAQBAJ&printsec=frontcover&hl=de&source=gbs_ge_summary_r&cad=0#v=onepage&q&f=false

Saddi J (2008) Autonomia, Independência ou Contrato: O que Devemos Esperar do Banco Central. Revista Electrônica sobre a Reforma do Estado No. 14. Available at http://www.direitodoestado.com/revista/rere-14-junho-2008-jairo%20saddi.pdf

Sappington D (1991) Incentives in principal-agent relationship. J Econ Perspect 5(2):45–66. Available at https://www.jstor.org/stable/1942685

Sargent T, Wallace N (1981) Some unpleasant monetarist arithmetic. Federal Reserve Bank of Minneapolis Quarterly Review, Available at https://www.minneapolisfed.org/research/qr/qr531.pdf

Shiller R (1997) Why do people dislike inflation? In: Romer C, Romer D (eds) Reducing inflation: motivation and strategy. University of Chicago Press, pp 13–70. Available at http://www.nber.org/chapters/c8881.pdf

Turrent y Diaz E (2005) Las Tres Etapas de la Autonomía del Banco Central en México. Análisis
    Económico 20(43):47–80. Available at http://www.analisiseconomico.com.mx/4303.html
Von Mises L (1953) The theory of money and credit. Yale University Press. Available at https://
    mises.org/library/theory-money-and-credit
Von Mises L (2008) Human action. The scholars edition, Scholars' Edition. Ludwig von Mises
    Institute. Available at https://mises.org/sites/default/files/Human%20Action_3.pdf
Walsh C (1995) Optimal contracts for central bankers. Am Econ Rev 85(1):150–167. Available at
    https://www.jstor.org/stable/2118001
Zúñiga F (2007) Autonomías Constitucionales e Instituciones Contramayoritarias (A Propósito de
    las Aporías de la "Democracia Constitucional"). Revista Ius et Praxis 13(2):223–244. https://
    doi.org/10.4067/S0718-00122007000200010

Chapter 5
Central Bank Statutes and Autonomy

5.1 Introduction

This chapter reviews the legal provisions of the statutes of the six Latin American central banks (status as of October 2019) to evaluate if the statutes provide certainty concerning central bank autonomy. The statutes allow reviewing the provisions related to personal, financial, and operational autonomy as well as the accountability arrangements of the central banks.[1] Importantly, the analysis of the statutes helps determine if the legal frameworks regarding central bank autonomy are consistent overall. For example, it is conceivable that a central bank has autonomy of constitutional rank but that the statutes place the bank within the public administration, i.e. under the control of the executive, or prescribe that the government decides on the staff, the finances, or the bank's operations, which diminishes certainty about the autonomy of the bank.

Personal and financial autonomy of the central banks is analyzed based on a large literature that aimed to code the main features of central bank autonomy.[2] This research determined the degree of personal autonomy from political interference and took into account variables like the appointment process, dismissal and office terms of the central banks' CEOs. The literature also measured financial autonomy in terms of whether provisions forbidding or limiting lending to the state did or did not exist.[3]

---

[1] See, e.g., Smits (1997), p. 176.

[2] Bade and Parkin were the first to code central bank autonomy. Their study included twelve industrial countries. See Bade and Parkin (1977).

I will often refer to the often-cited Cukierman-Index, see Cukierman et al. (1992). This study developed a detailed index on central bank autonomy for 72 countries between 1980 and 1989, including not only industrial economies but also emerging markets and developing countries.

[3] The influence of central banks' legal autonomy on inflation was higher in industrial countries than in developing economies. The main difference between them was the difference in institutional strength. See Cukierman et al. (1992).

A. L. Tapia-Hoffmann, *Legal Certainty and Central Bank Autonomy in Latin American Emerging Markets*, European Yearbook of International Economic Law 15, https://doi.org/10.1007/978-3-030-70986-0_5

Later studies took into account additional variables like central bank transparency to determine accountability.[4]

This chapter gathers the main statutory aspects to evaluate whether there is legal certainty concerning the autonomy of the central banks in our six Latin American countries. Ideally, the provisions embedded in the central bank law avoid legal vacuums.[5] The chapter shows that in most cases the statutes' provisions hardly reflect what the literature prescribes.

5.2 Personal Autonomy and Financial Autonomy

5.2.1 Personal Autonomy

Personal autonomy (also personal independence) guarantees that members of a central bank board can take decisions without having to feel morally or politically pressured in any way. Legal arrangements can shield the personal autonomy of a central bank's board members. Such arrangements include the appointment process for the board members in which veto players are involved, a term of office that must be long enough to not match the presidential period in office, and legal protection for individual board members against government retaliation in the development of their activities.[6] Moreover, the professional profile required to be a board member as well as regulations that limit other professional activities also play a role in allowing for self-determined decisions as central bank board member. The absence or the lack of clarity of these provisions in a central bank's statutes suggest problems with personal autonomy.[7]

5.2.1.1 Composition of the Central Bank Boards

One of the advantages of a decision-making board, as opposed to an individual decision-maker, is that a governance body has several veto players with different points of view. The diversity of opinions makes them better suited to repel the

---

[4]Studies on Latin America include Jácome (2001), p. 13. See also Jácome and Vásquez (2008). For further modifications and updates using additional countries, see Crowe and Meade (2007), pp. 71–72.

For a recent study using data up to 2010 and focusing on transparency as measure for accountability, see Dincer and Eichengreen (2014).

[5]Cukierman et al. (1992), pp. 355, 361–362.

[6]For an overview of the literature and the outlined characteristics of central bank autonomy in various papers, see Laurens et al. (2007).

[7]Apel (2007), pp. 52–53; see also Alesina and Summers (1993), pp. 152–153; Bade and Parkin (1988).

influence of various political players or private organizations.[8] Arguably, the ideal number of board members is unknown. Some studies suggest that it is five members. Other studies find seven members to be optimal.[9] For sure, it is an odd number to get decisions. Too many board members complicate decision making because it would require longer hours of discussion to achieve at an agreement. Moreover, representatives of the private sector should be excluded from any representation on the central bank board.[10]

In the six analyzed countries, the Board of Directors of the Central Bank of Chile and of the Bank of Mexico are composed of five members.[11] The boards of the Bank of the Republic of Colombia and the Central Reserve Bank of Peru each have seven members.[12] Brazil and Argentina's boards can be considered rather large for optimal decision-making. The Monetary Council of Brazil is composed of ten members;[13] the board of the Central Bank of Brazil has nine members;[14] and the board of the Central Bank of the Argentine Republic has ten members.[15]

5.2.1.2 Appointment of the Board Members

Even though absolute freedom from state intervention in the process of appointment of central bank board members is impossible, it is important to prevent all the board members from reflecting only the preferences of the executive branch in power.[16] To avoid that the influence over central bank authorities rests on only one person or institution, central bank statutes can allow the participation of several state institutions in appointing board members. In addition, veto players may intervene in the process of appointment of the board members of the central bank.

In federal states, each state may participate in the process of appointment. The inherent decentralization in federal countries may ensure less intervention of the central government.[17] The reason for this is that, in federal systems, a wide variety of

---

[8]Bini Smaghi (2007), p. 45.

[9]Crowe and Meade (2007), p. 86. For a study on the relationship of the number of board members and inflation, see also Berger and Nitsch (2011).

[10]Jácome (2001), p. 7.

[11]CBCH Law Sec. 7; BM Law Art. 38.

[12]BRC Act Art. 28; CRBP Law Art. 9.

[13]See LSFN Brazil Art. 6.

[14]Internal Rules of the Central Bank of Brazil Art. 5 [Regimento Interno do Banco Central do Brasil, Diário Oficial, 8 September 2011] [hereinafter RIBC Brazil].

[15]BCRA Law Sec. 6: *"The Bank shall be governed by a Board consisting of a Governor, a Deputy Governor and eight members [. . .]."*

[16]Bernhard (1998), p. 314.

[17]Fernández de Lis (1995), p. 11.

regional preferences are in competition. As regions differ, they might favor different monetary policies, cancelling out special interests.[18]

In centralized states, both the executive and legislative branches should participate to preserve an adequate balance of power.[19] The legislature is usually composed of people with different points of views. The diversity of interests can ensure that even though some of the elected members of the central bank board may agree with the policy ideas of the government, there will also be others with very different perspectives influencing monetary policy.[20]

Even though Mexico, Argentina and Brazil are federal states, none of them allows for a participation of the individual states in the confirmation of the central bank board. The central banks of Mexico and Argentina, however, require a dual process to appoint the board members. In the case of the Bank of Mexico, the President of Mexico must appoint the central bank board members, and the Senate must decide whether to approve the nominees.[21] The law prescribes a similar process in the case of the Central Bank of the Argentine Republic. According to Argentinean law, the President of the Republic appoints the members of the board but requires approval of the Senate. Argentina's central bank law makes an exception to the requirement of the legislative branch's approval. According to the law, the President appoints the central bank board members typically with the approval of the Senate of the Nation.[22] December 21, 2015 was the last time that a board member of the central bank was elected *in committee* (i.e., unilaterally) by the President. The reason for this was that, at the time, it was not possible to count on the agreement of the Senate because they were in recess.[23]

In more centralized countries, such as Chile and Peru, both the government and the legislature are involved in the appointment of the central bank board members. The board of the Central Bank of Chile is appointed in a dual process in which the President of the Republic requires the agreement of the Senate.[24] In the case of the board of the Central Reserve Bank of Peru, the executive branch appoints four of the seven members, while Congress appoints the other three.[25]

The appointment of the members of the board, except the manager, of the Colombian central bank relies unilaterally on the decision of the President of the Republic of Colombia.[26] The President of Colombia also holds the authority to

---

[18]Bernhard (1998), p. 324.

[19]Quintyn and Taylor (2002), p. 20. For more, see Crowe and Meade (2007), p. 70; Hasse (1990), p. 116.

[20]Bernhard (1998), p. 314.

[21]Const. Mexico Art. 28 para 7.

[22]BCRA Law Sec. 7.

[23]Executive Decree 179 of 2015, Argentina [Decreto Ejecutivo 179, 21 December 2015].

[24]CBCH Law Sec. 7.

[25]The Congress also must ratify the Executive's appointees. See CRBP Law Art. 9.

[26]Const. Colombia Art. 372.

renew members and replace board members in the event of death, illness, or dismissal.[27]

The Constitution of Brazil lays out that electing the president and the members of the central bank's board is in the exclusive responsibility of the Federal Senate.[28] However, in practice the nine board members of Brazil's central bank are appointed by the President of Brazil with the approval of the Federal Senate, following the internal rules of the bank.[29] The Monetary Council is composed of the Minister of Finance, the president of the private Bank of Brazil S.A., the president of the National Bank of Economic Development and seven extra members, all of whom are appointed by Brazil's president.[30]

5.2.1.3 Tenure and Renewal of Board Members

The terms of office for the board members of central banks should be long,[31] for instance 8 years,[32] without the possibility of renewal.[33] If the length of tenure of board members is equal to or less than the time in office of the president of a country, the government has the possibility to influence the central bank's decision-making via appointments. This threat to autonomy would be particularly strong if the executive unilaterally appoints or renews the board. The government could select people who will follow their orders.[34]

A longer tenure of board members has the advantage to ensure the continuity of monetary policy and enhance the credibility of the monetary institution.[35] A long tenure gives the central bankers enough time to build a reputation. A highly reputed board is better suited to defend its policies without fear of government retaliation because people trust in the central bank board.[36] The government is less likely to persecute a central banker with a good name because the board's credibility is valuable to control inflation and promote financial stability.[37]

A renewal of central bank board members leads to speculation about re-appointment. The board members with an interest in keeping their jobs would

---

[27]BRC Act Art. 35.

[28]The voting method to elect the members of the central bank board is secret ballot after a public hearing. See Const. Brazil Art. 52 (III d).

[29]RIBC Brazil Art. 5.

[30]LSFN Brazil Art. 6.

[31]Neumann (1991), p. 104.

[32]Smits (1997), p. 63.

[33]Hasse (1990), p. 116.

[34]Cukierman et al. (1992), p. 363; see also Neumann (1991), p. 104.

[35]Valencia (1998), p. 23.

[36]Massad (1989), p. 85; see also Cukierman et al. (1992), p. 363.

[37]Cukierman et al. (1992), p. 363.

thus be susceptible to political negotiation to preserve their seat.[38] If the possibility of renewal exists, the term in office of the central bank's members should not exceed a total of 10 years.[39]

Chile's, Mexico's and Argentina's legal arrangements concerning tenure of central bank board members are by and large in line with the outlined prescriptions. Although board members can be reelected, in all three countries the tenure of the board members is longer than the tenure of the president. There is no perfect overlap. The Constitutional Organic Law of the Central Bank of Chile prescribes the longest period in office of the central bank's board members among the studied countries: 10 years with the possibility of reappointment. Not all board members are appointed at once but there is a partial renewal of the board every 2 years.[40] By contrast, the term in office of the President of Chile is only 4 years.[41] The board members of the Bank of Mexico are selected for 8 years in office.[42] The period in office of the President of Mexico is 6 years.[43] Board members are appointed every 2 years. They start their period in office the first day of January of the first, third or fifth year of the President's tenure. The members of the Bank of Mexico's board can be reappointed.[44] The board members of the Central Bank of the Argentine Republic have a tenure of 6 years and can be reappointed.[45] The term of office for the President is 4 years in Argentina.[46]

The members of the boards of the Bank of the Republic of Colombia and the Central Reserve Bank of Peru have tenures that overlap with the presidential period. This overlap makes the central bank boards more vulnerable to potential interventions. The board of the Colombian central bank has a tenure of 4 years,[47] as does the President of Colombia.[48] Every 4 years, the President of the Republic can appoint two of the members. They can be reappointed for up to three periods in a row.[49] The members of the board of the Central Reserve Bank of Peru remain in office for

---

[38]Smits (1997), p. 157.

[39]Neumann (1991), p. 104.

[40]CBCH Law Sec. 8.

[41]In addition, the President of Chile cannot be immediately re-elected. See Const. Chile Art. 25 para 2.

[42]According to BM Law Art. 40, the board's governor will be appointed for a term of six years and the deputy governors for 8 years.

[43]Const. Mexico Art. 83 forbids presidential re-election.

[44]BM Law Art. 40.

[45]BCRA Law Sec. 7.

[46]Note that Const. Argentina Art. 90 allows for consecutive presidential re-election.

[47]BRC Act Art. 37.

[48]Const. Colombia Art. 190.

[49]BRC Act Art. 34.

4 years,[50] matching the period in office of the President of Peru.[51] The law does not mention anything about reappointment.

When it comes to Brazil, the law does not prescribe the tenure of the central bank's and the monetary council's board members, which is a problem in terms of legal certainty.

Table 5.1 provides a summary of the described arrangements concerning appointment and dismissal of board members.

5.2.1.4 Heads of the Central Bank Boards

The board of a central bank is commonly chaired by a central bank president or governor. Some central bank boards also have a general manager. According to the *Modified Cukierman Index*, a governor or president and a bank manager with a high degree of personal autonomy would be appointed by the board itself or, at least, in a dual process in which both the head of the executive, i.e. the president, and the legislature are involved. The head of the central bank is less autonomous if appointed unilaterally by the executive. The same is true when they are selected by a central bank board, which is itself directly and unilaterally chosen by the executive. As is the case of board members, the term of office of the head of the central bank should exceed the period in office of the president of the country. Therefore, a term of office of 6–8 years might be considered optimal, depending on the tenure of the country's president.[52]

As summarized in Table 5.2, central bank presidents are appointed by the president in each country or are members of the executive. From the perspective of legal certainty concerning personal autonomy these arrangements are troublesome. The central banks of Colombia, Chile and Peru have both a central bank president and a manager (CEO). The Minister of Finance is the president of the Colombian central bank.[53] The legal representative of the Colombian, Chilean and Peruvian central banks is the general manager, who is one of the board members and elected by the other members of the board.[54] The general managers of the Central Reserve Bank of Peru and the Central Bank of Chile are appointed by the board.[55] The president of the Central Reserve Bank of Peru is elected by Peru's president.[56] The President of Peru also proposes the general manager of the central bank who is

---

[50]BCR Peru Art. 9.

[51]Const. Peru Art. 86, para 2.

[52]Jácome and Vásquez (2008), p. 799.

[53]BRC Act Art. 28 (a).

[54]BRC Act Art. 37 para 2; CBCH Law Sec. 24; and CRBP Law Art. 38 (a).

[55]CRBP Law Art. 24 (s); CBCH Law Sec. 18 (4).

[56]According to the law, the president of the bank's board is one of the four members appointed by the President of the country. See CRBP Law Art. 9.

Table 5.1 Composition, appointment and tenure of board members

	Argentina	Brazil	Colombia	Chile	Mexico	Peru
Reason for dismissal	Disregard of the law Becoming part of the Government or Financial Sector Misconduct, Non-fulfillment of the duties of public officials		Unjustified absence in 2 sessions Offenses against professional ethics Disregard of Constitution, Laws and regulations Dis	False information in the affidavit Engaging in prohibitions Abusing position to get to privileges Not adhering to the board's rules Going against the bank's objective	Incapability of performing functions Engaging in forbidden activities Disrespect the confidentiality Providing false information Lack of fulfilling duties	Crime Serious misconduct such as granting loans that are forbidden
Dismissal	The President with Congress' advice	Ad natum (at discretion)	President of the Republic or the Superintendence by presidential delegation	Appellation Court of Santiago President with authorization of Congress or	Congress/ Political Trial	Congress
Removal	Yes		Yes (maximum 3 times)	Yes	Yes	No
Tenure	6 years		4 years	10 years	8 years	5 years
Appointment	President and Senate Exception: The President until Senate approved.	Senate According to the Internal Rules of the Bank: The President of the Republic	President	President and Congress	President and Congress	President and Congress
Number	10	9	7	5	5	7

Source: Author. Summary of findings from legal analysis as presented in respective country section

Table 5.2 Head of central bank boards

	President/ Governor	Manager	Appointed by
Argentina	Yes	No	President of the Republic with approval of the Senate
Brazil	Yes	No	President of the Republic
Colombia	Minister of Finance	Yes	President: President of the Republic Manager: Board
Chile	Yes	Yes	President: President of the Republic Manager: Board
Mexico	Yes	No	Executive
Peru	Yes	Yes	President: President of the Republic with ratification of the Congress Manager: The Board with proposal of the President of the Republic

Source: Author. Summary of findings from legal analysis as presented in respective country section

elected by the Bank's board.[57] The general manager is responsible for the administration of the central bank[58] as well as its legal representation.[59] Like in Peru, the President of Chile appoints the president of the central bank,[60] who is the *extra-judicial* representative of the bank.[61] The Board of Directors appoints the manager of the bank.[62] He is the legal representative of the bank and in charge of its administration and oversight.[63]

The Bank of Mexico has a governor who performs the functions of both president and manager. The governor of the Bank of Mexico is appointed by the executive.[64] In the case of the Argentinean central bank, the governor of the central bank is in charge of the bank's management with the support of the sub-managers.[65] He is also in charge of the bank's legal representation.[66] Again, the president of the bank is selected by the President of the Republic but with the approval of the Senate.[67] In

---

[57]CRBP Law Art. 24 (s).

[58]CRBP Law Art. 36.

[59]CRBP Law Art. 38 (a).

[60]CBCH Law Sec. 8.

[61]CBCH Law Sec. 22 (6).

[62]The law prescribes that the bank's board shall also *"[a]ppoint, accept resignations and terminate the working contracts of the General Manager, the General Counsel and the General Auditor."* See CBCH Law Sec.18 (4).

[63]CBCH Law Sec. 24.

[64]BM Law Arts. 38 and 47.

[65]The law states that the bank's governor is *"responsible for the management of the Bank"*. See BCRA Law Sec. 10 (a). However, the management of the bank will be exercised by the sub-managers, in line with BCRA Law Sec.16 which states that *"[t]he Bank shall be managed through deputy general managers [...]"*.

[66]BCRA Law Sec. 10 (d).

[67]BCRA Law Sec. 7.

Brazil, the Minister of Finance is the chairman of the Monetary Council.[68] Brazil's President appoints the central bank president.[69]

5.2.1.5 Confidentiality of the Opinions of Board Members

To protect individual board members from government retaliation targeted at them, the decisions made by the central bankers should be on behalf of the whole board and not the individual members. Moreover, although decisions of the central bank have to be transparent, the individual opinions of the board members should be kept confidential.[70]

Going through the statutes of the six central banks, only the law of the Central Reserve Bank of Peru establishes that the decisions and opinions of the Bank's board members do not represent any personal interest but the bank's.[71] In other words, everything communicated is communicated as a bank statement rather than a statement by a board member. The members of the central bank board are supposed to disclaim any private or political interest. The Constitution of Colombia demands that "members of the executive board shall represent the interest of the nation exclusively."[72] However, there are no legal provisions to protect the individual opinions of the board members.

5.2.1.6 Professional Profile of Board Members

Members of a central bank board must be adequately trained to fulfill their duties. Among the skills required are broad analytical abilities that allow them to understand macroeconomic issues, as well as knowledge about monetary policy and financial topics. Even if the board members can count on the assistant of advisers, they must be able to make their own judgments; otherwise, they face the risk of relying too much on the decisions of people who do not hold the same degree of responsibility. Therefore, the law should establish the professional characteristics of the board members based on expertise, merits, and technical knowledge.[73]

Experience is preferred over degrees for the members of the central bank boards of the countries in analysis. For instance, the internal rules of the Central Bank of Brazil use the phrase "well known capacity in economic and financial matters";[74] thus, stressing the importance of experience. Similarly, Argentina's central bank

---

[68]LSFN Brazil Art. 6 (I).

[69]Brazil's president also appoints all the other board members, see RIBC Brazil Art. 5.

[70]Apel (2007), p. 53.

[71]CRBP Law Art. 11.

[72]Const. Colombia Art. 372.

[73]Neumann (1991), p. 102.

[74]RIBC Brazil Art. 5.

Table 5.3 Professional profile

	Guarantee of Confidentiality of board members' opinions	Professional Profile
Argentina	No	Knowledge and experience in economics, finance or law
Brazil	No	Well known capacity in economic and financial issues
Colombia	No	Professional degree 10 years of experience in economic, monetary, financial, international, or legal issues
Chile	No	Does not specify
Mexico	No	3 members: Financial and monetary experience Previous high-profile positions 3 members: Medium level experience in monetary or financial issues
Peru	Yes	Expertise and experience in economic and financial issues

Source: Author. Summary of findings from legal analysis as presented in respective country section

charter mentions as requirements a "tested ability in monetary, banking or finance related legal matters, and a solid moral reputation",[75] rather than any particular degree. To be a member of the board of the Central Reserve Bank of Peru, it is not necessary to have any professional degree; rather, expertise and experience in economic and financial matters are required.[76] The preference for experience over certain university education is also clear in the case of the requirements for board membership at the Bank of Mexico. Three of the five members must have monetary or financial expertise and former high-level positions in public or private financial institutions. The two members who do not aspire to be governor of the bank must have a professional degree as well as some expertise in monetary policy, finance, or law.[77]

The central bank statutes that demand a professional degree for the board members do not seem to be concerned about the kind of degree board members hold. For instance, the board members of the Bank of the Republic of Colombia are required to have any professional degree, as well as at least 10 years of working experience in public and private institutions in, for instance, international trade, monetary policy, public finances, finance, or law.[78] The law of the Central Bank of Chile does not specify the professional profile of the members of the central bank board at all (see Table 5.3).

---

[75]BCRA Law Sec. 6.
[76]CRBP Law Art. 11.
[77]BM Law Art. 39 (II).
[78]BRC Act Arts. 29 (b) and (c).

Table 5.4 Forbidden and allowed activities

	Forbidden Activities	Allowed Activities
Argentina	Activities in financial institutions Activities in the public sector	University teaching
Brazil	N/A	N/A
Colombia	Running for or holding a political office	University teaching
Chile	Activities in the private sector Activities in the public sector Remunerated activities in general	Activities in nonprofits without remuneration University teaching
Mexico	Running for or holding a political office	Not specified in the law
Peru	Not specified in the law	Managers of firms as long as they are not bankrupt Managers of financial institutions without record of sanctions from the Superintendency of Banking and Insurance Shareholder of less than 5% in financial institutions

Source: Author. Summary of findings from legal analysis as presented in respective country section

5.2.1.7 Forbidden and Allowed Activities

The different indices of central bank autonomy do not include whether or not central bank board members are allowed or forbidden to pursue professional activities that differ from their duties at the bank. Being allowed to engage in activities outside the central banking role might lead to conflicts of interest. Therefore, additional activities typically require the permission of the board.[79]

The Table 5.4 shows that central bank statutes of the six countries limit extra activities of the central bank board members but to very different degrees. For instance, the central banks of Chile and Argentina include a prohibition of performing activities, remunerated or not, in the government or the public sector. In both cases, they are only allowed to teach at universities.[80] The board members of the Central Bank of Chile can also be part of nonprofit organizations.[81] The law of the Central Bank of Chile prescribes that, before taking office, the board members of the Central Bank of Chile must declare under oath (affidavit) that they are not working in the private sector, do not hold shares of financial institutions, and do not work for another public institution. The board members cannot perform any

---

[79]Additional activities of ECB members also require board approval, see Smits (1997), pp. 163–164.

[80]BCRA Law Sec. 8 (a).

[81]CBCH Law Sec. 14 para 1.

remunerated activity[82] or engage in activities that benefit themselves or others.[83] The board members of Argentina's central bank cannot be shareholders, managers, comptrollers, or work in finance.[84] They also cannot perform any function with the national, provincial, or local governments.[85]

The law of the Colombian central bank is also categorical in forbidding the board members to engage in any extra activity other than university teaching during their term of office as central bankers. The only political activity allowed is voting in general elections.[86] In the case of the Bank of Mexico, the board members cannot work in politics.[87] The law does not mention any prohibition of participating in activities related to the private sector.

The situation for the board members of the Peruvian central bank is different from those mentioned above. The president of the central bank board is the only official who works full time and exclusively for the bank.[88] The other members of the board are expected to develop other professional activities, but with some limitations. The board members of the Peruvian central bank can manage firms, except of firms that "fraudulently declared bankruptcy".[89] In a similar vein, they can also be managers of financial institutions that have not been "penalized by the Superintendency of Banking and Insurance".[90] The financial situation of board members or the firms they are shareholders of at also matters. A person cannot be board member if she or her firm have a substantial share in have outstanding debts that are in a "judicial procedure for collection".[91] Furthermore, the members of the Board of Directors of Peru's central bank are not allowed to own more than 5% of a financial institution.[92]

5.2.2   Financial Autonomy

A central bank is financially autonomous (or independent) when there are legal arrangements that isolate the bank from external influence in managing its finances. The bank should have sufficient funds available to pursue its objectives.[93] Going

---

[82]CBCH Law Sec. 14 para 5.

[83]CBCH Law Sec. 15.

[84]BCRA Law Sec. 8 (b).

[85]BCRA Law Sec. 8 (a).

[86]BRC Act Arts. 31 (a), (d) and (g).

[87]BM Law Art. 42.

[88]Only the president of the bank's board has a salary. The other members receive fees for their attendance to the board's meetings. See CRBP Law Art. 29.

[89]CRBP Law Art. 12 (e).

[90]CRBP Law Art. 12 (f).

[91]CRBP Law Arts. 12 (ll) and (m).

[92]CRBP Law Art. 12 (g).

[93]For more on financial autonomy of the central bank, see Amtenbrink (2010), p. 83.

through the legal provisions regarding government financing, guarantees to the bank's capital, rules on how to deal with profits and losses of the bank, as well as the responsibilities for the bank's budget allows analysing financial autonomy. Table 5.5 summarizes the findings.

5.2.2.1   Government Financing

Monetary and fiscal policy are interdependent. A highly indebted government may want to finance the deficit by selling bonds with below market rate yields or "by forcing debt down the throats of captive buyers, primarily commercial banks".[94] These possibilities entail inflation or financial repression that could undermine central bank autonomy.[95] However, when the government knows that the central bank is autonomous and devoted to pursuing the low inflation objective, the government will have to restrict public spending because the central bank will not monetize government debt. It is claimed that "lower rates of money growth sooner or later require lower deficits and the monetary authority imposes discipline on the fiscal authority."[96]

A central bank with a high degree of financial autonomy must be absolutely prohibited from lending to the government in the primary market.[97] If there is any possibility of indirect financing, such rules must be clarified. The law should specify the recipients, processes in lending, maturities and conditions for such loans.[98]

To maintain financial autonomy of the central bank, government financing should only take place in the secondary market and with strict and clear legal limits,[99] including that the credit must be secured.[100] The central bank board should be in a position to battle government demands of funding,[101] and the law should establish the limits and conditions of the loans. Among these limits is that the loans should not surpass a sensible percentage of central bank assets. Loans to the government could also be constrained by government profits and with interest rates at market prices, or by the requirement of a great majority of central bank board members. The worst option is that the central bank must negotiate with government about lending or that the government itself has the authority to take such lending decisions.

---

[94]Fry (1998), pp. 512–513.

[95]Fry (1998).

[96]Burdekin and Laney (1988), p. 648.

[97]Laurens et al. (2007), p. 283.

[98]Jácome and Vásquez (2008), pp. 800–801.

[99]It is claimed that even if the central bank is forbidden to directly finance the government and to buy general government securities in the primary market, buying general government debt in the secondary market can achieve the same economic results. Buiter (2004), p. 269.

[100]Burdekin and Laney (1988), p. 649.

[101]Fry (1998), pp. 512–513.

Table 5.5 Financial autonomy

	Prohibition of State Financing	Exceptions to the Prohibitions	State Guarantee of Bank's Capital	Distribution of Banks Profits	Budget
Argentina	Yes	Temporary loans up to 12% of the monetary base; temporary loans up to 10% of the gov.'s income in the last 12 months	No guarantee. Bank has to cover losses with its reserves or capital	50% go to the bank's reserves; 50% is transferred to the government	Proposed by board
Brazil	Yes	Not specified in the law	N/A	N/A	The board proposes; Monetary Council decides
Chile	Yes	State or risk of war declared by the Security Council	Implicit. If the bank decides it needs additional capital, the Treasury will be asked for resources.	10% are mandatory bank reserves; the board can transfer the rest to the government or make it part of the reserves	N/A but the bank is considered autonomous
Colombia	No	N/A	State covers bank's losses when the resources of the stabilization reserve are not enough	The bank sets up stabilization reserve to cover potential losses; the rest is transferred to the national government.	Elaborated by the CONFIS; approved by the board
Mexico	Yes	The bank can provide credit via the Treasury's checking account at the bank, given the government will be able to pay	N/A	Profits are transferred to the government; except those resulting from asset revaluation	Elaborated unilaterally by the board
Peru	Yes	Purchases of securities issued by the Treasury; the Constitution (Art. 78) mentions loans not specified in the law.	When capitalization reserves do not cover bank debt and losses, it is possible to use the revenue designated to the Treasury. If	75% to the bank's capitalization reserve; 25% go to the Treasury	The board is in charge.

(continued)

Table 5.5 (continued)

Prohibition of State Financing	Exceptions to the Prohibitions	State Guarantee of Bank's Capital	Distribution of Banks Profits	Budget
		necessary, the state covers the bank's debt and losses.		

Source: Author. Summary of findings from legal analysis as presented in respective country section

Out of the six Latin American countries analyzed, only the Constitution of Chile includes a general prohibition for the central bank to finance the government, directly or indirectly. The Central Bank of Chile may only buy government bonds except when there is war or the risk thereof.[102] Even though the Chilean central bank is forbidden to lend money to the Chilean government, it can lend money to other foreign states, central banks and financial institutions.[103]

The Constitution of Brazil forbids Brazil's central bank to give direct or indirect loans for public spending.[104] The law of the Central Bank of Brazil states that the bank only develops banking operations with financial institutions, either public or private. Operations with other non-financial institutions, of public or private law, are generally forbidden.[105]

The Central Reserve Bank of Peru is forbidden to directly finance the government.[106] However, it can buy treasury bonds in the secondary market, as long as their value never exceeds 5% of the monetary base of the previous year.[107]

The Mexican Constitution forbids every public authority to demand central bank financing.[108] The Bank of Mexico, however, is allowed to fund other financial

---

[102]Const. Chile Art. 109 paras 2 and 3: *"No public expenditure or loan shall be financed with direct or indirect credits of the Central Bank. However, in case of foreign war or threats of it, which will be qualified by the National Security Council, the central bank may obtain, grant or finance credits to the State and public or private entities."* See also CBCH Law Sec. 27.

[103]CBCH Law Sec. 38 (5) states that *"[…] with regard to international transactions, the bank shall be empowered to: […] 5. To concede loans to foreign States, foreign central banks or banking institutions, foreign or international financial entities, provided the purpose of the said loans is to assist in the fulfillment of the objectives of the Bank."*

[104]However, Const. Brazil Art. 164 para 2: *"The central bank may purchase and sell bonds issued by the National Treasury, for the purpose of regulating the money supply or the interest rate."*

[105]LSFN Brazil Art. 12: *"The Central Bank of the Republic of Brazil will operate exclusively with public and private financial institutions and is prohibited from performing banking operations of any type whatsoever with other persons governed by public or private law, with the exception of those operations expressly authorized by legislation."*

[106]CRBP Law Art. 77.

[107]According to CRBP Law Art. 61, the bonds that the Treasury shall provide for the bank's capitalization are not included within these limits.

[108]Const. Mexico Art. 28 para 6.

institutions, but only to fulfill the goals of monetary policy.[109] In contradiction to the constitutional mandate, the legislature has authorized the Bank of Mexico to finance the state.[110] First, the bank may provide loans to the Treasury via the Treasury's checking account at the central bank. If the Treasury runs into a deficit larger than 1.5% of government expenditure with the central bank, the central bank must issue bonds on behalf of the government.[111] Second, government securities owned by the bank are not considered loans to the government, according to the law.[112]

In Argentina, these prescriptions are not as straightforward. Although the statutes, in principle, forbid the central bank to fund any state institution or to guarantee government debt,[113] according to the website of the Central Bank of the Argentine Republic, the bank's assistance to the government was 150 billion pesos for 2017.[114]

Section 20 of the statutes includes generous exceptions to the rule that allow for such assistance. First, the Central Bank of the Argentine Republic can grant the government temporarily loans of up to 12% of the monetary base. Further the central bank can make a temporary loan of up to ten percent of the central government's revenues of the preceding 12 months. The government has 12 months to repay the loan. Failure to meet this obligation would not allow the central bank to provide new loans. If required, the central bank may provide an additional loan to the government amounting up to ten percent of the government's revenues over the last 12 months which should be repaid in no more than 18 months.[115]

Second, the law of the Argentinean central bank indirectly allows the bank to pay the government's internal and external debt. The law specifies the government's duty to repay the money to the central bank but says nothing about the terms and conditions.[116]

The Colombian central bank is not generally prohibited from lending to the government. The Colombian Constitution requires a unanimous vote of the board members to approve government loans.[117] The prescriptions to lending to the

---

[109]BM Law Art. 14.

[110]Note that BM Law Art. 7 para II states: *"Banco de México may perform the following activities: [. . .] II. Grant credit to the Federal government, [. . .]."*

[111]BM Law Arts. 11 and 12.

[112]BM Law Art. 11.

[113]BCRA Law Sec. 19 (a).

[114]Information provided by the bank online: http://www.bcra.gov.ar/PoliticaMonetaria/Politica_Monetaria.asp#d.

[115]BCRA Law Sec. 20.

[116]BCRA Law Sec. 24: *"The Bank shall charge the National Government's account with the fee for domestic and external public debt servicing on its behalf, as well as any expenses arising therefrom. The National Government shall provide to the Bank the necessary funds for meeting those expenses, and the Bank may make advances for those expenses subject to the restrictions set forth in Section 20."*

[117]Const. Colombia Art. 373: *"Financing operations for the benefit of the state shall mandate the unanimous approval of the executive board unless open market operations are involved. In no case may the legislature mandate credit quotas for the benefit of the State or individuals."*

government are clear but troublesome from the perspective of legal certainty concerning central bank autonomy, particularly considering that the board members are appointed by the president and headed by the Minister of Finance. Moreover, the Colombian central bank serves as fiscal agent for the government, issuing and placing government debt securities on the market,[118] which might be considered a way to guarantee that bonds are sold at a price the government approves of.

5.2.2.2   Dealing with Profits and Losses

The law should establish clear rules about how central bank profits and losses are dealt with.[119] Indices of central bank autonomy suggest that central banks should always be able to implement monetary policy without financial limitations. To guarantee this, central bank losses that might undermine the working of the central bank should be covered by the government. By contrast, high profits that won't be necessary in monetary policy operations should be transferred to the government.[120] Although autonomy indices consider the coverage of losses by governments important for financial autonomy, in practice central banks that are in need of recapitalization by the government might be pressured by the Treasury to not run losses. Indeed, some empirical studies found that central bank losses are associated with inflation or changes in policy.[121]

The law of the Bank of the Republic of Colombia prescribes that, with the profit from the Bank's operations, the Bank must build up some reserves.[122] The reserves are intended to cover losses the bank may make at some time. Resources that do not go to the reserves must be transferred to the national government. Only when the bank's losses exceed the amount in reserve is the government responsible for covering them.[123]

The Organic Law of the Central Reserve Bank of Peru rules that 25% of profit go to the public treasury and 75% to a capitalization reserve. The profit that is part of the public treasury can be used, if necessary, to pay the bank's debt.[124] If the reserves deposited in the Treasury are not sufficient to cover the bank's losses, the state must transfer non-negotiable debt to the bank within 30 days.[125]

The statutes of Chile's central bank prescribe a minimum capital. The bank's board can decide to increase the capital, requesting the Minister of Finance of Chile

---

[118]BRC Act Art. 13 (d).

[119]Jácome (2001), p. 9.

[120]*Ibid.*, p. 17.

[121]For a review of the literature on central bank losses, inflation, and independence, see Hoffmann and Löffler (2017).

[122]BRC Act Art. 27 para 8 (d).

[123]BRC Act Art. 27 para 8 (e).

[124]CRBP Law Art. 92.

[125]CRBP Law Art. 93.

to provide additional resources when necessary.[126] The Central Bank of Chile has some leeway in deciding where profits go. According to the Constitutional Organic Law of the Central Bank of Chile, the profit of the central bank is distributed as follows: Ten percent go to reserves, and then, if the board agrees, the rest is transferred to the government, unless the board decides that all the profits will constitute reserves or pay for the bank's losses.[127] However, the law does not establish the government's responsibility for covering the bank's losses.

According to the Organic Charter of the Central Bank of the Argentine Republic, the state guarantees "the commitments undertaken by Bank"[128] but not the bank's losses. According to the law, the profit that is not capitalized must be part of a reserve. Once the reserve reaches 50% of the bank's capital, additional earnings go to the government. The bank's losses must be covered by those reserves; when they are insufficient, additional losses must be covered by the bank's capital.[129]

The law that regulates the central bank establishes that the Central Bank of Brazil has to transfer revenues to the Treasury after covering the expenses from central bank operations.[130]

According to the Mexican legal framework, it is not obvious who covers potential losses. However, the government must ensure that almost all the payments the Bank of Mexico makes to international financial institutions, except to the International Monetary Fund, are repaid. The Bank of Mexico must use its own resources to cover the debt with the International Monetary Fund.[131] The law establishes that, as the Bank of Mexico is a non-profit institution, any profits must be transferred to the government, with the exception of the profits "resulting from the reevaluation of assets".[132] For example, the peso value of foreign reserves denominated in dollars increases when the U.S. dollar appreciates relative to the Mexican peso, leading to capital gains in the Bank of Mexico's revaluation account.

5.2.2.3 Board Control Over Budget and Salaries

An autonomous central bank should be able to decide about its own budget.[133] Specifically, the board of an autonomous agency, such as the central bank, should have the ability to decide, without public or private pressure, about the bank's resources, employees, and salaries, among other aspects related to the bank's budget. It is a complicated issue to avoid depending on political influence if the government

---

[126]CBCH Law Sec. 5.
[127]CBCH Law Sec. 77.
[128]BCRA Law Sec. 1 para 2.
[129]BCRA Law Sec. 38.
[130]LSFN Brazil Art. 8 para 2.
[131]BM Law Art. 13.
[132]BM Law Art. 55.
[133]Neumann (1991), p. 100; see also Jácome (2001), pp. 11–12.

pays the salaries and decides on the budget of the central bank. The best way of financing the central bank is through a fee or a tax on the banking industry.[134] If there is no way to avoid having the budget come from government, it should be based on a budget proposal made by the members of the agency.

In Colombia, the Consejo Superior de Politica Fiscal (CONFIS) reviews the development of the annual budget for the Bank of the Republic. The Bank, however, has to approve the budget.[135] According to the law, the bank's board members are considered public officials. Therefore, the President of Colombia makes decisions on their salaries.[136] Wages of the central bank staff are determined by the bank's administrative council, which is made up by 5 board members.[137]

The Central Reserve Bank of Peru was granted autonomy regarding the budget. Peru's central bank has some leeway for the management of its budget.[138] Specifically, the Board of Directors can "[a]pprove, modify and supervise the Bank's annual budget".[139] The bank is, therefore, allowed to determine the salary of the president of the bank, general manager, other bank officials.[140] The Bank can also decide about purchases, sales or the building of offices.[141]

According to the law, the Central Bank of Brazil has budgetary autonomy.[142] The budget of the bank is proposed by the board and decided by the Monetary Council.[143] The Internal Rules of the Central Bank of Brazil are very specific in regard to the budget management of the bank. The board member in charge of the bank's administration authorizes any budget modification.[144] Another board member, in charge of the organization of the financial system and credit operations, decides about the salaries of the board members.[145]

In Mexico, the board proposes, authorizes, or modifies the budget of Mexico's central bank.[146] A government committee determines the remuneration of the

---

[134]Quintyn and Taylor (2002), p. 21.

[135]BRC Act Art. 33 (b).

[136]BRC Act Art. 38 (a).

[137]BRC Act Art. 36 (c).

[138]According to CRBP Law Art. 86, the bank's board is in charge of the *"programming, formulation, approval, execution, expansion, modification and control of the institution's budget."*

[139]CRBP Law Art. 24 (ñ).

[140]CRBP Law Art. 24 (u).

[141]CRBP Law Art. 24 (y).

[142]LSFN Brazil Art. 8.

[143]RIBC Brazil Art. 12 (VI) (a).

[144]RIBC Brazil Art. 14 (I) (a).

[145]RIBC Brazil Art. 17 (VI).

[146]BM Law Art. 46 (XI): *"[. . .] The Board of Governors shall do the above in observance of the principle that the evolution of said budget remain consistent with that of the Federal Expenditure Budget."*

governor and board members.[147] The governor of the central bank makes the final decision about wages of the bank employees based on the proposal by the board.[148]

There is little on budget and salaries in the statutes of Chile's and Argentina's central banks. The President of Chile decides about the salaries of the board members with the advice of three former central bankers. The salary ought to be competitive salary, similar to the salary for high ranked bankers in the private sector.[149] The board decides about staff wages.[150] In Argentina the board sets up a budget plan including resources needed for the bank.[151]

5.3 Accountability

5.3.1 Autonomy Versus Accountability

An institution is accountable when its actions are controlled by an authority, and it has to take responsibility for potential misconduct. Accountability requires clarity of the bank's objectives to decide if actions were appropriate or if there was misconduct. For accountability of a central bank, transparency of monetary policy is required as much as clarity about who is responsible for monetary policy.[152]

By definition, accountability comes at the expense of some autonomy.[153] However, accountability is also important for the effectiveness of an autonomous institution.[154] While the autonomous status protects regulators and supervisors from the influence of the government, accountability prevents them from being influenced by other interest groups like the financial industry.[155] In a democratic system, both accountability and autonomy can only co-exist. The key for a harmonious coexistence of autonomy and accountability is the presence of accountability arrangements,[156] set up in a way that enables the establishment of responsibilities while

---

[147]The BM Law Art. 49 states that it is a *"committee made up of the Chairman of the National Banking Commission and two individuals appointed by the Secretary of Finance and Public Credit. The appointments of these individuals should not represent conflict of interest and they should be renowned for their experience in the labor market pertinent to public and private credit institutions as well as to the corresponding regulatory authority agencies."*

[148]BM Law Art. 47 (XII).

[149]CBCH Law Sec. 10.

[150]CBCH Law Sec. 18 (3).

[151]BCRA Law Sec. 15 (e).

[152]De Haan et al. (1999), pp. 171–172.

[153]Canova (2011), p. 253.

[154]Quintyn and Taylor (2002), pp. 3 and 5.

[155]*Ibid.*, pp. 9–10.

[156]*Ibid.*, p. 29.

preserving the advantages of an autonomous institution such as "continuity, coherence and expertise".[157]

The point of departure for designing the accountability arrangements for the central bank is the legal objective of the public organ. As *Bini Smaghi* explains,

> If the objectives of the authority are vague or multiple, it might be difficult to verify whether an agency is fully committed to the goals assigned to it. It would also be difficult to assess how the authorities make decisions in the presence of contradictory objectives.[158]

Certainty concerning the central bank's legal mandate makes it easier to recognize the legality or illegality of the central bank's conduct. Specifically, it is necessary to specify for what central bankers are accountable, to whom central bankers are accountable, and how they are accountable.[159]

The central banks should be accountable in their performance towards the achievement of their legal objectives. Not every action of the central bank should be controlled. Controlling every single action of the central bank would be very costly. Further, judging the central bank based on the achievement of its objectives provides incentives to future central bankers to achieve these objectives.[160] The ex-post control mechanism shall determine responsibilities in the event of misconduct or mistakes that can result in consequences for the institution. The members of the board and the legal representatives of central banks must be sanctioned if found responsible.[161] Such sanctions could affect the institution's budget or even lead to the removal of the responsible authority.[162]

There is a difference between *constitutional organs* and *organs of the public administration*.[163] Institutions with autonomy of constitutional rank should be placed outside of the public administration, whereas legal autarchies fit squarely within the public administration because of the statutory rank.[164] While the relationship between the executive and autarchies is one of subordination, indicating that the executive may pursue oversight and penalize its employees, the relationship with between institutions with constitutional autonomy and the executive should be one of coordination.[165]

---

[157]*Ibid.*, p. 30.
[158]Bini Smaghi (2007), p. 52.
[159]*Ibid.*, pp. 50–53.
[160]Miller (2005).
[161]Smits (1997), p.169.
[162]Elgie (2002), p. 189.
[163]Ugalde (2010), p. 260.
[164]Zúñiga (2007), p. 238.
[165]*Ibid.*, p. 237.

5.3.2 *Control*

The differences in legal rank of the central banks imply different legal provisions for control. An institution that enjoys constitutional autonomy should be controlled mainly internally or by other institutions with autonomy of constitutional rank that are independent from political influence.[166] By contrast, the control of autarchies which belong to the public administration might be done by the executive.[167]

In addition, the courts of justice should independently control the legality of the central bank decisions and policies. Judicial review ensures legal certainty through the judicial analysis of the consistency of central bank decisions.[168] Judicial precedents allow citizens to foresee to a reasonable degree how the court will decide in their individual cases.[169] Furthermore, control of legality seeks to ensure the central bank's effective attachment to the law.[170] In this sense, being answerable for their decisions before independent judges encourages authorities to respect the rules.[171] For the courts, legal certainty about the rules that regulate the central banks' performance plays a significant role in deciding about the legality and constitutionality of the central banks' decisions.[172] Apart from control and judicial review, central bank policies should be subject to public scrutiny.[173]

In Colombia, the Organic Law of the Bank of the Republic sets the standards for control, inspection, and oversight by the President of the Republic.[174] In

---

[166]Note that there is, and I would like to say surprisingly, a dispute among legal scholars whether or not an autonomous central bank should be part of the public administration or not for the case of Chile. If it is part of the public administration, control can be exercised via the executive. For a study that supports the idea that the central bank of Chile is part of the executive, see Ferrada Bórquez (1998), p. 339. For an opposite opinion see Zúñiga (2007), p. 230.

The courts have ruled that Chile's central bank is mostly outside the public administration. See *Control constitucionalidad enmienda "Ley General de Bancos"*, TC Chile, Sentencia Rol No. 216, 17 July 1995.

[167]Ugalde (2010), p. 260.

[168]Quintyn and Taylor (2002), p. 32.

[169]Santaella Quintero (2003), p. 170.

[170]Bini Smaghi (2007), p. 53.

[171]Frye (2004), pp. 454–455. See also North (1993). North claims in that article that the protection of property rights is critical to generate credible commitments.

[172]In this regard, see *Guillermo Alberto Duarte Quevedo v. Congreso de la República de Colombia*, CCC, Sentencia C-827, 8 August 2001: The autonomy of the central bank has to be taken into account by the constitutional judges during the control of constitutionality and all the other judges that have to make a decision in any issue related with the central bank.

[173]Quintyn and Taylor (2002), p. 31; see also Mitchell (1996), p. 252; Smits (1997), p. 169.

[174]According to the law of the Bank of the Republic, "[t]*he President of the Republic will perform the functions of inspection, surveillance, and control on the Banco de la República. This attribution includes the competency to supervise the observance of the Political Constitution, the laws and rules that govern the actions of the officials and employees of Banco de la República, to carry out the pertinent administrative investigations, and to apply the corresponding disciplinary regimen.*" See BRC Act Art. 46 para 1.

contradiction to the autonomy given by the constitution, the Constitutional Court of Colombia has consistently decided that the Bank of the Republic is part of the public administration and established that the Bank of the Republic is also under the control of the President of the Republic of Colombia. The Court held that, despite the constitutional autonomy of the central bank, the President has the right to set up a permanent administrative oversight over the central bank's actions to guarantee the legality of the central bank's decisions.[175]

The President inspects, controls, and surveils the legality of the actions of the authorities of the Bank of the Republic.[176] Both the General Comptroller and the President of the Republic perform the budgetary control of the Bank of the Republic. The General Comptroller oversees state assets,[177] and the President of the Republic delegates the assessment of the financial statements of the bank and the control of the management of the income resulting from the bank's operations to an auditor.[178] Control is not independent from political influence.

In contrast to the view that the central bank should be considered part of the public administration, and as such of the executive, as posited by the court in Colombia, the decisions of the Constitutional Tribunal of Chile (TC Chile) of 1986 and 1989 placed the central bank outside of the public administration, which is managed by the executive, in full consistency with the autonomy of constitutional rank.[179] In subsequent decisions in 1995, the TC Chile decided that the Constitutional Organic Act of General Rules for Public Administration does apply to the Central Bank of Chile. This organic act can be understood as a declaration of the

---

[175]*Jaime Horta Díaz v. Congreso de la República de Colombia*, CCC, Sentencia C-566, 17 May 2000.

[176]BRC Act Art. 46.

[177]Santaella Quintero (2003), p. 170.

[178]The law prescribes that "[. . .] [t]*he Auditor will be appointed by the President of the Republic and will have under his/her responsibility, among other issues, to certify the financial statements of the Banco, to perform the other functions indicated by the Code of Commerce for the Auditor, and to exercise the control on the management and the results of the Entity.*" See BRC Act Art. 48.

[179]The court manifested that, given the constitutional rank of the autonomy of the central bank, the "principle of hierarchy" and subordination to the main state administrator do not apply to the institution. It is part of the administration of the state, however, which is what was implied by including it in Article 1 of the Constitutional Organic Act of General Rules for Public Administration. The Constitutional Tribunal of Chile remarked that the central bank as an autonomous institution of constitutional rank is ruled only by the constitution and its organic constitutional act. See *Control constitucionalidad "Ley Orgánica Constitucional de bases generales de la Administración del Estado"*, TC Chile, Sentencia Rol No. 39, 2 October 1986.

In 1989, the Constitutional Tribunal decided that the bank is not part of the public administration, see *Control constitucionalidad "Ley Orgánica Banco central de Chile"*, Control constitucionalidad "Ley Orgánica Banco central de Chile", TC Chile, Sentencia Rol No. 78, 20 September 1989.

In a further decision, the Chilean constitutional judges determined that any conflict among constitutionally autonomous institutions, such as the central bank vs. the general comptroller, cannot be solved by administrative authorities but by the competent court of justice. See *Control constitucionalidad ley que establece normas para resolver cuestiones de competencia entre autoridades administrativas*, TC Chile, Sentencia Rol No. 80, 22 September 22, 1989.

principles that rule every organism of the public administration. Among these principles is, for example, the attachment to the constitution, the goal of the common good and the responsibility of the state for the errors of the public administration. However, in consistency with earlier decisions, the Constitutional Tribunal pointed to Article 18 of the Organic Act as well as Article 2 of the bank's charter, indicating that the central bank's own organic charter alone lays out how the central bank is organized and how it operates.[180] According to Article 2 of the Constitutional Organic Law of the Central Bank of Chile, all other legal provisions for the public administration are excluded from ruling the central bank under any circumstances.[181]

As a consequence, in Chile there is no executive control of the central bank. The board controls and oversees the policies and regulations issued by the Central Bank of Chile.[182] The board also appoints the general auditor of the bank and the general council.[183] The general council performs the ex-ante control of the legality of the bank's policies and decisions.[184] The general auditor controls the bank's accounts, operations and administrative regulations and informs the board about them.[185]

In line with the autonomy of constitutional rank, the central bank in Peru is under the control of the General Comptroller, who is also an organ with constitutional autonomy. The General Comptroller receives information from the Chief of the Internal Control Unit. This internal bank official must oversee the central bank's budget, net worth accounting, use of funds and custody of securities.[186] Moreover, the Superintendency of Banks and Insurance, which also has autonomy of constitutional rank, oversees the bank in all matters related to the attachment to the law.[187]

Statutory autonomies as organs of the public administration are under the control of an institution prescribed in the statutes by the legislature. In line with its status, the Central Bank of Brazil is controlled by the Monetary Council, which is subordinated to the executive. There is no detail or clarification in the bank statutes.[188]

---

[180]*Control constitucionalidad enmienda "Ley General de Bancos"*, TC Chile, Sentencia Rol No. 216, 17 July 1995.

[181]CBCH Law Sec. 2: *"The Bank shall, with regard to its duties and powers, be governed exclusively by the provisions of this act and it shall not be bound for any legal purposes, by general or special provisions, present of future, enacted for the public sector."*

[182]CBCH Law Sec. 18 (2).

[183]CBCH Law Sec. 18 (4).

[184]CBCH Law Sec. 25 (1): *"Ensuring that all the decisions, resolutions and contracts entered into by the Bank comply with all the applicable legal provisions in force. To this end, he shall acquaint himself with all such matters and shall make his observations known to the Board, for which purpose he shall attend the meetings thereof with the right to be heard."*

[185]CBCH Law Sec. 26.

[186]CRBP Law Art. 95 in connection with Art. 87.

[187]CRBP Law Art. 96.

[188]According to the law, the National Monetary Council is supposed to follow guidelines of the President in performing its functions. See LSFN Brazil Art. 4.

Auditors appointed by the President, provide memorandums on income and the balance sheet of Argentina's central bank.[189] The financial statements of the Central Bank of the Argentine Republic are subject to external audits by firms chosen by the central bank board from an official list created by the board itself. The auditing firms can only serve for four consecutive periods. The auditing reports must be submitted to the executive and legislative branches.[190] Further, the budget and the expenses of the central bank are in the responsibility of the Argentine General Audit Office, which assists the Congress in controlling the public budget. This office must also ensure that the bank's board provides the required financial information to the external auditor within the term of 1 year.[191]

In Mexico, the statutes and constitution are silent concerning the performance of control and oversight.

5.3.3 Dismissal

One of the cornerstones of personal autonomy is that the president of a country cannot arbitrarily get rid of its authorities.[192] Causes of dismissal can be very different from one legal framework to another. Although dismissal should not easily be allowed,[193] accountability implies that mistakes or bad behavior should have consequences. To allow for accountability without trading off personal autonomy, reasons for dismissal of the members of a central bank board should be free of subjectivity and clearly stated in the law, or left out completely.[194] The reasons should be related to the performance of their functions—such as not contributing to the achievement of the central bank objectives,[195] great misconduct or negligence—or related to situations in which the dismissed member no longer fulfills the requirements to be a board member.[196]

The ideal dismissal arrangement entails a process that starts with the central bank's board. Ideally, the courts of justice, as impartial players, independent of politics, make the final decision.[197] This final decision of the courts of justice seems more necessary when the government is legally allowed to start the process of dismissal.[198] When the courts of justice are not put in charge of making the final

---

[189]BCRA Law Sec. 36.

[190]BCRA Law Sec. 39.

[191]BCRA Law Sec. 40.

[192]Vermuele (2013), p. 1168.

[193]Neumann (1991), p. 103.

[194]Jácome and Vásquez (2008), p. 799.

[195]De Haan and Eijffinger (2002), p. 403; see also Hasse (1990), p. 116.

[196]Lybek and Morris (2004), pp. 35–36.

[197]Smits (1997), pp. 156 and 163.

[198]Jácome (2001), p. 7.

decision, there should be a process in which the central bank board is involved and the executive and legislative branch, in a dual process, make the final decision.[199] However, if the central bank is part of the public administration, we'd expect the executive to play a greater role in the dismissal process, undermining autonomy.

The courts of justice play a role in the dismissal of the central bank's board members only in the case of the Central Bank of Chile. The Court of Appeals of Santiago is in charge of making the decision regarding the dismissal of a board member of the Central Bank of Chile when the President of the Republic, the president of the bank or at least two board members file an accusation.[200] Reasons for dismissal are (1) providing false information in the affidavit upon employment as board member about fulfilling requirements for board members;[201] (2) engaging in prohibited activities for central bank board members;[202] or (3) abusing the central bank board membership in order to get privileges for themselves or others.[203]

Chile's President, with the authorization of the Senate, can also dismiss a board member of the Central Bank of Chile when (1) at least three other board members accuse the member of not abiding by the rules of the board or complying with the board's policies[204] or (2) the board member approves policies or rules that go against the primary legal objective of the Bank and cause great harm to the country's economy.[205]

The reasons for dismissal of board members of the Bank of Mexico are clearly specified in the law. Among these reasons are the inability to perform their functions because of mental or physical illness; engaging in activities other than those allowed in the constitution (e.g., representation of the bank, university teaching or participation in nonprofit organizations); disrespecting the confidentiality of information or providing information that they know is false; and not fulfilling their duties or not attending sessions, among others.[206] The board itself has the authority to decide about the removal of a board member without the intervention of other state institutions. However, Mexico's president can inform the board about a cause for dismissal of one of the board members and ask for the member's removal.[207] The

---

[199]Jácome and Vásquez (2008), p. 799.

[200]CBCH Law Sec. 15.

[201]CBCH Law Sec. 14.

[202]The inabilities and prohibitions for the members of the board of the Central Bank of Chile are in CBCH Law Sec. 13.

[203]CBCH Law Sec.15 para 1.

[204]CBCH Law Sec.16 para 1.

[205]CBCH Law Sec.17 para 1.

[206]BM Law Art. 43.

[207]BM Law Art. 44: *"The Board of Governors is entitled to determine whether the conditions for removal mentioned in the previous article have been met upon request by the President of the Republic or by at least two members of the Board. The opinion will be obtained by a majority of votes from the members of the Board of Governors and after having granted him/her the right to a hearing, without his/her participation in the vote."*

board member affected by sanctions can file for reconsideration, revocation, change or suspension of the dismissal.[208]

The Constitution of Mexico allows central bank board members to be impeached for serious misconduct.[209] According to the Constitution, the Chamber of Deputies questions the suspects and can decide to forward an accusation to the Senate. After an audience, and with the approval of two-thirds of the present members of the Senate, a sanction will be applied. The sanction laid out in the Constitution is dismissal and the permanent removal of the ability to exercise any public function.[210]

For accountability purposes, the statutes prescribe that the Bank of Mexico is part of the public administration and, therefore, subject to the Federal Law of Administrative Liabilities of Public Officers.[211] The purpose of this law is to subject all public officials to a unified accountability system, in accordance with the Mexican constitution.[212] This law lists the public officials that are subject to administrative liability, the general responsibilities of public servants, their obligations, and provides detailed information about the processes and penalties.[213] The public officials are accountable to the internal controlling departments of the Secretariat of Government Services.[214]

Public officials must fulfill the obligations relevant to all public servants. Among these obligations are the performance of the service they are responsible to provide; efficient management of resources; good behavior in the performance of their job; abstaining from hiring disqualified people; abstaining from receiving extra benefits in addition to those associated with the performance of their job; and adherence to the laws, regulations and administrative provisions related to public service, among others.[215] Among the sanctions are warnings, suspension from the job for between 3 days and 1 year, removal from the position, monetary penalty and ineligibility from holding public jobs.[216]

Following decisions of Mexico's Supreme Court, these prescriptions in the statutes of the BM are in conflict with the constitutional rank of the autonomy of the BM. The Mexican Supreme Court has clarified that only statutory autonomies

---

[208]BM Law Art. 64. In addition, according to Internal Rules of the Bank of Mexico Art. 28 II, such a "motion of reconsideration" has to be issued by the Directorate of Legal Affairs of the Bank.

[209]Const. Mexico Art. 28 para 7. See also Const. Mexico Art. 110.

[210]Const. Mexico Art. 110 paras 3, 4, and 5.

[211]BM Law Art. 61. See also Federal Law of Administrative Liabilities of Public Officers Art. 49 [Official translation of the Ley Federal de Responsabilidades Administrativas de los Servidores Públicos, Gaceta Oficial de la Federación, 23 March 2002] [hereinafter LFRSP Mexico].

[212]Const. Mexico Art. 108.

[213]LFRSP Mexico Art. 1. See also LFRSP Mexico Arts. 20 and 21. The Government Secretariat controls, for example, the property of public officials and monitors the growth of officials' wealth and questions suspicious rises. See LFRSP Mexico Arts. 41 and 42.

[214]LFRSP Mexico Art. 12.

[215]LFRSP Mexico Art. 8 (I), (III), (VI), (X), (XIV), and (XXIV).

[216]LFRSP Mexico Art. 13.

are part of the organisms of the decentralized public administration, also known as *para-estatal* administration.[217] Even though the centralized and decentralized institutions are both part of the public administration, the Court explained that the main difference between them is that the centralized institutions have a direct link with the public administration, whereas there is only an indirect link between decentralized institutions and the public administration.[218] The Court specified that the decentralized public organs are part of the public administration, but not part of the executive branch, the federal states or municipalities, which are understood as the holders of political power.[219] Constitutional autonomies in Mexico are not part of the decentralized or *para-estatales* institutions. They are, according to the Court, organs that are supposed to develop state functions that the branches of the state shall not perform.[220]

In Peru, the institution in charge of dismissing the members of the bank's board is the Congress, shielding the central bank from the executive.[221] But the decision of dismissal must be made with the agreement of two-thirds of the board members.[222] The Constitution of Peru prescribes that the board members of the Central Reserve Bank of Peru can be dismissed because of serious misconduct[223] such as committing a crime. A board member accused of a crime must first face Congress before facing the courts of justice and potentially being removed from the board.[224] Other serious misconduct includes granting credits that are not allowed in the law. This form of misconduct may include giving loans to the state in any way other than by purchasing treasury bonds in the secondary market;[225] providing loans to financial institutions that have not serviced their debt with the bank;[226] or giving loans to the board members.[227] The law also mentions that when one of the members does not attend four sessions in a row or six sessions within 6 months that member's position is

---

[217] *Inversora Bursátil, S.A.*, Amparo, SCJN México, Sentencia 2a. XV, Tomo XV, March 2002, p. 430.

[218] Jurisprudencia: Procurador General de la República, Acción de Inconstitucionalidad, Supreme Court of Justice of the Nation of Mexico [Suprema Corte de Justicia de la Nación de México], Sentencia P./J. 97, Tomo XX, September 2004, p. 809.

[219] *Banco Inbursa, S.A. and others*, Amparo, SCJN México, Sentencia 2a. CCXXIV, Tomo XIV, December 2001.

[220] *Municipio de Guadalajara, Estado de Jalisco*, Controversia Constitucional, SCJN México, Sentencia P. VIII, Tomo XXVII, February 2008, p. 1868.

[221] CRBP Law Art. 9.

[222] CRBP Law Art. 20.

[223] Const. Peru Art. 86; see also CRBP Law Art. 20.

[224] CRBP Law Art. 22. See also Const. Peru Art. 100 that describes the process of dismissal to follow in Congress.

[225] The Peruvian central bank is only allowed to buy securities issued by the Treasury in the secondary market, according to CRBP Law Art. 61.

[226] CRBP Law Art. 78.

[227] CRBP Law Art. 79.

vacated and subsequently opened. The only exception is when a board member is sick, but for no more than 3 months.[228]

Although Colombia's central bank is considered autonomous by the constitution, it is also considered part of the public administration. In line with the latter status, the President of Colombia and the state's prosecutor are responsible for conducting administrative investigations and to enforce discipline on the members of the board of the central bank.[229] The President of Colombia can dismiss and replace the board members of the Bank of the Republic because of unjustified absence from two board meetings,[230] misconduct and a lack of work ethics.[231]

The central bank's board members are also subject to the accountability regime established in the Single Disciplinary Code of Colombia.[232] The Single Disciplinary Code lays out the disciplinary offenses, processes and sanctions applied to all public authorities. A disciplinary offense is defined as the non-fulfillment of the public servant's duties, overstepping the scope of functions and violations to rules concerning prohibitions and conflicts of interest regulation.[233]

Consistent with the statutory autonomy of the central banks in Argentina and Brazil, the executive has broad powers in deciding about the dismissal of the central

---

[228]CRBP Law Art. 17 (e).

[229]BRC Act Art. 46.

[230]BRC Act Art. 35.

[231]BRC Act Art. 30 (b).

[232]Single Disciplinary Code of Colombia Art. 53 [Código Disciplinario Ùnico, Diario Oficial 44699, 4 February 2002] [hereinafter CDU].

[233]CDU Art. 23. In addition, according to the Single Disciplinary Code, offenses can be very serious, serious or slight. See CDU Art. 42.

Very serious offenses are those committed either deliberately or because of negligence. These include committing a crime; performing functions in spite of knowing about the possible existence of prohibitions; engaging in areas with conflicts of interest established in the constitution and the law; disregarding the instructions and guidelines established by the President of the Republic and the entities in charge of control, inspection and surveillance; misappropriation of public resources, offering gifts in exchange for personal benefits or not denouncing other officials who do so; performing one's functions in order to achieve different goals from those established in the law; overextending one's functions. See CDU Art. 55 (1) through (8).

Blocking the investigation of control organs and not providing information to the Congress when required for political control; unjust enrichment; unjustified investment of public resources in a way that does not guarantee the stability and liquidity of the market; hiding or manipulating data; and unjustified abandonment of office, among others, see CDU Art. 48 (2), (3), (27), (43), and (55).

Very serious offenses are sanctioned either with economic penalties, dismissal, or a prohibition from working in the public sector for 1–20 years. See CDU Art. 56.

In contrast to very serious offenses, serious and slight offenses are not detailed in the Single Disciplinary Code. The code only mentions the non-fulfilment of duties, abuse of rights, overreach of functions and violations of prohibitions as serious and slight offenses. The punishment is either a written warning or an economic penalty. See CDU Art. 44 (4) and (5).

The state's prosecutor office must evaluate the degree of culpability, the nature of the functions, the degree of damage to the goals of the public institution, the hierarchy of the public official, the social impact of the offense, the circumstances under which the offense took place, the reasons for the offense and whether the offense was committed by more than one person. See CDU Art. 43.

bank board members. In the case of Argentina's central bank, the President of the country can remove the members of the central bank board after receiving the advice of a commission of the Senate. The term *advice* (*consejo* in Spanish) refers to an opinion about how something should be done.[234] Advice is not the same as *approval*, i.e., granting permission.[235] Thus, the advice of the Senate is not binding for Argentina's President. The reasons for dismissal of board members are not fulfilling the rules established in the central bank statutes, becoming part of the government or the financial sector, or misconduct.[236] Moreover, the law of ethics applicable to all public officials adds that not fulfilling the duties of the public officials is a reason for dismissal.[237]

The board members of the Central Bank of Brazil can be dismissed *ad nutum*, which means immediately and at discretion, though it is not clear whether this refers to the discretion of the President of the Republic or the Senate.[238] The president of the National Monetary Council of Brazil is considered responsible for the decisions taken by the organism.[239]

5.3.4 Transparency and Public Scrutiny

Although central banks are not electorally accountable, the decisions of the central bank must be communicated to the public, making it possible to hold the central bank publicly accountable through the constant public exposure of its work.[240] The communication of central bank policies and decisions to the public allows other authorities and the public to scrutinize the fulfilment of the central bank's mandate.[241]

The publication of central bank statistics and other technical information should provide the public with information on policies and the rationale of these policies, increasing transparency of the central bank. Publishing central bank information also has the advantage to give the central bank board an opportunity to inform about potential conflicts with, for example, the government.[242] In this sense,

---

[234] *Cambridge Dictionaries Online*, Definition of *Advice*.

[235] *Cambridge Dictionaries Online*, Definition of *Approval*.

[236] The law prescribes that one of the reasons for dismissal of the board members is to fall within some ineligibility criteria. See BCRA Law Sec. 9. The reasons why a person cannot be a board member of the Argentinean central bank are specified in BCRA Law Sec. 8.

[237] Law of Ethics of the Public Function of Argentina Art. 2 [Ley de Ética de la Función Públicos, Boletín Oficial, 1 November 1999].

[238] RIBC Brazil Art. 5.

[239] LSFN Brazil Art. 5.

[240] Siklos and Sturm (2013), p. 1.

[241] Smits (1997), pp. 169–170.

[242] Bernhard (1998), p. 315.

communicating policy to the public can increase subjective legal certainty because people get a better idea of whether the central bank is following its mandate.[243]

The central bank laws of the six central banks analyzed differ greatly in their prescriptions to inform the public via publications on central bank decisions and policies. Some central banks do not have clear publication prescriptions. The statutes of the Brazilian monetary authority do not mention any provision concerning publication. Mexican central bank law demands that the central bank should coordinate with other authorities regarding the information and publication of economic and financial statistics.[244]

By contrast, the Central Bank of Chile has to publish decisions related to reserves, regulations, interest rates, foreign exchange transactions, restrictions on the exchange market, permitted exchange market operations, remittance payments and limits to bank holdings in the country and abroad.[245] The statutes of Chile's central bank further prescribe that the bank must publish technical information, including the daily exchange rate[246] and macro-economic statistics.[247]

According to Art. 3 of the charter of the Argentinean central bank, the bank is legally obliged to publish its monetary plan for the next period. This information must include the inflation target for the year. Every 3 months, the central bank must inform the public about changes or updates that have been made relative to their initial announcement as well as about the causes for those changes.[248] On its website, the bank provides reports about the state of the monetary, financial and exchange policy.

Since 2001, also the Peruvian central bank publishes its annual plan for monetary policy.[249] Further, the Central Reserve Bank of Peru is in charge of informing the public about the state of the finances and publishing macroeconomic statistics. The Bank also receives information from private and public institutions.[250]

The statutes of the Colombian central bank demand that its financial statement is "published in a nationwide circulating newspaper".[251]

---

[243]De Gregorio (2009), p. 7.

[244]BM Law Art. 62 (I).

[245]CBCH Law Sec. 67 para 1.

[246]CBCH Law Sec. 44 para 2.

[247]CBCH Law Sec. 53 para 1.

[248]BCRA Law Sec. 42.

[249]Information on the monetary program of the Central Bank of Reserve of Peru may be found at: http://www.bcrp.gob.pe/politica-monetaria.html.

[250]CRBP Law Art. 74 para 1.

[251]BRC Act Art. 27 (7).

5.4 Operational Autonomy and Economic Policy Coordination

5.4.1 Operational Autonomy

Most central banks are not free to choose their objectives but rather are subject to the objectives stated in the law.[252] They are autonomous in the sense that they have leeway to perform central bank operations available to pursue the banks' legal objectives.[253] For a central bank to have operational autonomy, the central bank should have the authority in using its instruments, for instance setting policy interest rates, intervening in foreign exchange markets, engaging in open market operations or determining required reserves, to reach the central bank objectives.[254]

In some cases, operational autonomy is rooted in the historical evolution of the bank and common practice, as in the case of the Federal Reserve. In other cases, operational autonomy is specified in the law,[255] as in the case of the ECB, the Bank of Japan, the Bank of England,[256] and the central banks in Latin America. The law should provide the central bank with legal guarantees to operate free from government intervention directly or indirectly.

The indirect guarantees include embedding central bank autonomy in the constitution or organic law instead of ordinary laws and giving the central bank a clear objective. However, central banks whose autonomy is embedded in statutes do not necessarily have a lower degree of operational autonomy than those whose autonomy is embedded in the constitution. Although central banks with autonomy of constitutional rank should, in principle, have full or almost full authority to decide about monetary policy and exchange rate instruments because they are neither subsidiary nor assisting the executive, as other organs of public administration do, they are, however, obliged to coordinate with other state institutions which may represent a limit to their autonomy.[257]

Therefore, the law can provide direct guarantees by giving central banks the exclusive authority over the operations and limiting the means to coordinate central bank policies with the general economic policies of the government as well as the government influence on central bank policies.

---

[252]Lastra (2015), p. 73.

[253]Quintyn and Taylor (2002), p. 202; see also Jácome (2001), p. 7. See also Hasse (1990), p. 117.

[254]Apel (2007), p. 41; see also Jácome (2001), pp. 7–11.

[255]When operational central bank independence is specified in the legal frameworks, the law can either be very specific and leave little room for central bankers' discretion or give more leeway to the central bank to choose measures. For instance, in case of emergency, broader discretion is regarded as positive to allow for a fast reaction. In times of financial unrest, strict legal rules in regard the operations of the central bank would require a complicated process of amendment. See Smits (1997), p. 157; see also Quintyn and Taylor (2002), pp. 14–16.

[256]Buiter (2004), pp. 260–261.

[257]Zúñiga (2007), p. 237.

5.4.2   Personal Autonomy and Operational Autonomy

Providing personal autonomy is a guarantee for operational autonomy. A lack of personal autonomy as well as unclear dismissal procedures can affect operational autonomy. If the president of a country, like in the countries analyzed, appoints board members or there is room to dismiss board members when their decisions deviate from those preferred by government, operational autonomy is in danger. Having a government representative in the central bank board who can directly influence policies or decide conflicts with operational autonomy.

Although linkages between central banks with, for example, a ministry of finance may help improve coordination with the government,[258] a central bank's operational autonomy is in danger when the executive can nudge central bank policies in favor of government policies. Therefore, the presence of the minister of finance on the central bank board, actively deciding policy, conflicts with both personal autonomy and operational autonomy, suggesting that central bank decisions are not free of government influence.[259]

Except for Peru, the Minister of Finance is present in the central bank boards of the countries analyzed. The statutes prescribe that the Argentinean and Mexican Ministers of Finance must be invited to attend to the meetings of the board.[260] They do not have the right to vote but their proposals must be heard, which may be considered a mean of coordination. In Chile, the Minister of Finance can suspend resolutions of the board for 15 days unless the board unanimously opposes the minister's decision.[261]

Most troublesome in terms of operational autonomy, in Colombia the Minister of Finance is one of the seven members and president of the central bank board.[262] Qualifying this point, the presence of the Minister of Finance on the central bank board may, however, also have positive side-effects, in preserving the central bank's reputation in case of unpopular decisions. The former Minister of Finance of Colombia, *Guillermo Perry*, remarked in this regard,

> When there is an excessively restrictive monetary policy that increases interest rates in an inconvenient moment, public opinion will blame the Government even though the decision had been made by the board of the Central Bank with a negative vote of the Minister [Own Translation].[263]

Thus, there may be a case for having the Minister of Finance present at board meetings with voice but not with vote to shield the central bank from an overly harsh public when decisions are made to reach objectives and help the coordination of

---

[258]Smits (1997), p. 169.

[259]Valencia (1998), p. 28.

[260]BCRA Law Sec. 12 para 2; see also BM Law Art. 45 para 3.

[261]CBCH Law Sec. 19.

[262]Const. Colombia Art. 372.

[263]Kalmanovitz (2000), p. 7.

government and central bank policies via communication.[264] Similarly, a central bank board member could be present in meetings of other policy organs to communicate views.[265]

Moreover, the National Monetary Council of Brazil includes the Minister of Finance as president, the Minister of Planning and the president of Brazil's central bank who is appointed by Brazil's President.[266]

5.4.3 Instrument Autonomy and Coordination

To allow for both operational autonomy and coordination with other state organs, the central bank must know which instruments are at its disposal to reach its objectives (and what the central bank cannot do). For example, the Bundesbank charter of 1957 is very straightforward in defining these instruments. Paragraph 3 summarizes the objectives of the Bundesbank as preserving the value of the currency and the stability and functioning of the payment system. The same paragraph mentions that the bank can reach these objectives using so-called *Währungspolitische Befugnisse*, i.e. monetary powers. Section 4, §§ 14–18 then provide a detailed description of these monetary powers, listing the main monetary policy instruments as well as functions necessary to reach the goals. Section 5 provides a closer description of the transactions the bank can engage in.[267]

Clear rules are also necessary in terms of coordination with other state branches. In this regard, different central bank objectives may require different operations, as well as diverse means of coordination with the government. For instance, while central banks employ instruments to reach price and monetary stability, contributing to economic development may also be considered a responsibility of government. Moreover, to be able to achieve the objective of financial stability central banks tend to have provisions to act as lender of last resort. To reach the financial stability objective and guarantee operational autonomy, the central bank needs clear rules regarding the performance of the lender of last resort,[268] which lay out the conditions and process for the central bank to rescue distressed financial institutions. To balance

---

[264]Jácome (2001), p. 18.

[265]Massad (1989), p. 89.

[266]Real Plan Law Art. 8 [Lei do Plano Real, Diário Oficial da União - Seção 1, 30 June 1995].

[267]§14 and §18 des Gesetzes über die Deutsche Bundesbank von 30. Juli 1957, p. 746.

[268]Central banks must act as the lender of last resort when there is a danger of systemic risk and an unexpected shock limits the capability of banking institutions to honor their liabilities. See Calomiris and Meltzer (2016), p. 1.

Banking panic can take place in a banking system in which a bank makes investments and gives credit with funds of the depositors and keeps a fraction as reserve. See Bordo (2014), p. 127. It is enough that one banking institution fails at giving bank deposits to depositors to trigger people's mistrust on the capability of other banks to do the same. The consequence is a massive withdrawal of deposits, known as bank panic. *Ibid.*, p. 127.

the need for coordination, for example when financial stability is threatened, and the importance of operational autonomy, legal rules should lay out the relationship between the central bank and other economic policy organs.[269]

Walter Bagehot, who believed that the unnatural existence of central banks has caused problems in markets in the first place,[270] proposed some rules a lender of last resort should follow to prevent its overuse and provide stability in markets, assuming that ending central banking is not a realistic option. According to Bagehot's rules, which are still considered a benchmark today,[271] central banks should provide loans freely and at high penalty interest rates against good assets, which function as collateral, to distressed financial institutions to promote financial stability.[272] Note that loans must be limited and oriented to help institutions with liquidity problems

---

To prevent the contagion of one failing bank to others, the central banks must be ready to lend to financial institutions to assure they have sufficient reserves. See Mishkin (2007), p. 381.

Injecting central bank liquidity would prevent financial institutions from non-payment of their debt and would guarantee the operation of capital markets. The existence of the discounting facility can prevent a systemic financial panic, but its main goals in to be a reactive measure. See Schwarcz (2008), p. 225.

Even though the lender of last resort can be successful at preventing financial crisis in developing countries, it is not the same case in countries with a weak institutional setting, for instance, developing countries. Countries with a weak institution in which most debt is denominated in foreign currency that have a history of high inflation may be unable to use this mechanism to prevent financial crisis. See Mishkin (1996), pp. 36–37.

[269]Quintyn and Taylor (2002), p. 32.

[270]Bagehot (1873), p. 32.

[271]Hogan et al. (2015), p. 333.

[272]In particular, Bagehot writes: *"Nothing, therefore, can be more certain than that the Bank of England has in this respect no peculiar privilege; that it is simply in the position of a Bank keeping the Banking reserve of the country; that it must in time of panic do what all other similar banks must do; that in time of panic it must advance freely and vigorously to the public out of the reserve. And with the Bank of England, as with other Banks in the same case, these advances, if they are to be made at all, should be made so as if possible, to obtain the object for which they are made. The end is to stay the panic; and the advances should, if possible, stay the panic. And for this purpose, there are two rules: First. That these loans should only be made at a very high rate of interest. This will operate as a heavy fine on unreasonable timidity and will prevent the greatest number of applications by persons who do not require it. The rate should be raised early in the panic, so that the fine may be paid early; that no one may borrow out of idle precaution without paying well for it; that the Banking reserve may be protected as far as possible. Secondly. That at this rate these advances should be made on all good banking securities, and as largely as the public ask for them. The reason is plain. The object is to stay alarm, and nothing therefore should be done to cause alarm. But the way to cause alarm is to refuse someone who has good security to offer. The news of this will spread in an instant through all the money market at a moment of terror; no one can say exactly who carries it, but in half an hour it will be carried on all sides, and will intensify the terror everywhere. No advances indeed need be made by which the Bank will ultimately lose. The amount of bad business in commercial countries is an infinitesimally small fraction of the whole business. That in a panic the bank, or banks, holding the ultimate reserve should refuse bad bills or bad securities will not make the panic really worse; the 'unsound' people are a feeble minority, and they are afraid even to look frightened for fear their unsoundness may be detected."* Bagehot (1873), pp. 96–97.

rather than financial institutions that are insolvent. Although the bank should announce the policy to provide sufficient funds in times of distress, it must have discretion in providing liquidity to those that match the criteria.[273] To promote legal certainty, these requirements should be specified in legal rules that allow the market participants to know what to expect.[274] In this regard, the mentioned guidelines for a lender of last resort do not only suggest how to react to turbulence. The guidelines are also indicative of the preventive function of clear rules for a lender of last resort. Clear rules promote better banking practices. They might restraint banks from taking unnecessary risks and provide an incentive to banks to hold an adequate level of reserves that would provide liquidity in case of a crisis as it is, first, not cheap to be in need of liquidity from the lender of last resort and, second, not guaranteed. Only illiquid, not insolvent, banks will be supported.[275] The statutes of the six Latin American central banks provide the banks with several instruments to achieve the main objectives.[276] They prescribe a number of functions and limits to the use of instruments. The degree of instrument autonomy is rather high in Peru, Mexico and Chile. When it comes to Colombia's, Argentina's and Brazil's monetary authorities, the law does not provide much certainty concerning instrument autonomy.

5.4.3.1 Peru

The Central Reserve Bank of Peru has one objective. It shall preserve monetary stability. The bank's functions are to manage the money supply and reserves, to issues notes and to provide financial statements and reports.[277] The statutes grant the central bank several duties and powers. Art. 24 of the central bank charter lists that the board shall, for example, formulate monetary policy, regulate credit conditions, regulate operations between banks[278] and administer the bank's international reserves. The powers are further specified in Arts. 42 et seq. To implement monetary policy the bank can, e.g., use open market operations,[279] buy foreign currencies,[280]

---

[273]Calomiris et al. (2016), p. 48.

[274]Calomiris et al. (2016), pp. 52–53; see also Bordo (2014), p. 127.

[275]Calomiris and Meltzer (2016), pp. 1–2.

[276]Monetary policy instruments are used to achieve primary objectives of central banks. The ECB's main monetary policy instruments are open market operations, minimum reserve requirements and standing facilities. See the website for an explanation:
  https://www.ecb.europa.eu/mopo/implement/html/index.en.html.

[277]Const. Peru Art. 84 para 2; see also CRBP Law Art. 2.

[278]CRBP Law Art. 24.

[279]CRBP Law Art. 62.

[280]CRBP Law Art. 66.

regulate interest rates[281] or set reserve requirements.[282] The Central Reserve Bank of Peru is the representative of the country at international organizations[283] and may be agent of the government to deal with multilateral credit institutions and financial entities of foreign governments.[284]

The law also sets limits to the operations of the Central Reserve Bank of Peru. The monetary operations of the central bank must preserve the financial autonomy of the bank. In particular, the bank is forbidden to grant financing to the state,[285] to provide loans to a financial institution that has not serviced its debt with the bank,[286] or to purchase shares,[287] among other prohibitions in the law.[288]

Preserving the health of the financial system is not an explicit objective of the Peruvian central bank. The law clarifies that the loans given by the central bank to financial institutions have the purpose to regulate monetary affairs.[289] Loans must fulfill several requirements including a thirty-day term limit and the need for good collateral to guarantee loans.[290] As demanded by *Bagehot*, liquidity is not provided against bad collateral. The bank makes clear that holding foreign reserves as well as foreign-currency deposits of banks serves the purpose to prevent liquidity problems in case of a withdrawal of funds. In this sense, the central bank explicitly acts as a lender of last resort.[291] Liquidity and external drain problems seem to be the main cause to provide lender of last resort support.

5.4.3.2　Colombia

When it comes to operational autonomy of the Colombian central bank in achieving its main objective, which is currency stability,[292] the law is much more restrictive

---

[281]However, the CRBP Law Art. 52 sets forth that *"the interest rates charged by the entities of the financial system for their operations be determined by free competition. Exceptionally, the Bank is empowered to fix maximum and minimum interest rates with the purpose of regulating the market."*

[282]CRBP Law Arts. 53 and 54.

[283]CRBP Law Art. 69.

[284]CRBP Law Art. 70.

[285]CRBP Law Art. 61; see also CRBP Law Art. 77.

[286]CRBP Law Art. 78.

[287]According to CRBP Law Art. 84, the central bank can only buy the shares *"issued by international financing organizations or those that are necessary for the rehabilitation of banking or financial institutions [. . .]."*

[288]CRBP Law Arts. 80, 81, 82, and 83.

[289]According to Law CRBP Peru Art. 58, the financial institutions that receive central bank financing must go under the Surveillance Regime established by the General Law of Banking, Financial and Insurance Institutions.

[290]CRBP Law Art. 59.

[291]Monetary Program of the BCRP. See http://www.bcrp.gob.pe/about-the-bcrp/frequently-asked-questions.html.

[292]Const. Colombia Art. 373.

than that of Peru, potentially undermining autonomy all together. The Bank of the Republic of Colombia has the legal attribution of being the monetary, exchange and credit authority. The Bank of the Republic is in charge of ensuring the "liquidity of the financial market and the normal operation of the internal and external payments of the national economy, taking care of the stability of the value of the currency."[293]

At first sight, it seems like the bank has substantial instrument autonomy. The bank manages, invests, stores and, in general, decides about international reserves.[294] Article 16 of the statutes lists the powers of the bank as well as its instruments. To provide liquidity to the financial system the bank can use open market operations,[295] manage inter-banking credit and determine liquidity requirements,[296] among others. Under exceptional circumstances, the bank can, for instance, limit the growth of bank portfolios and set maximum interest rates banks are allowed to charge.[297] The bank further determines conditions for public institutions to sell and buy securities[298] and establishes the method to calculate appropriate mortgage loan rates for the public mortgage loan system.[299]

However broad these powers seem; the Bank of the Republic of Colombia does not perform its operations autonomously. The Constitutional Court of Colombia has laid out that even though the bank is autonomous from the executive, it is part of the state. Therefore, according to the Court, the bank must contribute to the development plan established by the government.[300]

The statutes are also very detailed in setting the limits to operational autonomy, which are untypical for central banks with constitutional autonomy but in line with the notion that the central bank is part of the public administration. For example, the inflation targets the bank uses to anchor inflation expectations should always be lower than the last registered results.[301] Moreover, the Bank of the Republic must decide on the exchange rate regime with the Minister of Finance,[302] and every operation must be coordinated with the National Council of Economic and Social Policy (CONPES),[303] which is the highest planning authority of the government.[304] The bank even performs some functions on behalf of the government as long as they

---

[293]BRC Act Art. 16.

[294]BRC Act Art. 14.

[295]BRC Act Art. 16 (b).

[296]BRC Act Art. 16 (g).

[297]BRC Act Art. 16 (d) and (e).

[298]BRC Act Art. 16 (c).

[299]BRC Act Art. 16 (f).

[300]CCC, Judgment of 7 July 1999.

[301]BRC Act Art. 2 para 2.

[302]BRC Act Art.16 (i): "[. . .] *In case of a disagreement, the State's constitutional responsibility to see to the maintenance of the acquisitive capacity of the currency shall prevail.*"

[303]Specifically, the BRC Act Art. 4 states that the Bank of the Republic must perform its functions in agreement with CONPES' macroeconomic program.

[304]Departamento Nacional de Planeación: http://www.dnp.gov.co.

do not contradict the main objectives of the bank, including being the fiscal agent of the state. The Bank of the Republic may also receive state deposits under the conditions established by the board and issue, allocate and manage public debt securities.[305] The Bank of the Republic further represents Colombia at international financial institutions.[306]

The rules for the lender of last resort, established in the organic law, are rather unspecific. The Organic Law of the Bank of the Republic only states that the Colombian central bank can offer liquidity, credit lines and financial trust services to distressed public and private financial institutions. However, it says nothing about either the amount that can be lent, the terms for repayment or the guarantees of the loans.[307]

5.4.3.3   Chile

The Central Bank of Chile is the monetary, credit and exchange authority of the country. It must ensure "the stability of the currency" it issues and preserve the "normal functioning of internal and external payment systems".[308] To achieve these objectives, the bank's board is, according to the law, in charge of deciding the general policies and rules of the bank that will guide the performance of the bank's operations.[309] The Central Bank of Chile has the exclusive attribution of interpreting its own decisions, resolutions and regulations.[310] The Constitutional Organic Law of the Central Bank of Chile is categorical in regard to the binding nature of the decisions and policies of the bank over other state organs,[311] suggesting a high degree of operational autonomy.

Art. 34 of the Constitutional Organic Law of the Central Bank of Chile describes the main instruments at its disposal. The bank can use open market operations to provide liquidity, set interest rates, determine required reserves for financial institutions and open credit lines to financial institutions to reach its objectives.[312] Art. 35 summarizes the bank's powers in financial regulation. The bank can, for example, set the terms and conditions under which financial institutions may be "borrowing from the public".[313] The bank can also authorize banks "to pay interest on banking

---

[305]BRC Act Art. 13 (a), (c), and (d).

[306]BRC Act Art. 15.

[307]BRC Act Art. 12.

[308]CBCH Law Sec. 3.

[309]CBCH Law Sec. 18 (3).

[310]According to CBCH Law Sec. 83, the Chilean central bank exercises this competence "[...] *without prejudice of the legal competence of the courts of law.*"

[311]CBCH Law Sec. 82 para 1.

[312]CBCH Law Sec. 34 (1), (2), (5), and (7).

[313]CBCH Law Sec. 35 (1).

accounts",[314] establish the limits for interest rates on demand deposits,[315] and "regulate the functioning of clearinghouses".[316] Moreover, the Central Bank of Chile (CBCH) also regulates all aspects related to the formal exchange market. The bank is free to decide what foreign exchange operations can take place only in the formal market and has oversight to ensure that the values of export goods and services, commercial activities, transport, and technical assistance are the same as their value in international markets.[317]

The Organic Law gives the central bank the function to act as lender of last resort. To guarantee financial stability and stem liquidity problems the bank can provide credit for 90 days to distressed financial institutions. After that period, it is possible to renew the loans only with the approval of a majority of members of the central bank board and with a favorable report of the Superintendence of Banking and Financial Institutions. The law of the Central Bank of Chile does not specify guarantees for the loans given by the bank but does grant leeway to the institution to establish extra conditions to grant the loans.[318]

Like Colombia's central bank, the Central Bank of Chile is the fiscal agent of the state, whenever this function does not contradict the main goals of the central bank. The bank is in charge in all matters related to the servicing and renegotiation of external debt.[319] The Central Bank of Chile represents the government of Chile in international organizations. Furthermore, the bank can grant credit to foreign governments and central banks, if doing so contributes to the achievement of the bank's objective to maintain, manage and use international reserves.[320]

The law establishes two limits to the performance of the central bank's operations. First, in regard to the interpretations of the bank's decisions, resolutions and regulations, the law says that the only state organ authorized to overrule these interpretations are the courts of justice.[321] Second, in regard to the other functions of the Central Bank of Chile, the bank must take into account the government policies.[322]

5.4.3.4 Mexico

The main objective of the Bank of Mexico is to ensure the purchasing power of the Mexican peso which the bank issues. Preserving the health of the financial system

---

[314]CBCH Law Sec. 35 (2).

[315]CBCH Law Sec. 35 (4).

[316]CBCH Law Sec. 35 (8).

[317]For more detail about the bank's foreign exchange policy, see CBCH Law Sec. 42.

[318]CBCH Law Sec. 36 (1).

[319]CBCH Law Sec. 37.

[320]CBCH Law Sec. 38 (5).

[321]CBCH Law Sec. 83.

[322]CBCH Law Sec. 6 para 2.

and the proper functioning of the payments system are secondary purposes of the bank stated only in the central bank statutes.[323] Art. 3 of the Law of the Bank of Mexico lists the functions of the bank[324] and Art. 46 outlines the specific powers of the central bank board.[325]

The Law of the Bank of Mexico summarizes the instruments the bank may use to reach its objective in Art. 7. The bank may deal with securities, provide credit to credit institutions or the government, receive credit from important financial institutions or international organizations, deposit money at financial institutions, issue bonds, receive deposits, or use repurchase agreements (repos) in foreign exchange matters.

To preserve the stability of the financial system, the Mexican central bank is supposed to regulate intermediation and financial services,[326] including the fees, interest rates and prices of financial transactions. The performance of these functions must be carried out according to the Financial Services Transparency and Regulation Law. Considering the opinions of the National Banking and Securities Commission, the National Commission for the Protection for Users of Financial Services or the Federal Antitrust Commission is also required.[327] The Bank of Mexico also acts as the lender of last resort for financial institutions.[328] But the statutes do not mention any conditions for providing last resort financing. All what the statutes require is that financial institutions that receive central bank loans must provide some guarantee.[329] This broad rule leaves room to speculate regarding the rules for providing loans. As in the case of Colombia and Chile, the rules for the lender of last resort function are not specified.

The Bank of Mexico can act as the fiscal agent of the state.[330] The bank is the only institution allowed to issue, buy, sell and service government debt on behalf of the government.[331] The function as fiscal agent of the state may undermine operational autonomy. If government bonds do not sell well in the market, the central bank may

---

[323]Const. Mexico Art. 28; see also BM Law Art. 2.

[324]According to the BM Law Art. 3, the Mexican central bank has six functions: First, to regulate and issue the currency as well as foreign exchange and the payment system. Second, to be the lender of last resort for banks. Third, to be the government's fiscal agent. Fourth, to provide advice to the government. Fifth, participate in meetings of international organizations such as the International Monetary Fund. And sixth, cooperate with other institutions.

[325]BM Law Art. 46.

[326]BM Law Art. 3 (I); see also BM Law Art. 24.

[327]BM Law Art. 26 para 2.

[328]BM Law Art. 3 (II).

[329]BM Law Art. 16 states that *"[f]inancing granted by Banco de México to credit institutions shall be guaranteed by deposits of money and securities that said institutions have at the Central Bank. As the aforementioned financing becomes due, the Bank is entitled to charge the corresponding amounts to the accounts in which the money deposits have been recorded."*

[330]According to the law, the Bank of Mexico can also provide Treasury Services. See BM Law Art. 3 (III).

[331]BM Law Art. 10.

be forced to buy securities back as they are issued to fulfill this function even if this is in conflict with monetary policy objectives.[332]

The international reserves held by the Bank of Mexico should contribute to preserving the purchasing power of the currency by balancing in- and outflows of foreign exchange.[333] The statutes prescribe that the Bank of Mexico must, for as long as possible, maintain the real value of its own capital plus its liquid reserves. The law further establishes that the bank needs approval form the Minister of Finance for the management of its reserves.[334] According to the law, in every foreign exchange operation, the bank has to follow the guidelines of a so-called Exchange Commission, which includes three officials of the Ministry of Finance and three members of the Bank's board, including the governor of the bank.[335] The Minister of Finance, who is president of the Commission, makes the final decision in the event of a tie.[336]

5.4.3.5   Argentina

The statutes of the Argentinean and Brazilian monetary authorities guarantee little operational autonomy. In Argentina, the legal rank of the central bank as well as its objectives imply a need for coordination with government policies.

The State Attorney of Argentina clarifies that any autarchy, which is also the status of the central bank, is part of the country's public administration. Because the executive branch is at the top of the hierarchy of the public administration, the State Attorney suggests that this hierarchy implies a subordination of all autarchies under the executive to assure a *unity of action* of all institutions that are part of the public administration.[337]

However, Section 1 of the Organic Charter of the Central Bank of the Argentine Republic exempts the bank from general regulations of the public administration whenever these regulations interfere with the bank's mission. Moreover, the law also states that the central bank is not subject to orders or guidelines of the executive branch unless the National Congress gives its authorization.[338] Section 3 further states that the bank is supposed to work toward reaching its objectives, constrained

---

[332]Note that, however, it is not unusual that a central bank issues bonds. The Bundesbank did so as well, see Sec. 5 § 20 (2) des Gesetzes über die Deutsche Bundesbank von 30. Juli 1957, p. 745.

[333]BM Law Art. 18.

[334]BM Law Art. 53.

[335]BM Law Art. 21.

[336]According to BM Law Art. 21, "[s]*essions of the Commission shall be presided by the Ministry of Finance, in case of his absence by the Governor of the Bank of Mexico, and in absence of both by the secretary appointed by the head of the Ministry. Who presides the meeting will have the deciding vote in case of a tie.*"

[337]General Procuration of the National Treasury of Argentina [Procuracion del Tesoro de la Nación Dictamen 178/2012 – Tomo 282, 20 July 2012].

[338]BCRA Law Sec. 1 in combination with BCRA Law Sec. 4.

by the powers given to the bank and within the government's policy framework.[339] Thus, developing policies in line with the directions of the government is not perceived to interfere with the bank's mission.

In addition to the position of the central bank within the public administration, the objectives of the central bank suggest a need for coordination. Section 3 of the statutes of the Argentinean central bank lists several objectives without clear priority order, namely "monetary and financial stability, employment, and economic development with social equality."[340] Employment or social equality can hardly be reached by central bank policy alone.

To reach these objectives, Section 4 of the statutes gives the bank several powers. The bank regulates the payment system, the financial system, money, credit and interest rates in the economy. It is also a "financial agent for the National Government".[341] Section 14 summarizes the duties of the central bank board, which includes setting interest rates, the conditions on lending as well as deciding on reserve requirements. These sections do not differ much from those of other banks.

The operations of the bank are clarified further in Chapter V, Sections 17 to 27. Section 17 lists the issuance of currency and ways to mitigate liquidity problems by loans from the central bank, thus describing its functions as lender of last resort. The Central Bank of the Argentine Republic can assist a financial institution with funds up to "the value of its assets" if it is temporarily illiquid.[342] As guarantees the bank accepts government bonds and other securities.[343] To promote productive investment the law suggests that the central bank can only make advances to financial institutions if they have the required collateral.[344]

The Superintendence of Financial and Exchange Institutions is a sub-department of the Central Bank of the Argentine Republic that supervises the financial system.[345] It is, for example, in charge of rating financial institutions, canceling authorization to perform exchange operations, approving financial institutions'

---

[339]BCRA Law Sec. 3.

[340]BCRA Law Sec. 3.

[341]BCRA Law Sec. 4 (c).

[342]BCRA Law Sec. 17 (b).

[343]The central bank requires public bonds and other securities as guarantee when a loan granted by the central bank to a financial institution exceeds the value of the institution's assets. See BCRA Law Sec. 17 (c).

[344]The BCRA Law Sec. 17 (f) states that the central bank shall be empowered to "[m]ake advances to financial institutions, upon the submission of collateral, assignment, pledge or any other special encumbrance of: I) receivables or other financial assets owed or guaranteed by the National Government, or II) debt securities or share certificates issued by financial trusts, whose assets consist of receivables or other financial assets owed or guaranteed by the National Government in order to promote mid-term and long-term lending for production investment. In the case of advances for production investment, the Board may accept that, out of the total guarantee required, up to TWENTY-FIVE PER CENT (25%) consist of the assets referred to in the first paragraph of (c) above, taking into account for such purposes the time frames related to such transaction."

[345]BCRA Law Sec. 43.

regularization and restructuring plans and implementing and applying financial regulations.[346]

5.4.3.6 Brazil

The monetary authorities of Brazil have to coordinate their policies with the executive branch. They are not meant to operate autonomously. The law is clear on this. In Brazil, the National Monetary Council formulates monetary policy monetary and credit policy to support the "economic and social progress of the country";[347] the central bank is the council's executive arm.[348]

Article 3 (VII) of Lei No. 4595 that governs Brazil's monetary, banking, and credit institutions rules that the National Monetary Council has to coordinate "monetary, credit, budget, fiscal and domestic and external public debt policies."[349] Article 4 further states that the monetary council should follow the guidelines of the President of Brazil in authorizing policies and setting guidelines for the central bank. Moreover, the Monetary Council must coordinate all policies with the government's "investment policy".[350]

Article 10 summarizes the responsibilities of the central bank. The Central Bank of Brazil issues bank notes, performs discount operations and grants loans to financial institutions.[351] The bank controls credit and "foreign capital operations",[352] applies financial regulation and may penalize institutions if necessary.[353] The central bank also buys and sells government bonds as monetary policy instrument (open market operations)[354] and has a very detailed set of reserve requirements at its disposal to affect liquidity conditions in the financial sector.[355] As a government agent the central bank negotiates with financial institutions and places state bonds on the market.[356]

Article 11 of the Internal Rules of the Central Bank of Brazil provides a long list of powers and functions of the central bank board. The article gives the board the

---

[346]BCRA Law Sec. 46 and BCRA Law Sec. 47, for more about the powers and attribution of the Superintendence.

[347]LSFN Brazil Art. 2.

[348]According to LSFN Brazil Art. 9, "[i]*t is the responsibility of the Central Bank of the Republic of Brazil to comply with and ensure compliance with the provisions attributed to it by current legislation and norms issued by the National Monetary Council.*" See also LSFN Brazil Art. 10 for more detail on the central bank responsibilities.

[349]LSFN Brazil Art. 3 (VII).

[350]LSFN Brazil Art. 4 (VII).

[351]LSFN Brazil Art. 10 (I) through (V).

[352]LSFN Brazil Art. 10 (VI) and (VII).

[353]LSFN Brazil Art. 10 (IX).

[354]LSFN Brazil Art. 10 (XII); see also RIBC Brazil Art. 99 (I).

[355]There is a department responsible, see RIBC Brazil Art. 96 (II) (b).

[356]LSFN Brazil Art. 11 (I) and (II).

authority to set the main refinancing rate for banks, the SELIC rate.[357] The board shall also develop monetary, credit and foreign exchange policies and grant credit to financial institutions following the guidelines of the Monetary Council,[358] indicating little operational autonomy.

The central bank acts as Brazil's bankers' bank. But provisions are open to interpretation. The central bank holds bank reserves and monitors and runs the payment system.[359] Article 3 (VI) of Lei No. 4595 includes that the National Monetary Council is in charge of ensuring the liquidity and solvency of financial institutions, suggesting that the operational arm of the Monetary Council, the central bank, has to provide liquidity assistance when necessary.[360] Including the word solvency indicates that the monetary authorities are not subject to Bagehot's rules.

5.4.4 Communication

Well-suited information and advice channels enable an accurate feedback among all the institutions in charge of economic policies.[361] Ideally, the information should flow in both directions; central banks having to inform the executive and legislative branches about policies and regulations, but they also receive reports on public spending, economic resources, and public debt status in return.

A government's unilateral capacity to override the authority of the central bank in case of a conflict of points of view would diminish the operational autonomy of the monetary authority. In case of conflict about policy formulation, it is better if the conflict is solved with the intervention of more than one veto player: the central bank board, the executive branch, the parliament.[362] The participation of the courts might be desirable. The best option concerning a central bank's operational autonomy is, of course, to let the central bank opinion prevail.

The statutes in the countries differ substantially in clarifying the means of communication. On the one hand, there are no legal provisions about the flow of information between the central bank, the legislature and the government for the Monetary Council and Central Bank of Brazil. On the other hand, the organic law of

---

[357]RIBC Brazil Art. 11 (I)

[358]RIBC Brazil Art. 11 (III) (a) and (c).

[359]To perform this function the Brazilian Central Bank has the Department of Banking Operations and the Payment System. To know more about the functions of this department, see RIBC Brazil Art. 96.

[360]LSFN Brazil Art. 3 (VI).

[361]Hasse (1990), pp. 126–127.

[362]Jácome and Vásquez (2008), p. 800.

Chile's central bank is the only one to define a process for solving conflicts in the development of economic policy between different state organs.[363]

Except for Brazil's, central bank statutes in the countries analyzed demand informing the executive or/and legislature.

The statutes of the Central Reserve Bank of Peru prescribe that the bank must report to the Minister of Finance about all economic policy aspects carried out by other institutions that prevent the central bank from fulfilling its role and achieving its objectives.[364]

By contrast, Colombia's Bank of the Republic is supposed to inform the Congress of Colombia about guidelines, evaluations of results and objectives of the monetary, credit and exchange policies. The bank must also update Congress if any change in these policies occurs. The bank's board must further inform Congress about management issues, the financial situation of the bank and the state of the international reserves. Congress, in general, can demand information from the bank whenever Congress deems it necessary.[365] In addition, the Bank of the Republic provides technical advice to the government on all topics related to its expertise.[366] The Bank of the Republic further provides an opinion about the general budget of the state.[367]

The manager of the Bank of Mexico is supposed to inform the legislative commissions annually about the adherence to its mandate.[368] Congress must receive reports about inflation, economic development and economic indicators. In addition, at any time, the House of Representatives or the Senate of Mexico can ask the bank's manager to provide information on any topic or activity related to the central bank. The executive and legislature must receive, three times per year, reports about the exercise of monetary policy, the activities of the bank and the bank's budget.[369]

The Central Bank of Chile has the duty to inform the Minister of Finance and Senate about its activities and plans, including the monetary policy plan for the next

---

[363]The law establishes that the bank's decisions can only be objected to by the Ministry of Finance in front of a commission made up by the National Economic Comptroller, the Minister of Finance, and the Minister of Foreign Affairs. The bank can appeal the decision of this commission in front of the Appeals Court of Santiago. See CBCH Law Sec. 46.

In Colombia's central bank statutes, a potential disagreement about the foreign exchange policies between the Bank of the Republic of Colombia and its Finance Ministry is resolved in favour of the position that is conducive to stabilizing the purchasing power of the currency. See BRC Act Art. 16 (i).

[364]CRBP Law Art. 94.

[365]BRC Act Art. 5.

[366]BRC Act Art. 13 (e).

[367]BRC Act Art. 16 (k).

[368]BM Law Art. 47 (XIII).

[369]BM Law Art. 51.

year.[370] The Central Bank of Chile also informs and advises the country's president at his request[371] and publishes macroeconomic statistics.[372]

The governor of the Central Bank of the Argentine Republic must annually inform Congress about the bank's operations. He must appear in front of a legislative commission once per year or whenever they require his presence.[373] The central bank must also report to the Minister of Finance about the monetary, liquidity and credit situation of the country.[374] Further, the bank must advise the Minister of Economy and Congress regarding the exchange rate regime.[375]

When it comes to obligation of the government to provide information to the central bank there is less in the statutes. The Bank of the Republic of Colombia can demand information from every state institution, and the institutions are obliged to provide it.[376] The Central Reserve Bank of Peru can demand information from public institutions, the private sector[377] as well as the Superintendency of Banking and Insurances of Peru.[378]

In Argentina, the Ministry of Finance is legally obliged to report to the Central Bank of the Argentine Republic (BCRA) about public spending, economic resources, public debt status and other information that the central bank may consider important, every 3 months.[379] As Chile's central bank has the authority over exchange rate policies, the bank is allowed by law to scrutinize and inspect, with no restriction, all the accounts, documents, books, files and correspondence of the state organs bound by the central banks' exchange policies and regulations. The central bank can also demand all types of information and clarifications of explicit circumstances from managers and staff of those public organs. The central bank further receives information from authorities supervising the public agencies bound by the central bank's foreign exchange policies and regulations.[380]

---

[370] According to CBCH Law Sec. 80, this information may include *"the general economic projections on which such information is based and the possible effects they may have on major items in the financial statements of the Bank projected for such period."*

[371] CBCH Law Sec. 4.

[372] According to CBCH Law Sec. 53 para 3, *"*[i]*n order to perform the functions referred to in this Section, the Bank shall have the authority to request and obtain from the various agencies and departments of the Public Service Administration, decentralized entities, and generally the public sector, any information it may deem necessary."*

[373] BCRA Law Sec. 10 (i).

[374] BCRA Law Sec. 26.

[375] BCRA Law Sec. 29.

[376] BRC Act Art. 18.

[377] CRBP Law Art. 74.

[378] CRBP Law Art. 97.

[379] BCRA Law Sec. 27.

[380] CBCH Law Sec. 82.

5.5   Evaluation of Coherence of Legal Frameworks

For there to be legal certainty concerning central bank autonomy, the statutes of central banks with autonomy of constitutional rank should provide a high degree of autonomy from other state organs.

Of the four central banks with autonomy of constitutional rank, this chapter has shown that only the statutes of Chile's central bank guarantee a high level of autonomy for the central bank. For example, in terms of financial autonomy, there are clear provisions that prevent lending to the state, shielding the bank from credit demands of governments. When it comes to personal autonomy, a dual process of election of the board members and a tenure in office of 10 years, which does not overlap with presidential tenure, guarantee that there is little room for interventions of other state branches in the appointment of board members that might undermine central bank autonomy.

The chapter has shown that the statutes of the CRBP seem to provide autonomy to the central bank in many ways. Financial, operational and accountability arrangements are in line with the constitutional rank of the central bank's autonomy. However, the statutes provide little personal autonomy. The time in office of the central bank's board members matches with the period in office of the President of Perú. The president of the CRBP's board is unilaterally appointed by the president of country. Moreover, the board's president is also the only exclusive official of the bank, the other members can perform other functions, such as managing financial institutions. Neither of these problems in the statutes that fail to guarantee *de jure* personal autonomy are sufficient to claim that there is interference of the government or the private sector in the bank's operations in practice. However, there may be conflicts of interest. The law does not provide absolute certainty concerning autonomy.

Most provisions in the statutes of the BM provide a relatively high degree of central bank autonomy. However, some provisions in the statutes are inconsistent with the constitutional provisions. First, the statutes add an objective. Second, the statutes allow the bank to finance the state despite the general constitutional prohibition. And third, the bank is subject to the rules of the public administration for accountability purposes, although organs with constitutional autonomy are placed outside the public administration according to the Supreme Court of Justice of the Nation. The contradictions may lead to concerns about the degree of central bank autonomy.

The chapter has indicated that the statutes of the Colombian central bank contradict the constitutional rank of the autonomy of the bank, undermining legal certainty. The set-up is rather consistent with the idea that the Colombian central bank is part of the public administration and, therefore, heavily controlled by the executive. The executive is powerful in appointing, controlling and dismissing board members. The bank can lend to the government and must coordinate decisions with the highest planning authority of Colombia, which is also an organ dependent on the executive branch.

The Central Bank of the Argentine Republic (BCRA) and the Central Bank of Brazil have only statutory autonomy. From this perspective, the statutes do not have to guarantee as much political independence to be consistent with the rank of the banks. But if the legislator wanted a central bank that is autonomous, autonomy should be guaranteed in the statutes, nevertheless. In Brazil, there is no evidence of autonomy in the statutes. The central bank is not meant to be autonomous. However, the Argentinean central bank statutes include provisions that provide autonomy beyond what the rank implies. For example, the executive and legislative elect the board members in a dual process. The board members of Argentina's central bank also have a tenure of 6 years, a period that does not overlap with the term of office of the President of Argentina. Moreover, there is a general prohibition of lending to the state. However, undermining legal certainty, the BCRA's statutes include numerous exceptions to the rules.

Legal References

Constitutions

Constitution of Argentina with Amendments through 1994 [English Translation of Diario Oficial No. 27.959, 23 August 1994]. Constitute Project, University of Texas at Austin, available at http://www.constituteproject.org/constitution/Argentina_1994.pdf

Constitution of Chile with Amendments through 2015 [English Translation of the Constitución Política de la República de Chile, Gazeta Official, 20 October 2015]. Constitute Project, University of Texas at Austin, available at https://www.constituteproject.org/search?lang=en&q=chile

Constitution of Colombia with Amendments through 2015 [English Translation of Constitución Política de Colombia, Diario Oficial No. 49.554, 25 June 2015]. Constitute Project, University of Texas at Austin, available at https://www.constituteproject.org/constitution/Colombia_2015.pdf

Constitution of Mexico [English Translation of the Political Constitution of the Mexican States, Gazeta de la Federación, 5 February 1917], Constitute Project, University of Texas at Austin, available at https://www.constituteproject.org/constitution/Mexico_2015.pdf?lang=en

Constitution of Peru [English Translation of Constitución Política del Perú, Diario Oficial, 30 December 1993], Congress of the Republic of Peru, available at http://www.congreso.gob.pe/Docs/files/CONSTITUTION_27_11_2012_ENG.pdf

The Constitution of Brazil [English Translation of the Constituição da República Federativa do Brasil, Diario Oficial da União, 5 October 1988]. Chamber of Deputies, available at http://english.tse.jus.br/arquivos/federal-constitution

Legislation

Argentina

Law of Ethic of the Public Function of Argentina [Ley de Ética de la Función Públicos, Boletín Oficial, 1 November 1999].

Organic Charter of the Central Bank of the Republic Argentina [Official Translation of the Carta Orgánica del Banco Central de la República Argentina, Boletín Oficial, 28 March 2012], available at https://www.bcra.gob.ar/Institucional/BCRALaw.asp

Brazil

Internal Rules of the Central Bank of Brazil [Regimento Interno do Banco Central do Brasil, Diário Oficial, 8 September 2011].

Law of the National Financial System of Brazil [Official Translation of the Lei 4.595, Lei do Sistema Financeiro Nacional, Diário Oficial da União - Seção 1 – Suplemento, 31 December 1964], available at https://www.bcb.gov.br/ingles/norms/LAW4595EN.asp

Real Plan Law Art. 8 [Lei do Plano Real, Diário Oficial da União - Seção 1, 30 June 1995].

Chile

Basic Constitutional Act of the Central Bank of Chile [Official Translation of the Ley Orgánica Constitutional del Banco Central de Chile, Diario Oficial 6 January 1990].

Colombia

Organic Act of the Bank of the Republic of Colombia [Official Translation of the Ley Orgánica del Banco de la República, Ley 31 de 1992, Diario Oficial No. CXXVIII, 29 December 1992].

Single Disciplinary Code of Colombia [Código Disciplinario Ùnico, Diario Oficial No. 44.699, 5 February 2002].

Germany

Gesetz über die Deutsche Bundesbank vom 30. Juli 1957.

Mexico

Federal Law of Administrative Liabilities of Public Officers [Official Translation of the Ley Federal de Responsabilidades Administrativas de los Servidores Públicos, Gaceta Oficial de la Federación, 23 March 2002].
Law of the Bank of Mexico [Official Translation of the Ley del Banco de México, Official Gazette, 23 December 1993].

Peru

Organic Law of the Central Reserve Bank of Peru [Official Translation of the Ley Orgánica del banco central de reserve del Perú, Diario Oficial, 30 December 1992].

Other

General Procuration of the National Treasury of Argentina [Procuracion del Tesoro de la Nación Dictamen 178/2012 – Tomo 282, July 20, 2012].

Executive Decrees

Argentina

Executive Decree 179 of 2015, Argentina [Decreto Ejecutivo 179, Diario Oficial, 21 December 2015].

Case Law

Tribunal Constitucional de Chile [Constitutional Tribunal of Chile]

Control constitucionalidad "Ley Orgánica Constitucional de bases generales de la Administración del Estado", TC Chile, Sentencia Rol No. 39, 2 October 1986.
Control constitucionalidad autonomía Banco Central en la "Ley Orgánica Constitucional del Banco Central", TC Chile, Sentencia Rol No. 78, 20 September 1989.

Control constitucionalidad ley que establece normas para resolver cuestiones de competencia entre autoridades administrativas, TC Chile, Sentencia Rol No. 80, 22 September 22, 1989.
Control constitucionalidad enmienda "Ley General de Bancos", TC Chile, Sentencia Rol No. 216, 17 July 1995.

Corte Constitucional de Colombia [Constitutional Court of Colombia]

René Vargas Pérez v. Congreso de la República de Colombia, CCC, Sentencia C-481, 7 July 1999.
Jaime Horta Díaz v. Congreso de la República de Colombia, CCC, Sentencia C-566, 17 May 2000.
Guillermo Alberto Duarte Quevedo v. Congreso de la República de Colombia, CCC, Sentencia C-827, 8 August 2001.

Suprema Corte de Justicia de la Nación de México [Supreme Court of Justice of the Nation]

Banco Inbursa, S.A. and others, Amparo, SCJN México, Sentencia 2a. CCXXIV, Tomo XIV, December 2001, p. 370.
Inversora Bursátil, S.A., Amparo, SCJN México, Sentencia 2a. XV, Tomo XV, March 2002, p.430.
Procurador General de la República, Acción de Inconstitucionalidad, SCJN México, Sentencia P./J. 97, Tomo XX, September 2004, p. 809
Municipio de Guadalajara, Estado de Jalisco, Controversia constitucional, SCJN México, Sentencia P. VIII, Tomo XXVII, February 2008, p. 1868.

References

Alesina A, Summers L (1993) Central bank independence and macroeconomic performance: some comparative evidence. J Money Credit Banking 25(2):151–162. https://doi.org/10.2307/2077833
Amtenbrink F (2010) Securing financial independence in the legal basis of a Central Bank. In: Milton S, Sinclair P (eds) The capital needs of Central Banks. Routledge, London, pp 83–92
Apel E (2007) Central banking systems compared: the ECB, the Pre-Euro Bundesbank and the Federal Reserve System. Routledge International Studies in Money and Banking
Bade R, Parkin M (1977) Central Bank laws and Monetary policies: a preliminary investigation. University of Western Ontario Working Paper. Available at https://ir.lib.uwo.ca/cgi/viewcontent.cgi?article=1548&context=economicsresrpt
Bade R, Parkin M (1988) Central Bank Laws and Monetary Policy. University of Western Ontario. Available at https://www.researchgate.net/profile/Michael_Parkin3/publication/245629808_Central_Bank_Laws_and_Monetary_Policy/links/564a30e208ae127ff98687e5.pdf
Bagehot W (1873) Lombard street. Scribner, Armstrong & Company

Berger H, Nitsch V (2011) Too many cooks? Committees in Monetary Policy. South Econ J 78 (2):452–475. https://doi.org/10.4284/0038-4038-78.2.452

Bernhard W (1998) A political explanation of variations in Central Bank independence. Am Polit Sci Rev 92(2):311–327. https://doi.org/10.2307/2585666

Bini Smaghi L (2007) Independence and accountability in supervision: general principles and European setting. In: Masciandaro D, Quintyn M (eds) Designing financial supervision institutions: independence, accountability and governance. Edward Elgar, Cheltenham, pp 41–62

Bordo M (2014) Rules for a lender of last resort: an historical perspective. J Econ Dyn Control 49:126–134. https://doi.org/10.1016/j.jedc.2014.09.023

Buiter W (2004) Two Naked Emperors? concerns about the stability & growth pact and second thoughts about Central Bank independence. Fiscal Stud J Appl Public Econ 25(3):249–277. https://doi.org/10.1111/j.1475-5890.2004.tb00539.x

Burdekin R, Laney L (1988) Fiscal policymaking and the Central Bank institutional constraint. Kyklos 41(4):647–662. https://doi.org/10.1111/j.1467-6435.1988.tb02734.x

Calomiris C, Meltzer A (2016) Rules for the lender of last resort: introduction. J Financ Intermed 28:1–3. https://doi.org/10.1016/j.jfi.2016.08.003

Calomiris C, Flandreau M, Laeven L (2016) Political foundations of the lender of last resort: a global historical narrative. J Financ Intermed 28:48–65. https://doi.org/10.1016/j.jfi.2016.09.002

Canova T (2011) Black Swans and Black Elephants in plain sight: an empirical review of Central Bank Independence. Legal Studies Research Paper Series, Chapman Law Review, Vol. 14, Chapman University School of Law 11-09:237–310. Available at https://papers.ssrn.com/Sol3/papers.cfm?abstract_id=1783691

Crowe C, Meade E (2007) The evolution of Central Bank governance around the world. J Econ Perspect 21(4):69–90. Available at http://www.jstor.org/stable/30033752

Cukierman A, Webb S, Neyapti B (1992) Measuring the Independence of Central Banks and its effects on policy outcomes. World Bank Econ Rev 6(3):352–398. https://doi.org/10.1093/wber/6.3.353

De Gregorio J (2009) A Veinte Años de la Autonomía del Banco Central de Chile. CEMLA Boletín 12(3):5–10. Available at http://www.cemla.org/PDF/boletin/PUB_BOL_LV04.pdf#page=4

De Haan J, Eijffinger S (2002) The democratic accountability of the European Central Bank: a comment on two fairy tale. J Common Mark Stud 38(3):393–407. https://doi.org/10.1111/1468-5965.00227

De Haan J, Amtenbrink F, Eijffinger S (1999) Accountability of Central Banks: Aspects and Quantifications. BNL Quarterly Review, Banca Nazionale del Lavoro 52(209):169–193. Available at http://ideas.repec.org/p/dgr/kubcen/199854.html

Dincer N, Eichengreen B (2014) Central Bank transparency and independence: updates and measures. Int J Central Bank 10(1):189–259. Available at http://econpapers.repec.org/article/ijcijcjou/y_3a2014_3aq_3a1_3aa_3a6.htm

Elgie R (2002) The politics of the European Central Bank: principal-agent theory and the democratic deficit. J Eur Public Policy 9(2):186–200. https://doi.org/10.1080/13501760110120219

Fernández de Lis S (1995) Classifications of Central Banks by Autonomy: A Comparative Analysis. Banco de España, Servicio de Estudios Documento de Trabajo 9604. Available at https://www.bde.es/f/webbde/SES/Secciones/Publicaciones/PublicacionesSeriadas/DocumentosTrabajo/96/Fich/dt9604e.pdf

Ferrada Bórquez J C (1998) La Autonomía en el Reparto de las Potestades Públicas: El Caso del Banco Central de Chile. Revista Chilena de Derecho 25(1):335–344. Available at https://dialnet.unirioja.es/servlet/articulo?codigo=2650072

Fry M (1998) Assessing Central Bank independence in developing countries: do actions speak louder than words? Oxford Econ Pap 50(3):512–529. Available http://www.jstor.org/stable/3488585

Frye T (2004) Credible commitment and property rights: evidence from Russia. Am Polit Sci Rev 98(3):453–466. Available at https://www.jstor.org/stable/4145340?seq=1

Hasse R (1990) The European Central Bank: perspectives for a further development of the European Monetary System, strategies and options for the future of Europe. Bertelsmann Foundation Publishers

Hoffmann A, Löffler A (2017) Surplus liquidity, Central Bank Losses and the use of reserve requirements in emerging markets. Rev Int Econ 25(5):990–998. https://doi.org/10.1111/roie. 12292

Hogan T, Linh L, Salter A (2015) Ben Bernanke and Bagehot's Rules. J Money Credit Bank 47 (2-3):333–348. https://doi.org/10.1111/jmcb.12178

Jácome L (2001) Legal Central Bank Independence and Inflation in Latin America during the 1990s. IMF Working Paper 212. Available at https://www.imf.org/external/pubs/ft/wp/2001/ wp01212.pdf

Jácome L, Vásquez F (2008) Is there any link between legal Central Bank independence and inflation? Evidence from Latina America and the Caribbean. Eur J Polit Econ 24(4):788–801. https://doi.org/10.1016/j.ejpoleco.2008.07.003

Kalmanovitz S (2000) La Independencia del Banco Central y al Democracia en América Latina. Preparado para el Colloque Mondialisation économique et gouvernement des sociétés: l'Amérique latine, un laboraotire? GREITD l'IRDet les Universités de Paris. Available at http://www.hacer.org/pdf/ibc.pdf

Lastra R (2015) International financial and monetary law, 2nd edn. Oxford University Press

Laurens B, Sommer M, Arnone M, Segalotto JF (2007) Central Bank autonomy: lessons from global trends. IMF Staff Pap 56(2):263–296. Available at https://www.imf.org/en/Publications/ WP/Issues/2016/12/31/Central-Bank-Autonomy-Lessons-from-Global-Trends-20632

Lybek T, Morris J (2004) Central Bank Governance: A Survey of Boards and Management. IMF Working Paper No. 04/226. Available at https://papers.ssrn.com/sol3/papers.cfm?abstract_ id=879051

Massad C (1989) La Función Técnica y la Función Política del Banco Central: Anatomía Prenatal. Cuadernos de Economía 26(77):75–90. Available at http://www.jstor.org/stable/23830298? seq=1#page_scan_tab_contents

Miller G (2005) The political evolution of principle-agent models. Ann Rev Polit Sci 8:203–225. https://doi.org/10.1146/annurev.polisci.8.082103.104840

Mishkin F (1996) Understanding Financial Crisis: A Developing Country Perspective. NBER Working Paper No. 5600. doi:https://doi.org/10.3386/w5600

Mishkin F (2007) The economics of money, banking and financial markets, 8th edn. The Addison-Wesley Series in Economics

Mitchell J (1996) Understanding Maastricht. Contemp Eur Hist 5(2):243–257. https://doi.org/10. 1017/S0960777300003799

Neumann M (1991) Precommitment by Central Bank Independence. Open Econ Rev 2(2):95–112. Available at http://link.springer.com/article/10.1007%2FBF01886895

North D (1993) Institutions and credible commitment. J Inst Theoret Econ 149(1):11–23. Available at https://www.jstor.org/stable/40751576

Pedroza de la Llave ST (2002) Los Órganos Constitucionales Autónomos en México. In: Serna de la Garza JM, Caballero Juarez JA (eds) Estado de Derecho y Transición Jurídica, Serie Doctrina Jurídica 95:173–194. Available at http://biblio.juridicas.unam.mx/libros/1/306/1.pdf

Quintyn M, Taylor M (2002) Regulatory and Supervisory Independence and Financial Stability. IMF Working Paper No. 02/46. Available at https://www.imf.org/external/pubs/ft/wp/2002/ wp0246.pdf

Santaella Quintero H (2003) Autonomía, Estado Social y Corte Constitucional. Vicisitudes del proceso de consolidación de la banca central independiente en Colombia. Revisto Derecho del Estado 14:155–176. Available at http://heinonline.org/HOL/LandingPage?handle=hein. journals/revderest14&div=9&id=&page=

Schwarcz S (2008) Systemic risk. Georgetown Law J 97:193–249. Available at http://heinonline. org/HOL/LandingPage?handle=hein.journals/glj97&div=7&id=&page=

Siklos P, Sturm JE (eds) (2013) Central Bank Communication, Decision Making and Governance: Issues, Challenges and Case Studies. CESIfo Seminar Series, The MIT Press. Available at https://www.jstor.org/stable/j.ctt5hhkb0

Smits R (1997) The European Central Bank: institutional aspects. Kluwer Law International

Ugalde F (2010) Órganos Constitucionales Autónomos. Revista del Instituto de la Judicatura Federal 29:253–264. Available at http://www.ijf.cjf.gob.mx/publicaciones/revista/29/Filiberto%20Valent%C3%ADn%20Ugalde%20Calder%C3%B3n.pdf

Valencia G (1998) La Banca Central en Colombia. Banco de la Republica, Subgerencia de Estudios Económicos. Available at http://www.banrep.gov.co/docum/ftp/borra097.pdf

Vermuele A (2013) Convention of agency independence. Columbia Law Rev 113(5):1163–1238. Available at http://www.jstor.org/stable/23479725

Zúñiga F (2007) Autonomías Constitucionales e Instituciones Contramayoritarias (A Propósito de las Aporías de la "Democracia Constitucional"). Revista Ius et Praxis 13(2):223–244. https://doi.org/10.4067/S0718-00122007000200010

Chapter 6
The Constitutional Court of Colombia Versus Central Bank Autonomy

6.1 Introduction

Colombia is a young democracy that has faced, and still faces, many challenges. These challenges include 50 years of conflict between the state and the guerrilla FARC, a lack of access to fundamental rights, a persistent gap between rich and poor, and periods of macroeconomic instability.[1] The Colombian Constitution of 1991 included novel provisions to help stabilize Colombia and improve the country's social situation. Among the innovations was the creation of an autonomous central bank, the Bank of the Republic,[2] with the single objective of preserving the purchasing power of the currency to improve macroeconomic stability.[3]

At the heart of the new constitution, however, is the principle of the social rule of law, which was meant to help overcome inequalities.[4] This social rule of law is comprised of a set of positive rights, such as the right to health care,[5] social security,[6]

---

[1]Carbonari and Vargas (2009), pp. 231–234.

[2]Const. Colombia Art. 371. Before the constitutional reform of 1991, monetary policy was conducted by a monetary council created in 1963. This council was mostly made up by government members. Inflation was high (20%) but stable. The key for the stability were several economic restrictions, such as capital controls. These arrangements were incompatible with economic liberalization. See Alesina et al. (2005), pp. 347–348.

[3]The Colombian Constitution states that preserving the purchasing power of the currency is a duty of the Colombian state. The Bank of the Republic is the state's "intermediary" in the performance of this function. See Const. Colombia Art. 373.

[4]The original Spanish version of the Constitution of Colombia says that "Colombia es un estado social de derecho." Some translate this to English in what I would consider being inaccurate: "Colombia is a social state under the rule of law." The right translation would be: Colombia is a state based on a social rule of law. *See*: Const. Colombia Art. 1.

[5]According to Const. Colombia Art. 49, *"[p]ublic health and environmental protection are public services for which the State is responsible [. . .]."*

[6]Const. Colombia Art. 48.

© The Author(s), under exclusive license to Springer Nature Switzerland AG 2021
A. L. Tapia-Hoffmann, *Legal Certainty and Central Bank Autonomy in Latin American Emerging Markets*, European Yearbook of International Economic Law 15, https://doi.org/10.1007/978-3-030-70986-0_6

and housing,[7] among others. Under the Constitution of 1991, it is the state's obligation to enforce those rights.[8] The Constitutional Court of Colombia (CCC) was created to ensure that state organs do not deviate from their constitutional role and work together to realize the values of the social rule of law.[9]

The Court has emphasized that certainty in the law is an ex-ante requirement to ensuring the commitments of state authorities. Yet arguably, several Court decisions have added an extra dose of uncertainty. When performing judicial review, the CCC has, for example, directly modified established legal rules or contradicted executive decrees, for instance those related to reform the bureaucratic system,[10] as well as judgments of other judges.[11] The CCC has also abstractly reviewed legislation enacted by Congress and made decisions with difficult economic implications.[12]

---

[7]Const. Colombia Art. 51: *"All Colombian citizens are entitled to live in dignity. The State shall determine the conditions necessary to give effect to this right and shall promote plans for public housing, appropriate systems of long-term financing, and community plans for the execution of these housing programs."*

[8]The Const. Colombia Art. 2 says that *"essential goals of the State are to serve the community, promote the general prosperity, and guarantee the effectiveness of the principles, rights, and duties stipulated by the Constitution [...]"*. The authorities of the Republic are there to protect the life, honor, property, beliefs and other rights and freedoms, and to ensure the compliance of the state and particulars with social obligations.

According to the Colombian Constitution of 1886, the Supreme Court of Colombia oversaw the constitutionality of laws passed by Congress. However, it was necessary that the executive branch previously challenged the law for not being in agreement with the constitution. See Constitution of Colombia of 1886 Art. 151 (4) [Constitución de Colombia de 1886, Diario Oficial No. 6758 y 6759, August 7, 1886]: *"Make the final decision on the constitutionality of legislative acts that have been challenged by the government as unconstitutional [Own Translation]."*

[9]*Celmira Waldo de Valoyes v. Caja Nacaional de Previsión Social-Seccional Chocó*, CCC, Sentencia SU-111, 6 March 1997.

[10]Kugler and Rosenthal (2005), p. 76.

[11]López Daza (2011), pp. 176–177.

[12]Constitutional judgments about economic issues are not a novelty. They have taken place in the United States, for instance, where the Supreme Court nullified labor laws that tried to establish guarantees to workers, arguing the violation of freedom of contract. It has also occurred in Spain where the court has declared laws about social security unconstitutional for conflicting with the Spanish Constitution. See Uprimny (2006), pp. 41–44.

The difficulty of adjudicating the constitutionality of economic aspects was recently evidenced in Europe as consequence of the decision of the German Federal Court about the Outright Monetary Transactions Program (OMT) which implied that the central bank could purchase bonds issued by member states in the secondary market. The Court of Justice of the European Union decided that this central bank measure was in line with the EU Treaties. On the other hand, the German Federal Court decided that the OMT might violate the law of the EU. For more detail, see *Peter Gauweiler and Others v Deutscher Bundestag*. BVerfG, C-62/14. This particular case raised the issue about whether the courts of justice should limit their basis for a decision to the rationality of the measure of the central bank or fully review monetary policy. One of the arguments in favor of a full judicial review of monetary policy can be found in the idea that full judicial review is a requirement to balance central bank autonomy with democracy. The argument against it points to the constitution rank of the ECB (via the Maastricht Treaty) which limits the scope of judicial review to the word of the legal rule that grants the bank independence. A technical argument against it is that judges are

Some decision of the CCC seem to have led to unexpected changes in the budget or the ignorance of international commitments.[13]

Such activism does not help bolster the trust in the stability and coherence of the legal system[14] and raised doubts as to whether it is appropriate to allow constitutional judges to scrutinize certain technical issues. For instance, one argument is that judges may lack the necessary knowledge to take such decisions, and thus their judgments could lead to bad policies.[15] Further, judges may make constitutional decisions that impede into other state organs' area. In addition, making economic policy subject to constitutional review reduces its flexibility. Making policies viable may then require constitutional amendments.[16]

This chapter deals with the interventions of the CCC in decisions of the Colombian central bank. Constitutional judges, in their eagerness to harmonize every action of the state organs with the social rule of law, have interfered with the Bank of the Republic's autonomy, operations and legal objectives, causing uncertainty about the independence and role of the institution. By intervening with the operations of the central bank, the Court has produced contradictory judgments. On the one hand, the Court has ratified the autonomy of the central bank by putting clear limits to legislative and executive intervention—which are more commonly considered a threat to central bank independence. On the other hand, the Court has modified the objective of the central bank, limiting its autonomy to achieve goals in line with the social rule of law.

In particular, this chapter elaborates on the constitutional decisions regarding mortgage loan rates in the so-called UPAC mortgage system, in which the CCC interfered with central bank decisions in order to guarantee the constitutional right to decent housing. The Court instructed the central bank on limits of loan interest rates despite the bank's autonomy. As Justices Cifuentes and Naranjo stated, these judgments made the CCC the superior regulating organ of the state.[17] Such judgments undermine the central bank objective to reach low inflation, as low mortgage loan interest rates may contribute to an increase in mortgage lending and accelerating

---

not qualified to disentangle complicated economic aspects. The court's lack of knowledge can be evident, and the court's credibility can suffer when an expert in monetary policy matters challenges the court's decision. For more detail on this topic, see Goldmann (2014), pp. 265–274.

[13]Cerra Nolasco (2001), p. 171.

[14]Uprimny (2006), pp. 40–41.

[15]*Ibid.*, p. 39.

[16]*Ibid.*, p. 40.

[17]*Alejandro Baquero Nariño and other v. Congreso de la República de Colombia*, CCC, Sentencia C-955, 26 July 2000, quote in Spanish: *"La sentencia anuncia con claridad que ha nacido en el panorama de los órganos reguladores del Estado, uno superior a todos, dotado de poderes de intervención, cuyas resoluciones incluso no experimentan las limitaciones que se pueden hacer valer ante las autoridades competentes."* Regarding the opinion of Justices Cifuentes and Naranjo, the CCC manifested that those opinions are against the rule of law, antidemocratic and disrespectful of the CCC. Their opinion threatens the building of institutions of the country according to a majority of CCC justices.

house price inflation. The interventions in the central bank's autonomy have also opened the door for further constitutional rights' lawsuits against the central bank, which continue to threaten the central bank's autonomy.

The first part of the chapter provides a review of the general characteristics and limits of constitutional review, and the problems with judicial activism. Elaborating on the use of constitutional review in Colombia and the nature of the social rule of law as the main principle of the Colombian constitution, the chapter draws on the type of judgments the CCC undertakes to harmonize the legal framework with the social rule of law, and how the CCC demarcates the central bank's autonomy based on this principle. Specifically, the CCC has referred to the rights to decent housing and the principle of credit democratization established in the Constitution of 1991 to justify interventions into the central bank's policies undermining legal certainty concerning the central bank's autonomy.

6.2   Constitutional Review and Judicial Activism

6.2.1   Constitutional Review

Constitutional review is the attribution that an organ of the state has to preserve the supremacy of the constitution in the legal framework.[18] *Robertson* defines constitutional review as,

> a process by which an institution, commonly called constitutional court, has the constitutional authority to decide whether statutes or other decrees created by the rule-making institutions identified by the constitution are valid given the terms of the constitution.[19]

In the tradition model of constitutional review, a constitutional court is made up by judges that evaluate the constitutionality of laws. They do not act as legislators.[20] Constitutional review protects a specific set of negative rights, i.e., the right to life, the right to enjoy personal freedom, and the right to property. From a natural rights perspective, these negative rights were not given by the state. The state's only (potential) role lies in protecting them from aggression.[21] Constitutional courts are also not appellation courts, which mean they are not supposed to review the facts of a lawsuit.[22] Constitutional courts review only two things: the protection of constitutional rights and the distribution of authority among state organs.[23]

---

[18]Cerra Nolasco (2001), p. 167.

[19]Robertson (2010), p. 5.

[20]Martinez Caballero (2000), p. 11.

[21]Mavčič (2001), p. 11.

[22]Robertson (2010), pp. 12–13.

[23]Mavčič (2001), p. 11.

In the context of negative rights, constitutional review can ensure certainty in the law. Judges can protect people's fundamental rights from intervention of the state and guarantee a legitimate exercise of the power of authorities. When there is only a limited amount of legislation, legal gaps are scarce.

However, drawing on the ideas of John Maynard Keynes, a new institutional setting arose that partially replaced the market mechanisms with government control and regulation.[24] Reflecting the burgeoning trend of regulating the economy, the scope of constitutions throughout the world widened after the two World Wars. In addition to the classic function of protecting fundamental rights and limiting the scope of action of the state, the constitutions included rules and principles for the public economic order. The public economic order entailed several social rights, as well as institutions in charge of economic policy. A new constitutionalism emerged in which public authorities were moved from a neutral position in the economy to a broader engagement in a menu of economic issues.[25] Today, most constitutions include a catalogue of social and economic rights that enjoy constitutional protection.[26]

6.2.2 Activist Courts and Legal Certainty

The sheer number of constitutional guarantees has triggered an activist control of constitutionality, also known as judicial activism. Judicial activism is often an elusive concept. Activist judges are those who seek to achieve some social goal, mainly social welfare, through their judgments. In this sense, constitutional justices direct other state institutions to perform their functions towards the achievement of social welfare,[27] even to the point of guiding or interfering in policymaking.[28]

Kmiec identifies what makes a judge activist. Activist judges nullify legal rules created by other state organs without a clear constitutional reason. It is also considered judicial activism when judges make law, a function usually attributed to the legislative branch.[29] Further, judicial activism occurs when judges disregard mandatory precedents, such as previous judgments of a higher court.[30]

The activist role of the constitutional courts prevents them from achieving legal certainty.[31] This is so primarily because judicial activism blurs the dividing line

---

[24]Catrile and Pita (2011), p. 123.

[25]Rivero Ortega (2013), p. 55.

[26]Mavčič (2001), p. 11.

[27]Cerra Nolasco (2001), p. 169.

[28]Robertson (2010), p. 10.

[29]In this sense, the activist justices attempt to clarify legal texts or create new legal norms by complementing the constitutional text with judicial opinions.

[30]Kmiec (2004), pp. 1463–1476.

[31]Kugler and Rosenthal (2005), p. 90.

between law making and law applying. Applying the constitutional rules, constitutional courts must make decisions with strict attachment to the constitution and the law. However, when they pursue an objective, they go from being guardians of the constitution to political actors. Moreover, activist courts cannot guarantee the stability of the legal system because an activist court do neither respect primary rules created by the legislators, nor precedents created by the courts themselves.

Avoiding judicial activism contributes to legal certainty.[32] Therefore, constitutional judges should—as much as possible—follow the literal meaning of constitutional provisions. By doing so, they directly enforce the constitution. However, constitutions that include a broad set of rights are extensive documents, often ambiguous, and, therefore, hard to apply directly.[33] These constitutions may lack formal legal certainty. In this context, those who defend constitutional activism claim that as the straightforward enforcement of the constitution is impossible, the activism of the constitutional court is the water in the middle of the literal application of constitutional provisions and the particularities of each law, decree, or judgment subject to constitutional review. Courts fill this space in between with constitutional doctrine.[34]

K. Roosevelt differentiates the court's doctrine from the meaning of the constitution. The court's doctrine is its interpretation of the constitution. When the court analyzes the constitutionality of legal rules, the court does not invoke the constitution directly, but the doctrine of the court.[35] The constitutional doctrine is necessary because of the lack of certainty if constitutional review becomes activist, departing from the real meaning of the constitution[36] and its literal prescriptions. By developing their doctrines, constitutional courts have faced harsh criticisms for their activist roles. They have been criticized for imposing their ideologies about the constitution and being subject to their own will instead of to the rule of law.[37]

Judicial activism may also pursue legal certainty in times of change. *Escobar Martinez* explains that in societies in process of democratization, courts often take the lead using consistent interpretation to help make effective the new institutional setting, as was the case in Austria and Germany after World War II.[38] Not surprisingly, judicial activism seems to be more likely in young liberal democracies plagued with political and social instability, such as a considerable gap between the rich and poor, crime, or internal conflicts. South Africa had to face the social consequences of apartheid. In Colombia, the civil war between the Farc and a division between rich and poor complicated the process of institution building.

---

[32]See my explanation in the chapter on legal certainty about limits that judges should have when deciding about the actions of public policy to not usurp the functions of technical agencies.

[33]Peters (2016), pp. 23–26.

[34]Roosevelt (2008), p. 12.

[35]*Ibid.*, pp. 18–21.

[36]*Ibid.*, p. 169.

[37]Roosevelt (2008), p. 12.

[38]Escobar Martinez (2006), pp. 94–96.

Both countries tried to overcome their problems through constitutions that are mainly catalogs of promises and good intentions, and therefore very hard to enforce.[39]

Robertson suggests that a new constitutional mandate can demand an active constitutional court that seeks to entrench the constitution in the institutional setting of the country. In Poland and Czech Republic, for instance, this type of constitutional review was necessary to answer unclear questions about the structure of the state, such as the appointment and dismissal of authorities.[40]

Comparing the performance of the Supreme Court of the UK with the Supreme Courts of other common law countries such as Australia, Ireland, Israel, and South Africa, *Dickson* provides evidence that the quality of the legal framework and the characteristics of the constitutions strongly influence the degree of judicial activism.[41] Judges that operate in the institutional setting of the UK, Australia, and Ireland, for example, tend to avoid striking down legislation passed by their parliaments. On the other hand, common law judges in South Africa or Israel are activist because the institutions are weak, and judges must preserve a stable legal order and keep democracy working. In South Africa, for instance, constitutional judges took on the challenge of shaping a society after apartheid. In Israel, the complicated democratic and legal setting after 1948 demanded a very active control of constitutionality to fill gaps and give coherence to the legal framework. Moreover, even in countries like Canada, judges took on an activist stance to, for instance, enable the social assimilation of the Constitution of 1982, which included fundamental rights.[42]

Institutional characteristics of the courts themselves and their functions particularly influence judicial activism. Among these characteristics are the judge's experience and knowledge, the process of appointment and removal, and tenure. Moreover, legal uncertainty about the functions of the courts and scope of the rights can also increase the likelihood of an activist court. When the tasks of the constitutional courts are not clearly specified, other authorities may try to contest their decisions, which they may regard as illegitimate. This motivates the court to justify its actions through judgments.[43] Further, if the rights embedded in the constitution are ambiguous, too broad, or difficult to understand, it is more likely that the court must intervene to clarify them. This is usually the case with economic and social guarantees that require some state action to make them viable.[44]

---

[39]Bonilla (2013), pp. 26–27.

[40]Robertson (2010), pp. 84–85.

[41]In common law systems, the law-making role of the courts diminishes the degree of judicial independence. The court requires a joint process of decision making, coordination and increased ways of communication. When they declare a law unconstitutional, a debate between judges and the members of the parliament responsible to fill the spaces left by the declaration of unconstitutionality is often necessary. See Dickson (2007), p. 11.

[42]Dickson (2007), pp. 12–13.

[43]Ruggiero (2012), pp. 27–28.

[44]*Ibid.*, pp. 33–34.

The literature also discusses other institutional aspects that make judicial activism more likely. *Ruggiero* suggests that in centralized governments where political representation is less dispersed, courts have less room to review legislation and, therefore, less opportunity to influence legislative outcomes.[45] *Vanberg* implies that in an institutional environment where the probability of legislative compliance with constitutional judgments is low, judicial activism is the optimal strategy for the courts.[46]

6.2.3 Consistent Interpretation and Coherence of the Legal System

Consistently interpreting the constitution can be a way for constitutional courts to exercise judicial activism. The main particularity of consistent interpretation is that a legal rule with unconstitutional characteristics is not expelled from the legal system. Instead, the rule remains in the legal framework, but with changes and conditions that the constitutional court adds in order to align the rule with the constitutional mandate.[47] The technique of consistent interpretation seeks to solve the inconsistency of two different legal rules without opening legislative gaps.[48] Consistent interpretation has been applied in Europe since around 1925, and in the US since the nineteenth century. In Colombia, the technique of consistent interpretation has been used by the Supreme Court and the Administrative Court (Consejo de Estado) since 1912 and 1947, respectively.[49]

---

[45]*Ibid.*, pp. 20–21.

[46]In his study, Vanberg explains that constitutional review is a game of imperfect information in which it is not possible for the Congress to know how the court is going to review legislation. At the same time, the court cannot know whether or not the Congress is going to comply with the judicial decision. The court could either be friendly with the legislators or declare the law constitutional. The court could also be hostile and nullify laws enacted by the Congress. The court could also be sure of public support and, not only declare the law unconstitutional, but also be ready to engage in an institutional conflict with the legislative branch if the Congress does not comply. On the other hand, the court cannot know if the Congress is going to comply and whether it will face electoral accountability in case of noncompliance. For electoral accountability, the functioning of the legislative branch must be transparent, and the citizens must follow up its performance. When the constitutional court enjoys public support and the performance of the Congress is transparent, the danger of electoral punishment is high, and the Congress has incentives to comply with the court's decisions. When the court is not well-known, and the transparency of the legislative branch is not high enough, the Congress has little incentives to comply with the constitutional decision. See Vanberg (2001), p. 346 for a detailed explanation of the game.

[47]Olano Garcia (2004), pp. 576–577.

[48]Betlem (2002), pp. 397–398.

[49]For more on how the Colombian administrative court has been modulating judicial decisions, see Escobar Martinez (2006), pp. 91–93.

Critics of this practice claim that despite trying to promote certainty in the law, consistent interpretation can produce legal uncertainty when the court is too creative and misinterprets the legislative intention at the moment of creating a legal rule.[50] This has eroded the principle of division of branches and motivated a sort of *de facto* capture of legislative power by the Supreme Court.[51] For this reason, the U.S. Congress monitors the judicial decisions of the Supreme Court.[52]

6.3 Constitutional Review in the Light of the Social Rule of Law

6.3.1 Constitutional Review in Colombia

Before the Constitution of 1991 was in place, the Supreme Court of Justice of Colombia was in charge of evaluating the constitutionality of laws, judicial decisions, and administrative acts. With the enactment of the constitution of 1991, the Supreme Court remained the highest court for civil, criminal, and administrative matters, but the task of constitutional review was given to the newly created Constitutional Court of Colombia (CCC).[53]

The CCC is a powerful state organ. The Court can overturn legislative bills and enacted legislation relatively easily. First, when the constitutional court reviews the constitutionality of a legislative bill, the President is obliged to enact the law by the mere decision of the court. If the court finds that the bill of law is unconstitutional, the bill is tabled. If the court considers that only part of the bill is unconstitutional, the Congress must correct the problem and rewrite the text following the CCC.[54] Court decisions are made with absolute majority. Five of the nine members have to agree.[55] This majority is rather small, considering the court's power to overrule other state organs. The court can make decisions about legislation unilaterally. As the justices of the CCC have a relatively short period in office,[56] they might be susceptible to political influence.

---

[50]Escobar Martinez (2006), p. 107; see also Olano Garcia (2004), p. 577.

[51]Ruggiero (2012), pp. 16–17.

[52]Eskridge (1991), p. 343.

[53]Martinez Caballero (2000), p. 10; see also Bonilla (2013), p. 26.

[54]According to Const. Colombia Art. 167, in the case in which "[a] *bill has been opposed as unconstitutional. In such an event, should the Houses insist, the bill shall be sent to the Constitutional Court so that the latter, within the six (6) following days, may decide about its constitutionality. The decision of the Court obliges the President to approve the statute. If the Court declares the bill unconstitutional, it shall be filed away.*"

[55]General Rulings of the Constitutional Court of Colombia Art. 3 [Reglamento Interno de la Corte Constitucional de Colombia, Acuerdo 01, 1992].

[56]Const. Colombia Art. 233: "*The judges of the Constitutional Court, the Supreme Court of Justice, and of the Council of State shall be elected for a period of eight years.*"

The CCC performs the abstract control of constitutionality of legal rules and reviews the judicial decisions concerning the *writs of Amparo*,[57] which is a protection of constitutional rights.[58] This remedy originated in Mexico, thus the name. In Colombia, it is known as writ of protection (*tutela juridica*).[59] Concerning the abstract control of constitutionality, the court determines the material content and the procedure of laws, executive and legislative decrees, and international treaties. In the case of constitutional amendments and referendums, the court can only rule on the constitutionality of the process.[60]

Constitutional review in Colombia pursues legal certainty. The CCC is supposed to realize the supremacy of the constitution as the factor that determines the validity of the other legal rules of the legal framework.[61] Further, the CCC is supposed to make sure that the entire legal system is consistent with the constitution.[62]

To do so, the CCC has several privileges and enjoys a prominent position among the other state institutions. All administrative authorities are obliged to respect constitutional decisions. Further, the decisions of the constitutional court are mandatory precedent, which means that all judges must take them into account when making judgments.[63] The decisions of the CCC are also difficult to contest. The law says that there is no way of appealing a decision of the constitutional court.[64] Nevertheless, there is a process to nullify the CCC's decisions. This process shall start before a decision has been enacted and must be based on procedural mistakes. The procedural mistakes that admit revision of the constitutional decision are, for example, when the decision has been made by a lower majority than required; when there is an inconsistency between the motivation of the decision and its resolution, or

---

[57] According to Const. Colombia Art. 241 (9), one of the functions the CCC should perform is to "[r] *evise, in the form determined by statute, the judicial decisions connected with the protection of constitutional rights."*

[58] Azcuna (1993), p. 1.

[59] Const. Colombia Art. 86: *"Every individual may claim legal protection before the judge, at any time or place, through a preferential and summary proceeding, for himself/herself or by whoever acts in his/her name, the immediate protection of his/her fundamental constitutional rights when the individual fears the latter may be jeopardized or threatened by the action or omission of any public authority."*

[60] According to Const. Colombia Art. 241 (1), to safeguard the constitution the Constitutional Court may *"[d]ecide on the petitions of unconstitutionality brought by citizens against measures amending the Constitution, no matter what their origin, exclusively for errors of procedure in their formation."*

[61] Const. Colombia Art. 4.

[62] Const. Colombia Art. 241: *"The safeguarding of the integrity and supremacy of the Constitution is entrusted to the Constitutional [. . .]"*.

[63] Cerra Nolasco (2001), pp. 169–170.

[64] Executive Decree 2067 of 1991 Art. 49 [Decreto Ejecutivo 2067 de 1991]: *"The judgments of the constitutional court cannot be appealed. Constitutional court proceedings may only be nullified before the ruling of the court. Only irregularities involving violation of the due process may be a basis for the court to nullify the process* [Own Translation]*."*

when the decision commands duties to people not involved in the conflict.[65] Finally, given the level of independence and the fact that the court is not democratically elected, there may be an issue with accountability.[66]

6.3.2 Consistent Interpretation in Colombia and Legal Certainty

When the CCC declares a legal rule unconstitutional, the rule is expelled from the legal framework. Such decision is *res judicata,* which means that the conflict has arrived at an end and the same topic cannot be decided upon again.[67] However, *res iudicata* in the Colombian framework does not necessarily imply that decisions remain unchanged. Indeed, *res iudicata* can also be deferred. Thus, even though a legal rule is regarded unconstitutional, it does not immediately leave the legal framework. The legal rule remains temporarily binding when the court determines that getting rid of it right away affects constitutional rights. This was the case, for instance, with the reform of the Mining Law in Colombia. In this case, the court decided that immediately removing the law from the legal framework could have negative effects on the environment, interfering with the right to live in an environment free of pollution. The court delayed the legal consequences of unconstitutionality for 2 years to prevent such negative externalities.[68]

A rule that is constitutional, on the other hand, is preserved in the legal framework. It does not get the status of *res judicata.* Therefore, further decisions may be made on the same issue[69] if there are new facts or new legal norms that demand new judicial reasoning.[70]

Legal rules that are declared constitutional are often subject to modifications through integrative judgments. Through integrative judgments, the court seeks to preserve the supremacy of the constitution and legal certainty. In this sense, the constitutional judges are supposed to infuse the constitutional mandate into inferior

---

[65]German Arango Rojas v. Corte Constitucional de la República de Colombia, CCC, Sentencia A-195, 20 May 2009. See also Olano Garcia (2004), p. 572.

[66]Peters (2016), p. 25.

[67]Cerra Nolasco (2001), pp. 172–173.

[68]*Felipe Ortega Escobar and other v. Congreso de la República de Colombia,* CCC, Sentencia C-027, 27 January 2012.

[69]*Ibid.,* p. 173.

[70]Under exceptional conditions, *res iudicata* applies to a legal rule declared constitutional: (1) The constitutional court has to decide about the constitutionality of a legal rule that is identical to one previously declared constitutional; (2) The facts that motivate a new constitutional lawsuit are identical; (3) There are no important economic, social, cultural, political or even ideological changes that require a modification in the judicial reasoning to adapt it to the new circumstances. See *María Camila Silva Mogollón v. Congreso de la República de Colombia,* CCC, Sentencia C-860, 18 October 2006.

legal rules wherever the judges meet indeterminacy or obscurity.[71] Another objective is to make sure that the legal framework is a harmonious set of rules and that the constitutional court has no excuse to not administer justice, arguing in a legal vacuum.[72]

Through this technique, the court can either set conditions to restrict the effects of legal rules or modify their content to align them with the constitutional mandate. In the first case, the constitutional judges declare that a legal rule is constitutional but some of its effects are not. Therefore, through motivated declarations of constitutionality, the court clarifies the reasons for the permanence of a rule in the legal framework and nullifies interpretations that are not constitutional.[73] Regarding the second case, the court has claimed that its role is to trespass or project the constitutional mandate wherever there is obscurity or inconsistency, even if by doing so, it looks like the court is legislating. According to the CCC, this is not creating legal rules, which is the role of the legislative branch, but fulfilling its role as guardians of the constitution. This may even be applied retroactively to infuse the new constitutional mandate into the entire legal framework.[74]

The CCC has also justified the use of integrative judgments for consistent interpretation of legal rules that need clarification of their meanings. However, the Court defines clarity of the legal rules in terms of efficiency. In this sense, the Court has claimed that a legal rule is not clear, and is therefore inefficient, when its literal application produces effects contrary to those expected with the creation of the disposition. When this is the case, the judges of the CCC can interpret the legal rule in a way that achieves the goal for which it was created and that, at the same time, is consistent with the legal framework.[75]

The CCC views the Constitution as a document that requires a flexible interpretation in order to achieve justice and social equity in response to every-day changes.[76] According to the court, new economic, social, and ideological circumstances demand updating the meaning of the constitutional mandate.[77] In this sense, the new function of the state is not to act mechanically according to the set of rules, but according to the demands of real life. Reality, not statutes, is the court's justification of the normative system.[78] This means that the CCC justifies the

---

[71]*Marcela Barona Montua v. Congreso de la República de Colombia*, CCC, Sentencia C-109, 15 March 1995.

[72]*Pablo Antonio Bustos Sánchez v. Congreso de la República de Colombia*, CCC, Sentencia C-083, 1 March 1995.

[73]Martinez Caballero (2000), p. 13.

[74]*Marcela Barona Montua v. Congreso de la República de Colombia*, CCC, Sentencia C-109, 15 March 1995.

[75]*Carlos Eduardo Naranjo Florez v. Congreso de la República de Colombia*, CCC, Sentencia C-151, 5 April 1995.

[76]*AA v. Instituto Colombiano de Bienestar Familiar*, CCC, Sentencia T-389, 27 May 1999.

[77]*Camilo Velásquez Reyes v. Corte Constitucional de la República de Colombia*, CCC, Sentencia A-256, 4 August 2009.

[78]*AA v. Instituto Colombiano de Bienestar Familiar*, CCC, Sentencia T-389, 27 May 1999.

legitimacy of its decisions according to a standard of reasonability in which the Constitution is not the only factor that determines whether the court revokes the action of a state authority.[79]

According to the doctrine, the CCC can review acts of the other state organs, as well as omissions. Legislative omissions occur when the constitution has given a specific, concrete, and definite mandate to Congress, which was not fulfilled within the deadline. In case of absolute legislative omission, the CCC can order Congress to fulfill the constitutional mandate.[80] It is also possible that Congress has incurred in a relative omission. This means that the legislators have created a law demanded by the constitution, but excluded for no reason some beneficiaries, e.g., a labor law that provides benefits for workers except those of the public sector. In these cases, the CCC does not need to ask Congress to fill the gap. The CCC can fill the gap itself.[81]

Furthermore, when Congress enacted a law that excluded some options for no reason, for instance some groups of people, the CCC referred to this as a *legislative omission* and considered it an unjustified discrimination that allowed the court to fill the gap,[82] or make the necessary changes and additions in the light of the principle of equality.[83] The court fills the gaps left by legislative omissions (1) when a law that is applicable to several people or groups of people has consequences for only some of them and (2) when a law misses an element or condition that is necessary to harmonize it with the constitution. These omissions of the legislator must (1) lack reason and cause inequality among the people involved in the legal rule or (2) reflect non-compliance with a duty imposed by the constitutional court.[84]

6.3.3 The Social Rule of Law: Main Parameter of Judicial Interpretation

In addition to the notion of the democratic rule of law in Latin America, which entails the judicial protection of civil and political rights of citizens, the Colombian Constitution of 1991 included a new element, the social character of the rule of law.[85] The Constitution of 1991 broadened the catalogue of constitutional rights,

---

[79]Roosevelt (2008), p. 3.

[80]*Armando José Soto Jiménez v. Congreso de la República de Colombia*, CCC, Sentencia C-1064, 10 October 2001.

[81]Olano Garcia (2004), pp. 578–579.

[82]*Armando José Soto Jiménez v. Congreso de la República de Colombia*, CCC, Sentencia C-1064, 10 October 2001.

[83]Martinez Caballero (2000), p. 24; see also Olano Garcia (2004), p. 577.

[84]*Ivan Santiago Martínez Vásquez v. Congreso de la República de Colombia*, CCC, Sentencia C-100, 23 February 2011.

[85]The conception of the social rule of law is exclusive to the Colombian legal framework. However, the Mexican Constitution of 1917 was the first to coin the term "social function of property" as the cornerstone of the economic system. See Castillo Calle (2013), p. 6.

e.g., the right to full employment, social justice, etc. Moreover, the new constitution also allowed citizens and administrative authorities to file constitutional lawsuits.[86] Due to this new set of constitutional rights and the fact that more people can start proceedings for protection, almost every aspect of daily life can be subject to constitutional review and almost every institution is under the scrutiny of the constitutional court.[87]

The concept of the social rule of law implicitly suggests that legal subjects live in conditions of material inequality. They cannot enjoy real freedom unless the state is committed to help them overcome these conditions.[88] While legal certainty, explained as people's capacity of foreseeing the legal consequences of their acts, is at the core of the classical liberal view of the rule of law, at the center of the social rule of law we also find people's dignity, understood as meeting a certain social and economic threshold.[89]

Within constitutions some substantive principles determine the interpretation of the constitution and the coherence of the entire legal system.[90] The social rule of law in the Colombian legal framework performs the function of the most important principle for constitutional interpretation, which explains the implications of the other constitutional rules.[91] This principle has the power of directing the actions of every state organ in a way to ensure that Colombians can participate in general prosperity and have equal economic opportunities.[92] This includes, for example, access to education, health care, and housing. In order to put the social rule of law at work at its premises, there seems to be an increasing need for government to help create social plans implemented through public policy.[93]

The Brazilian Constitution of 1946 put "social justice" at the core of economic activity. See Constitution of Brazil of 1946 Art. 145 [Constituição dos Estados Unidos do Brasil, 18 September 1946]: *"The economic order must be organized according to the principles of social justice, reconciling freedom of initiative with the valorization of human labor* [Own Translation]."

The Chilean Constitution of 1925 did not introduce the socialization of property but guaranteed public economic goods like protecting labor markets and social welfare. See Constitution of Chile of 1925 Art. 10 [Constitución de Chile de 1925, 18 September 1925]: The value of public importance that the constitution protected was the "socialization of property" that allowed the state to intervene in economic issues to achieve a plethora of socially desirable objectives.

[86]Const. Colombia. Art. 40: *"Any citizen has the right to participate in the establishment, exercise, and control of political power. To make this decree effective the citizen may:* [. . .] (6.) *Undertake public measures in defense of the Constitution and the law."*

[87]López Daza (2011), pp. 170–175.

[88]*Andrés de Zubiría Samper v. Congreso de la República de Colombia,* CCC, Sentencia C-776, 9 September 2003.

[89]*Andrés de Zubiría Samper v. Congreso de la República de Colombia,* CCC, Sentencia C-776, 9 September 2003.

[90]Palombella (2016), p. 8.

[91]Ribeiro (2003), p. 42.

[92]*Armando José Soto Jiménez v. Congreso de la República de Colombia,* CCC, Sentencia C-1064, 10 October 2001.

[93]Carbonari and Vargas (2009), pp. 234–236.

From a legal perspective, it was necessary to give the social and economic rights that compose the social rule of law a clear legal basis, which enables the enforcement of those rights.[94] Therefore, the Colombian Congress created several laws with social purpose, such as the Education Law (Law 115 of 1994) that guarantees the access to education for all Colombian citizens,[95] and the Law of an Integral Social Security System (Law 100 of 1993) that guarantees human dignity through the state's responsibility of covering the economic and health needs of its citizens.[96]

According to the CCC, administrative organs should be able to fulfill their roles through means that are in line with the social rule of law.[97] In many cases, this may require the state to intervene in the economy, via taxation for example, in order to eliminate sources of material inequality[98] or to fix market mistakes; the state may also have to limit economic freedom to ensure fair competition and the like.[99]

The CCC has used the social rule of law as the main constitutional principle to guide the court's interpretation. In this sense, the Court has invoked that principle to guide the democratic use of power and to balance social justice with the law.[100] According to the Court, encouraging the development of social policies and enhancing the common good are the main benefits derived from the application of the social rule of law.[101] Therefore, the CCC took on the ambitious role of eliminating general inequalities via its decisions, affecting a broad group of people, and aiming to coordinate the action of several state organs towards the achievement of social rights.[102]

Although the CCC asserts that the economic and social rights prescribed in the Constitution shall not apply directly, as they are limited by how the legislator's rule

---

[94]*Ibid.*, p. 236.

[95]Law of Education Art. 4 [Ley de Educación, Colombia Diario Oficial, 8 February 1994]: *"The state, society and family must ensure quality of education and promote access to public education, and it is the responsibility of the Nation to ensure its coverage [Own Translation]."*

[96]Note that also the Law of Integral Social Security System Art. 1 [Ley de Seguridad Social Integral, Colombia Diario Oficial 41.148, 23 December 1993] states the following: *"The system of integral social security has the objective of guaranteeing the people and communities rights to be able to have a life quality that is in agreement with human dignity through the protection of the contingencies that affect them [Own Translation]."*

[97]*José Alirio Montoya Restrepo and others v. Caja Nacional de Previsión*, CCC, Sentencia T-068, 5 March 1998.

[98]*Andrés de Zubiría Samper v. Congreso de la República de Colombia*, CCC, Sentencia C-776, 9 September 2003.

[99]*Armando José Soto Jiménez v. Congreso de la República de Colombia*, CCC, Sentencia C-1064, 10 October 2001.

[100]*José Alirio Montoya Restrepo and others v. Caja Nacional de Previsión*, CCC, Sentencia T-068, 5 March 1998.

[101]*Marcela Barona Montua v. Congreso de la República de Colombia*, CCC, Sentencia C-109, 15 March 1995.

[102]Rodriguez Garavito and Rodríguez Franco (2015), pp. 6–7.

and by the financial conditions of the state,[103] in practice the Court itself has not always taken into account this assessment. For instance, the Court has ruled that the economic situation of the country cannot be an obstacle for the payment of retirement pensions or to protect the right of a punctual payment of retired people.[104]

6.3.4   Central Bank Autonomy in the Light of the Social Rule of Law

The CCC ratified the constitutional autonomy of the Bank of the Republic. The Court explained that the Bank of the Republic is a constitutionally autonomous organ of the state because freeing the institution from political interests is the only way to achieve its goal of preserving a sound currency.[105] The bank is recognized as an administrative autonomy, which means that it is not part of other state organs. Therefore, the Bank of the Republic is not subject to the executive branch's instructions. Members of the bank's board have leeway in making decisions on the use of the instruments that the law has granted the bank in order to achieve its noninflationary objective. The Court stated that the bank is independent in the use of its economic resources. The income the bank obtained from managing its economic resources should make up a part of the bank's reserves needed to react in times of economic turmoil. According to the Court, the bank enjoys this high degree of autonomy in order to increase people's confidence in the bank's capacity to preserve the purchasing power of the currency.[106]

However, the CCC has also been clear about the formal and material limits of the bank's autonomy. The bank's *formal* limits are found in legislation and the CCC's judicial decisions. The *material* limits are based on the need to coordinate monetary policy with the general economic policy of the country, respecting the social rule of law.[107] Therefore, conditions of constitutionality determined by the CCC are considered the formal limits for the autonomy of the Colombian central bank.[108] The court clarified the dimension of the material limits of autonomy when it evaluated the bank's legal objective. The second article of the Organic Law of the

---

[103]*Celmira Waldo de Valoyes v. Caja Nacional de Previsión Social-Seccional Chocó*, CCC, Sentencia SU-111, 6 March 1997.

[104]*Emperatriz Castillo Burbano v. Gobierno de la República de Colombia*, CCC, Sentencia C-747, 6 October 1999.

[105]*René Vargas Pérez v. Congreso de la República de Colombia*, CCC, Sentencia C-481, 7 July 1999.

[106]*Jaime Rafael Pedraza Vanegas v. Congreso de la República de Colombia*, CCC, Sentencia C-050, 10 February 1994.

[107]*René Vargas Pérez v. Congreso de la República de Colombia*, CCC, Sentencia C-481, 7 July 1999.

[108]*Alejandro Baquero Nariño and other v. Congreso de la República de Colombia*, CCC, Sentencia C-955, 26 July 2000.

Bank of the Republic that describes the objective of the central bank was subject to abstract constitutional control, which the Court finally declared constitutional. However, through an integrative sentence, the Court specified the limits of the Bank of the Republic's objective. The court declared that although the single objective of the Colombian central bank is to preserve the purchasing power of the currency, the board could not be indifferent to the other objectives of economic policy. It is, according to the Court, the central bank's obligation to pursue the social objectives of the Colombian state in line with the social rule of law, as entrenched in the Constitution of 1991. The Court, therefore, mentioned that even though keeping inflation low is important for the economy, other objectives of the general economic policy, such as employment, are also important.[109]

The social rule of law, therefore, may be interpreted as a demarcation of central bank autonomy. The CCC is clear when it explains that the Economic Development Plan of the country, designed every year by the government,[110] is the limit of the autonomy of the Bank of the Republic. Specifically, the CCC has ruled that even though the Colombian central bank has autonomy of constitutional rank and pursues the goal of preserving the purchasing power of the currency, the central bank autonomy is a peculiar one. According to the court, the Colombian monetary authority is neither extremely independent nor dependent on the government, but something in the middle. It is subordinated to the Economic Development Plan of the government.[111] Regarding the characteristics of the government's development plan the CCC has said that this plan is not only based on economic considerations but must be balanced with all the constitutional dispositions related to the social rule of law.[112]

6.4   The Court's Interventions in Central Bank Autonomy

6.4.1   Public Housing Policy and the Mortgage Loan Problems

A review of the context helps to understand how central bank policies may have been against the rights to decent housing or credit democratization.

---

[109]*Andrés Quintero Rubiano v. Congreso de la República de Colombia*, CCC, Sentencia C-208, 1 March 2000.

[110]Providing housing to the most vulnerable people is one of the main interests of the economic development plan. See Departamento Nacional de Planificación, Bases del Plan Nacional de Desarrollo, p. 28, 49.

[111]*René Vargas Pérez v. Congreso de la República de Colombia*, CCC, Sentencia C-481, 7 July 1999.

[112]*Juan Carlos Ramírez Gómez v. Congreso de la República de Colombia*, CCC, Sentencia C-191, 8 May 1996.

6.4.1.1   Saving and Housing Corporations (CAVs) and the UPAC System

In the 1970s, few Colombians were able to afford necessary down payments required to get a mortgage loan. Most people were rather poor and had no access to financial markets to finance housing. The Colombian government led by President M. Pastrana, therefore, aimed to strengthen the development of the Colombian economy via a stimulation of the construction sector,[113] providing incentives for people to channel savings toward mortgage banks that financed social housing.[114]

In particular, the government gave financial institutions known as *Savings and Housing Corporations* (CAVs) the task to provide (subprime) mortgage loans of up to 15 years in duration.[115] The CAVs had to allocate at least 23% of their mortgage portfolio to the financing of social housing.[116] A central element of the newly developed mortgage system was that mortgage loans and savings in CAV accounts were denominated in terms of UPAC, an internal unit of constant purchasing power, which adjusted the nominal value of savings and mortgage loans to an index of consumer price inflation.[117] The precise method of calculating the UPAC was changed 21 times between 1972 and 1999.[118] For instance, the UPAC's calculation was originally based on consumer price inflation in the previous quarter.[119] Later, this was modified to take into account the previous 24 months[120] and, again later, the previous 12 months were considered.[121]

---

[113]Fique Pinto (2008), p. 76.

[114]Executive Decree 677 of 1972 Art. 1 [Decreto Ejecutivo 677 de 1972, Diario Oficial No. 33.594, 18 May 1972] [hereinafter Colombia, Executive Decree of 18 May 1972]: *"The government, through its acting agencies, will encourage savings with the purpose of channeling part of them to construction* [Own Translation].*"* Another strategy was to provide direct housing subsidies to the poorest people in order to allow them to afford housing. See Fique Pinto (2008), p. 77.

[115]Forero (2004), p. 36; see also Bank of the Republic (2000).

[116]Held (2000), p. 40.

[117]Forero (2004), p. 36.

[118]Urrutia and Namen (2012), p. 296.

[119]Executive Decree 1229 of 1972 Art. 3 [Decreto Ejecutivo 1229 de 1972, Diario Oficial No. 33.663, 16 August 1972]: *"The Board of Savings and Housing will calculate the value of the UPAC monthly [. . .] based on the changes in the consumer price index for employees and workers as prepared by the National Administrative Department of Statistics (DANE) for the previous quarter and inform the CAVs* [Own Translation].*"*

[120]Executive Decree 269 of 1974 Art. 1 [Decreto Ejecutivo 269 de 1974, Diario Oficial No. 3.072, 21 February 1974]: *"The Board of Savings and Housing will calculate the value of the UPAC monthly [. . .] based on the changes in the consumer price index for employees and workers as prepared by the National Administrative Department of Statistics (DANE) for the previous 24 months and inform the CAVs* [Own Translation].*"*

[121]Executive Decree 58 of 1976 Art. 1 [Decreto Ejecutivo 58 de 1976, Diario Oficial No. 34.489, 1 February 1976] [hereinafter Colombia, Executive Decree of 1 February 1976]: *"The Board of Savings and Housing will calculate the value of the UPAC monthly [. . .] based on the changes in the consumer price index for employees and workers as prepared by the National Administrative Department of Statistics (DANE) for the previous 12 months* [Own Translation].*"* Furthermore, Art.

Given Colombia's history of double-digit inflation rates, the main objective of applying this monetary correction was to attract private resources to finance the construction of houses by protecting credit from inflation.[122] In an environment of financial repression, when financial markets were underdeveloped, and deposit interest rates did not compensate for inflation, the CAVs' exclusive right to index savings and use the new UPAC system attracted substantial amounts of savings. Given that no interest rate was charged additional to the inflationary correction in the monthly mortgage payments and corresponding mortgage loan values, demand for mortgage loans of Colombian households that would otherwise not be able to finance mortgages increased. The UPAC system rose to dominate the banking market, at its height making up a third of the market share.[123]

However, in the 1970s and 1980s, inflation rates in Colombia often reached 20% and could even surpass 30%. The UPAC mortgage loan system itself seemed to have contributed to inflation[124] by using past inflation rates to determine the value of loans and deposits, producing even more inflation in the future. More troublesome to the government was that high rates of adjustments meant high, albeit only nominal, mortgage loan rates and increases in loan values. The government, therefore, set limits on the adjustment of the UPAC. In 1975, the limit was set at 19%,[125] in 1976 at 18%,[126] in 1980 at 21%[127] and in 1982 at 23%.[128] Indeed, the consumer price index grew by a factor of 114, or from 3.34 in September 1972 to 379.52 [pesos] in August of 1994, but the UPAC only grew 60 times, going up from 100.49 to 5979.7 pesos, in the same period.[129]

---

2 of this decree states that *"without prejudice to the provisions of the preceding article, the increase of the unit of constant purchasing power (UPAC) should be have an upper-limit of 18% annually* [Own Translation]."

[122]Held (2000), p. 40.

[123]Forero (2004), pp. 32–33.

[124]Urrutia and Namen (2012), p. 296.

[125]Executive Decree 1685 of 1975 Art. 1 [Decreto 1685 de 1975, Diario Oficial No. 34.402, 18 September 1975]: *"Regarding the system for calculating the UPAC, the increase of its value has to be limited to a maximum of 19% annually* [Own Translation]."

[126]Colombia, Executive Decree of 1 February 1976 Art. 1: "[. . .] *the increase of the unit of constant purchasing power (UPAC) should be maximal 18% annually* [Own Translation]."

[127]Executive Decree 2475 of 1980 Art. 1 [Decreto Ejecutivo 2475 de 1980, Diario Oficial No. 35.610, 29 September 1980].

[128]Executive Decree 2929 of 1982 Art. 1 [Decreto Ejecutivo 1919 de 1982, Diario Oficial No. 36.115, 22 October 1982].

[129]Mora (2010), p. 18.

6.4.1.2   Bank of the Republic and the UPAC

Originally, a Board of Savings and Housing was in charge of calculating the UPAC and informing the CAVs of its value.[130] In 1984, this task was attributed to the Bank of the Republic. At that time, the Bank of the Republic was considered a private institution. Its board was mostly made up by private bankers, while the state was only a minority shareholder.[131] However, the bank had public functions as the monopoly issuer of currency, as well as the fiscal agent of the state. The bank was the executive arm of the so-called Monetary Council, which was in charge of monetary policy.[132]

To provide (bail-out) funding to the CAVs[133] whenever they were in risk of a bank run, the Bank of the Republic was in charge of creating the Fund for Savings and Housing (FAVI),[134] which was initially funded by bond sales by the bank.[135] In addition, FAVI was funded by income of the bank's credit operations,[136] external and internal loans[137] and by a portion of the bank's budget.[138]

Financial reforms in the early 1990s and the end of financial repression opened other investment options. The resulting development of the financial sector and rise in bank deposit interest rates above inflation rates challenged the competitiveness of the UPAC system. To stay competitive and fulfill its task in providing mortgage loans to underprivileged households, the CAVs demanded to have the ability to compete for funds on fair grounds and use market interest rates rather than inflation rates to calculate the UPAC.

After several modifications in the method of calculation of UPAC, the Bank of the Republic decided to include interest rates in the calculation of the UPAC.[139]

---

[130]In 1976, this state organism was eliminated, and all its functions passed to the Monetary Council, according to the Art. 5 of the Decree 1110 of 1976.

[131]*AA v. Instituto Colombiano de Bienestar Familiar*, CCC, Sentencia T-389, 27 May 1999.

[132]See website of the Banco de la Republica: http://www.banrep.gov.co/es/reformas.

[133]Forero (2004), p. 34.

[134]Colombia, Executive Decree of 18 May 1972 Art. 6: *"For the purposes specified in this decree, there will be a Fund of Savings and Housing in the Bank of the Republic [Own Translation]."*

[135]*Ibid.*, Art. 8: *"The Monetary Council will authorize the Bank of the Republic to issue and allocate bonds up to an amount of 60,000,000 of pesos, in three portions of 20,000,000 pesos for the initial allocation of resources for the FAVI [Own Translation]."*

[136]Colombia, Executive Decree of 18 May 1972, Art. 7: *"The resources of the Fund of Savings and Housing will come: c) from the reimbursements, interests and fees of the credit operations the* [the bank] *executes [Own Translation]."*

[137]*Ibid.*, Art. 13: *"The Bank of the Republic's Fund of Savings and Housing, after getting the authorization of the Board for Savings and Housing, will be able to: a) Get internal and external loans [. . .] [Own Translation]".*

[138]*Ibid.*, Art. 7: *"The resources of the Fund of Savings and Housing will come from: d) part of the budget that is assigned to the Bank of the Republic and that the Bank decides to grant it in the fund [Own Translation]."*

[139]Executive Decree 1131 of 1984 Art. 1 [Decreto Ejecutivo 1131 de 1984, Diario Oficial No. 36.115, 5 June 1984]: *"The Bank of the Republic will calculate monthly and report with*

From 1984 on, the importance of the consumer price index in the calculation of UPAC diminished and the importance of interest rates increased. In 1988, the UPAC adjustment index was made up of, by and large, equal proportions of the fixed-term deposit interest rates and the consumer price index.[140]

With the enactment of the new Constitution in 1991, the Bank of the Republic became a public institution with constitutional autonomy.[141] The protection of the purchasing power of the currency became the new central bank's single objective.[142] Based on the new Constitution of 1991, Congress had the obligation to enact legislation that systematically organized all the aspects related to financial activities in line with the new constitution. When the legislative branch failed to do so, the executive enacted Decree 1730 of 1991. This decree included the method of calculating the UPAC, stating the Bank of the Republic was supposed to calculate the UPAC based on consumer prices and deposit rates.[143]

The Organic Law of the Bank of the Republic (Law 31 of 1992) ratified the bank's attribution as monetary, credit, and exchange rate authority of the country, as well as its task to calculate the UPAC. The law included the mandate that the UPAC should reflect movements in interest rates in the economy.[144] In 1994, the UPAC

---

identical frequency the value in legal tender of the UPAC to the CAVs, for each day of the following month [. . .] calculated based on the changes in the consumer price index as is relevant for employees and workers, prepared by the National Statistics Department (DANE) for the period of the twelve (12) previous months. To that it will add 1.5% of the squared difference between the average variation in the mentioned price index and the effective weighted average of the deposit certificates up to ninety (90) days issued by commercial banks and financial corporations, calculated by the Bank of the Republic for the next month [Own Translation].*"*

[140]Executive Decree 1319 of 1989 Art. 1 [Decreto Ejecutivo 1319 de 1989, Diario Oficial No. 38.869, 22 June 1989]: "[. . .] *calculated like this: forty percent (40%) of the resulting variation in the national index of consumer prices (total weighted) prepared by the National Administrative Department of Statistics for the period of the next twelve (12) months. To that thirty-five (35%) of the average of the variable rate of DFT calculated by the Bank of the Republic for the next month are to be added* [Own Translation].*"*

[141]Const. Colombia Art. 371: *"The Bank of the Republic shall exercise the functions of a central bank. It shall be organized as a legal public entity with administrative, patrimonial, and technical autonomy, subject to its own legal regime."*

[142]Const. Colombia Art. 373: *"The State, through the intermediary of the Bank of the Republic, shall oversee the maintenance of the purchasing power of the currency."*

[143]Executive Decree 1730 of 1991 Art. 2.1.2.3.7 [Decreto Ejecutivo 1730 de 1991, Diario Oficial No. 39.889, 4 July 1991] "[. . .] *calculated as follows: forty-five percent (45%) of the resulting variation of the national consumer price index (weighted total) prepared by the National Department of Statistics DANE for the period of twelve 12 months. To this 35% of the average rate of the fixed term deposits calculated by the Bank of the Republic for the precious month will be added* [Own Translation].*"*

[144]BRC Act Art. 16: *"The Banco de la Republica will study and adopt monetary, credit and exchange measures aimed at regulating the circulation of money, The Banco de la República will study and adopt the monetary, credit, and and, in general, the liquidity of the financial market and the normal operation of the internal and external payments of the national economy, taking care of the stability of the value of the currency. To such effect, the Board of Directors will: [. . .] f) Set forth*

ceased to be related to inflation, becoming solely adjusted to fixed-term deposit interest rates.[145]

6.4.1.3 Financial Crises of 1997/8 and UPAC System

Following the outbreak of the East Asian crisis of 1997–1998 and the Russian flu of 1998, emerging market currencies around the world came under severe pressure. An increase in perceived emerging market risk contributed to capital outflows that lowered the supply of foreign funds in Colombia and contributed to increasing deposit interest rates. The Bank of the Republic sold dollar reserves for pesos to stem the depreciation of the peso against the dollar. Additionally, the bank increased interest rates to prevent further capital outflows. As the crisis evolved, deposit interest rates, which are used to calculate the value of the UPAC loans as well as the monthly installment payments, rose rapidly. Nominal interest rates reached 33% in 1999.[146]

Given the corresponding rise in mortgage loan rates, an increasing share of borrowers could not service the debt. As housing prices tended to decline when mortgage-servicing costs increased, it was also hardly possible to use collateral to get new loans to roll over the debt. The share of non-performing loans of the CAVs quadrupled from about 6% in 1996 to 22% in 1999.[147] The collapse of the mortgage market contributed to a severe crisis in Colombia.

In this context, *Forero* suggests that the

UPAC system suffered from the fact that monetary adjustment was linked to liability interest rates, because they deviated a great deal from inflation. In this context housing prices, which had been increasing rapidly before 1998, and the volume of construction, which had been enormous, collapsed immediately. This gave rise, on the one hand, to a huge increase in the liabilities and installments to be paid by clients and, on the other, to a fall in the price of the housing acting as collateral. At the same time, unemployment in the country was rising.[148]

However, this assessment focuses only on the eventual crisis period. To attract savings, the UPAC system had to include market interest rates in calculations. Otherwise, it would have failed to attract funding and collapsed much sooner. The public housing policies that were able to stimulate (an excessive) demand for

---

the methodology for determining the value of the Constant Purchasing Power Unit (UPAC) in local currency, intending that it also reflects the movements of the interest rate in the economy."

[145]Decision No. 26 of 1994 of the Bank of the Republic [Resolución Externa No. 26 de 1994]: "The Bank of the Republic will calculate monthly for every day of the following month and inform with the same frequency the Savings and Housing Corporations (CAVs), of the value in terms of legal tender of the UPAC, which is equivalent to seventy-four percent (74%) of the moving average of fixed term deposits rates [. . .][Own Translation]".

[146]Forero (2004), p. 36.

[147]Hofstetter et al. (2011), p. 6.

[148]Forero (2004), p. 36.

housing failed when the period of financial repression came to an end.[149] The UPAC system that was supposed to allow low income households to finance housing eventually backfired on the very same people it was supposed to help, as they were no longer able to service mortgage loans. Many debtors had to pass over their houses to the financial institutions.[150]

6.4.2   UPAC Problems and Integrative Judgments

6.4.2.1   The Social Rule of Law Versus Central Bank Autonomy

The Constitution of 1991 set forth that Colombians are entitled to live in dignity in decent housing.[151] This was taken to mean, first, that people have a right to housing of good quality, and second, that the state is responsible for implementing the plans that allow underprivileged people to have access to decent housing.[152] Given the problems of low income households in servicing their mortgage debt in terms of UPAC and the ongoing mortgage crisis, in 1999 the CCC reviewed the constitutionality of Article 16: Letter f of the Bank's law.

The Court declared Art. 16f unconstitutional for two reasons. First, noting that the UPAC should reflect interest rates, Congress gave the bank hints on how to calculate the UPAC, which conflicted with the autonomy of the institution. The legislative branch may establish the tasks the bank is supposed to exercise, such as determining the method of calculating the UPAC. But the legislator cannot choose the instruments or rule for calculating the UPAC.[153] Along similar lines, the Court also declared Art.16e of the Organic Charter of the bank unconstitutional. According to the Court, the legislative branch interfered with the bank's autonomy by establishing that, only in exceptional circumstances and for periods that do not exceed 120 days per year, the bank could set interest rates that banking institutions charge or pay clients.[154]

The second, and more interesting, reason for declaring Art. 16f unconstitutional was that the inclusion of the element of interest rates in the calculation of the UPAC was not in line with the principle of the social rule of law, specifically the right to have access to decent housing (Art. 51) and the principle of credit democratization

---

[149]Hofstetter et al. (2011), p. 7.

[150]Mora (2010), p. 19.

[151]Const. Colombia Art. 51: *"All Colombian citizens are entitled to live in dignity. The State shall determine the conditions necessary to give effect to this right and shall promote plans for public housing, appropriate systems of long-term financing, and community plans for the execution of these housing programs."*

[152]Fique Pinto (2008), p. 73.

[153]*AA v. Instituto Colombiano de Bienestar Familiar*, CCC, Sentencia T-389, 27 May 1999.

[154]*Andrés Quintero Rubiano v. Congreso de la República de Colombia*, CCC, Sentencia C-208, 1 March 2000.

(Art. 335). According to the Court, upgrading the value of debt according to the interest rates established by the market increases the debt mountain so that debtors end up paying much more than they originally received as loan. The CCC emphasized that the state is in charge of designing plans that, progressively, accomplish the fulfillment of these rights by promoting social housing and setting up a system that allows low-income households to have access to long-term housing financing.[155]

To comply with the Court's decision, the Bank of the Republic started to calculate the UPAC by taking the arithmetical average of the year-over-year inflation rates over the last 12 months.[156] As long as housing prices developed in line with the average price level or slower, there was no problem in reaching the objective of price stability. But as accelerating housing prices may translate into inflation in the medium term, not being able to counteract increases in housing prices by raising interest rates may undermine the central bank in achieving its price stability target. Therefore, being obliged to regulate the mortgage market in customer-favorable terms reduces legal certainty about the central bank's autonomy in reaching its main objective.

Regarding Decree 1730 of 1991,[157] the CCC argued in a similar fashion.[158] In line with the constitution, the Court stated that even though the President of the Republic is responsible for organizing public credit,[159] it is the role of Congress to regulate financial activities.[160] The calculation of the UPAC as outlined in the decree was found to be in conflict with new constitutional prescriptions regarding credit democratization and the right of all Colombians to have access to housing.[161] The Court did not forbid the application of the UPAC system with its judgment. Instead, the Court deferred the effects of the decisions to avoid economic turbulence, maintaining that the system should remain in place until Congress created a new system.[162]

---

[155]*AA v. Instituto Colombiano de Bienestar Familiar*, CCC, Sentencia T-389, 27 May 1999.

[156]Decision No. 10 of 1999 of the Bank of the Republic Art. 1 [Resolución Externa No. 10 de 1999]: *"The Bank of the Republic will calculate monthly for every day of the following month and will inform the Savings and Housing Corporations (CAVs) at the same frequency on the value the Unit of Constant Purchasing Power UPAC in terms of legal tender. For this purpose, the monetary correction will be equivalent to the arithmetic average of the annual inflation rate based on the consumer price index of the twelve (12) previous months* [Own Translation]."

[157]Executive Decree 1730 of 1991 Art. 2.1.2.3.7 [Decreto Ejecutivo 1730 de 1991, Diario Oficial No. 39.889, 4 July 1991].

[158]*Humberto de Jesús Longas Londono v. Gobierno de la República de Colombia*, CCC, Sentencia C-700, 16 September 1999.

[159]See also, the Const. Colombia Art. 189 (25) which states that the President of the Republic must *"[o]rganize the public credit [. . .]"*.

[160]According to Const. Colombia Art. 150 (19 d), Congress must *"regulate activities concerning finance [. . .]"*.

[161]*Humberto de Jesús Longas Londono v. Gobierno de la República de Colombia*, CCC, Sentencia C-700, 16 September 1999.

[162]*Humberto de Jesús Longas Londono v. Gobierno de la República de Colombia*, CCC, Sentencia C-700, 16 September 1999; see also Uprimny (2006), p. 46.

6.4.2.2   The End of the UPAC System and Central Bank Responsibility

The UPAC system finally ended in 1999 when the CCC declared Article 134 of Decree 663 of 1993 unconstitutional. This article allowed financial institutions to capitalize on housing loans, which was at the core of UPAC in which the nominal value of loans was adjusted by inflation or interest rates.[163] The court said that capitalizing interest does not generally conflict with the constitutional mandate. However, when financial institutions put interest on loans extended to people to pay for their houses, people's right to affordable housing and credit democratization are undermined.[164]

This declaration of unconstitutionality of the UPAC system threatened to have consequences for the Bank of the Republic. The CCC stated that people that were harmed by UPAC, because they had to pay high interests to the financial institutions that gave them housing loans, have the right to sue the state for state liability. Accordingly, the state has the obligation of paying compensation and the right to personally sue the authorities involved in the damage caused by not taking into account people's right to affordable housing. Given that it was argued that the UPAC system failed during the crisis because of the inclusion of the deposit interest rate in its calculation, the bank was viewed as responsible.[165]

6.4.3   A New System: CCC Continues Taking on BRC Functions

To stem the mortgage crisis, the Colombian Congress enacted the Housing Law (Law 546 of 1999 of Colombia). This law created the Unit of Real Value (UVR) as a replacement for the UPAC.[166] It also protected the beneficiaries of housing credit from paying much more than the original amount of credit due to the payment of interest rates that make the debt unpayable.[167] The law further created the Counsel of Economic and Social Policy (CONPES) as the authority in charge of calculating the

---

[163]Executive Decree 663 of 1993 [Decreto Ejecutivo 663 de 1993, Diario Oficial No. 40.820, 5 April 1993].

[164]*Emperatriz Castillo Burbano v. Gobierno de la República de Colombia*, CCC, Sentencia C-747, 6 October 1999.

[165]*Sixto Acuna Acevedo and others v. Congreso de la República de Colombia*, CCC, Sentencia C-1140, 30 August 2000.

[166]Law 546 of 1999 of Colombia Art. 3 [Ley 546 de 1999, Diario Oficial 43.827, 23 December 1999] [hereinafter Law 546]: *"The unit of real value UVR is a unit of account that reflects the purchasing power of the currency, based solely on the variation of the consumer price index: 1. Protect the patrimony of families represented in housing. 3. Protect the users of housing loans. [Own Translation]"*.

[167]Law 546 Art. 2: *"Objectives and criteria of this law: the National government will regulate the long-term specialized housing finance system to set the necessary conditions to implement the*

UVR and gave the government the attribution to determine the exchange rate between the old UPAC and the new UVR.

The UVR, like the UPAC, is not a means of payment, but a unit of account to express the deposits, loans, quotas, and interest rates of financial institutions and its clients. The credits are denominated in pesos. According to the Bank of the Republic, the success of the UVR is, therefore, closely related to the bank's objective to keep inflation at bay. Lower inflation helped advance capital markets. Growing markets for securities and mortgage bonds were important to allow financial institutions to raise funds, pay interest rates, and allocate the funds in UVRs.[168]

CONPES, which belongs to the executive branch, initially was given the task to determine the method of calculating the new unit of account for long-term housing financing.[169] Consistent with the CCC's earlier decisions, this part of Article 3 of Law 546 of 1999 was declared unconstitutional. The Court argued the Bank of the Republic had the exclusive task of calculating the UVR, as well as determining the exchange rate between UVR and UPAC,[170] a decision that seemed to strengthen the central bank's autonomy.

However, remember that one of the formal limits to the autonomy of the Bank of the Republic is constitutional judgment. The second limit is the social rule law. Therefore, the CCC ordered that the Bank of the Republic shall help work towards the fulfillment of the right to affordable, decent housing and credit democratization. According to the Court, loan rates should not be subject to the volatility of markets. In order to avoid the severe fluctuations in interest rates for the UVR, the CCC maintained that the bank had to reduce the liability interest rates applicable to mortgages below the lowest of all the other real interest rates in the market. The Bank of the Republic was to further set an upper limit on loan rates and make sure the UVR is easy to calculate. In particular, it should be based only on the consumer price index, rather than on "complicated mathematical formulas [Own Translation]".[171]

This constitutional decision also had retroactive effects in fixing the damage cause by the introduction of fixed-term deposits rates caused in the calculation of the UPAC. The Court decided that the UPAC adjustments from 1988 on had to be recalculated using the change in the consumer price index. The Court specified this in detail, prescribing exactly how to determine the value of loans in terms of UPAC. It ruled that from 1988 to 1990, the calculation of the UPAC should include 75%,

---

constitutional right for decent housing in accordance with the following objectives and criteria [. . .] [Own Translation]".

[168]Bank of the Republic (2000).

[169]The UVR replaced the UPAC, which was declared unconstitutional in the constitutional decision. See *Humberto de Jesús Longas Londoño v. Gobierno de la República de Colombia*, CCC, Sentencia C-700, 16 September 1999.

[170]*Alejandro Baquero Nariño and other v. Congreso de la República de Colombia*, CCC, Sentencia C-955, 26 July 2000.

[171]*Alejandro Baquero Nariño and other v. Congreso de la República de Colombia*, CCC, Sentencia C-955, 26 July 2000.

from 1990 to 1993 80%, from 1993 to 1994 90%; from 1994 to 1999 74% and from June 1999 to December 1999 100% of the changes in the consumer price index.[172]

The bank established a resolution to attach to CCC's decision. In doing so, the Bank of the Republic set an upper limit for the long-term loan interest rate for credit in UVR of 13.1% per year.[173]

6.4.4 The Long Shadow of the Court's Decisions: A Series of Lawsuits

The Court's interventions have not been without consequences. In the following years, the central bank faced a series of lawsuits brought on by citizens and financial institutions.

The first series of lawsuits directly followed the CCC's decision to declare the UPAC system unconstitutional due to the inclusion of interest rates in the calculation of the UPAC. In 1999, the inability of some debtors to service their mortgage loans triggered foreclosure lawsuits. As the Colombian central bank was viewed as—at least partly—responsible for the troubles in the mortgage market, debtors sued the Bank of the Republic seeking compensation for the damages caused by the calculation of the UPAC.[174] Moreover, financial institutions whose foreclosures lawsuits failed[175] also sued the Bank of the Republic if they calculated mortgage interest rates based on the UPAC prescribed by the Bank of the Republic before it was declared unconstitutional. Financial institutions that were sued by their clients for charging too high interest rates brought lawsuits against the Bank of the Republic arguing that the bank had the responsibility and was supposed to act as guarantor that should compensate the debtors and financial institutions.[176]

In 1999, the bank had also signed an insurance contract for the risks in the performance of its professional tasks. Thus, the bank asked several insurance

---

[172]*Ibid.*

[173]Decision No. 14 of 2000 of the Bank of the Republic Art. 1 [Resolución Externa No. 14 de 2000].

[174]For instance, *Gunar Raul Ramírez and others v. Bank of the Republic of Colombia and other*, Consejo de Estado de Colombia, File N: 76001-23-31-000-2001-02078-01(26174), 2 February 2004; *Myriam Valencia de Zafra v. Bank of the Republic and other*, Consejo de Estado de Colombia, File N: 76001-23-31-000-2001-00804-01(28298), 13 April 2006; *Hugo Yesid Suarez Sierra v. Bank of the Republic and other*, Consejo de Estado de Colombia, File N: 25000-23-26-000-2001-01147-01(25614), 10 June 2004; among others.

[175]For instance, the CCC in a writ of protection of the constitutional rights of the debtors revoked the foreclosure declaration made in favor of the Savings and Housing Corporation "Colmena". See *Jorge Enrique Pineda Rodríguez v. Juzgado Sexto Civil del Circuito de Bucaramanga and other*, CCC, Sentencia T-597, 27 July 2006.

[176]For instance, *Granahorrar Banco Comercial S.A., and others v. Tribunal Administrativo de Cundinamarca*, Consejo de Estado de Colombia, File N: 25000-23-25-000-2001-9014-01 (AG-035), 20 June 2002.

companies to pay for the bank's spending in regard to legal costs and compensations following the unconstitutionality of the UPAC system. The insurance companies refused to compensate the bank. The bank then filed a statement of claim. The arbitration tribunal denied all the bank's claims, stating that the insurance company was not supposed to compensate the bank for the loss suffered in the performance of its policy, and condemned the bank to pay a penalty fee of 1,044 million of pesos.

The bank appealed the arbitration tribunal's decision to the Council of State of Colombia, the highest body of contentious administrative jurisdiction. In 2014, the Council of State ratified the decision of the arbitration tribunal and condemned the bank to pay an extra 25 million pesos in trial costs.[177] Therefore, not only did the CCC's decisions provide the room to sue the bank for past policies, fear of compensation claims and penalties or court fees have raised concerns within the bank and affected future policies, undermining its autonomy due to budget constraints.

In addition, the Bank of the Republic faced administrative lawsuits over the following 10 years for its policies after 1999, referring to earlier decisions. This provides evidence that the central bank does not seem uncontestable by citizens, and the CCC's decisions have had effects well beyond the issues decided in 1999. In 2004, citizens sued the bank in front of the Council of the State of Colombia, which is the country's highest body of contentious administrative jurisdiction, arguing that the calculation method of the UPAC decided upon by the bank in its decision No. 13 of 2000[178] had to take into account simple instead of compound interest rates in order to fulfill the mandate of the constitutional court in decision C-955 of 2000.[179] According to the plaintiffs, the compound interest increased their debt and was not in line with the social rule of law, based on which the CCC intervened with central bank policies. The court, however, declined the pretensions of the lawsuit.[180]

The same plaintiff filed another lawsuit in 2006 against the bank's External Resolution No. 3 of 2005,[181] in which the bank laid out the calculation of the new UVR for the new period. In this resolution, the bank set mortgage interest rates at 11%. The plaintiff argued that another financial institution, Bancafe, offered mortgage loans with an interest rate of 7%. Therefore, the bank did not fulfill its duty to set an interest rate lower than the lowest offered by any other financial institution. However, the court also denied this claim.[182]

---

[177]*Bank of the Republic v. Seguros Generales Suramericana S.A. and other*, File N: 11001-03-26-000-2014-00195-00(52969), 8 July 2015.

[178]Decision No. 13 of 2000 of the Bank of the Republic [Resolución Externa No. 13 de 2000].

[179]*Alejandro Baquero Nariño and other v. Congreso de la República de Colombia*, CCC, Sentencia C-955, 26 July 2000.

[180]*Ninfa Inés Andrade Navarrete and other v Bank of the Republic*, Consejo de Estado de Colombia, File N: 11001-03-27-000-2004-00074-00(14824), 23 August 2012.

[181]Decision No. 3 of 2005 of the Bank of the Republic [Resolución Externa No. 3 de 2005].

[182]*Ninfa Inés Andrade Navarrete v. Bank of the Republic*, Consejo de Estado de Colombia, File N: 11001-03-27-000-2006-00009-00(15971), 1 January 2008.

6.5 Summary and Outlook

This chapter provides a legal analysis of court interventions in central bank autonomy in Latin American Emerging Markets. Although it is rather common that governments aim to interfere with central bank autonomy, in Colombia the CCC limited central bank autonomy with reference to the social rule of law. Furthermore, the CCC has given green light to the intervention of the government in the central bank's policies by subjecting monetary policy to the government's development plan. Regarding the decisions that affected the autonomy of the Bank of the Republic, the CCC maintained that the legislative branch cannot interfere with the technical autonomy of the bank. However, the CCC reserved the right to intervene in the autonomy of the bank when ordering that the bank had to reduce mortgage interest rates, helping to ensure the rights to decent housing and credit democratization.

The Court implicitly augmented the bank's objective to achieve price stability, adding economic policy objectives. The rights to decent housing and credit democratization are often argued to benefit the common good. Yet, the Court's decisions were only to the benefit of some people who cannot afford decent housing or won't get mortgage loans in the market. Moreover, the additional objective may even be at odds with strategies to avoid inflation. Preserving the purchasing power of the currency and keeping inflation at bay, without doubt benefits the Colombian society in general. In addition, the CCC blamed the bank's board members for the household debt problems during the mortgage crisis, interfering with the personal autonomy of board members. Board members seem less autonomous if they can be punished in their patrimony, which adds an extra source of accountability not considered in the Organic Law of the bank.

The Courts decisions—based on the social rule of law—undermined legal certainty about the central bank's autonomy and led the bank to face a number of lawsuits over its policies. Legal certainty is, thus, in danger due to the very existence of the ambiguous social rule of law as very backbone of the Colombian Constitution. Given the lack of certainty from the principle of the social rule of law, the CCC has suggested that the written law is not what guides their constitutional interpretation, but reality.[183] Not surprisingly, decisions of the CCC have repeatedly led to an "institutional trains' crash [Own Translation]" that has made newspaper headlines since the enactment of the Colombian Constitution of 1991.[184]

When it comes to other Latin American countries there is a case in Peru where the courts implicitly intervened in the autonomy of the central bank. The Organic Law of the Central Reserve Bank of Peru states that it is a task of the Peruvian central bank

---

[183]*AA v. Instituto Colombiano de Bienestar Familiar*, CCC, Sentencia T-389, 27 May 1999.

[184]He refers to "choque de trenes institucionales" López Daza (2011), p. 177.

to decide on interest rates and its upper limits in contracts.[185] Although Peru's Congress has put forward that interest rates charged on unfulfilled obligations have to be within the limits set by the Peruvian central bank,[186] and the Peruvian central bank determined a maximum annual interest rate that people may charge in contracts and economic operations,[187] in Law 29,947 Congress set a different interest rate that universities could charge to students for student loans. According to this law, the interest rate that universities can charge should not be higher than the interest rates that banks charge in the inter-bank market.[188] The Constitutional Tribunal of Peru declared the law constitutional on August 27, 2014. The Court remained silent as to whether the law violates the autonomy of the Peruvian central bank.[189]

Legal References

Constitutions

Constitution of Colombia of 1886 [Constitución de Colombia de 1886, Diario Oficial No. 6758 y 6759, 7 August 1886]. Constitute Project, University of Texas at Austin.

Constitution of Colombia with Amendments through 2015 [English Translation of Constitución Política de Colombia, Diario Oficial No. 49.554, 25 June 2015]. Constitute Project, University of Texas at Austin, available at https://www.constituteproject.org/constitution/Colombia_2015.pdf

Legislation

Colombia

General Rulings of the Constitutional Court of Colombia [Reglamento Interno de la Corte Constitucional de Colombia, Acuerdo 01, 15 October 1992].

---

[185]CRBP Law Art. 24: *"The attributions and duties of the board are: g): Set the interest rates and the debt readjustment index set forth in the civil code for operations carried out by operators, excluding financial entities."*

[186]Civ. Code Peru Art. 1243: *"The conventional maximum loan interest rate is set by the Bank of Reserve of Peru.* [Own Translation]*"*.

[187]Circular letter 021-2007 of the CRBP [Circular No. 021-2007-BCRP].

[188]Law 29,947 of Peru [Ley 29.947, Diario Oficial No. 479.481, 28 November 2012].

[189]Colegio de Abogados de Lima Norte v. Congreso de la República del Perú, TC Peru, Sentencia Exp. No. 011-2013, 27 August 2014.

Law 546 of 1999, Colombia [Ley 546 de 1999, Diario Oficial No. 43.827, 23 December 1999].

Law of Education [Ley de Educación, Colombia Diario Oficial No. 41.214, 8 February 1994].

Law of Integral Social Security System [Ley de Seguridad Social Integral, Colombia Diario Oficial No. 41.148, 23 December 1993].

Organic Act of the Bank of the Republic of Colombia [Official Translation of the Ley Orgánica del Banco de la República, Ley 31 de 1992, Diario Oficial No. CXXVIII, 29 December 1992].

Peru

Organic Law of the Central Reserve Bank of Peru [Official Translation of the Ley Orgánica del banco central de reserve del Perú, Diario Oficial, 30 December 1992].

Law 29,947 of Peru [Ley 29.947, Diario Oficial No. 479.481, 28 November 2012].

Executive Decrees

Colombia

Executive Decree 677 of 1972 [Decreto Ejecutivo 677 de 1972, Diario Oficial No. 33.594, 18 May 1972].

Executive Decree 1229 of 1972 [Decreto Ejecutivo 1229 de 1972, Diario Oficial No. 33.663, 16 August 1972].

Executive Decree 269 of 1974 [Decreto Ejecutivo 269 de 1974, Diario Oficial No. 3.072, 21 February 1974].

Executive Decree 1685 of 1975 [Decreto 1685 de 1975, Diario Oficial No. 34.402, 18 September 1975].

Executive Decree 58 of 1976 [Decreto Ejecutivo 58 de 1976, Diario Oficial No. 34.489, 1 February 1976].

Executive Decree 2475 of 1980 [Decreto Ejecutivo 2475 de 1980, Diario Oficial No. 35.610, 29 September 1980].

Executive Decree 2929 of 1982 [Decreto Ejecutivo 2929 de 1982, Diario Oficial No. 36.115, 22 October 1982].

Executive Decree 1131 of 1984 [Decreto Ejecutivo 1131 de 1984, Diario Oficial No. 36.637, 5 June 1984].

Executive Decree 1319 of 1989 [Decreto Ejecutivo 1319 de 1989, Diario Oficial No. 38.869, 22 June 1989].

Executive Decree 1730 of 1991 [Decreto Ejecutivo 1730 de 1991, Diario Oficial No. 39.889, 4 July 1991].

Executive Decree 2067 of 1991 [Decreto Ejecutivo 2067, Diario Oficial No. 40.012, 4 September 1991].

Executive Decree 663 of 1993 [Decreto Ejecutivo 663 de 1993, Diario Oficial No. 40.820, 5 April 1993].

External Resolutions

Colombia

Decision No. 26 of 1994, Bank of the Republic of Colombia [Resolución Externa No. 26 de 1994].
Decision No. 10 of 1999, Bank of the Republic of Colombia [Resolución Externa No. 10 de 1999].
Decision No. 13 of 2000, Bank of the Republic of Colombia [Resolución Externa No. 13 de 2000].
Decision No. 14 of 2000, Bank of the Republic of Colombia [Resolución Externa No. 14 de 2000].
Decision No. 3 of 2005, Bank of the Republic of Colombia [Resolución Externa No. 3 de 2005].

Peru

Circular Letter 021-2007 of the Central Reserve Bank of Peru [Circular No. 021-2007-BCRP].

Case Law

Colombia

Consejo de Estado de Colombia [Council of State of Colombia]

Granahorrar Banco Comercial S.A., and others v. Tribunal Administrativo de Cundinamarca, Consejo de Estado de Colombia, File N: 25000-23-25-000-2001-9014-01(AG-035), 20 June 2002,
Gunar Raul Ramírez and others v. Bank of the Republic of Colombia and other, Consejo de Estado de Colombia, File N: 76001-23-31-000-2001-02078-01 (26174), 2 February 2004.
Hugo Yesid Suarez Sierra v. Bank of the Republic and other, Consejo de Estado de Colombia, File N: 25000-23-26-000-2001-01147-01(25614), 10 June 2004.
Myriam Valencia de Zafra v. Bank of the Republic and other, Consejo de Estado de Colombia, File N: 76001-23-31-000-2001-00804-01(28298), 13 April 2006.
Ninfa Inés Andrade Navarrete v. Bank of the Republic, Consejo de Estado de Colombia, File N: 11001-03-27-000-2006-00009-00(15971), 1 January 2008.

Ninfa Inés Andrade Navarrete and other v. Bank of the Republic, Consejo de Estado de Colombia, File N: 11001-03-27-000-2004-00074-00(14824), 23 August 2012.
Bank of the Republic v. Seguros Generales Suramericana S.A. and other, File N: 11001-03-26-000-2014-00195-00(52969), 8 July 2015.

Corte Constitucional de Colombia [Constitutional Court of Colombia]

Jaime Rafael Pedraza Vanegas v. Congreso de la República de Colombia, CCC, Sentencia C-050, 10 February 1994.
Pablo Antonio Bustos Sánchez v. Congreso de la República de Colombia, CCC, Sentencia C-083, 1 March 1995.
Marcela Barona Montua v. Congreso de la República de Colombia, CCC, Sentencia C-109, 15 March 1995.
Carlos Eduardo Naranjo Florez v. Congreso de la República de Colombia, CCC, Sentencia C-151, 5 April 1995.
Juan Carlos Ramírez Gómez v. Congreso de la República de Colombia, CCC, Sentencia C-191, 8 May 1996.
José Alirio Montoya Restrepo and others v. Caja Nacional de Previsión, CCC, Sentencia T-068, 5 March 1998.
Celmira Waldo de Valoyes v. Caja Nacaional de Previsión Social-Seccional Chocó, CCC, Sentencia SU-111, 6 March 1997.
AA v. Instituto Colombiano de Bienestar Familiar, CCC, Sentencia T-389, 27 May 1999.
René Vargas Pérez v. Congreso de la República de Colombia, CCC, Sentencia C-481, 7 July 1999.
Humberto de Jesús Longas Londono v. Gobierno de la República de Colombia, CCC, Sentencia C-700, 16 September 1999.
Emperatriz Castillo Burbano v. Gobierno de la República de Colombia, CCC, Sentencia C-747, 6 October 1999.
Luisa del Carmen Anaya Atencio and others v. Sala de Casación Laboral de la Corte Suprema de Justicia and others, CCC, Sentencia T-525, 23 July 1999.
Andrés Quintero Rubiano v. Congreso de la República de Colombia, CCC, Sentencia C-208, 1 March 2000.
Alejandro Baquero Nariño and other v. Congreso de la República de Colombia, CCC, Sentencia C-955, 26 July 2000.
Sixto Acuna Acevedo and others v. Congreso de la República de Colombia, CCC, Sentencia C-1140, 30 August 2000.
Armando José Soto Jiménez v. Congreso de la República de Colombia, CCC, Sentencia C-1064, 10 October 2001.
Andrés de Zubiría Samper v. Congreso de la República de Colombia, CCC, Sentencia C-776, 9 September 2003.
Jorge Enrique Pineda Rodríguez v. Juzgado Sexto Civil del Circuito de Bucaramanga and other, CCC, Sentencia T-597, 27 July 2006.

María Camila Silva Mogollón v. Congreso de la República de Colombia, CCC, Sentencia C-860, 18 October 2006.

German Arango Rojas v. Corte Constitucional de la República de Colombia, CCC, Sentencia A-195, 20 May 2009.

Camilo Velásquez Reyes v. Corte Constitucional de la República de Colombia, CCC, Sentencia A-256, 4 August 2009.

Ivan Santiago Martínez Vásquez v. Congreso de la República de Colombia, CCC, Sentencia C-100, 23 February 2011.

Felipe Ortega Escobar and other v. Congreso de la República de Colombia, CCC, Sentencia C-027, 27 January 2012.

Peru

Tribunal Constitucional del Perú [Constitutional Tribunal of Peru]

Colegio de Abogados de Lima Norte v. Congreso de la República del Perú,TC Peru, Sentencia Exp. No. 011-2013, 27 August 2014.

References

Alesina A, Carrasquilla A, Steiner R (2005) Toward a truly independent Central Bank in Colombia. In: Alesina A (ed) Institutional reforms: the case of Colombia. The MIT Press, pp 337–360

Azcuna A (1993) The Writ of Amparo: a remedy to enforce Fundamental Rights. Ateneo Law J 37 (13):1. Available at http://ateneolawjournal.com/Media/uploads/d1568003d7212bca8050a05a7f68dcd9.pdf

Bank of the Republic (2000) Los Codirectores del Banco de la Republica fijan su criterio sobre UVR ante la Corte Constitucional. Press Release, 29 February 2000. Available at http://www.banrep.gov.co/es/node/6293

Betlem G (2002) The Doctrine of consistent interpretation – managing legal uncertainty. Oxford J Legal Stud 22(3):397–418. https://doi.org/10.1093/ojls/22.3.397

Bonilla D (2013) Introduction. In: Bonilla D (ed) Constitutionalism of the global south: the activist tribunals of India, South Africa and Colombia. Cambridge University Press

Carbonari F, Vargas J (2009) A bridge to peace through citizenship building: guaranteeing health and education rights in Colombia. In: Gacitúa-Marió E, Georgieva S, Norton A (eds) Building equality and opportunity through social guarantees. The World Bank, pp 231–257

Castillo Calle MA (2013) El Derecho Constitucional Económico en el Perú. Nómadas, Revista Crítica de Ciencias Sociales y Jurídicas 1–9. https://doi.org/10.5209/rev_NOMA.2013.42352

Catrile F, Pita JJ (2011) Historia de la Creación del Banco Central de la República Argentina. Investigaciones Económicas del BCRA:117–138. Available at http://www.bcra.gov.ar/pdfs/investigaciones/64_Liddle.pdf

Cerra Nolasco E (2001) El Control de Constitucionalidad. Análisis de la Doctrina de la Corte en los 10 Años de Vigencia Constitucionalidad. Revista de Derecho Universidad del Norte 16:162–179

Dickson B (2007) Judicial activism in common law Supreme Courts. Oxford University Press

Escobar Martinez LM (2006) La Modulacion de Sentencias: Una Antigua Practica Europea. Universitas Revista de Ciencias Juridicas Law Review 55(112):91–110. Available at http://revistas.javeriana.edu.co/index.php/vnijuri/article/view/14644

Eskridge W (1991) Overriding Supreme Court statutory interpretation decisions. Yale Law J 101 (2):331–455. https://doi.org/10.2307/796805

Fique Pinto LF (2008) La Política Pública de Vivienda en Colombia: Conflicto de Objetivos. Bitácora Urbano Territorial 2(13):73–89. Available at http://search.proquest.com/openview/ca75e7d77e5b93f11ddc14eaeda7ec25/1?pq-origsite=gscholar&cbl=2035745

Forero E (2004) Evolution of the mortgage system in Colombia: from the UPAC to the UVR system. Hous Finance Int 18(3):32–41. Available at https://www.researchgate.net/publication/228457381_Evolution_of_the_mortgage_system_in_Colombia_From_the_UPAC_to_the_UVR_System

Goldmann M (2014) Adjudicating economics? Central Bank independence and the appropriate standard of judicial review. Germ Law J 15(2):265–280. Available at http://heinonline.org/HOL/LandingPage?handle=hein.journals/germlajo15&div=20&id=&page=

Held G (2000) Políticas de Vivienda de Interés Social Orientadas al Mercado: Experiencias Recientes de Subsidios a la Demanda en Chile, Costa Rica y Colombia. CEPAL-SERIE Financiamento del Desarrollo No. 96, 3–53. Available at http://repositorio.cepal.org/bitstream/handle/11362/5304/1/S00050485_es.pdf

Hofstetter M, Tobar J, Urrutia M (2011) Effects of a Mortgage interest rate subsidy: evidence from Colombia. IDB Working Paper Series No. IDB-WP-257. Available at https://publications.iadb.org/bitstream/handle/11319/3106/Effects%20of%20a%20Mortgage%20Interest%20Rate%20Subsidy%3A%20Evidence%20from%20Colombia.pdf?sequence

Kmiec K (2004) The origin and common meanings of judicial activism. Calif Law Rev 92 (5):1441–1477. https://doi.org/10.2307/3481421

Kugler M, Rosenthal H (2005) Checks and balances: an assessment of the institutional separation of political powers in Colombia. In: Alesina A (ed) Institutional reforms: the case of Colombia. The MIT Press, pp 75–102

López Daza G (2011) El Juez Constitucional Colombiano como Legislador Positivo: Un Gobierno de los Jueces? Revista Mexicana de Derecho Constitucional 24:169–193. Available at http://www.scielo.org.mx/scielo.php?pid=S1405-91932011000100005&script=sci_arttext

Martinez Caballero A (2000) Tipos de Sentencias en el Control Constitucional de las Leyes: la Experiencia Colombiana. Revista Estudios Socio-Jurídicos 2(1):9–32. Available at: https://scholar.google.com/scholar?hl=de&q=tipos+de+sentencias+en+el+control+constitucional+de+las+leyes&btnG=&lr=

Mavčič A (2001) Constitutional review. Bookworld Publications

Mora A (2010) El UPAC y la UVR: Aspectos Generales sobre el Origen y Desarrollo del Crédito Hipotecario Colombia. Revista MBA EAFIT 1:12–27. Available at http://www.eafit.edu.co/revistas/revistamba/Documents/upac-uvr.pdf

Olano Garcia H (2004) Tipologia de Nuestras Sentencias Constitucionales. Universitas Revista de Ciencias Juridicas Law Rev 53(108):572–602. Available at http://revistas.javeriana.edu.co/index.php/vnijuri/article/view/14750

Palombella G (2016) Principles and disagreements in international law (with a view from Dworkin's Legal Theory). In: Pineschi L (ed) General principles of law–the role of the Judiciary, Ius Gentium: Comp Perspect Law Just 46:3–21. Available at https://link.springer.com/chapter/10.1007/978-3-319-19180-5_1

Peters C (2016) Legal formalism, procedural principles, and judicial constraint in American adjudication. In: Pineschi L (ed) General principles of law - the role of the judiciary, Ius Gentium: Comparative Perspectives on Law and Justice, vol. 46. Springer, pp 23–44. https://doi.org/10.1007/978-3-319-19180-5_2

Ribeiro M (2003) Limiting arbitrary power: the vagueness Doctrine in Canadian constitutional law. UBC Press

Rivero Ortega R (2013) Derecho Administrativo Económico, Sexta Edición. Marcial Pons

Robertson D (2010) The judge as political theorist: contemporary constitutional review. Princeton University Press

Rodriguez Garavito C, Rodríguez Franco D (2015) Radical deprivation on trial. Cambridge University Press

Roosevelt K (2008) The myth of judicial activism: making sense of supreme court decisions. Yale University Press

Ruggiero C (2012) Judicial power in a federal system: Canada, United States and Germany. LFB Scholarly Publishing LLC

Uprimny R (2006) Legitimidad y Conveniencia del Control Constitucional a la Economía. In: Buitrago F (ed) En la Encrucijada: Colombia en el Siglo XXI, Uniandes Journals, pp 38–68

Urrutia M, Namen O (2012) História do Crédito Hipotecário na Colombia. Ensayos sobre Política Económica 30(67):280–306. Available at http://www.banrep.gov.co/sites/default/files/publicaciones/archivos/espe_art9_67.pdf?_ga=2.80682007.1050366040.1496611677-1707481394.1494063075

Vanberg G (2001) Legislative- judicial relations: a game-theoretic approach to constitutional review. Am J Polit Sci 45(2):346–361. https://doi.org/10.2307/2669345

Chapter 7
Economic Emergency and Central Bank Autonomy in Argentina

7.1 Introduction

Argentina's economic history is a success story gone wrong. With its independence from Spain, Argentina could overcome the centralist and authoritarian rule of the Spanish conquerors.[1] After struggling with a dictatorship in the early years as an independent republic (Juan Manuel Rosas from 1829 to 1852),[2] a relatively long period of economic growth and stability began in Argentina arguably because of the classical liberal principles of the country's first constitution. The Constitution of 1853 institutionalized the protection of property rights, stabilized the legal rules, provided economic liberty and encouraged foreign immigration.[3]

---

[1]In Argentina, the crisis of 2001 was not a consequence of Menem's liberal policies but the result of a gradual rejection of the cultural and legal liberal values. Argentina's modernization could get rid of absolutism, mercantilism and disregard of the law that were the negative features of the Spanish heritage. See García Hamilton (2005), pp. 521–527.

[2]*Ibid.*, p. 528.

[3]Juan Bautista Alberdi set the philosophical basis for the liberal constitution of 1853. See Gelli (2003), p. 166.

In his book "Bases and Starting Points for the Political Organization of the Argentina Republic", Alberdi developed the fundamental structure of the new constitution of the country based on classical liberal principles. To read more about the philosophy behind the Argentinean constitution. See J. Alberdi, Bases y Puntos de Partida para la Organización Política de la República Argentina. To read more about the economic basis of the constitution. See Alberdi (1858). In sum, it is possible to see that in Constitution of 1853 provided the institutional basis for economic development and the rule of law. By 1910 Argentina was on the way to become a world economic power. J. García explains that Argentina at that time was the main exporter of grains and meat. Her GDP was equivalent to 50% of the GDP of the rest of Latin America and her level of trade rose to 7% of world trade. See García Hamilton (2005), p. 528.

© The Author(s), under exclusive license to Springer Nature Switzerland AG 2021
A. L. Tapia-Hoffmann, *Legal Certainty and Central Bank Autonomy in Latin American Emerging Markets*, European Yearbook of International Economic Law 15, https://doi.org/10.1007/978-3-030-70986-0_7

After some successful years, authoritarian governments wrecked[4] the poster child of economic development in Latin America by governing with a centralist style.[5] The mismanagement of the economy by authoritarian leaders undermined the institutional structure of the country and triggered recurrent episodes of hyperinflation and crisis.[6] Argentina has defaulted several times on its debt obligations (four times since 1980).[7]

During crisis episodes, governments have taken far-reaching policy measures. Although emergency decrees are executive orders that are typically issued by governments to deal with difficult situations under exceptional circumstances, over the last 35 years, the use of emergency decrees has been common in Argentina. Emergency decrees are exceptions to the rule of law that entail a high degree of legal uncertainty because of the suspension of the constitutional order.[8]

The use of emergency decrees increased during the 1980s and 1990s. Raul Alfonsin signed ten emergency decrees during his presidency between 1983 and 1989. However, during the 10-year presidency of Carlos Saul Menem[9] (1989 to 1999) the use of emergency decrees increased[10] to 545 in total.[11] Menem

---

[4]It is argued that the seed to Argentina's decline was an educational reform that started in 1907. This reform tried to integrate immigrants by exaggerating nationalist feelings. Those feelings triggered the cult to the personality of national heroes and politicians and substituted hard work and respect for property rights by entitlements and pride of natural resources. See *ibid.*, p. 529.

[5]The worst occurred during the government of Juan Domingo Perón who started the wave of nationalization of private enterprises and the seemingly unstoppable expansion of the public deficit, commonly financed through monetary expansion. Perón disregarded the rule of law. Perón managed to reform the Constitution of 1853 in a way that property rights and contracts were not guaranteed anymore. Further, Perón took advantage of his broad political capital to remove judges and replace them with much friendlier judges. See *ibid.*, pp. 531–532.

[6]According to the data presented by S. Edwards and G. Tabellini, the annual rate of Argentina's inflation between 1983 and 1987 was 380%. See Edwards and Tabellini (1991), p. 19.

[7]Thomas and Cachanosky (2006), pp. 70–71. See also Feldstein (2002), p. 10.

[8]Grossman (1986), p. 36.

[9]Carlos Saul Menem inherited a country highly convulsed and indebted which motivated him to change the dynamics of Argentinean markets. Among the measures taken by Menem were to open the economy to international trade and privatize troubled public companies. Through the Convertibility Law, in 1991, Menem replaced a central bank in charge of monetary policy by a central bank in charge of managing the currency board. See Thomas and Cachanosky (2006), pp. 70–71. See also Feldstein (2002), p. 10.

[10]Ferreira Rubio and Goretti (1996), p. 448.

[11]Avalos (2012), p. 153.

systematically broke the rule of law through emergency decrees issued unilaterally[12] and without any constitutional or legal authorization.[13]

The use of emergency decrees has continued after the turn of the millennium. During his 2-year presidency between 1999 and 2001, Fernando de la Rúa issued 73 decrees of emergency, most of which aimed to control the crisis by reducing public spending. Eduardo Duhalde issued 154 decrees of emergency while he served as the President of Argentina for approximately a year and a half between January 2002 and May 2003. Nestor Kirchner, who was the President of Argentina between 2003 and 2007, issued 270 emergency decrees. Christina Fernandez de Kirchner, who took office at the end of 2007, issued 29 emergency decrees until 2011.[14]

This chapter suggests that the use of emergency decrees as well as emergency laws is a threat to central bank autonomy in Argentina. Elaborating on the use and legitimization of economic emergency decrees/laws during crisis periods concerning central bank law and the convertibility law in Argentina, the chapter shows that a continuous state of emergency has undermined legal certainty about the central bank's autonomy and objectives, which deteriorated central bank credibility.

7.2 The State of Public Emergency

7.2.1 Definition and Requirements of State of Public Emergency

The Cambridge Dictionary defines *state of emergency*[15] as "a temporary system of rules to deal with an extremely dangerous or difficult situation."[16] The state of

---

[12]The Congress of Argentina opened the doors for the president of the country's only rule through the Administrative and Economic Emergency laws that were enacted in the middle of the economic crisis left by Alfonsin's government, by both main political forces in the Argentinean Congress (Radicals and Justicialists) almost without opposition. The new legal rules would allow the president to set measures if the Congress was not fast enough to react to mitigate a crisis. Based on this the government issued several economic emergency decrees, arguing that the Congress was not fast enough to face the economic crisis. Further, using the presidential attribution of vetoing the legislation enacted by the Congress, Menem partially or totally vetoed the legislation that was against his emergency economic plan. See Ferreira Rubio and Goretti (1996), pp. 445–446.

[13]Menem used emergency decrees, for instance, to appoint general prosecutor of the Supreme Court, members of the control organisms, among other authorities that required Senate approval to be appointed. See *ibid.*, pp. 443–444.

[14]Avalos (2012), p. 156.

[15]A synonym for state of emergency is state of siege. Arguably the term state of emergency is used to refer to a state that is less serious than a state of siege. See Fitzpatrick (1994), p. 1. The term siege, according to the *Oxford Dictionary* on Lexico.com, entails some form of forced military action. It also entails total control.

[16]*Cambridge Dictionary,* Definition of *state of emergency* in English.

emergency should be the exception and not the rule. Otherwise, the legal order will become obsolete and will be replaced by an authoritarian rule.[17]

According to the Paris Minimum Standards of Human Rights Norms in a State of Emergency,[18] a public emergency is an "exceptional situation of crisis or public danger, actual or imminent, which affects the whole population and the whole population of the area to which the declaration applies and constitutes a threat to the organized life of the community of which the state is composed."[19]

Traditionally, the executive branch declares the state of emergency. This declaration allows the head of government to take emergency measures through decree, which is an "official statement that something must happen."[20] Decrees are unilateral decisions taken by the executive branch in exercise of the administrative function of the state. Emergency decrees are normative orders that embody exceptional measures taken in times of deep crisis. In this sense, emergency decrees deal with topics that in normal circumstances are within the exclusive competence of the legislative branch, but in extraordinary cases demand radical and fast measures that require the competence of the executive branch.[21]

Public emergencies can have different origins. The most common emergencies are those triggered by an external attack, a war, a natural disaster or economic meltdowns. Emergencies caused by economic meltdowns are similar to emergencies triggered by natural disasters and external conflicts, if they threaten the very constitution of the country. Economic emergences may make necessary the implementation of economic plans that would not be accepted under normal circumstances,[22] for instance the economic measures taken during the Great Depression in the United States by President Franklin D. Roosevelt.[23] On the other hand, the nature of the

---

[17]Agamben mentions that the declaration of state of emergency or exception can be a tool that even governments elected democratically tend to use to overturn the law temporary or even permanently. The Third Reich is a case of permanent state of exception that abolished the rule of law. Through a decree, Hitler suspended the articles of the Weimar constitution that guaranteed fundamental rights. This decree was in force during all the time that Hitler was in office. See Agamben and Borrás (2003), pp. 58–59.

[18]The International Law Association approved parameters to which governments must attach during the declaration of a state of emergency at its 61st conference. The Committee on the Enforcement of Human Rights Law was involved in the creation of this set of minimum standards. The objective of establishing this non-binding rule is to help to preserve the rule of law even in cases when government must suspend some rights because of an exceptional and unforeseeable circumstance, such as an emergency. See Lillich (1985), p. 1072.

[19]The Paris Minimum Standards of Human Rights Norms in a State of Emergency Sec. (A) 1 (b) [Version published by The American Journal of International Law, October 1985] [hereinafter Paris Minimum Standards].

[20]*Cambridge Dictionary*, Definition of *decree* in English.

[21]Avalos (2012), p. 149.

[22]Scheuerman (1999–2000), p. 1869.

[23]A very famous case that supports the emergency doctrine and speaks to the view that the constitution survives times of crisis is the management of the Great Depression by Franklin Delano Roosevelt (FDR). The crisis justified breaking the constitution, for instance, by eliminating the

emergency tends to be difficult to determine. For example, a hurricane, which can lead to a natural disaster, has political and economic consequences. Moreover, economic breakdowns can trigger a political crisis.[24]

According to the Siracusa Principles on the Limitation and Derogation of Provisions in the International Covenant on Civil and Political Rights, the declaration of a state of emergency must involve an "actual and imminent danger which threatens the life of the nation."[25] A *threat to the life of the nation* should here be understood as a real and not hypothetical event of great magnitude that distresses the whole population by threatening them physically, their territory, the independence of the nation and the proper system of protection of human rights.[26] The Siracusa Principles imply that simple internal disturbances are not enough to justify disregarding human rights treaties. Neither are mere economic conflicts.[27]

The Paris Minimum Standards of Human Rights and the Siracusa Principles on the Limitation and Derogation of Provisions in the International Covenant on Civil and Political Rights present requirements and limits to the exercise of the declaration of a state of emergency and the application of extraordinary measures. Among them are, first, a clear time frame that should not be disregarded. If the period of the emergency has to be extended, a new declaration of emergency must be issued and approved by the legislative branch. Second, the legislative branch should not be dissolved. Third, the measures taken during the state of emergency must be subject to judicial review.[28] Fourth, the emergency measures must be proportionate and strictly necessary to deal with the crisis. Fifth, ordinary means are not available to deal with the emergency.[29]

---

equilibrium between the executive and legislative branches, ignoring people's right against illegal searches and seizures, or allowing confiscations. FDR made several decisions without legislative approval even though it was required. This behavior triggered uncertainty about the validity of measures. FDR even issued the Emergency Banking Act through which he intervened in the legislative attribution of pursuing monetary policy and eliminated the gold standard in contractual clauses. This affected contracts retroactively and caused a stock market crash due to the rapid devaluation of the American dollar. Despite its initial opposition, the Supreme Court had to support the debunking of the gold standard to prevent the President from starting a public and populistic war against the court. FDR threatened to address the nation to blame the Supreme Court justices for not allowing the government to counteract the crisis. See Roots (2000), pp. 262–283; Humphreys (2006), pp. 677; and 678–679. See also: Meyler (2007), p. 540.

[24]Meyler (2007), p. 547.

[25]Siracusa Principles on the Limitation and Derogation of Provisions in the International Covenant on Civil and Political Rights II A 39 (a) [Posted by the American Association for the International Commission of Jurists, April 1985] [hereinafter Siracusa Principles].

[26]Siracusa Principles II A 39 (a), and (b) [Posted by the American Association for the International Commission of Jurists, April 1985].

[27]Siracusa Principles II A 40, and 41.

[28]Paris Minimum Standards Sec. (A) 3, 5, and 7.

[29]Siracusa Principles II C 51, 53, 54, and 56.

7.2.2   Preserving the Rule of Law in a Public Emergency

7.2.2.1   Protection of Basic Rights

> Those who would give up essential liberty to purchase a little temporary safety deserve neither liberty nor safety.[30]

A crisis that threatens the life of the nation requires rapid action by authorities. Therefore, a public emergency entails more limits on the exercise of rights than those imposed by the constitution and requires a modification of the state's power structure and the authorities' competences.[31] At the center of the concern about public emergency literature is the way in which governments can take effective measures to stop a crisis but at the same time assure that the rule of law will prevail.[32] Despite modification of the rules, a country should not end up with a lawless regime.[33]

Constitutional rules must be stable to be a credible constraint to state power. However, from the perspective of an emergency, constitutional rules must also provide some degree of flexibility to allow authorities to deal with uncommon circumstances.[34] Thus, the constitution should not be a "suicide pact" that ties the hands of government in good times and does not allow it to untie its own hands when strict measures must be taken.[35]

The flexibility of constitutional rules to mitigate crises creates uncertainty about the legal framework,[36] especially about the prevalence of fundamental rights.[37] Indeed, human rights are most vulnerable during a crisis, because authorities may

---

[30]Franklin and Temple Franklin (1818), p. 270.

[31]Gross and Ní Aoláin (2006), p. 17.

[32]*Ibid.*, p. 33.

[33]Humphreys (2006), p. 679.

[34]Gross and Ní Aoláin (2006), p. 68.

[35]J. Elster uses the term *suicide pact* suggesting, for example, that even though granting autonomy in the constitution gives the central bank more autonomy, this statement is challenged in times of emergency. Assuring the central bank commitment to its legal objective, ideally price stability, is for some regarded as dangerous in times of economic crisis because it ties the hands of the government in a way that they cannot efficiently stop the crisis. It is even argued that allowing the central bank to care for employment can be positive in times of economic crisis when unemployment rises. When the central bank objective is strict about pursuing low inflation and the central bank board willing to pursue the goal to maintain reputation, keeping the possibility of legislative removal of the board members is considered necessary. See Elster (1994), pp. 220–222.

[36]Meyler (2007), pp. 539–540.

[37]In cases of emergency caused by terrorism, for instance, some basic guarantees of personal freedom have not prevailed. Through a military order president George W. Bush got rid of basic guarantee of the due process such as the protection against arbitrary detention and subjecting civil foreigners to military courts just on the belief that they could somehow be related to terrorism. The military order issued in times of emergency due to terrorism denied potential detainees the right of having a lawyer, of being protected against unusual punishment, which are rights guaranteed by the Constitution of the United States. See also Agamben and Borrás (2003), p. 59.

take extreme measures that often sacrifice people's rights. Therefore, constitutional rules must protect people's rights in times of crisis. *Cole* notes,

> It is in times of crisis that constitutional rights and liberties are most needed, because the temptation to sacrifice them in the name of national security will be at its most acute. To government officials, civil rights and liberties often appear to be mere obstacles to effective protection of the national interest.[38]

International human rights treaties aim to deal with the legal uncertainty stemming from an uncontrolled use of the state of emergency. Article 27 (1) of the American Convention on Human Rights states, "In time of war, public danger, or other emergency [...] a State [...] may take measures derogating from its obligations under the present Convention [...]".[39] The term *derogation* in international law emphasizes that this can only be a controlled and temporally limited suspension of human rights during an emergency as opposed to an arbitrary application of martial law or the state of emergency. The finality of using the term *derogation* is intended to allow governments to suspend lawfully and credibly some human rights with the commitment to restore them when the crisis ends. By adhering to derogation, governments signal that the measures taken respond to an exceptional situation during which it is not possible to follow the standard legal processes.[40] The process of derogation entails the public disclosure of the emergency policies.[41]

Some rights cannot be derogated under any circumstances. According to the Siracusa Principles and Paris Minimum Standards, these rights are life; freedom from torture, cruel, inhuman or degrading treatment or punishment; freedom from medical and scientific experimentation without free consent; freedom from slavery or involuntary servitude; the right not to be imprisoned because of contractual debt; the right not to be convicted or sentenced to a heavier penalty by virtue of retroactive criminal legislation; the right to recognition as a person before the law; freedom of thought, conscience and religion;[42] the right to personal liberty and to a fair trial; rights of minorities, families and children; right to nationality; right to participate in the government; and right to judicial protection, habeas corpus and Writ of Amparo.[43]

Countries with strong institutions tend to derogate more than countries with weak institutions. In countries with high electoral accountability and judicial oversight of public authorities, the government tends to protect itself by derogating. On the other hand, countries with weak institutions, in which authorities are not effectively

---

[38]Cole (2003), p. 2567.
[39]ACHR Art. 27 para 1.
[40]See Siracusa Principles II B 42, 43, 44, and 45.
[41]Hafner-Burton et al. (2011), p. 680.
[42]Siracusa Principles II D 58.
[43]Paris Minimum Standards Sec. (C).

subject to control and accountability, tend to not derogate, because they are accustomed to disrespect human rights on an everyday basis.[44]

From the list of rights protected in the event of derogation we can see that economic emergencies and the protection of property rights are treated differently to the point of not being protected at all in times of emergency if taking the protection of property to the extreme risks a breakdown of the economic system.[45] For example, American law relieves the government of the obligation to pay the owner for damage to or the loss of his or her property. But the police power of the state cannot be abused. As long as a decision was sound and not arbitrary, it will be enforced even if it turns out later to have been unnecessary. Public officials must be able to act swiftly and effectively during a crisis.[46]

Argentina's Constitution of 1853 generally guarantees people's property rights.[47] Between 1876 and 2007, Argentina has derogated from human rights treaties during national emergencies six times for a total period of 3 years.[48] Although property rights were undermined during this period, the infringement of property rights had to

---

[44]Hafner-Burton et al. (2011), p. 682. The article employs statistical tools and case studies based on systematic empirical data on derogations of human rights treaties in times of emergency, showing that the main objective of well-established democracies with stable institutions in derogating from responsibilities is to solve potential domestic problems such as censure from voters, interest groups and judges instead of preserving international reputation. See *Ibid.*, p. 703.

[45]Meyler (2007), p. 540.

[46]Lee (2015), p. 391.

[47]Constitution of Argentina of 1853 Art. 17 [Copy of the Original Manuscript of the Constitución de la Federación Argentina published by the Congress Library (Biblioteca del Congreso de Argentina)] [hereinafter Const. Argentina 1853]. This constitution also allowed free navigation in Argentinean rivers of every ship that has trade purposes; (See: Const Argentina 1853 Art. 26) giving the government the obligation of signing free trade agreements (See Const Argentina 1853 Art. 27) and placing no restrictions on immigration especially from Europe (See Const. Argentina 1853 Art. 25 and Art. 64 (16)).

[48]Hafner-Burton et al. (2011), p. 679.

This data was obtained from the website of the United Nations Treaty Section and the Council of Europe Treaty Office, the Annual Reports of the Inter-American Commission of Human Rights, notices of derogation provided by the Organization of American States, among others. See *ibid.*, p. 687.

According to the Annual Reports of the Inter-American Court of Human Rights, the Argentinean government has abused the declaration of state of emergency. The military government declared the state of emergency in 1976 and this had been extended with no valid reason until at least 1981. See Inter-American Commission on Human Rights (IACHR), Annual Report of the Inter-American Commission on Human Rights 1980–1981, 16 October 1981.

The Court criticized the unjustified state of emergency in Argentina during which military trials of civilians, forced disappearance and denegation of the habeas corpus took place. See Inter-American Commission on Human Rights (IACHR), Annual Report of the Inter-American Commission on Human Rights 1981–1982, 20 September 1982.

According to the database of "The State of Emergency Data Project" based on the archives of the United Nations, between 1995 and 2013 Argentina derogated twice because of "manmade" emergency. Fernando de la Rúa issued the derogation in 2001 twice. See Zwitter et al. (2014). See also State of Emergency Mapping Project (STEMP) at http://emergencymapping.org/database2.html.

be within the scope of necessity. Generally, the courts did protect contract and property rights, ruling in favor of property owners that faced unreasonable lawsuits following emergency decrees.[49]

7.2.2.2   Public Emergency and the Counterweight System

From a constitutional perspective, keeping a system of checks and balances guarantees the protection of human rights and the rule of law during a public emergency. The head of the public administration, which is either a president or the respective head of government, must take or delegate the emergency measures.[50] The legislative branch approves the measures, and the judiciary supervises them.[51]

Commonly, the function of the executive branch in the legislative process is limited to the vetoing power of the President, but in times of emergency, the President also has the attribution of creating legislation through decrees.[52] While the legislative branch delegates the law-making attribution to the executive branch in case of emergency, the legislative branch is also responsible to confirm or approve the official declaration of the state of emergency made by the executive branch.[53]

Judicial review is a critical element of the debate about economic emergency. The courts have the responsibility to preserve the rights that should prevail even in times

---

De la Rúa declared a state of emergency (siege) for thirty days via the emergency decree 1678 of December 2001, as consequence of the unrest that the country was facing because of the economic crisis. See Emergency Decree 1678 of 2001, Argentina [Decreto de Emergencia 1678, Diario Oficial, 19 December 2001].

Yet even though there were several declarations of state of emergency in Argentina in recent years, there is no report of any notice of derogation.

[49] See CSJN Argentina, *Agustin Ercolano v. Julieta Lanteri de Renshaw*, Fallos: 137:170, 28 April 1922. In the context of the housing crisis an emergency law was enacted to lower rent payments. Following the disposition of the emergency law Jose Horta sued the house owner Ernesto Harguindeguy to demand reduced rent payments. The Plaintiff won in first instance and the defendant appealed in front of the Supreme Court. The Supreme Court revoked the first decision arguing that the law was retroactive and affected a previous renting contract and, therefore, the property rights of the defendant. Further, the Court argued that setting a maximum for monthly rent payments can only be a temporary measure and should only affect future rent contracts. See also CSJN Argentina, *José Horta v. Ernesto Harguindeguy*, Fallos: 136:170, 21 August 1922.

The plaintiff Leonardo Mango sued Ernesto Traba. The judge decided in favor of the plaintiff. However, an emergency law enacted to solve the housing crisis extended the renting terms, quashing that judicial decision. The plaintiff appealed in front of the Supreme Court of Justice of Argentina. The Court finally revoked the first judicial decision and nullified the first decision which was in favor of the plaintiff. See CSJN Argentina, *Leonardo Mango v. Ernesto Traba*, Fallos: 144:220, 26 August 1925.

[50] ACHR Art. 27: Note that the convention says only "State Party" and does not specify which state organ oversees declaring a state of emergency.

[51] Grossman (1986), p. 35.

[52] Negretto (2002), pp. 377–379.

[53] Paris Minimum Standards Sec. (A) 2.

of crisis.[54] The role of the courts, as institutions independent from political influences, is to protect the rights of people, especially those in vulnerable situations.[55] Therefore, every person who has been affected by emergency measures should be able to challenge them in front of a court of justice.[56]

In practice, the effective division of branches is put aside in times of emergency, either because the government requires leeway to act quickly or because the other state organs are unable to react.[57] The government accumulates great political power to set the legislative agenda and pass legislation that otherwise would have not been created.[58] As it is the common goal of all three branches during a public emergency to return to stability, the authorization or ratification of executive decrees by the legislative branch and oversight of the courts seem to be just formalities. Governments tend to receive constant authorization from the legislatures to implement economic modifications through emergency decrees.[59] Commonly, the legislature adheres to the demands of the government and supports the emergency policies even without having time to debate.[60]

Judges heavily rely on classified documents that are usually available only to the executive branch and lack qualified information to support decisions in times of emergency. In addition, they are ineffective at restoring the rights of those affected by emergency measures when the popular desire for security is greater than the desire to preserve basic rights.[61] The latter is a general problem. There are incentives to support the government when an emergency contributes to overwhelming support and patriotic feelings among the population.[62]

During crisis periods, the courts' decisions also lack the necessary influence over the government which can de facto choose whether or not to act in accordance with judicial decisions. In fact, the courts' reliability is deeply affected by government decisions. If the government decides to follow a court's ruling that blocks a government's action, the outcome of the emergency is completely the court's

---

[54]Grossman (1986), p. 40.

[55]Cole (2003), p. 2567; see also Gross and Ní Aoláin (2006), p. 63.

[56]Cole explains that most people agree to sacrifice liberty when there is a public need for security. In this situation, the courts are useless because people are not ready to demand the protection of their rights. According to Cole, this was the case during the American Civil War when Lincoln abolished the habeas corpus. The courts and the public ignored the situation. See Cole (2003), pp. 2568–2569.

[57]Meyler (2007), p. 544.

[58]Negretto (2002), pp. 377–379.

[59]This has been the case, for instance, during the Kirchner years when the President has constantly received Congress authorization to unilaterally increase taxes and tariffs. Thomas and Cachanosky mention Resolution 125 of 2008 that imposed a tariff of 90% on exports for the agricultural sector for prices higher than 600 USD. See Thomas and Cachanosky (2006), p. 74.

[60]Humphreys (2006), p. 684.

[61]Judicial decisions taken when a crisis is over are argued to have a higher probability to succeed at protecting human rights as they may be used as precedents that limits the scope of emergency measures in future crisis. See Cole (2003), pp. 2565–2566.

[62]Gross and Ní Aoláin (2006), p. 64.

responsibility. On the other hand, if the government is not satisfied with the court's decision, the government can rebel against the court and disobey the ruling. Both situations can affect the court's public legitimacy forever.[63] Because of all of the pressure that courts face during an emergency to violate or ignore the constitution and the law, the judiciary tends to support the government's measures.[64] Moreover, when legal provisions about the role the government can play during an emergency are not straightforward, the judiciary can help to accommodate the law by interpreting the legal rules to legalize the exercise of emergency powers.[65]

7.2.3 Argentina's Constitution of 1853 and the State of Emergency

The original Constitution of 1853 did not refer to a state of (economic) emergency. In Article 23, the Constitution merely prescribed that in the event of domestic unrest or external attack, which puts the constitutional order at risk, a *state of siege* could be declared.[66]

The Argentinean Constitution of 1853 set several rules for the declaration of the state of siege. First, the Constitution established a territorial limit. A state of siege and suspension of constitutional rights was limited to the territorial area where this takes place.[67] The Constitution also established that the National Congress of Argentina, which consists of the House of Deputies and the Senate, had the exclusive attribution of declaring the state of siege.[68] The National Congress had the competence to declare public emergencies and to grant emergency loans to allow the state to deal with the emergency.[69]

The government could declare the public emergency just by exception if the Congress was in legislative recess. However, even in this case, Congress was supposed to approve the declaration of emergency.[70] The President of Argentina had only one role according to the constitutional prescriptions. He could order the arrest of people and transport them from one place to the other within the Argentinean territory. However, the President of the Republic was not allowed to administer justice and decide on the sanction of the arrested people.[71]

---

[63]Cole (2003), pp. 2570–2571. It may, of course, also undermine the government's legitimacy. But the point is that courts feel pressured to follow.

[64]Gross and Ní Aoláin (2006), pp. 62–63.

[65]*Ibid.*, p. 72.

[66]Const. Argentina of 1853 Art. 23.

[67]Const. Argentina of 1853 Art. 23.

[68]Const. Argentina of 1853 Art. 64 (26).

[69]Const. Argentina of 1853 Art. 4.

[70]*Ibid.*, p. 69.

[71]*Ibid.*, p. 68.

In consonance with the Constitution, the President of the Republic of Argentina could only issue decrees to enforce laws enacted by the legislature if they did not contradict the law.[72] Through decrees, the President could also regulate some aspects over which the Constitution had given the executive branch exclusive attribution and exercise legislative functions via delegation by the legislature.[73]

Pointing to the *police power of the state*, the Supreme Court of Justice of Argentina has justified the use of emergency rules that go beyond the state of siege. This police power of the state embodies all the legal restrictions on people's rights that are necessary to preserve order, trust, economic and financial stability,[74] among others. Referring to the police power of the state, Argentina's Supreme Court of Justice tried to provide certainty through its decisions by following the doctrine of consistent jurisprudence. To adapt the constitutional text to the changes in society, the Court adopted a more flexible vision of the Constitution.[75]

The Supreme Court of Justice set parameters to the application of emergency laws under the original Constitution of 1853. According to the Court, emergency laws are supposed to be a remedy to the emergency; they should not substantially modify legal relationships. In addition, emergency laws must lay down a clear timeframe during which the extraordinary measures will be in force. Given the impossibility of knowing specifically when the emergency is going to stop, it must at least be clearly stated that, as soon as the crisis is over, the government will cease the emergency measure. Further, the legislative branch, not the government, was supposed to declare the emergency and decide the scope of the emergency measures.[76] The Supreme Court also clarified that, even though the Court did not have the competence to examine the opportunity, necessity, convenience or efficiency of the measures taken in case of emergency, the Court was competent to perform judicial review of the reasonableness of the measures.[77]

---

[72]Bestard (2008), pp. 581–583. See also Const. Argentina Art. 100 (8), according to which the Chief of the Cabinet of Ministers can *"approve decrees establishing implementing regulations for laws, decrees that provide for the extension of ordinary sessions of Congress or the convening of extraordinary sessions, and the messages of the President promoting a legislative initiative."*

[73]Ferreira Rubio and Goretti (1996), p. 449.

[74]According to the Supreme Court of Justice of Argentina, Congress delegated the power to provide operating licenses to financial institutions, regulate banking activity and sanction non-compliant financial institutions to the central bank. See CSJN Argentina, *Sergi Vinciguerra Antonio v. Central Bank of the Argentine Republic*, Fallos: 3192:3196, 17 March 1998.

[75]Jacobs (2003), pp. 409–412.

[76]In the "Zappa" *case*, the court laid down that it is the exclusive attribution of the legislative branch to declare an economic emergency and decide how people's rights are supposed to be limited in pursuit of the common good. See CSJN Argentina, *Rolon Zappa, Victor F. v. National State*, Fallos: 308:1848, 30 September 1986.

[77]According to the court, *reasonability* is the proportion between the means and the objective of a law. For instance, the general prohibition of enacting laws that retroactively modify contractual terms, does not apply in times of crisis when limiting contracting rights to pursue the common good is reasonable. See CSJN Argentina, *Oscar Agustin Avico v. Saúl de la Pesa*, Fallos: 172:21, 7 December 1934. On the other hand, when the salaries of public employees were reduced via

7.3 Monetary Problems and the State of Emergency in Argentina

7.3.1 Monetary Instability and the Central Bank Solution

Before the creation of the Central Bank of the Argentine Republic in 1935,[78] several currencies circulated in the Argentinean territory. Several commercial banks and the Bank of the Province of Buenos Aires (BPBA) competed in issuing currency. To provide stability to the monetary system, Argentina attempted to adopt the gold standard in 1863.[79] This attempt failed at the beginning because it was not possible for Argentina to accumulate enough gold to back the currency. However, in 1867 the effort succeeded.[80] Argentina never became a core member of the gold standard. Instead, it went on and off the gold standard several times. At first, the parity of the Argentinean currency to gold lasted 9 years until 1876. Argentina returned to the gold standard in 1883 but had to go off again in 1885. When most countries joined the gold standard, also Argentina gave it another try. From 1899 until World War I, Argentina was a member of the gold club. In the inter-war period, the gold standard was reintroduced the last time. After adopting the gold standard in 1927, Argentina left again 2 years later, making it one of the first countries to go off gold during the Great Depression.[81]

As Argentina was unable or unwilling to adhere to the gold standard for longer periods, the gold standard, by itself, was not able to provide a stable monetary system. Argentina set up a central bank to deal with monetary issues in 1935. Monetary stability could still not be achieved. According to *Hanke*, the peso depreciated against the dollar by a factor of 9,000,000,000,000 between 1935 and 2004.[82]

Argentina's monetary authorities have been short of credibility. On the one hand, the failure of fiscal and monetary stabilization plans deteriorated credibility. On the other hand, the exorbitant use of the state of emergency to deal with monetary and fiscal problems, the repeated modifications of the rules for the monetary authorities

---

Emergency Decree 896 of 2001, Argentina [Decreto de Emergencia 896, Diario Oficial, 13 July 2001] and Economic Emergency Law 25,453 of Argentina [Ley de Emergencia Económica 25.453, 31 July 2001], the Court declared that both, the decree, and the law lacked reasonability because the salary reduction prevented the plaintiff to live under basic conditions. See CSJN Argentina, *Gustavo Nordensthol v. Subterraneos de Buenos Aires*, Fallos: 307:326, 2 April 1985.

[78]Historical Information about the Argentinean central bank: http://www.bcra.gov.ar/Institucional/Historia.asp.

[79]Having a gold standard system means that the currency issued by the monetary authority is backed by gold. Having the currency backed by gold does not allow for monetary expansion and might be effective at preserving stability of prices. See Bordo and Kydland (1995), p. 423.

[80]Della Paolera (1994), pp. 539–541.

[81]Bordo and Kydland (1995), p. 437.

[82]Hanke (2003), p. 55.

and the use of the central bank to mitigate crises and finance deficits imply a low degree of autonomy.[83]

7.3.2   Economic Emergency Decrees Under Alfonsin and Menem

Until the 1980s, the governments used emergency decrees seldom and only when natural catastrophes occurred. However, since the hyperinflation crisis of the 1980s, governments used them during economic crises to set up stabilization plans or modify the law. The governments of Alfonsin and Menem until 1994 justified the issuance of emergency decrees with the *police power of the state*. Emergency regulation related to functions of the central bank had become *business as usual*.

7.3.2.1   Austral and Bonex Plans

Between 1981 and 1985, Argentina was in a hyperinflationary crisis that followed several years of excessive indebtedness financed by the Central Bank of the Argentine Republic (BCRA) during the military dictatorship of the *junta*.[84] After losing the Falklands War, the junta called for elections. When Raul Alfonsin was elected in 1983, he first wanted to bring down inflation gradually, retaining the government's spending. However, negative external conditions, such as high interest rates in the world economy and a decline in international trade limited the availability of external credit. As the new government continued to finance deficits by central bank money, annual rates of inflation in Argentina increased from 100% to more than 1000% in 1985.[85]

Alfonsin's Austral Plan was a change in strategy away from gradualism to a radical stabilization policy. To recover the credibility in the value of the currency, Alfonsin aimed for a reliable monetary and fiscal plan that combined monetary stabilization with income policies. Using income policies, such as wage and price

---

[83]Miguel Kiguel explains that in 1959 President Frondizi tried to stop inflation through monetary discipline, fiscal restrictions, and deep devaluation of the currency. This attempt brought monetary stability to the country only for two years when inflation went from 113% to 14%. In 1967, President Vasena tried to apply a similar method and reduced salaries considerably to contain inflation. But success was only temporary. Hyperinflation picked at the end of the 1970s. The Peronist government first tried to promote monetary stability but without success. Its populist plans required fiscal expansion. After these attempts, President Martinez de Hoz tried to promote monetary policy conservatism and fixed exchange rate strategies, a strategy that worked until 1981 when inflation increased unstoppable. See Kiguel (1991), p. 969.

[84]Fitzpatrick (1994), p. 38.

[85]Kiguel (1991), p. 970. For the data, see: http://www.tradingeconomics.com/argentina/inflation-cpiu.

controls, the government wanted to break the inertia of inflation. For example, wage negotiations assumed high inflation rates in the first place, which sustained inflation even under tight monetary and fiscal policy.[86] The emergency decrees further embodied an anti-inflationary strategy based on the commitment of the government to no longer finance deficits with BCRA money. To reach this objective, the Austral Plan, implemented via Emergency Decree No. 1096 of 1985,[87] assured that the BCRA could no longer provide transitionary loans to the government.[88] The Argentinean peso was replaced by the *Austral*[89] at a fixed parity of 1 Austral to 1000 Argentinean pesos. The emergency decree required the BCRA to issue new currency denominated in Australes instead of Argentinean pesos.[90]

Launching the *Plan Austral* (Austral plan), the executive branch took over from the legislature the constitutional tasks of issuing the national currency and preserving its value.[91] The legislative branch had already delegated this function to a central bank by enacting the Organic Charter of the BCRA. The BCRA was an autonomous organ of statutory rank[92] without a clear objective[93] and under the guidance of the executive branch.[94] According to the law, the executive branch appointed the BCRA's board members.[95] Although the *Plan Austral* interfered with the competences of the National Congress, Congress did not challenge the executive's decision to deal with the hyperinflationary crisis. Indeed, the Plan was successful at first, reducing inflation to 3.1% within a few months in 1985.[96]

The Austral plan was successful during the first several years.[97] The income policies successfully broke the inertia of inflation. However, the government was unable to use the time that it gained to adopt reforms that would stabilize the budget. Fiscal spending soon went out of control again.[98] Although it seems that the government had good intentions, it lacked the final will or political capital to limit

---

[86]Dornbusch and de Pablo (1990), pp. 91–107.

[87]Emergency Decree 1096 of 1985, Argentina [Decreto de Emergencia 1678, Diario Oficial, 17 June 1985].

[88]Lagos and Galetovic (1989), p. 231.

[89]Kiguel (1991), p. 970; see also Ferreira Rubio and Goretti (1996), p. 448.

[90]Emergency Decree 1096 of 1985, Argentina [Decreto de Emergencia 1678, Diario Oficial, 17 June 1985].

[91]Const. Argentina of 1853 Art. 64 (10).

[92]Organic Charter of the Central Bank of the Republic of Argentina of 1973 Art. 1 [Carta Orgánica del Banco Central de la República Argentina, Diario Oficial, 10 October 1973] [hereinafter BCRA Law (1973)].

[93]BCRA Law (1973) Art. 3.

[94]BCRA Law (1973) Art. 4.

[95]BCRA Law (1973) Art. 7. During his time in office President Alfonsin appointed José Luis Machinea as president of the BCRA and all the directors via emergency decree. Then unilaterally dismissed Machinea and appointed Javier González Fraga.

[96]Kiguel (1991), p. 970; Gelli (2003), p. 190.

[97]Frenkel and Fanelli (1986), p. 82.

[98]Dornbusch and de Pablo (1990), pp. 107 et seq.

fiscal expansion. When inflation spurred again, the trust in Alfonsin's government eroded.[99]

The failure of *Plan Austral* was followed by several years of hyperinflation and rampant devaluation. The new government of Carlos Saúl Menen aimed to achieve currency stability through *Plan Bonex*, which tried to contain inflation by extending the term structure of liquidity in the economy to prevent people from spending, i.e., making assets less liquid. To do so, the government froze bank deposits and replaced short-term deposits in Argentinean pesos with medium term government bonds in American dollars using Emergency Decree No. 36 of 1990.[100] In addition, the government decided to postpone payments to improve the budget. The government measures contributed to a state of illiquidity. Argentineans repatriated money from abroad. The capital inflow stopped the devaluation of the Argentinean currency. However, any successes were short-lived. Public debt rose, inflation returned, and the currency continued to be very volatile.[101]

7.3.2.2 The Supreme Court and Emergency Decrees

The lack of constitutional basis for the emergency decrees by Alfonsin and Menem motivated the Supreme Court of Justice of Argentina to institutionalize the state of economic emergency and clarify the scope of the policy power of the state for the government. In the *Peralta* case[102] of 1990, approving the constitutionality of the conversion of deposits into government bonds under Menem, the Court first established that the President of Argentina can issue decrees of necessity and economic emergency under two conditions: the social danger must be imminent, and the National Congress has not taken any legislative measure to prevent it.

The Court ruled that through the law on the functioning of central bank, Congress delegated the performance of monetary policy to an organ dependent on the executive branch.[103] Based on this decision, governments could make use of decrees to affect central bank law and monetary policy. According to its critics, the Court viewed emergency measures too favorably despite the unconstitutionality of government decisions that were not authorized by the legislature. In this regard, Argentina's Supreme Court of Justice has been criticized for its lack of independence from political interference.[104]

---

[99]Lagos and Galetovic (1989), pp. 240–241.

[100]Emergency Decree 36 of 1990, Argentina [Decreto de Emergencia 36, Diario Oficial, 5 January 1990].

[101]Calcagno (1997), p. 67.

[102]*Luis A. Peralta and others v. Estado Nacional (Ministerio de Economía-B.C.R.A)*, CSJN Argentina, Fallos: 313:1513, 27 December 1990.

[103]*René Roberto Colina and others v. Estado Nacional (Ministerio de Economía-B.C.R.A)*, CSJN Argentina, Fallos: 324:4520, 28 December 2001.

[104]See Jacobs (2003), pp. 393–394. Jacobs explains how the Supreme Court of Argentina has been influenced by the executive and legislative branches since the beginning of its existence. However,

As a consequence, the exercise of the police power of the state in times of emergency allowed the government to (1) enforce the law;[105] (2) create legal rules, different from legislation, that regulate aspects that have to be handled by the public administration;[106] and (3) issue emergency decrees in case of the disruption of the social order to preserve the common good.[107]

Although the executive power of the government is the broadest among the state branches,[108] even in times of crisis, the power of the government has constitutional limitations that prevent it, for instance, from confiscating private property.[109] Moreover, emergency decrees require the approval of a congressional committee to be in force. This legislative committee had the competence to reform the decree, if necessary, within ten days; otherwise, the presidential emergency decree would be understood as *tacitly* approved.[110] However, most of the decrees of necessity and emergency sent to Congress have been tacitly approved ever since.[111]

---

it is claimed that the independence of the courts was significantly diminished since Juan Domingo Perón was in power. The Peronist period was full of disagreements between Peron's populist plans and the court's defense, for instance, of property rights. Peron started the impeachment mechanism that has been used almost by every Argentinean president since then, to get rid of a Supreme Court that blocks presidential intentions. Judges and justices have been arbitrarily removed from the courts despite the constitutional protection of their tenure that prevents them from being arbitrarily dismissed. In line with the Argentinean constitution (Art. 110), the Supreme Court justices preserve their offices as long as they show "good behavior". Further, their salaries are established by the law and they are untouchable. The political instability in Argentina has taken its toll in the judiciary and led to the dismissal of judges after each episode of social unrest. Menem, for instance, manipulated the formation of the board of the Supreme Court to have a majority that would pass his emergency decrees. See Jacobs (2003), pp. 407–408.

[105] Barnett (2003), p. 451.

[106] Gordillo (2012), p. 205.

[107] *Ibid.*, p. 215; see also Meyler (2007), pp. 549–550.

[108] According to the Federalist Papers by Alexander Hamilton, the head of the executive branch is the most powerful of all: The President participates in the law-making process, is the commander in chief of the army, has the attribution of appointing ambassadors, etc. Nevertheless, the President is always subject to accountability and relies on decisions of the constituencies to stay in power. Moreover, the President performs most of his functions under the oversight and authorization of the Congress. See Hamilton et al. (2001), p. 69.

For attributions of the President of Argentina, see Const. Argentina Art. 99. For example, Art. 99 (1) states that the President is the head of the public administration. The President further participates in the execution and enactment of the law, see Art. 99 (2) and (3). The President also appoints (jointly with the Senate), the justices of the Supreme Court of Argentina. See Const. Argentina Art. 99 (4).

[109] Barnett (2003), p. 455.

[110] *Luis A Peralta and other v. Estado Nacional*, CJSN Argentina, Fallos: 313:1513, 27 December 1990.

[111] Negretto (2002), pp. 395–397. For instance, Emergency Decree 2192 of 1986 abolished the "incentive fund" that provided an extra remuneration to public servants. In the case "Levy Horacio" of 15 July 1997, the Supreme Court of Justice of Argentina decided that the decree was constitutional because Congress never abolished Emergency Decree 2192 of 1986. Not abolishing the decree was considered an example of tacit approbation of the emergency decree. See Avalos (2012),

7.3.3   Currency Board and Emergency Regulation

To prevent further devaluation and to stabilize the economy, the government of Menem decided to install a currency board.[112] The Convertibility Law (March 27, 1991) fixed the exchange rate between the Austral and the U.S. dollar at 10,000 Austral per dollar.[113] The BCRA was now put in charge of preserving the Currency Board.[114] According to the Convertibility Law, the BCRA reserves of foreign currency and gold had to be equivalent to at least one hundred percent of the monetary base.[115]

7.3.3.1   Currency Board

Currency boards are an option to provide monetary stability in countries where the credibility of the monetary authority has been damaged because of hyperinflation.[116] Installing a currency board is a way to import monetary stability from an anchor currency[117] and the rule of law of the country with the anchor currency. The same logic of the functional decentralization of power that underlies the delegation of functions to an independent institution can explain the use of a currency board. With a currency board, the monetary attributions, which are sovereign powers of a particular state, are delegated to an international entity, such as a foreign state.[118]

Using a currency board, the nominal value of the domestic currency is pegged to the nominal value of the anchor currency, which should be a hard currency, such as the U.S. dollar or the Euro. Thus, currency boards belong to the class of pegged exchange rate systems. The traditional role of the central bank in a currency board

---

p. 153. See *Levy Horacio and other v. Estado Nacional*, CSJN Argentina, Fallos 320:1426, July 15, 1997.

[112]Calcagno (1997), p. 65; see also Austral Convertibility Law [Ley 23.928 Ley de Convertibilidad del Austral, Boletín Oficial, 28 March 1991] [hereinafter Convertibility Law]. The convertibility law "lei" is really an act.

[113]Convertibility Law Art. 1: "*As of April 1, 1991 the provisions of this law establish the convertibility between the peso and the US dollar with an exchange ratio of one peso per dollar ($1)* [Own Translation]".

[114]Thomas and Cachanosky (2006), pp. 70–71. See also Convertibility Law Art. 4; see also Feldstein (2002), p. 10.

[115]Convertibility Law Art. 4.

[116]Dollarization is the adoption of the U.S. dollar as a country's money and "solution to the problems created by a lack of transparency and commitment to the exchange-rate target." Dollarization is a stronger commitment to a fixed exchange rate than the currency board. A currency board can be abandoned by "allowing a change in the value of the currency." This is not as easy with dollarization. See Mishkin (2007), p. 485.

[117]Council of Economic Advisers of the United States Government, Economic Report of the President, 1999, pp. 289–290.

[118]Lastra (2015), p. 105.

system is to issue currency that is convertible to the anchor currency at a fixed exchange rate.[119] The central bank must ensure that the monetary base[120] is backed by reserves, which are commonly "low risk interest bearing bonds in the anchor currency and gold."[121]

In principle, both a conservative central bank and a currency board seek to prevent inflation by limiting monetary expansion and forbidding central bank financing of the state budget.[122] However, in developing countries, currency boards are regarded as more effective instruments than independent central banks to preserve the stability of prices because under a currency board system it is not possible to perform discretionary monetary policy, since, first, the fixed exchange rate is established by law.[123] Currency boards have the advantage over an autonomous central bank of being able to avoid conflicts between monetary policy and exchange rate policy, thereby preventing balance-of-payment crises.[124]

The currency board, therefore, limited the BCRA's duties to buying foreign currencies at market prices[125] and to preserving reserves that should be equivalent to at least 100% of the monetary base.[126] Only a central bank shielded from executive instructions is in a position to keep the necessary reserves to preserve the currency board.[127]

From a legal perspective, the currency board provides an additional dose of legal certainty and makes the state's commitment towards price stability more credible[128] for several reasons. First, because the currency board, as an almost mechanical device, binds the national currency to a fixed exchange rate, it leaves the central bank with no room for exchange rate manipulation.[129] Second, the currency board system enhances transparency, because, to determine whether the central bank is

---

[119]Jacobs (2003), p. 398; see also Hanke (2002), p. 88.

[120]The monetary base is the currency in circulation plus the deposits.

[121]Hanke (2002), p. 88.

[122]Buiter and Grafe (2001), p. 18.

[123]Council of Economic Advisers of the United States Government, Economic Report of the President, 1999, p. 289.

[124]Hanke (2002), pp. 91–92. They are less prone to crises because there is no need to speculate on the durability of the fixed exchange rate regime if the currency is fully backed by reserves.

[125]Convertibility Law Art. 3: *"The Central Bank of the Argentine Republic may buy foreign currency at market price, out of its own resources, by order and for the account of the National Government, or by issuing the necessary Australs to meet that end* [Own Translation].*"*

[126]Convertibility Law Art. 4: *"The unrestricted reserves of the Central Bank of the Argentine Republic in gold and foreign currency shall always be equivalent to, at least, a hundred percent (100%) of the reserve money. To the purposes of this Law, whenever reserves are invested in deposits, other interest-earning operations, domestic and foreign government bonds payable in gold, precious metals, U.S. dollars or other similarly sound currency, the estimation thereof shall be based on market values* [Own Translation].*"*

[127]Calcagno (1997), p. 66.

[128]Lastra (2015), p. 105. According to Lastra, the currency board borrows the 'credibility' of the anchor currency, which is commonly a strong currency such as the American dollar or the Euro.

[129]Calcagno (1997), p. 67; see also Thomas and Cachanosky (2006), p. 71.

performing its functions within the rules set by the currency board, it is enough to look at the central bank's balance sheet. The balance sheet will show the central bank's liabilities and its assets in detail.[130] Third, a currency board system prevents the central bank from lending to the government and acting as a lender of last resort, which ensures the central bank's financial autonomy and forces the government to reduce spending if necessary.[131] Finally, a currency board is difficult to modify. Eliminating it requires a reform of the law not a central bank decision.[132]

7.3.3.2 Legal Modifications and the Currency Board

Central Bank Charter

The 1973 charter of the BCRA was enacted by Law 20,539. This charter established clearly that the bank develops its functions under the rule of the Ministry of Finance.[133] All of the members of the board were selected unilaterally by the executive branch.[134] The central bank was not independent. The main objectives of the bank were to regulate credit to allow for economic development, to oversee the liquidity of the banking sector and to implement the exchange rate policy authorized by the government.[135] Under a currency board, the dependence of the central bank as well as its function in supporting economic development would be a problem and in conflict with the idea of a currency board. Changes in central bank law were supposed to increase the credibility of the currency board.

Law 23,697 of 1989 ordered the enactment of the charter for the BCRA. In this law, Congress laid down that a commission composed of the president and vice-president of the bank, the president of the Commission of Economics Affairs of the Senate and the president of the Commission of Economics Affairs of the House of Deputies, had to draft a new central bank law. This commission had to send the bill to the President of Argentina, who was in charge of making comments and modifications before sending the bill to the Congress for approval. The central bank charter was supposed to grant a higher level of autonomy to the central bank to allow it to achieve the single goal of preserving the stability of the currency. The law was also supposed to set clear limits on lending to the government and order reports to the Congress about the plan put in force to achieve Congress' monetary and credit policy.[136]

---

[130]Hanke (2002), pp. 89–90.

[131]*Ibid.*, pp. 91–92.

[132]Lastra (2015), p. 104. See also Calcagno (1997), p. 65.

[133]BCRA Law (1973) Arts. 1 and 4.

[134]BCRA Law (1973) Art. 8.

[135]BCRA Law (1973) Art. 3.

[136]Economic Emergency Law 23,697 of Argentina Art. 3 (a), (b), and (e). [Ley de Emergencia Económica 23.697, Boletín Oficial, 25 September 1989].

The organic charter of the BCRA was enacted in 1992. The charter followed the guidelines of Law 23,697 of 1989 in providing more independence to the monetary authority as well as a single objective.[137] The BCRA should not receive any instruction from the executive branch in the development of monetary policy.[138] The 1992 charter also established a general prohibition of lending to the government.[139] This prohibition, however, was not absolute, because the law laid down an exception for the purchase of government securities at market price until a maximum of 10% of the BCRA's capital or a third of available reserves.[140] At first sight, the gain in autonomy seemed to match the currency board arrangements.

However, the BCRA rules did not respect the main principles of the currency board. To have an orthodox currency board, the law must clearly specify that the BCRA cannot intervene or regulate the financial sector, finance public spending or act as lender of last resort.[141] The last two requirements are necessary to ensure that there are enough reserves to back up the currency in circulation.

The 1992 charter of the BCRA preserved the function of the lender of last resort by allowing the BCRA to extend loans to distressed institutions.[142] Taking government bonds as securities is a way of financing the government.[143] Article 60 of the BCRA Law of 1992 established that 20 percent of the reserves of the bank could be held as government bonds.[144] Only when it is necessary to use reserves to provide liquidity to the financial system can a maximum of one-third of the reserves be exchanged for government bonds, a maximum limit set in Article 33.[145]

The way the central bank law was designed during the convertibility period[146] from 1991 to 2002 suggests that Argentina did not have a full-fledged currency board. Instead, Argentina had a central bank with discretion to perform monetary policy and a pegged exchange rate regime. The only special feature of the system was the conversion on demand of Argentinean pesos into American dollars. *Hanke* explains that it is common that pegged exchange rates suffer from conflicts between the anchor currency and the domestic monetary policy.[147]

---

[137]BCRA Law (1992) Art. 3.

[138]BCRA Law (1992) Art. 3 para 3.

[139]BCRA Law (1992) Art. 19 (a).

[140]BCRA Law (1992) Art. 20.

[141]Hanke and Schuler (2002), p. 43; Mishkin (2007), pp. 485–486. See also Buiter and Grafe (2001), p. 19.

[142]BCRA Law (1992) Art. 17 (b) and (c).

[143]Hanke and Schuler (2002), p. 44.

[144]BCRA Law (1992) Art. 60.

[145]BCRA Law (1992) Art. 33.

[146]By convertibility period we mean the time during which the convertibility law was enforced.

[147]Hanke (2003), p. 50.

Constitutional Amendments

Apart from flaws in central bank law, the 1994 amendments to the Constitution ratified Congress's duty to defend the value of the currency,[148] coin money and regulate the value of domestic and foreign currency.[149] Such provisions cast doubts on legal certainty concerning the currency board arrangements.

More far-reaching were the amendments concerning the reasons for a state of siege as well as for a state of emergency. The amended Constitution prescribed that the declaration of the state of siege can take place in the event of internal unrest and external attack. Only in this event is it possible to suspend the protection of certain rights. The President of the Republic can ask the Senate to approve the state of siege. The Senate has the attribution of approving it and suspending it when necessary.[150]

Regarding the state of emergency, Article 76 of the amended Constitution of Argentina established that the legislative branch can delegate lawmaking functions to the executive branch in times of administrative problems or "public emergency"[151] that make it impossible to follow the ordinary lawmaking process. These circumstances are internal commotion, such as a social or economic crisis, or external attack.[152] From this point onward, the Constitution has allowed the President of the Republic to issue economic emergency decrees.[153]

7.3.3.3 Management of the Tequila Crisis of 1994

A lender of last resort function of the central bank undermines the credibility of a currency board. However, without far-reaching lender of last resort functions, the central bank was not able to mitigate banking crises.[154] This problem led to modifications of central bank law during the so-called Tequila Crisis[155] when capital flight reduced banking liquidity and produced a bank run on approximately 18% of the Argentinean banking deposits.[156] Banks tried to recover liquidity by demanding inter-banking loans at high interest rates and finally asked the BCRA for help.[157]

---

[148]Const. Argentina Art. 75 (19).

[149]Const. Argentina Art. 75 (11).

[150]Const. Argentina Arts. 61 and 75 (29).

[151]Const. Argentina Art. 76 para 1.

[152]Gelli (2003), p. 180.

[153]These decrees cannot be applied in "exceptional circumstances" involving "criminal, tax, or electoral matters or the regime governing political parties [...]" See Const. Argentina Art. 99 (3) para 3.

[154]Lastra (2015), pp. 109–110.

[155]It is called Tequila crisis because it started with capital flight from Mexico, depreciating the peso against the U.S. dollar. The crisis spread to other emerging markets.

[156]See Perry and Serven (2003).

[157]Calcagno (1997), pp. 79–80.

Even though the BCRA Law allowed for liquidity transfers to distressed financial institutions, in the context of the crisis, the amounts that the BCRA could lend were not enough. Banks collapsed, and the economy went to crisis.

Consequently, the executive branch issued Decree No. 290 of March 1995 which modified the Organic Charter of the BCRA. Following Article 26 of the decree, the BCRA can increase limits and terms for emergency liquidity, provided, however, that the BCRA does not jeopardize the reserves that back the monetary base in the currency board framework.[158]

Although the intervention of the BCRA helped Argentina overcome the negative spillovers of Mexico's Tequila Crisis and return to the growth path with rates well above 5 percent,[159] the intervention of the government via executive decree might signal that the government was ready to use monetary policy and undermine the currency board arrangements when necessary. To increase the confidence in the convertibility law, the government reformed financial markets, tightening capital requirements and bank regulation. Weak Argentinean banks were taken over by foreign banks. The banking system became more crisis-prone until the crisis of 2001,[160] suggesting that the lender of last resort function was less important.

7.3.3.4 Management of the Crisis of 2001/2002

Since convertibility was established, Argentina grew faster than other Latin American countries.[161] To provide credibility and work properly, however, fiscal discipline would have been necessary under the currency board arrangement. Nevertheless, Argentina accumulated fiscal deficits and failed to reduce public spending.[162] In 1993, Argentina's total external debt was at 28% of GDP. Until 2001, external debt rose to 53% of GDP, most of which was government debt. Debt-servicing became more and more difficult.[163]

During the late 1990s, Argentina had to face a series of outside shocks. Commodity prices leveled, driving down revenues. International financing costs went up for emerging markets, specifically after Russia and Brazil went to crisis. Capital flight from the emerging markets put an appreciation pressure on the dollar and, therefore, on Argentina's currency. Devaluation was not possible under the currency board to promote exports. The economy went to crisis.[164]

President Fernando De la Rúa came to office in December 1999. Shortly thereafter, he appointed Domingo Cavallo to deal with the high public debt inherited from

---

[158]Emergency Decree 290 of 1995, Argentina [Decreto de Emergencia 290, 27 February 1995].

[159]Hanke (2002), p. 102.

[160]De la Torre et al. (2003), p. 47.

[161]Perry and Serven (2003), p. 4.

[162]Jacobs (2003), pp. 398–399.

[163]See Perry and Serven (2003), p. 41.

[164]See Thomas and Cachanosky (2006), p. 71.

the previous administration.[165] The legislative branch decided that the executive should be in a better position to deal with the crisis. Through Law 25,414, enacted in March 2001, the legislative branch delegated legislative functions to the executive branch until March 1, 2002. Through this law, the government received authority that belonged to the legislative branch, which included ruling over autarchic institutions, such as the BCRA. The executive branch was permitted to create and decide about the functions and the centralization of institutions with some degree of autonomy.[166]

Cavallo first aimed to restore growth via tariffs and two main reforms of the Convertibility Law. Exports, except oil exports, were carried out at an undervalued peso and imports at an overvalued peso. The government supported the exporters and made importers pay extra. On June 21, 2001, Congress enacted an emergency law, Law 25,445, to modify the Convertibility Law. Article 1 of Law 25,445 redefines the convertibility of the peso as a simple average of the euro and the dollar.[167] This law was a source of uncertainty because markets saw these measures as first steps toward ending the currency board. In fear of devaluation, foreign investors sold Argentinean government bonds. To prevent a default the government made the private sector take on additional debt to finance the public deficit, gradually undermining the stability of the banking sector. These actions led to bank runs, a high demand for U.S. dollars, a rise in inflation and increases in interest rates.[168]

To preserve the dollar reserves, President de la Rúa issued Decree No. 1570 in December 2001, which limited the withdrawal to 250 *U.S. dollars* per week and account.[169] The deposit freeze, Corralito, proved that the Convertibility Law would not remain unchallenged. People protested on the streets. President de la Rúa and his Minister of Economy resigned.[170] The Supreme Court declared this decree

---

[165]Perry and Serven (2003), p. 54. De la Rúa's government measure to face the imminent economic crisis was high taxation on income, consumer goods, health insurance and transportation. See Perry and Serven (2003), p. 54. Instead of contributing to the payment of the government debt, tax collection reduced considerably. See Hanke and Schuler (2002), p. 47.

[166]Economic Emergency Law 25,414 of Argentina Art. 1 (I) a, b, c, d [Ley de Emergencia Económica 25.414, Boletín Oficial, 30 March 2001] [hereinafter LEE 25,414] With this emergency law the executive branch got, also, the attribution to take measures to improve the country's competitiveness by introducing tax exemptions, reducing taxes and tariffs, or easing bureaucratic processes related with trade, etc. See LEE 25,414 Art. 2 (II) a, b, c, d.

[167]See Economic Emergency Law 25,445 Art. 1. [Ley de Emergencia Económica 25.445, Boletín Oficial, 22 June 2001] [hereinafter LEE 25,445]. See also Hanke (2002), p. 102 as well as Perry and Serven (2003), p. 49.

[168]Hanke (2003), p. 102. See also Perry and Serven (2003), p. 41 and p. 49.

[169]Jacobs (2003), pp. 400–401.

[170]Emergency Decree 803 of 2001, Argentina [Decreto de Emergencia 803, 21 June 2001]. The lack of revenue pushed the country into recession and made it unable to honor its debt. In 2002, the currency board was gone, GDP fell by 10.9%, the unemployment rate was at 18.3%, and the currency was devalued. The economic situation led to social unrest and the resignation of De la Rúa. See Thomas and Cachanosky (2006), p. 72.

unconstitutional,[171] as the result of which, the legislative branch decided to strengthen the power of the executive to take the necessary measures to deal with the crisis. On December 23rd, 2001, interim-President Saá declared Argentina's default. He had to resign a couple of days later.[172]

Through Law 25,561 of January 6, 2002, the National Congress finally ended the currency board in Argentina and established that all bank accounts denominated in American dollars will be converted into Argentinean pesos.[173] In this law, the National Congress renewed the delegation of legislative powers to the executive branch until December 31, 2003 to restructure and reactivate the financial, banking and exchange market, create conditions for sustainable growth of the economy, restructure the debt,[174] and establish a new exchange rate between the Argentinean peso and foreign currencies.[175] Further, as the functions of the BCRA changed with the abolition of the Convertibility Law, Congress prescribed that the new role of the BCRA was to buy and sell foreign currency according to the guidelines established by the executive branch.[176]

The IMF stopped providing financing because the government had failed in paying previous loans and Argentina had to default in the payment of its sovereign debt. See Jacobs (2003), pp. 400–401.

[171]First, the Supreme Court of Justice of Argentina declared this emergency decree unconstitutional. The Court did so by revoking a decision of a lower ranked judge made regarding the writ of Amparo that suspended the effects of Article 2 of Emergency Decree 1570 and allowed the withdrawal of higher than the allowed sums from the Banco de la Ciudad de Buenos Aires. See Emergency Decree 1570 of 2001, Argentina [Decreto de Emergencia 1570, 1 December 2001]. The affected bank asked for the Supreme Court's direct intervention to declare the validity of DE 1 December 2001. The Supreme Court declared Article 2 constitutional and ordered the restitution of the money withdrawn from the bank. See *René Roberto Colina and others v. Estado Nacional*, CJSN Argentina, Fallos: 324:4520, 28 December 2001.

Few months later, in a controversial decision triggered by public pressures, the Court argued that according the Art. 17 of the Argentinean Constitution, people had the right to their deposits. Therefore, DE 1 December 2001 and all the other dispositions that derived from it were unconstitutional. The Court argued that this was not reasonable. Legal uncertainty regarding people's deposits in banking institutions was produced. See Jacobs (2003), p. 416. See also *Smith, Carlos Antonio v. Poder Ejecutivo Nacional o Estado Nacional*, CJSN Argentina, Fallos: 325:28. 1 February 2002.

This court's decision triggered a lawsuit against the court's justices. President Duhalde justified the lawsuit arguing that the court's decision was politically motivated. See Jacobs (2003), p. 402.

[172]Thomas and Cachanosky (2006), p. 73.

[173]Economic Emergency Law 25,561 of Argentina Art. 6-11 [Ley de Emergencia Económica 25.561, Boletín Oficial, 7 January 2002] [hereinafter LEE 25,561].

[174]LEE 25,561 Art. 1.

[175]LEE 25,561 Art. 2.

[176]LEE 25,561 Art. 3.

7.4   A Permanent State of Emergency

The Argentinean example shows that one of the main risks of the declaration of a state of emergency is that it might never end.[177] Emergency regulation has undermined the autonomy of the central bank since the 2001/2002 financial crisis.

Argentina's Economic Emergency Law 25,561 was enacted on January 6, 2002, delegating legislative functions to the executive branch until December 2003. The law has since been renewed over and over again. The first renewal was in November of 2003 and extended until December 2003.[178] Then, the emergency law was extended until December 2004,[179] then until December 2006,[180] December 2007,[181] December 2008,[182] December 2009,[183] December 2011,[184] December 2013,[185] December 2015,[186] finally until December 31, 2017.[187] The content of the emergency law did not change. Therefore, the government has controlled the exchange rate, which is usually the role of an autonomous central bank, since 2002.

Under the permanent state of emergency, the legislative and executive branches have teamed up to provide a legal framework for the new monetary regime pretending that an independent central bank exists. In practice, the BCRA has almost no autonomy from political power. On January 23, 2002, the legislative branch enacted Law 25,562,[188] which reformed the charter of the BCRA. The day that Law 25,562 was enacted, the executive branch issued Decree No. 71 and established the

---

[177]Meyler (2007), p. 564.

[178]Economic Emergency Law 25,820 of Argentina [Ley de Emergencia Económica 25.820, Boletín Oficial, 4 December 2003].

[179]Economic Emergency Law 25,972 of Argentina [Ley de Emergencia Económica 25.972, Boletín Oficial, 17 December 2004].

[180]Economic Emergency Law 26,077 of Argentina [Ley de Emergencia Económica 26.077, Boletín Oficial, 10 January 2005].

[181]Economic Emergency Law 26,204 of Argentina [Ley de Emergencia Económica 26.204, Boletín Oficial, 20 December 2006].

[182]Economic Emergency Law 26,339 of Argentina [Ley de Emergencia Económica 26.339, Boletín Oficial, 4 January 2008].

[183]Economic Emergency Law 26,456 of Argentina [Ley de Emergencia Económica 26.456, Boletín Oficial, 16 December 2008].

[184]Economic Emergency Law 26,563 of Argentina [Ley de Emergencia Económica 26.563, Boletín Oficial, 22 December 2009].

[185]Economic Emergency Law 26,729 of Argentina [Ley de Emergencia Económica 26.729, Boletín Oficial, 28 December 2011].

[186]Economic Emergency Law 26,896 of Argentina [Ley de Emergencia Económica 26.896, Boletín Oficial, 22 October 2013].

[187]Economic Emergency Law 27,200 of Argentina [Ley de Emergencia Económica 27.200, Boletín Oficial, 4 November 2015].

[188]Economic Emergency Law 25,562 of Argentina Art. 20 [Ley de Emergencia Económica 25.562, Boletín Oficial, 8 February 2002].

exchange rate regime. This decree ordered the BCRA to purchase and sell foreign currency in the exchange market for 1.40 pesos per U.S. dollar.[189]

The reform via Law 25,562 of 2002 granted the BCRA new means to finance the government deficit. The general prohibition of lending to the government remained. However, the BCRA can provide transitory loans of up to ten percent of the government's annual cash resources (tax money) that must be repaid within 12 months, and a new loan was allowed only if the government paid off the previous loans within the 12 months.[190] Later, in February 2002, the government issued Decree No. 401, which allowed the BCRA to inject liquidity in the financial system by issuing BCRA bonds and securities, nullifying prohibitions in Article 19 of the BCRA Law.[191]

Decree No. 214 of February 2002 further broadened the scope of the Law 25,561 by ordering that every payment obligation, including deposits, which were originally made in dollars, should be transformed into pesos at 1.40 pesos for each U.S. dollar. To make this possible, the BCRA was supposed to define a *reference stabilization coefficient* (CER), an index to adjust credits to inflation daily.[192] In 2003, conditions to lend to the government were modified again. The reform allowed the BCRA to make temporary loans to the government. The BCRA could grant loans of no more than twelve percent of the monetary base with a duration of 12 months. New loans meeting these conditions could be granted only when previous loans were paid off.[193]

President Nestor Kirchner financed the government deficit using such loans because Argentina had no access to foreign credit following the default during the crisis.[194] Despite the economic situation, Kirchner considerably increased public spending and taxes. Although tax revenues increased from 26% of GDP in 2003 to 45% of GDP in 2014, the deficit was high. The BCRA managed the exchange rate and kept the rate of currency depreciation below the rate of inflation. As goods prices in the country rose faster than the external value of the currency fell, the exchange rate appreciated in real terms, which made it harder to export.[195]

In 2006, the National Congress of Argentina enacted the rules that the executive branch must follow to issue emergency decrees. These rules are based on Article 99 of the Constitution, which gives the President the authority to participate in the lawmaking process,[196] and on Article 100, which gives the Ministers the duty to

---

[189]Emergency Decree 71 of 2002, Argentina [Decreto de Emergencia 71, 9 January 2002].

[190]Economic Emergency Law 25,562 of Argentina Art. 20 [Ley de Emergencia Económica 25.562, Boletín Oficial, 8 February 2002].

[191]Emergency Decree 401 of 2002, Argentina [Decreto de Emergencia 401, 28 February 2002].

[192]Emergency Decree 214 of 2002, Argentina [Decreto de Emergencia 214, 3 February 2002].

[193]Economic Emergency Law of Argentina 25,780 Art. 15. [Ley de Emergencia Económica 25.780, Boletín Oficial, 8 September 2003].

[194]Thomas and Cachanosky (2006), p. 72.

[195]*Ibid.*, p. 73.

[196]Const. Argentina Art. 99 (3).

legalize the decrees issued by the President to exercise the legislative delegation of Congress and emergency decrees. According to the Constitution, these decrees must be subject to the analysis of a Bicameral Commission of the Legislature within ten days of issuance by the government.[197]

The Bicameral Commission of the National Congress has ten days to decide on the validity of each delegation.[198] Eight members of each house, the House of Deputies and the Senate, compose the commission.[199] In line with these rules, the legislative delegation that operates only during an emergency[200] is an initiative of the executive branch. The legislature has to approve or decline it, if the bicameral commission decides that the delegation is valid[201] without making any change.[202] Each of the chambers must explicitly decide about the legislative delegation, implying a system of checks and balances.[203] Only after the communication to the executive branch[204] and publication will the emergency decree be in force.[205]

De-facto nothing had changed. The legislature and executive have continued to work hand in hand. In November 2008, Law 26,422 allowed the BCRA to give the government a loan of up to ten percent of government resources in the last 12 months. The government had to repay the loan within 18 months.[206] Through Decree No. 2010 of 2009,[207] also known as the *Bicentenario Decree of Debt Reduction and Stabilization*, the Argentinean government decided that the reserves of the BCRA were no longer untouchable and that its reserves should be used to pay domestic and external debt due in 2010. In consonance with this decree, the government received 6569 USD millions from the reserves of the BCRA, in return for which, the BCRA received a bill of exchange for 10 years.

Decree No. 2010 of 2009 led to a conflict between the executive branch and the president of the BCRA, who argued that the emergency decree was illegal and violated the autonomy of the BCRA. Specifically, the president of the BCRA

---

[197]Const. Argentina Art. 100 (12) and (13).

[198]Legal Regime of the Decrees of Necessity and Urgency, Legislative Delegation and Partial Law Enforcement Art. 19 [Régimen Legal de los Decretos de Necesidad y Urgencia, de Delegación Legislativa y de Promulgación Parcial de Leyes, Boletín Oficial, 26 July 2006] [hereinafter DNU Law].

[199]DNU Law Art. 3.

[200]Const. Argentina Art. 76.

[201]DNU Law Art. 10.

[202]DNU Law Art. 23.

[203]DNU Law Art. 11; see also Const. Argentina Art. 82. According to the new rules, the precedent created by the *Luis A Peralta and other v. Estado Nacional*, CJSN Argentina, Fallos: 313:1513, 27 December 1990 (Case Peralta) that allowed the tacit delegation of legislative functions in case of emergency, does not apply anymore.

[204]DNU Law Art. 25.

[205]DNU Law Art. 26.

[206]Law 26,422 of Argentina Art. 72 [Ley 26.422, Boletín Oficial, 21 November 2008].

[207]Executive Decree 2010 of 2009, Argentina [Decreto Ejecutivo 2010, Diario Oficial, 14 December 2009].

maintained that Articles 18 and 33 of the central bank's charter prescribe that the BCRA can hold only liquid government securities purchased on the market and that the un-transferable bill of exchange with a 10-year maturity was an illiquid document.[208] It is telling that the refusal of the BCRA president led to his dismissal by the President of the Republic through Decree No. 18 of 2010. This decision was made in accordance with Article 11 of the central bank charter, which prescribes the dismissal of board members in case of misconduct or non-fulfillment of the duties of a public official.[209]

In the light of the cumulative changes via emergency regulation, the final reform made to the Organic Charter of the BCRA in 2012 is to be considered a way to guarantee that the central bank supports the government's policies without the need for further decrees. Until 2012, the BCRA had the clear and single objective of preserving the stability of the currency.[210] Through this reform, the National Congress changed the BCRA's objective. The BCRA was given the ambiguous objective of preserving the monetary and financial stability while promoting employment and economic development.[211]

7.5 Summary

The creation of Argentina's central bank in 1935 was supposed to solve problems of monetary instability. This goal was not achieved. The persistent monetary problems of Argentina may be explained by the fact that the monetary authority of Argentina has never enjoyed a high degree of autonomy from political influence because its central bank functions were delegated by the legislative branch to the central bank, which the Constitution of 1853[212] put in charge of monetary policy.[213] Although the central bank is considered to have statutory autonomy, Argentina's Supreme Court of Justice has clarified that the central bank is an organ subordinated to the executive.[214] Therefore, fiscal policy considerations of the government have dominated monetary policy, which is a recipe for higher inflation.[215]

This chapter has further outlined that in times of emergency, the executive and legislative branches introduced stabilization plans via emergency regulation, like the

---

[208]Executive Decree 2010 of 2009, Argentina [Decreto Ejecutivo 2010, Diario Oficial, 14 December 2009] Art. 2.

[209]Executive Decree 18 of 2010, Argentina [Decreto Ejecutivo 18, Diario Oficial, 7 January 2010].

[210]BCRA Law (1992) Art. 3.

[211]BCRA Law Art. 3.

[212]Const. Argentina of 1853 Arts. 64 (3) and 69 (6).

[213]Const. Argentina Arts. 6, 11, and 19.

[214]*Luis A Peralta and other v. Estado Nacional*, CJSN Argentina, Fallos: 313:1513, 27 December 1990.

[215]Sargent and Wallace (1981), p. 2.

Austral Plan of 1985, or modified the central bank charter when deemed necessary. The monetary stabilization plans were only temporarily successful. Moreover, repeated changes in the central bank charter have threatened legal certainty concerning the autonomy of the central bank and its objectives. The low degree of de jure autonomy and the continuous modifications of the central bank charter have rendered the BCRA unable to create a sound currency and to inspire the people's confidence in the stability of prices.

Specifically, the use of economic emergency decrees since 2001 to modify the central bank charter or to influence the development of monetary policy will also make it hard for monetary authorities to credibly commit to reigning in inflation in the future. Unless the use of emergency regulation will be restricted, even a new central bank charter that aims for more de jure autonomy, as suggested by President M. Macri in 2017, would unlikely be able to increase credibility in the central bank's ability to provide monetary stability.

To promote legal certainty concerning the central bank's autonomy, Argentina might need a constitutional reform of broader scope. Granting the central bank autonomy of constitutional rank might be a good first step. But such a simple modification might not be enough because of Argentina's history of using emergency decrees and laws. Therefore, to ensure legal certainty about central bank autonomy, emergency rules in the Constitution of Argentina must include limits. Emergency decrees should not allow modifying the charter of the central bank.

To solve problems of credibility, Argentina could adopt Chile's provisions related to the state of emergency. Article 44 of the Constitution of Chile prescribes that emergency legislation "shall not affect the competences and the functioning of the constitutional organs nor the rights and immunities of their respective titular".[216] Moreover, the Constitutional Tribunal of Chile ruled that the government cannot enact emergency decrees that affect what is established in organic constitutional laws.[217] As the central bank law is among them, Chile's government cannot modify the central bank law using emergency decrees.

Legal References

Treaties and Conventions

Pact of San José Costa Rica [Version published by the Organization of American States of the American Convention on Human Rights, Pact of San José Costa Rica, entry into force on 18 July 1978].

---

[216]Const. Chile Art. 44. Emergency legislation is referred to as "state of exception".

[217]*Senado de la República de Chile v. Ministerio Trabajo y Previsión Social*, TC Chile, Sentencia Rol No. 231, 18 March 1996.

Siracusa Principles on the Limitation and Derogation of Provisions in the International Covenant on Civil and Political Rights [Version published by the American Association for the International Commission of Jurists, April 1985].

The Paris Minimum Standards of Human Rights Norms in a State of Emergency [Version published by The American Journal of International Law, October 1985].

Constitutions

Constitution of Argentina of 1853 [Manuscript of the Constitución de la Federación Argentina published by the Congress Library, Biblioteca del Congreso de Argentina].

Constitution of Argentina with Amendments through 1994 [English Translation of Diario Oficial No. 27.959, 23 August 1994]. Constitute Project, University of Texas at Austin, available at http://www.constituteproject.org/constitution/Argentina_1994.pdf

Constitution of Chile with Amendments through 2015 [English Translation of the Constitución Política de la República de Chile, Gazeta Official, 20 October 2015]. Constitute Project, University of Texas at Austin, available at https://www.constituteproject.org/search?lang=en&q=chile

Legislation

Argentina

Austral Convertibility Law [Ley 23.928, Ley de Convertibilidad del Austral, Boletín Oficial, 28 March 1991].

Law 26,422 of Argentina [Ley 26.422, Boletín Oficial, 21 November 2008].

Legal Regime of the Decrees of Necessity and Urgency, Legislative Delegation and Partial Law Enforcement [Régimen Legal de los Decretos de Necesidad y Urgencia, de Delegación Legislativa y de Promulgación Parcial de Leyes, Boletín Oficial, 26 July 2006].

Organic Charter of the Central Bank of the Republic Argentina [Official Translation of the Carta Organic Charter of the Central Bank of the Republic Argentina [Official Translation of the Carta Orgánica del Banco Central de la República Argentina, Boletín Oficial, 28 March 2012], available at https://www.bcra.gob.ar/Institucional/BCRALaw.asp

Organic Charter of the Central Bank of the Republic of Argentina of 1973 [Carta Orgánica del Banco Central de la República Argentina, Boletín Oficial, 10 October 1973].

Organic Charter of the Central Bank of the Republic Argentina of 1992 [Carta Orgánica del Banco Central de la República Argentina de 1992, Boletín Oficial, 23 September 1992].

Argentina

Economic Emergency Legislation

Economic Emergency Law 23,697 of Argentina [Ley de Emergencia Económica 23.697, Boletín Oficial, 25 September 1989].

Economic Emergency Law 25,414 of Argentina [Ley de Emergencia Económica 25.414, Boletín Oficial, 30 March 2001].

Economic Emergency Law 25,445 of Argentina [Ley de Emergencia Económica 25.445, Boletín Oficial, 22 June 2001].

Economic Emergency Law 25,453 of Argentina [Ley de Emergéncia Económica 25.453, Boletín Oficial, 31 July 2001].

Economic Emergency Law 25,561 of Argentina [Ley de Emergencia Económica 25.561, Boletín Oficial, 7 January 2002].

Economic Emergency Law 25,562 of Argentina [Ley de Emergencia Económica 25.562, Boletín Oficial, 8 February 2002].

Economic Emergency Law 25,780 of Argentina [Ley de Emergencia Económica 25.780, Boletín Oficial, 8 September 2003].

Economic Emergency Law 25,820 of Argentina [Ley de Emergencia Económica 25.820, Boletín Oficial, 4 December 2003].

Economic Emergency Law 25,972 of Argentina [Ley de Emergencia Económica 25.972, Boletín Oficial, 17 December 2004].

Economic Emergency Law 26,077 of Argentina [Ley de Emergencia Económica 26.077, Boletín Oficial, 10 January 2005].

Economic Emergency Law 26,204 of Argentina [Ley de Emergencia Económica 26.204, Boletín Oficial, 20 December 2006].

Economic Emergency Law 26,339 of Argentina [Ley de Emergencia Económica 26.339, Boletín Oficial, 4 January 2008].

Economic Emergency Law 26,456 of Argentina [Ley de Emergencia Económica 26.456, Boletín Oficial, 16 December 2008].

Economic Emergency Law 26,563 of Argentina [Ley de Emergencia Económica 26.563, Boletín Oficial, 22 December 2009].

Economic Emergency Law 26,729 of Argentina [Ley de Emergencia Económica 26.729, Boletín Oficial, 28 December 2011].

Economic Emergency Law 26,896 of Argentina [Ley de Emergencia Económica 26.896, Boletín Oficial, 22 October 2013].

Economic Emergency Law 27,200 of Argentina [Ley de Emergencia Económica 27.200, Boletín Oficial, 4 November 2015].

Emergency Decrees

Argentina

Emergency Decree 1096 of 1985, Argentina [Decreto de Emergencia 1096, Diario Oficial, 14 June 1985].

Emergency Decree 36 of 1990, Argentina [Decreto de Emergencia 36, Diario Oficial, 5 January 1990].

Emergency Decree 290 of 1995, Argentina [Decreto de Emergencia 290, Diario Oficial, 27 February 1995].

Emergency Decree 803 of 2001, Argentina [Decreto de Emergencia 803, Diario Oficial, 21 June 2001].

Emergency Decree 896 of 2001, Argentina [Decreto de Emergencia 896, Diario Oficial, 13 July 2001].

Emergency Decree 1570 of 2001, Argentina [Decreto de Emergencia 1570, Diario Oficial, 1 December 2001].

Emergency Decree 1678 of 2001, Argentina [Decreto de Emergencia 1678, Diario Oficial, 19 December 2001].

Emergency Decree 71 of 2002, Argentina [Decreto de Emergencia 71, Diario Oficial, 9 January 2002].

Emergency Decree 214 of 2002, Argentina [Decreto de Emergencia 214, 3 February 2002].

Emergency Decree 401 of 2002, Argentina [Decreto de Emergencia 401, Diario Oficial, 28 February 2002].

Executive Decrees

Argentina

Executive Decree 2010 of 2009, Argentina [Decreto Ejecutivo 2010, Diario Oficial, 14 December 2009].

Executive Decree 18 of 2010, Argentina [Decreto Ejecutivo 18, Diario Oficial, 7 January 2010].

Case Law

Argentina

José Horta v. Ernesto Harguindeguy, CJSJN Argentina, Fallos: 136:170, 21 August 1922.

Agustin Ercolano v. Julieta Lanteri de Renshaw, CSJN Argentina, Fallos: 137:170, 28 April 1922.

Leonardo Mango v. Ernesto Traba, CSJN Argentina, Fallos: 144:220, 26 August 1925.

Oscar Agustin Avico v. Saúl de la Pesa, CJSN Argentina, Fallos: 172:21, 7 December 1934.

Gustavo Nordensthol v. Subterraneos de Buenos Aires, CSJN Argentina, Fallos: 307:326, 2 April 1985.

Rolon Zappa, Victor F. v. Estado Nacional, CJSN Argentina, Fallos: 308:1848, 30 September 1986.

Luis A Peralta and other v. Estado Nacional, CJSN Argentina, Fallos: 313:1513, 27 December 1990.

Levy Horacio and other v. Estado Nacional, CSJN Argentina, Fallos 320:1426, July 15, 1997.

Sergi Vinciguerra Antonio v. Central Bank of the Argentine Republic, CJSN Argentina, Fallos: 3192:3196, 17 March 1998.

René Roberto Colina and others v. Estado Nacional, CJSN Argentina, Fallos: 324:4520, 28 December 2001.

Smith, Carlos Antonio v. Poder Ejecutivo Nacional o Estado Nacional, CJSN Argentina, Fallos: 325:28. 1 February 2002.

Chile

Senado de la República de Chile v. Ministerio Trabajo y Previsión Social, TC Chile, Sentencia Rol No. 231, 18 March 1996.

References

Agamben G, Borrás MR (2003) El estado de excepción. Mientras Tanto 86:57–66. Available at https://www.jstor.org/stable/27820667

Alberdi JB (1858) Sistema Económico y Rentístico de la Confederación Argentina según su Constitución de 1853. Imprenta de José Jacquin, Besanzon. available at https://books.google.de/books?id=T0QLxiNIaEwC&printsec=frontcover&hl=de&source=gbs_ge_summary_r&cad=0#v=onepage&q&f=false

Avalos E (2012) Los Decretos de Necesidad y Urgencia en Argentina: Desde 1853 a Nuestros Días. Revista de la Facultad de Derecho 3(1):147–157. available at https://revistas.unc.edu.ar/index.php/refade/article/view/5972

Barnett R (2003) The proper scope of the police power. Notre Dame Law Rev 79(2):429–496. https://doi.org/10.2139/ssrn.437201

Bestard AM (2008) Delegación de Facultades Legislativas en el Poder Ejecutivo, El Poder Legislativo. In: Aportes para el Conocimiento del Congreso de la Nación Argentina 6:579–595. Available at http://www.derecho.uba.ar/investigacion/investigadores/publicaciones/bestard- delegacion_de_facultades.pdf

Bordo M, Kydland F (1995) The gold standard as a rule: an essay in exploration. Explorat Econ Hist 32(4):423–464. https://doi.org/10.1006/exeh.1995.1019

Buiter W, Grafe C (2001) Central Banking and the Choice of Currency Regime in Accession Countries. In: Revue d'économie financière (English ed.). https://doi.org/10.3406/ecofi.2001.4564

Calcagno AF (1997) El Régimen de Convertibilidad y el Sistema Bancario en la Argentina. Revista de la Cepal 61:63–89. available at http://repositorio.cepal.org/bitstream/handle/11362/12047/061063089_es.pdf?sequence=1&isAllowed=y

Cole D (2003) Judging the next emergency: Judicial review and individual rights in times of crisis. Mich Law Rev 101(8):2565–2595. https://doi.org/10.2307/3595389

De la Torre A, Levy Yeyati E, Schmukler S, Ades A, Kaminsky G (2003) Living and dying with hard pegs: the rise and fall of Argentina's currency board. Brookings Institution Press 3 (2):43–107. Available at http://www.jstor.org/stable/20065441

Della Paolera G (1994) Experimentos Monetarios y Bancarios en Argentina: 1861-1930. Revista de Historia Económica. J Iberian Latin Am Econ Hist 12(3):539–589. https://doi.org/10.1017/S0212610900004754

Dornbusch R, de Pablo J (1990) The austral plan. In: Sachs J (ed) Developing country debt and economic performance, Vol. 2: The Country Studies – Argentina, Bolivia, Brazil, Mexico, pp 91–114

Edwards S, Tabellini G (1991) Explaining fiscal policies and inflation in developing countries. J Int Money Financ 10(1):16–48. https://doi.org/10.1016/0261-5606(91)90045-L

Elster J (1994) The impact of constitutions on economic performance. World Bank Econ Rev 8 (1):209–226. https://doi.org/10.1093/wber/8.suppl_1.209

Feldstein M (2002) Argentina's fall: lessons from the latest financial crisis. Foreign Aff 81(2):8–14. available at http://www.nber.org/feldstein/argentina.pdf

Ferreira Rubio D, Goretti M (1996) Cuando el Presidente Gobierna Solo: Menen y los Decretos de Necesidad y Urgencia hasta la Reforma Constitucional (julio 1989 - agosto 1994). Desarrollo Económico 36(41):443–474. https://doi.org/10.2307/3467401

Fitzpatrick J (1994) Human rights in crisis: the international system for protecting rights during states of emergency. University of Pennsylvania Press. Available at https://books.google.de/books?id=ORb8OrquqxAC&printsec=frontcover&hl=de&source=gbs_ge_summary_r&cad=0#v=onepage&q&f=false

Franklin B, Temple Franklin W (1818) Memoirs of the life and writings of Benjamin Franklin. H. Colburn

Frenkel R, Fanelli J (1986) El Plan Austral, Seminario sobre Crisis Externa y Política Económica: Los Casos da Argentina, Brazil y México. Available at https://repositorio.cepal.org/bitstream/handle/11362/33116/S8600682_es.pdf?sequence=1&isAllowed=y

García Hamilton J (2005) Historical reflections on the Splendor and Decline of Argentina. Cato J 25 (3):521–540. Available at https://object.cato.org/sites/cato.org/files/serials/files/cato-journal/2005/11/cj25n3-11.pdf

Gelli MA (2003) La Corte Suprema de la República Argentina en las Emergencias Económicas. Anuario Iberoamericano de Justicia Constitucional 7:165–207. Available at https://dialnet.unirioja.es/servlet/articulo?codigo=761396

Gordillo A (2012) Tratado de Derecho Administrativo y Obras Selectas. Tomo 5, Primeras Obras, Fundación de Derecho Administrativo. Available at http://www.gordillo.com/pdf_tomo5/tomo5.pdf

Gross O, Ní Aoláin F (2006) Law in times of crisis: emergency powers in theory and practice. Cambridge University Press. Available at https://books.google.de/books?id=XgbEUxcKBgAC&printsec=frontcover&source=gbs_ge_summary_r&cad=0#v=onepage&q&f=false

Grossman C (1986) A framework for the examination of states of emergency under the American Convention of Human Rights. Am Univ Int Law Rev 1(1):35–55. Available at https://digitalcommons.wcl.american.edu/cgi/viewcontent.cgi?referer=https://scholar.google.de/&httpsredir=1&article=1644&context=auilr

Hafner-Burton EM, Helfer L, Fariss CJ (2011) Emergency and escape: explaining derogation from human rights treaties. Int Organ 65(4):673–707. https://doi.org/10.1017/S002081831100021X

Hamilton A, Jay J, Madison J (2001) The federalist papers. In: George WC McCellan J (eds) The Gideon Edition, Liberty Fund Inc, Indianapolis. Available at http://files.libertyfund.org/files/788/0084_LFeBk.pdf

Hanke S (2002) Currency boards. Ann Am Acad Polit Sci 579(1):87–105. https://doi.org/10.1177/000271620257900107

Hanke S (2003) The Argentine straw man: a response to currency board critics. Cato J 23(1):47–57. Available at http://citeseerx.ist.psu.edu/viewdoc/download?doi=10.1.1.352.6338&rep=rep1&type=pdf

Hanke S, Schuler K (2002) What went wrong in Argentina? Central Bank J 12(3):43–48. Available at http://latlibre.org/wp-content/uploads/2019/02/103Schuler03.pdf https://digitalcommons.wcl.american.edu/cgi/viewcontent.cgi?referer=https://scholar.google.de/&httpsredir=1&article=1644&context=auilr

Humphreys S (2006) Legalizing lawlessness: On Giorgio Agamben's state of exception. Eur J Int Law 17(3):677–687. https://doi.org/10.1093/ejil/chl020

Inter-American Commission on Human Rights (IACHR) (1981) Annual Report of the Inter-American Commission on Human Rights 1980–1981. Available at https://www.cidh.oas.org/annualrep/80.81eng/TOC.htm

Inter-American Commission on Human Rights (IACHR) (1982) Annual Report of the Inter-American Commission on Human Rights 1981–1982. Available at http://www.cidh.org/annualrep/81.82sp/indice.htm

Jacobs B (2003) Pesification and economic crisis in Argentina: the moral Hazard posed by a politicized supreme court. Univ Miami Inter-Am Law Rev 34(3):391–434. Available at http://www.jstor.org/stable/pdf/40176544.pdf?refreqid=excelsior%3Af09cfc36cfd873a478b5653d3189ceb5

Kiguel M (1991) Inflation in Argentina: stop and go since the austral plan. World Dev 19(8):969–986. https://doi.org/10.1016/0305-750X(91)90120-7

Lagos LF, Galetovic A (1989) Las Planes Austral y el Cruzado: ¿Por qué no Detuvieron la Inflación? Cuadernos de Economía 26(78):217–242. Available at http://www.jstor.org/stable/23830344?seq=1#page_scan_tab_contents

Lastra R (2015) International financial and monetary law, 2nd edn. Oxford University Press

Lee B (2015) Emergency takings. Mich Law Rev 114(391):391–454. Available at http://brooklynworks.brooklaw.edu/cgi/viewcontent.cgi?article=1534&context=faculty

Lillich R (1985) The Paris minimum standards of human rights norms in a state of emergency. Am J Int Law 79(4):1072–1081. https://doi.org/10.2307/2201848

Meyler B (2007) Economic emergency and the rule of law. DePaul Law Rev 56(2):539–568. Available at http://via.library.depaul.edu/cgi/viewcontent.cgi?article=1306&context=law-review

Mishkin F (2007) The economics of money, banking and financial markets, 8th edn. The Addison-Wesley Series in Economics

Negretto G (2002) ¿Gobierna Solo el Presidente? Poderes de Decreto y Diseno Institucional en Brasil y Argentina. Desarrollo Económico 42(167):377–404. https://doi.org/10.2307/3455843

Perry G, Serven L (2003) The Anatomy of a Multiple Crisis: Why was Argentina Special and What Can We Learn from It? World Bank Policy Research Working Paper No. 3081. https://doi.org/10.1596/1813-9450-3081

Roots R (2000) Government by permanent emergency: the forgotten history of the new deal constitution. Suffolk Univ Law Rev 33:259–417

Sargent T, Wallace N (1981) Some Unpleasant Monetarist Arithmetic. Federal Reserve Bank of Minneapolis Quarterly Review. Available at https://www.minneapolisfed.org/research/qr/qr531.pdf

Scheuerman W (1999–2000) The economic state of emergency. Cardozo Law Rev 21:1868–1894. Available at https://heinonline.org/HOL/LandingPage?handle=hein.journals/cdozo21&div=79&id=&page

Thomas C, Cachanosky N (2006) Argentina's Post-2001 economy and the 2014 default. Q Rev Econ Financ 60:70–80. https://doi.org/10.1016/j.qref.2015.08.002

Zwitter A, Prins A, Pannwitz H (2014) State of Emergency Mapping Database. University of Groningen Faculty of Law Research Paper. Available at https://papers.ssrn.com/sol3/papers.cfm?abstract_id=2428254

Chapter 8
Towards Monetary Stability in Latin America

8.1 General Summary

The book emphasizes the importance of legal certainty concerning the rules that guarantee autonomy of central banks to provide for a framework of monetary stability.

The principle of legal certainty guides how the law must be made, interpreted, and applied. A look at different notions of legal certainty in Chap. 2 clarifies this. *Formal* legal certainty demands that the law consists of clear, consistent, and stable legal rules. *Substantive* legal certainty demands consistency in judicial decisions. Veredicts should respect the principle legal rules and precedents. Both formal and substantive legal certainty are the basis for subjective legal certainty. *Subjective* legal certainty is related to the confidence people have in the legal system if they feel that there are no unforeseeable legal risks stemming from great inconsistencies or ambiguity in the law, its interpretation, or application.

Chapter 3 shows that a high degree of legal certainty improves the conditions for authorities to commit to their promises and for citizens to believe these legal commitments. To make commitments credible, commitments should be included in the legal framework in such a way that it is hard to modify the commitments. From this perspective, the constitution is most effective in restraining authorities domestically.

Chapter 4 emphasizes the importance of the legal rank of central bank autonomy, as well as the close-knit relationship between the banks' objectives and central bank autonomy. Because legislation can be easily modified, there is little legal certainty concerning central bank autonomy if central bank autonomy does not have constitutional rank. A history of non-interventionism, stability, and good central bank performance might compensate for a lower legal rank and provide sufficient (subjective) legal certainty for the bank to perform well. But given the history of monetary instability in Latin America, a strong commitment to central bank autonomy seems necessary.

When it comes to central bank objectives, some objectives provide more legal certainty than others. Although all central banks are supposed to contribute to the stable economic development of their respective countries in one way or another, they may do so by either stabilizing inflation rates or supporting employment or social progress. Most importantly, from the perspective of legal certainty, a central bank needs one clear or a few consistent objectives. If there is more than one objective without ordering, it is hard to know what the central bank will do when a specific problem arrives that makes trading-off one objective against the other necessary. If objectives are very broadly defined—for example, contributing to social progress—it is less clear if at any point the central bank acts according to the will of the government or autonomously.

Chapter 5 provides a detailed analysis of the statutes governing Latin American central banks to determine if central bank autonomy is guaranteed in the law or if there are conflicts with autonomy as guaranteed, for instance, in the constitution. It is conceivable that a central bank is labeled autonomous, but the legislator has provided numerous ways for governments to influence the central bank. For instance, when a president appoints board members, autonomy is questionable. Similarly, rules that allow for the dismissal of board members at a president's will would undermine autonomy. Any rules that require the central bank to finance the government are not conducive to providing legal certainty concerning central bank autonomy.

Chapters 6 and 7 focus on specific threats to the certainty of central bank autonomy stemming from exceptions in the law and conflicts between laws, which tend to be ignored when in studies of central bank autonomy. For the case of Colombia, Chap. 6 has identified conflicting laws and court interventions as a threat. Specifically, the Constitutional Court of Colombia (CCC) acknowledged that the Colombian central bank as autonomous and set clear limits on legislative and executive intervention. But the Court also modified the central bank's objective, saying central bank policies must be in line with the social rule of law, which comprises a number of positive rights, such as the rights to health care, social security, and housing. In particular instances the Court declared unconstitutional high mortgage interest rates, which were administered by the central bank, arguing that the central bank's decisions must be in line with the social rule of law. Because of these court decisions, the bank faced several lawsuits over its policies. Avoiding the use of obscure concepts such as the *social rule of law*, as well as a less activist court, may help improve certainty about the autonomy of the central bank.

In addition, Chap. 7 provides evidence that the use of economic emergency decrees in Argentina since 2001 has allowed for the continuous modification of the central bank charter. The existence of such legal rules, therefore, leads to uncertainty regarding central bank autonomy in times of crisis when emergency rules do not include limits.

Drawing on previous chapters, this final chapter compiles the findings and provides proposals to improve certainty concerning autonomy for the central banks in the region (status as of October 2019).

8.2 A Benchmark Framework

Compiling the main findings from the analyses presented in the book, key ingredients for an *ideal* framework that provides certainty concerning central bank are: (1) autonomy of constitutional rank; (2) a clear objective; (3) strong guarantees for personal and financial autonomy; and (4) accurate arrangements to balance coordination and accountability without sacrificing independence. Naturally, the rules should be consistent with one another and there should be no loopholes that allow a government to influence a central bank under certain conditions.

8.2.1 Autonomy of Constitutional Rank

The autonomy of a central bank can be entrenched in legal documents of different rank. Whether central bank autonomy is embedded in the constitution, organic or ordinary legislation is the most fundamental hint about the degree to which authorities wanted to tie their hands regarding monetary policy. Each of these documents entail a different degree of consensus and stability related to their costs of modification.

An increased cost in the modification of the legal obligations makes legal obligations more credible. While international agreements may be able to tie the hands of government in an international environment, a constitution restrains authorities domestically. Amending the constitution is normally more difficult than amending legislation, either organic or ordinary, because of the increased number of veto players involved and the stiff process of amendment. Those that delegate autonomy to a central bank show a willingness to not intervene in monetary policy. However, embedding autonomy and the objective of the central bank in the constitution signals a stronger commitment to central bank autonomy over time.

8.2.2 Clear (Single) Objective

Ideally, central banks have a single objective, which should not require much explanation—such as holding inflation low. Having a central bank that also pursues other objectives, such as employment or an ambiguous economic development goal, makes the monetary authority face tradeoffs. Such legal rules might fail in guiding people's expectations.

Furthermore, the reality of our six Latin American countries and their inflationary history show that the traditional objective of preserving monetary stability is the best option for the central banks in those countries. Monetary authorities would have to focus on preventing inflation and force governments to keep the house in order by pursuing modest fiscal policies. Monetary stability is a key necessity for the Latin American countries to graduate from emerging market status.[1]

8.2.3   Guarantees of Personal and Financial Autonomy

At times, the constitution or the first two articles of the statutes of a central bank imply that a central bank is autonomous. But the rest of the law is plagued with dispositions that make this autonomy impossible or undermine its credibility. As such, several aspects in terms of personal autonomy and financial autonomy that are important to promote certainty in such autonomy.

First, rules concerning the appointment and tenure of board members matter. Rules must assure that board members are elected in a process that involves more than one veto player. The more people involved, the more diverse and independent is each member of the central bank board from those that appoint the member. In countries with a federal system, the federal states might take part in the appointment process. Central bank board members should have long terms in office. Most importantly, their time in office should not match the presidential period and there should be no possibility of reelection.

Second, the board members should display certain personal characteristics. On the one hand, they need to have technical knowledge and expertise in monetary policy. They should be able show that they are experts in the field. On the other hand, they should not be allowed to develop other professional activities, except, for instance, university teaching, while they are board members to prevent conflicts of interest.

In terms of financial autonomy, there is a need for clear rules that prohibit lending to the government. Ideally, the prohibition will have no exceptions. Moreover, the central bank board should be able to handle its own budget and determine the salaries of board members. To guarantee that the central bank can do its job, the central bank should have enough reserves available for monetary policy implementation without economic boundaries.

---

[1]Reinhart and Rogoff (2011), pp. 283–284.

8.2.4   Coordination and Accountability

Central bank autonomy comes with responsibilities. The responsibilities of a politically independent central bank are of two kinds: coordination of monetary policy with the economic policy of other state organs, and accountability for their actions. However, for there to be legal certainty concerning central bank autonomy the arrangements for coordination should not diminish a central bank's operational and financial autonomy, and the accountability arrangements should not diminish personal autonomy of the central bank's board members.

To allow for coordination without undermining autonomy, communication with the other state organs should be the main mean of coordination of central banks. Channels of communication could be mutual reports, advice, and appearances of board members. Accountability rules should provide that central bank board members are not accountable for the content but for the legality of their decisions. The board members of the central banks should be accountable in front of the courts of justice for the control of legality, and occasionally in front of both the executive and the legislative, but never only in front of the executive. Giving the executive too much space diminishes personal autonomy.

8.3   Main Findings and Proposals: The Good, the Bad, and the Ugly

Legal frameworks and their interpretations can hardly be perfect. The comparison of the legal frameworks of central banks provided in this book points to key shortcomings in the law as well as substantial differences between the countries in the region. As such, the following proposals for improvement suggest merely slight adjustments for some countries, while proposals for other countries are rather general.

8.3.1   The Good: Chile and Peru

At the first glance, the central bank frameworks of Chile and Peru are very similar and leave little doubts concerning central bank autonomy. This section could thus be very short. But their organic charters provide lots of detail that will be used to indicate specifically what good central bank law looks like. Although the central bank laws represent the side of the spectrum that closely fits the benchmark model, a comparison of findings on the two frameworks, with one another and with the benchmark model, reveals some room for improvement, specifically in terms of personal autonomy in Peru.

8.3.1.1 Constitutional Rank and Clarity of Objective

Both central banks have been granted autonomy of constitutional rank. The constitutions of both countries provide a similar degree of stability because the processes for constitutional amendment are similar. In both countries, amending the constitution requires two sessions, high majorities, and the possibility of a referendum, which indicates substantial modification costs for the constitution and a strong commitment of promises entrenched in the constitutions.

The objectives of the central banks also enjoy a high degree of stability. The legal objectives of the Central Reserve Bank of Peru (CRBP) have remained unchanged since 1993, and the objective of the Central Bank of Chile (CBCH) was defined in 1989. Nevertheless, it is possible to say that the objective of the Peruvian central bank is slightly more advantageous in terms of legal certainty. The reasons are twofold. First, the CRBP has a single and clear objective, preserving the purchasing power of the currency, while the CBCH has a double objective, monetary stability and preserving the normal functioning of the internal and external payment system. Even though both objectives of the Chilean central bank are, at large, compatible, having more than one objective cannot beat the clarity of the objective of the Peruvian central bank. The other reason is that the objective of the CRBP is entrenched in the constitution, while the objective of the CBCH is in the organic law of the bank. Although, organic law provides more legal certainty than ordinary legislation, as modification necessitates larger majorities, organic law does not guarantee the stability of the constitution.

In both Peru and Chile, the legal rules that guarantee the personal, financial, and operational autonomy of the central bank and determine the means of coordination and accountability are entrenched in organic law. These legal rules are, by and large, consistent with both the banks' objectives and the constitutional autonomy.

8.3.1.2 Addressing Issues in Personal Autonomy

The legal framework of the CBCH, however, has more guarantees for personal autonomy of the board members than the legal rules that govern the CRBP. While the legal framework of the CRBP provides that the tenure of the board members overlaps with the presidential period and is only 5 years, the tenure of the board members of the CBCH does not overlap with the presidential period. It is also longer—10 years. Peru should reform central bank law in this respect.

The members of both central banks are elected in a dual process, which means they are elected with the participation of both the executive and the legislative branches. But the process differs. The President of the country elects four of the seven CRBP board members and the legislature the other three. To provide certainty about personal autonomy, it is recommended that all central bank board members be elected by both the President of the country and the legislature. According to the legal arrangements of the CBCH, the President of the country appoints all the central bank board members, but the appointments must be approved by the legislature. The legislature could block the President's appointment, increasing the likelihood that members who are independent from the government are appointed to the board. In order to further improve the legal rules concerning CBCH's personal autonomy, reappointment of the central bank's board members could be eliminated. Moreover, the president of the central bank board should not be appointed by the President. As all other arrangements are close to the ideal, except for possibility of reappointment, there is no risk of political arrangements to remain in office stemming from the law.

The Peruvian arrangements are more troublesome because the country's President unilaterally appoints some central bank board members, including the president of the board. It would be better if board members elect the central bank president. Moreover, according to CRBP law, only the president of the board is an exclusive official of the bank. The other board members can perform other functions such as managing firms or financial institutions. They may even own shares of less than the 5% in a financial institution. Such arrangements should be revisited. Peru gives too much more power to the central bank president and may allow for conflicts of interests of other board members.

By contrast, the legal arrangements to guarantee personal autonomy of CBCH board members are preferable. CBCH board members are exclusive officials of the central bank. The law prohibits them from owning shares in financial institutions and performing activities, remunerated or not, in the government or the public sectors. The members of the board of the Central Bank of Chile are only allowed to teach at the university and to be part of nonprofits. Another advantage of the CBCH in guaranteeing the personal autonomy of board members is that the law protects their opinions as confidential and clarifies that they do not represent their personal points of view but the central bank's perspective. The law of the CRBP does not have such a provision.

Considering the demands for technical knowledge of the board members, CRBP law only mentions that board members should have experience in economic and financial matters. This requirement may be insufficient. Requiring a professional degree and certain years of experience may be more appropriate. The law of the CBCH, however, remains silent on any demands for qualification.

8.3.1.3 Improving Financial Autonomy

The law of the Chilean central bank is the clearest among the six Latin American countries considered in terms of prohibiting the financing of the state directly or indirectly. There is one exception to the rule: the risk of war qualified by the National Security Council of Chile. In the Peruvian law, there is also a general prohibition, but with one exception: buying treasury bonds in the secondary market up to a limit of 5% of monetary base of the previous year.

While the CRBP is autonomous in managing its funds and determining the salaries of its staff and authorities, Chile's President sets the salaries for the board members of the CBCH. In this regard, Peru's provisions are preferable. By contrast, regarding the management of revenue, the CBCH has leeway to make decisions regarding its funds, while the CRBP must follow clear legal rules. 25 percent of profits goes to the public Treasury and the other 75% to a capitalization reserve. The law of the CRBP guarantees the capital of the bank by guaranteeing the bank's liabilities—if the reserves deposited in the Treasury are not enough to cover the bank's losses, the state has to transfer negotiable debt to the bank. The law of the CBCH does not include an explicit guarantee. Thus, it might be advisable to guarantee the funds that the central bank requires to perform monetary policy, including a state obligation to cover the bank's losses when the central bank's revenue is not sufficient.

8.3.1.4 Additional Suggestions

Both legal frameworks provide guarantees for operational autonomy and a set of instruments for the banks to reach their objectives. The legal arrangements concerning the function as a lender of last resort are also very clear in the central bank laws of both countries. In the case of the Peruvian central bank, the legal arrangements respect that the bank's objective is not financial stability. The law stipulates that the central bank is the lender of last resort only to preserve monetary stability and sets clear rules for the bank's performance of this function. For example, only financial institutions that are under the control of the Superintendence of Banking and Insurance of Peru can receive stabilization loans from the CRBP.

The legal arrangements concerning the lender of last resort (LLR) function of the CBCH clearly state that the loans given to financial institutions are granted only because of transitory illiquidity and provide terms and conditions. However, the law does not clarify the guarantees that the bank has to receive for the loans but leaves it to the discretion of the board members whether to demand guarantees or not. This void should be filled.

It is possible to conclude that the arrangements for coordination of the CRBP and the CBCH with other state organs in charge of economic policy respect the autonomy of constitutional rank of both central banks. In this sense, the main channel of coordination is via mutual reports. The law of the CRBP even gives the bank the opportunity to complain to the Ministry of Finance if the economic policies of other organs jeopardize the achievement of its goals. The board of the CBCH can invite the Minister of Finance to some sessions with voice but no vote. Therefore, the influence of the executive branch in the bank's decisions is minimal. An advantage of the CBCH; coordination arrangements over those of the CRBP is that the constitutional organic law of the CBCH lays out a process for solving conflicts in the development of economic policy. Specifically, the law establishes that the bank's operations can only be objected to by the Ministry of Finance in front of a commission made up by the National Economic Comptroller, the Ministry of Finance, and the Ministry of Foreign Affairs. The Bank can appeal the decision of this commission in front of the Appealing Court of Santiago.

The budget of the CBCH is under the control of the General Auditor, who is appointed by the central bank's board. The budget of the Peruvian central bank is under the control of the General Comptroller of the Republic that oversees the central bank's budget, net worth accounting, use of funds, and custody of securities. This organ is also constitutionally autonomous; therefore, it enjoys the same degree of independence from political intervention as the central bank. The policies and regulations issued by the Central Bank of Chile are only controlled by the board. And the control of legality is under the oversight of a General Council, who is also appointed by the central bank's board.

The process to dismiss board members is relatively clear and stiff. The Congress of Peru is responsible for removing board members, along with the agreement of two-thirds of board members. A high voting bar makes it difficult to remove board members. The appropriate and legal reasons for dismissal are also clear. One is serious misconduct, such as crimes and the granting of credits that are not allowed by law. A board member accused of crime must be judged first in the Congress before facing the courts of justice and removed from the board. The appropriate reasons for dismissal of the board members of the CBCH are also clearly stated in the law. The Appealing Court of Santiago is in charge of determining whether to dismiss a board member of the Central Bank of Chile in cases of perjury and traffic of influences. The President of the country and the legislature are responsible in cases the legal rules governing the bank have not be adhered to. In the case of the dismissal arrangements of CBCH board members, the law also states that a position for the bank's board opens when a member fails to attend four sessions in a row or six sessions within six months. However, the process of dismissal in this case is not set forth in the law.

8.3.2 The Bad: Argentina & Brazil

In contrast to the legal frameworks of the CBCH and CRBP, the laws of the Central Bank of the Argentine Republic (BCRA) and Central Bank of Brazil (CBB) have little in common with the benchmark framework outlined. The rules do not provide a reason to be confident that the central bank will act autonomously and maintain price stability over time. Specifically, in the case of Brazil, the law does not even reveal an intention by the legislator to create a central bank that operates independent from government.

8.3.2.1 Statutory Autonomy and Multiple Objectives

Neither the Central Bank of Brazil nor the Central Bank of the Argentine Republic was granted autonomy in their countries' respective constitutions. The Constitution of Argentina provides that the National Congress shall preserve the stability of the currency. Monetary policy was only delegated to the central bank via an ordinary law. The charter of the BCRA suggests that the bank has the status of an autarchy, meaning that it has statutory autonomy and should manage itself. The bank is also considered part of the public administration, which means it depends on the executive branch. Contrary to the rules that govern the BM and the BRC, placing

Argentina's central bank within the public administration is not in conflict with the legal rank of its autonomy.

Brazil's central bank is also considered to have statutory autonomy, but it is only the executive arm of the Monetary Council of Brazil. As the Monetary Council has no autonomy whatsoever, but is composed by members of the executive, the autonomous status of the CBB is meaningless as far as providing certainty about the achievement of the bank's legal objectives. The central bank does not make any monetary policy decisions.

Whereas there seems to be no intention to have an autonomous central bank in Brazil, in Argentina the exclusion of central bank autonomy in the constitution could stem from difficulties in modifying the constitution. Even if governments and the legislature wanted the autonomy of the central bank to be embedded in the constitution, amendments could only be made via a democratically elected constitutional assembly.

8.3.2.2 Multiple Objectives

In Brazil, the Monetary Council pursues several objectives with a clear priority order. Its main objective, the economic and social progress of the country, is consistent with the fact that the Monetary Council is part of the government. Preserving price stability, however, is only a subordinated goal. Similarly, the Central Bank of the Argentine Republic has multiple objectives, including price stability, employment, and supporting the economic development of the country. However, it is not clear which of these objectives is the bank's main priority. Given that Argentina's central bank has a history of financing the government, which has triggered episodes of monetary instability, this is a problem that should be addressed. A clear commitment to monetary stability would move the statutes of the bank closer to the benchmark model and improve confidence in the bank's autonomy.

8.3.2.3 Central Bank Autonomy in Brazil

In line with Brazil's central bank's rank and its relationship to other state branches, the statutes do not guarantee central bank autonomy in any way. The central bank's board is elected by the Federal Senate or the President of Brazil, and the Minister of Finance is the chairman of the Monetary Council. Board members can be dismissed at the discretion of the government. The Monetary Council does not only have to coordinate all policies with the government but must also follow the guidelines of the President of Brazil. On the bright side, amending Brazil's Constitution carries the lowest modification costs of all six countries. If it is the will of the executive and legislature to have an autonomous central bank, they won't face problems in achieving this. Unfortunately, this also implies that creating a bank with autonomy of constitutional rank would not provide much legal certainty concerning central bank autonomy.

8.3.2.4 Improving the Rules for the BCRA

Statutes governing the BCRA leave doubts about the autonomy of the bank. On the one hand, provisions regarding the appointment process and tenure, as well as prohibitions on activities of BCRA board members are by and large in line with the benchmark model. Moreover, the arrangements concerning communication between the BCRA and other state organs are reasonable. It is noteworthy that the BCRA does not only prepare reports for the executive, but the Ministry of Finance is also obliged to report to the BCRA, and financial statements are audited by a board-appointed auditor. In these aspects, the law of the BCRA is as close to the benchmark model as the law of the CBCH.

On the other hand, the executive controls the bank. The President of Argentina can remove board members at will. Such provisions are consistent with the legal rank of the central bank and its place within the public administration, but they suggest there is less certainty about the autonomy of the bank. Even more troublesome are provisions regarding financial and operational autonomy. On the upside, the statutes forbid the central bank from granting loans to any state institution. However, there are numerous exceptions that allow for the financing of the government. It is also worrisome, from the perspective of certainty concerning central bank autonomy, that the BCRA is allowed to service government debt on behalf of the government. Such exceptions should be dropped from the statutes. When it comes to operational autonomy, the legal rank of the central bank, as well as its objectives, imply a need for coordination with government policies. Although the central bank does not have to follow the order of the executive branch, the bank is supposed to develop its policies in line with government policies.

8.3.2.5 A Special Threat: Emergency Decrees

The use of economic emergency decrees in Argentina poses a special threat to the central bank autonomy. Emergency decrees have been used repeatedly to modify the central bank charter and affect monetary policy. Therefore, a new central bank charter as proposed by the former President of Argentina, M. Macri, giving the bank autonomy of constitutional rank will hardly suffice to provide certainty about central bank autonomy, as long as emergency decrees can modify the bank charter. To provide a clear signal of change and certainty concerning autonomy, emergency decrees should not allow for the modification of the charter of the central bank. Argentina could also learn from Chile's provisions related to the state of emergency. In Chile, the government cannot modify central bank law using emergency decrees.

8.3.3 The Ugly: Mexico & Colombia

Like the CRBP and the CBCH, the (Bank of Mexico) BM and (Bank of the Republic of Colombia) BRC were also granted autonomy in their countries' constitutions. However, in contrast to the legal frameworks of the CRBP and the CBCH, the rules laid out in the Mexican constitution and the law of the BM contradict each other. And although constitutional provisions for the BRC seem to be in line with the benchmark model at first look, suggesting that the drafters of the constitution mean for the bank to be somewhat autonomous, decisions of the Constitutional Court of Colombia indicate that these provisions do not necessarily mean that the bank has autonomy in reaching its constitutional objectives.

8.3.3.1 Three Main Contradictions

Starting with the BM, there are three main contradictions between constitutional prescriptions and the central bank law. First, the constitutional rank of the BM means that the bank is a constitutional organ and should not be considered a part of the public administration. However, the BM is subject to the Federal Law of Administrative Liabilities of Public Officers. This gives rise to doubts concerning the bank's rank generally, and in terms of control and personal autonomy specifically. According to this law, public officials are accountable to the Secretariat of Government Services, which is composed of officials appointed unilaterally by the President of Mexico. The bases for dismissal are outline ambiguously in the law (e.g., bad behavior), which leaves a lot of room for speculation about what a board member subject to the law is allowed to do.

A second contradiction is related to the central bank's objective. Although the constitution gives the Mexican central bank a single objective of preserving the value of the currency, the law of the BM adds the objective of preserving the health of the financial system. It is, of course, clear that the constitutional provisions should prevail over legislation. Moreover, as shown in Chap. 4, there are good reasons to consider preserving the stability of the currency and the health of the financial system as compatible objectives.

And third, the Mexican constitution forbids every public authority from asking for central bank financing. Again, however, the legislative branch authorized the BM to finance the state. Ignoring the constitution, the legislature allowed the BM to provide funding to the government via loans, security purchases, or by crediting the checking account of the Treasury.

The principle of constitutional supremacy states that constitutional prescriptions prevail over legislation. But legal certainty requires that the legislative branch respects constitutional mandates and that a legislative initiative adheres to the limits set by the constitution. It is likely that the legislators tried to evade the stiff process of constitutional amendment required to change the Mexican constitution. Indeed, amending the Mexican constitution is harder than doing so in most of the other countries analyzed (except Argentina). Amending the Mexican constitution requires a large majority, as well as the approval of the 16 of 30 federal states. However, to improve legal certainty for the autonomy of the BM, the Supreme Court of Mexico should declare unconstitutional the articles of the charter of the BM that conflict with the constitutional provisions.

These inconsistencies in the law seem minor relative to the three main contradictions in Colombian law. The BRC's autonomy and the legal objective are entrenched in the Constitution of Colombia. In line with the benchmark framework, the BRC also has the single objective of preserving price stability. Therefore, like the BM, the constitutional provisions seem very straightforward.

However, as is the case with the BM, the constitutional entrenchment does not provide as much certainty as it suggests. First, the constitutional entrenchment of autonomy is, like the BM's, inconsistent with rules that place the central bank within the public administration, which is controlled by the executive branch.

Second, court decisions on the prevalence of the social rule of law cast doubts on both the bank's objectives as well as its autonomy. Specifically, the Constitutional Court of Colombia (CCC) demanded that every state institution contributes to the achievement of social and economic rights of the Colombian people, as the so-called social rule of law is the backbone of the Colombian legal system. At the center of the social rule of law is people's dignity, which is understood as meeting a certain social and economic threshold. In contrast with the bank's constitutional objective, the CCC ruled that the bank, as a state institution, should also consider the social rule of law and contribute to social and economic justice, not just price stability. With reference to the social rule of law, Colombia's government sets up annual development plans that shall, for example, make housing affordable. According to the court, the bank should contribute to the fulfillment of government development plans.

And third, the rules governing the bank may be easier to change than a constitutional entrenchment typically implies. The reason is that there are three ways to amend the Constitution of Colombia. One calls for a constitutional assembly—a high burden. Another way is to amend the constitution via a referendum. The referendum is reserved for few aspects and amending the central bank rules is not one of them. Finally, amending the Constitution may neither require a referendum nor a constitutional assembly. In such cases, amending the Colombian constitution is no more difficult than amending an organic or statutory law. It entails, however, a higher guarantee of stability than amending an ordinary law.

8.3.3.2 Additional Suggestions

Even when these major conflicts in the law are settled, there will still be work to be done on the statutes.

The BM law could be further improved to provide legal certainty concerning central bank autonomy by providing more detail and modifying rules to guarantee personal autonomy. Indeed, many aspects, such as the guarantee of bank capital or who performs control and oversight, could be elaborated upon in the law. Although monetary policy operations in principle are specified clearly in BM law, providing substantial operational autonomy, the specific conditions under which the bank can act as a lender of last resort and provide emergency lending are not specified. Neither does the BM law establish a confidentiality protection for the opinions of the central bank board members, as does Peruvian law. Nor does the law specify a process to resolve conflicts between the bank and other economic policy organs, as does Chilean law.

The law of the BM also has aspects that are very much in line with the benchmark model. For example, the bank's board alone can dismiss board members in cases related to the performance of their functions. Regarding financial autonomy, BM Law does specify that the board determines the budget, giving financial autonomy to the bank. In terms of personal autonomy, the appointment of the board members of the BM requires a dual process, which is similar to the prescriptions of CBCH Law. The President of the country chooses the board members. The legislature must approve or reject the candidates. The board members of the BM also have a tenure of eight years, which does not overlap the presidential period of 6 years.

However, there are three issues concerning personal autonomy that could be addressed. The first issue is concerned with the appointment process of the board. Like CBCH board members, BM board members can be reelected, which might undermine personal autonomy for members who want to be nominated again. Second, as in all six central banks analyzed, the central bank president is appointed by the executive rather than by the board members. Small changes in BM Law would help deal with these problems. And third, like the law of the CRBP, BM Law also lacks a prohibition on board members' performance of private activities that could pose a conflict of interest with the bank's functions.

Again, the provisions in the statutes governing the Bank of the Republic of Colombia provide even more serious doubts about the intention of the legislator to create an autonomous central bank. The law does not grant personal autonomy. The rules are mostly the exact opposite to those of the benchmark case. On the upside, the statutes ensure that members of the board are well versed and have lots of working experience in related fields. But the central bank is also heavily controlled by the executive, which appoints, controls, and dismisses the board members. Financial autonomy is at risk, as the bank can lend to the government. And the bank must coordinate decisions with the highest planning authority of Colombia, which is also an organ dependent on the executive branch.

Considering these shortcomings, a wholesale redraft of the central bank law is to be recommended, specifically regarding personal autonomy, financial autonomy, and coordination arrangements, to reduce the influence of the executive branch over the BRC and, therefore, bring the bank's statutes in line with the constitutional rank of the autonomy.

Specifically, to improve the rules concerning personal autonomy, the President of Colombia should not have the sole authority to appoint board members. Instead, they should be appointed in a dual process with the participation of both the executive and the legislature. Importantly, the Minister of Finance should not serve as the president of the board, and board members should have terms of more than four years (ideally 10 years), which should not overlap with the presidential period. Finally, board members should not have the option to be reappointed to avoid political arrangements.

When it comes to financial autonomy, there should be a general prohibition on lending to the government. If there is an exception to this prohibition, it should be clearly stated in the law, like in the case of Chile. The current arrangement, which allows the central bank's board to decide whether to grant credit to the government, jeopardizes certainty about the autonomy. Such rules are more dangerous given the role of the Minister of Finance and the fact that the President of Colombia appoints the board members unilaterally that would make such a decision.

Rules that guarantee autonomy would also not ask the BRC to coordinate central bank operations with the National Council of Economic and Social Policy (CONPES) or other members of the executive. Instead, the law should establish proper channels of communication that allow for an exchange of information.

8.4 Final Remarks

Although monetary stability has improved since the 2000s in the Latin America emerging markets, there are serious doubts about the ability of Latin American central banks to maintain price stability over time. Granting autonomy to a central bank is recognized as the most important means to allow a central bank to commit credibly to the fulfillment of its objectives. Authorities in many Latin American countries will be able to affect central bank decisions. Most importantly, a lack of clarity, inconsistencies, or generous exceptions in the law provide ways for authorities to affect central banks even without bending or disregarding the rules.

However, the legal frameworks of the countries analyzed differ substantially. Peru's and Chile's central bank frameworks (as of 2019) provide certainty concerning the autonomy of the bank. We may be confident that such certainty provides a sound basis to provide for monetary stability.

By contrast, it should come as no surprise if we see a rise in inflation in Argentina and Brazil as soon as it is in their governments' interest. Their central banks are labeled autonomous but are not meant to operate independent from the government. Finally, the Colombian and Mexican central banks are autonomous at first glance only. If governments want to interfere with central bank policies, they can. The lack of legal certainty undermines any autonomy that might be granted in the law. Those that believe that monetary instability is merely a phantom of the past might be proven wrong again.

Reference

Reinhart C, Rogoff K (2011) This time is different: eight centuries of financial folly. Princeton University Press

Printed by Printforce, the Netherlands